WORLD PREHISTORY

WORLD PREHISTORY

A Brief Introduction

SEVENTH EDITION

BRIAN M. FAGAN

University of California, Santa Barbara

PEARSON

Prentice
Hall

Upper Saddle River, New Jersey 07458

Library of Congress Cataloging-in-Publication Data

Fagan, Brian M.
    World Prehistory: a brief introduction/Brian M. Fagan.—7th ed.
        p. cm.
    Includes bibliographical references and index.
    ISBN 978-0-13-225708-4
    1. Prehistoric peoples.   2. Anthropology, Prehistoric.   3. Human evolution.   4. Antiquities,
Prehistoric.   I. Title.
    GN470.F34 2008
    930—dc22   2007011891

Editorial Director: Leah Jewell
Publisher: Nancy Roberts
Editorial Assistant: Lee Peterson
Director of Marketing: Brandy Dawson
Marketing Manager: Lindsey Prudhomme
Assistant Marketing Manager: Jessica Muraviov
Project Manager: Barbara Reilly
Operations Specialist: Ben Smith
Cover and Interior Design: Ilze Lemensis
Cover Photo: Feline Effigy, Moche Site of Huaca de La Luna (c.a. 500 A.D.). Excavated by Santiago Uceda.
    Photograph by Steve Bourget.
Director, Image Resource Center: Melinda Patelli
Manager, Rights and Permissions: Zina Arabia
Manager, Visual Research: Beth Brenzel
Manager, Cover Visual Research and Permissions: Karen Sanatar
Image Permission Coordinator: Michelina Viscusi
Photo Researcher: Francelle Carapetyan
Composition/Full-Service Project Management: Kari Callaghan Mazzola and John P. Mazzola
Printer/Binder: Courier Companies, Inc.
Cover Printer: Phoenix Color Corp.

This book was set in 10/12 Palatino.

*Grateful acknowledgment is made to the copyright holders on pages 376–378, which are hereby a continuation
of this copyright page.*

Pearson Education LTD.
Pearson Education Singapore, Pte. Ltd
Pearson Education, Canada, Ltd
Pearson Education—Japan
Pearson Education Australia PTY, Limited

Pearson Education North Asia Ltd
Pearson Educación de Mexico, S.A. de C.V.
Pearson Education Malaysia, Pte. Ltd
Pearson Education, Upper Saddle River, NJ

10 9 8 7 6 5 4 3
ISBN 13: 978-0-13-225708-4
ISBN 10:   0-13-225708-4

To Victoria Pryor
with thanks for creative inspiration
and many kindnesses

There is not yet one person, one animal. . . . Only the sky alone is there; the face of the earth is not clear. Only the sea alone is pooled under all the sky; there is nothing whatever gathered together. It is at rest; not a single thing stirs. . . . Whatever there is that might be is simply not there: only the pooled water. . . .

From the Quiche Maya legend of the creation
DENNIS TEDLOCK (1985, p. 127)

Contents

Preface

Three thousand, four thousand years maybe, have passed and gone since human feet last trod the floor on which you stand, and yet, as you note the signs of recent life around you—the half-filled bowl of mortar for the door, the blackened lamp, the finger-mark on the freshly painted surface, the farewell garland dropped on the threshold—you feel it might have been but yesterday. . . . Time is annihilated by little intimate details such as these, and you feel an intruder.

Egyptologist Howard Carter, notebook entry on Tutankhamun's tomb, November 26, 1922

Golden pharaohs, lost cities, grinning human skeletons: Archaeology is the stuff of romance and legend! Many people still think of archaeologists as adventurers and treasure hunters, like Indiana Jones of Hollywood movie fame seeking the elusive Holy Grail. This enduring image goes back to the late nineteenth century, when archaeologists like Heinrich Schliemann could still find lost civilizations like Troy and excavate three royal palaces in a week. Today no archaeologists behave like Indiana Jones. They are scientists, not adventurers, as comfortable in an air-conditioned laboratory as they are on a remote excavation. The development of scientific archaeology from its Victorian beginnings ranks among the greatest triumphs of twentieth-century science.

Archaeology has changed our understanding of the human experience in profound ways. A century ago, most scientists believed humans were no more than 100,000 years old. Today we know that our origins go back at least 5 million years. Our predecessors assumed the Americas were settled in about 8000 B.C. and that farming began around 4000 B.C. New excavations date the first Americans to at least 12,000 B.C. and the beginnings of agriculture to about 10,000 B.C. Most important, archaeology has changed our perceptions of ourselves, especially of our biological and cultural diversity. Welcome to the fascinating world of archaeology!

The seventh edition of *World Prehistory* continues a long tradition of providing an interesting, jargon-free journey through the 5-million-year-old landscape of the human past. I hope you enjoy your sojourn in its pages.

Highlights of the Seventh Edition

The seventh edition of *World Prehistory* has been revised throughout to reflect the latest advances in the field. It includes suggestions by dozens of archaeologists and students who have taken the trouble to contact me after using previous editions.

This is an exciting time to be writing about archaeology. Many scientific advances are changing our perceptions about the past. The seventh edition contains important new discoveries about early human evolution, the late Ice Age, and the origins of agriculture. New and updated coverage of the field appears in every chapter, with an up-to-date Guide to Further Reading at the end of the book, along with a glossary of technical terms and one of archaeological sites and cultural terms.

Updating and Rewriting

- **New perceptions of world prehistory.**   Chapter 1 includes important discussions of archaeology and alternative perspectives on the past, reflecting new thinking on this important topic.

- **Early human evolution.**   Chapter 2 discusses the latest advances in the study of human origins, including the latest fossil discoveries in Ethiopia and Kenya.

- **Origins of modern humans.**   Chapter 3 covers new research into the controversial issue of the earliest modern humans and fresh perceptions of Neanderthal ancestry and behavior.

- **Origins of food production.**   Chapter 5 incorporates expanded coverage of the latest theories on the origins of agriculture and animal domestication. Chapter 6, which describes the first farmers, incorporates the latest dates for early agriculture obtained from accelerator mass spectrometry (AMS) radiocarbon dates and the results of new research in eastern Turkey, where some of the earliest farming settlements in the world are being found.

- **Origins of states and civilization.**   Chapter 8 includes current theoretical debates on the origins of state-organized societies, including the issues of factionalism and charismatic leadership. Chapters 9 to 14 offer an up-to-date description and analysis of the first civilizations, with expanded coverage of ancient Egyptian civilization and of South and Southeast Asian states. Chapters 12 and 13 offer more comprehensive analysis of highland and lowland Mesoamerican civilizations than in previous editions.

- **Revision and updating throughout.**   The entire text and Guide to Further Reading have been revised and updated on a page-by-page basis.

Feature Boxes

Three types of feature boxes, designed to amplify the narrative, enhance the book:

- **Science.**   These boxes introduce key dating methods and other scientific approaches, such as radiocarbon and AMS dating, and also environmental reconstruction.

- **Site.**   Most of the chapters include one or more boxes describing sites of unusual importance, and some aspects of unusual interest.

- **Voices.**   The Mesopotamian, Egyptian, and highland Mesoamerican chapters include special boxes that quote from writings of ancient times, giving each an unusual "voice."

New and Revised Art Program

The seventh edition's art program has been revised with new photographs and fresh or revised line art. The new illustrations provide additional background on recent discoveries, amplify the narrative, or replace older art with new pictures. Some expanded captions serve to integrate the illustrations more closely into the text.

Ancillary Materials

The ancillary materials that accompany this textbook have been carefully created to enhance the topics being discussed.

Instructor's Manual with Tests (0-13-225675-4)   For each chapter in the text, this manual provides a detailed outline, list of objectives, discussion questions, classroom activities, and additional resources. The test bank includes multiple-choice, true–false, and essay questions for each chapter.

TestGEN-EQ (0-13-225677-0)   This computerized software allows instructors to create their own personalized exams, to edit any or all of the existing test questions, and to add new questions. Other special features of this program include random generation of test questions, creation of alternate versions of the same test, scrambling question sequence, and test preview before printing.

The Fagan Companion Website™   This Web site correlates the text with related material available on the Internet. Features of the *Companion Website™* include chapter objectives and study questions, as well as links to interesting material and information from other sites on the Web that can reinforce and enhance the content of each chapter. Address: www.prenhall.com/fagan

Research Navigator™   *Research Navigator™* can help students to complete research assignments efficiently and with confidence by providing three exclusive databases of high-quality scholarly and popular articles accessed by easy-to-use search engines.

- **EBSCO's *ContentSelect*™ Academic Journal Database,** organized by subject, contains 50–100 of the leading academic journals for anthropology. Instructors and students can search the on-line journals by keyword, topic, or multiple topics. Articles include abstract and citation information and can be cut, pasted, e-mailed, or saved for later use.

- **The *New York Times* Search-by-Subject Archive** provides articles specific to anthropology and is searchable by keyword or multiple keywords. Instructors and students can view full-text articles from the world's leading journalists writing for the *New York Times.*

- **Link Library** offers editorially selected "Best of the Web" sites for anthropology. Link Libraries are continually scanned and kept up-to-date, providing the most relevant and accurate links for research assignments.

Gain access to *Research Navigator* by using the access code found in the front of the brief guide called *The Prentice Hall Guide to Research Navigator*™. The access code for *Research Navigator* is included with every guide and can be packaged for no extra charge with *World Prehistory, Seventh Edition*. Please contact your Prentice Hall representative for more information.

Acknowledgments

Many colleagues, too numerous to list here, have advised me on this revision. I am deeply grateful for their encouragement and assistance. I would like to thank the following reviewers for their help in revising this new edition. I appreciate their frank comments: Elliot Abrams, Ohio University; Carol A. Morrow, Southeast Missouri State University; Henry W. Schulz, City College of San Francisco; Tamra L. Walter, Texas Tech University; Peter S. Wells, University of Minnesota.

Lastly, my thanks to my editor, Nancy Roberts, and her colleagues at Prentice Hall. They have turned a complex manuscript into an attractive book and have done all they can to minimize unexpected difficulties.

As always, I would be most grateful for criticisms, comments, or details of new work, sent to me at brian@brianfagan.com.

Brian M. Fagan

A Note on Chronologies and Measurements

The narrative of prehistory in these pages is organized in as linear a fashion chronologically as is practicable. It is based on radiocarbon, potassium-argon, and tree-ring dates, as well as on historical documents. Although every effort has been made to make dates accurate, many of them should be recognized for what they are—statistical approximations. The time scales of prehistory are presented in two ways:

- At the beginning of most chapters, a time line shows the reader the relative position of the developments described in that chapter within the broad time frame of prehistoric times.

- Chronological tables placed at strategic points in the book provide a comparative view of developments in different areas of the world. Each is linked to its predecessors and successors, so that they provide background continuity for the narrative.

The following conventions are used for dates in this book:

B.P.—Years before Present. In general, years before 40,000 B.P. are given in years before present, while dates after 12,000 B.P. are invariably expressed as A.D./B.C., unless the context is obvious.

Mya—Million years ago.

Kya—Thousand years ago.

B.C./A.D.—To avoid confusion, I use the common B.C./A.D. identification for dates. Another common convention is B.C.E./C.E. (Before the Common Era/Common Era), which is not used in this book.

"Present"—By scientific convention, "present" is A.D. 1950.

For clarity, all radiocarbon and potassium-argon dates are quoted here without their statistical errors. However, readers should be aware that such calculations exist for every chronometric date in this book.

All measurements are given in metric, with miles, yards, feet, and inch equivalents, since this is now a common scientific convention.

Calibration of Radiocarbon Dates

The calibration of radiocarbon dates has now reached a high degree of refinement, as scientists develop ever more accurate time scales for the past 15,000 years, using tree-ring, coral, and ice-core data. See page xxii for the latest calibration table, based on those published in the special calibration issue of the journal *Radiocarbon* in 1998.

It should be stressed that these calibrations are provisional, statistically based, and subject to modification, especially before 7,000 B.C.

Tree-Ring Calibrations

Radiocarbon Age (Years A.D./B.C.)	Calibrated Age in Years
A.D. 1760	A.D. 1945
1505	1435
1000	1105
500	635
1	15
505 B.C.	767 B.C.
1007	1267
1507	1867
2007	2477
3005	3795
4005	4935
5005	5876
6050	7056
7001	8247
8007	9368
9062	9968

Barbados Coral Calibrations Using Uranium/Thorium and AMS Carbon 14

AMS Radiocarbon Dates	Uranium Thorium Calibration
7760 B.C.	9140 B.C.
8270	10,310
9320	11,150
10,250	12,285
13,220	16,300
14,410	17,050
15,280	18,660
23,920	28,280
(increasing differences after 25,000 B.C. [calibrated])	

About the Author

Brian Fagan is one of the world's leading archaeological writers and an internationally recognized authority on world prehistory. He studied archaeology and anthropology at Pembroke College, Cambridge University, and then spent seven years in sub-Saharan Africa working in museums and in monuments conservation while excavating early farming sites in Zambia and East Africa. He was one of the pioneers of multidisciplinary African history in the 1960s. Since 1967, he has been Professor and Emeritus Professor of Anthropology at the University of California, Santa Barbara, where he has specialized in writing and lecturing about archaeology to wide audiences.

Professor Fagan has written several best-selling textbooks: *Ancient Lives: An Introduction to Archaeology and Prehistory*, 3/E; *In the Beginning*, 11/E (with Christopher DeCorse); *Archaeology: A Brief Introduction*, 8/E; *People of the Earth: An Introduction to World Prehistory*, 12/E; *Ancient Civilizations*, 3/E (with Chris Scarre); *A Brief History of Archaeology*; *Archaeology and You*; and this volume. They are all published by Prentice Hall and are used around the world. His general books include *The Rape of the Nile*, a classic history of Egyptology; *The Adventure of Archaeology*; *Time Detectives*; *Floods, Famines, and Emperors: El Niño and the Fate of Civilizations*; *The Long Summer*; and *Fish on Friday: Feasting, Fasting, and the Discovery of the New World*. He is General Editor of the *Oxford Companion to Archaeology*. In addition, he has published several scholarly monographs on African archaeology and numerous specialized articles in national and international journals. He is also an expert on multimedia teaching and has received the Society for American Archaeology's first Public Education Award for his indefatigable efforts on behalf of archaeology and education.

Brian Fagan's other interests include bicycling, sailing, kayaking, and good food. He is married and lives in Santa Barbara with his wife and daughter, four cats (who supervise his writing), and last but not least, a minimum of five rabbits.

PART I PREHISTORY

Six million years is a vast span of time. In order to begin to comprehend it, to grasp its salient pattern of events, it helps to think of those events as constituting a play, a drama of our past. A very special play, for no one wrote the script: 6 million years of Improvisation. Our ancestors are the actors, their tools are the props and the incessant changes of environment through which they lived the changes of scenery. But as a play do not think of it as a "whodunit," in which action and ending are all. For we already know the ending—we are living it. The . . . Stone Age actors have all died out leaving just one single survivor, *Homo sapiens.*

STEVEN MITHEN (1996, p. 17)

1 Introducing World Prehistory

PROLOGUE

Egypt: the Valley of the Kings, November 1922. The two men paused in front of the doorway that bore the seals of the long-dead pharaoh. They had waited six long years, from 1917 to 1922, for this moment. Silently, Howard Carter pried a hole through the ancient plaster. Hot air rushed out of the small cavity and massaged his face. Carter shone a flashlight through the hole and peered into the tomb. Gold objects swam in front of his eyes, and he was struck dumb with amazement.

Lord Carnarvon moved impatiently behind him as Carter remained silent.

"Can you see anything?" he asked, hoarse with excitement.

"Yes, wonderful things," whispered Carter as he stepped back from the doorway.

They soon broke down the door. In a daze of wonderment, Carter and Lord Carnarvon wandered through the antechamber of Tutankhamun's tomb. They fingered golden funerary beds, admired beautifully inlaid chests, and examined the pharaoh's chariots stacked against the wall. Gold was everywhere—on wooden statues, inlaid on thrones and boxes, in jewelry, even on children's stools. Soon Tutankhamun was known as the golden pharaoh, and archaeology as the domain of buried treasure and royal sepulchers. Tutankhamun's magnificent tomb is a symbol of the excitement and romance of archaeology.

Since time immemorial, humans have been intensely curious about their origins, about the mysterious and sometimes threatening world in which they exist. They know that earlier generations lived before them, that their children, grandchildren, and their progeny in turn will, in due course, dwell on earth. But how did this world come about? Who created the familiar landscape of rivers, fields, mountains, plants, and animals? Who fashioned the oceans and seacoasts, deep lakes, and fast-flowing streams? Above all, how did the first men and women settle the land? Who created them, how did they come into being? Every society has creation stories to account for human origins. However, archaeology and biological anthropology have replaced legend with an intricate account of human evolution and cultural development that extends back more than 2.5 million years. This chapter describes how archaeologists study and interpret human prehistory.

"In the Beginning" . . .

> "After the Great Fire destroyed the world and before the little bird Icanchu flew away, he roamed the wasteland in search of First Place. The homeland lay beyond recognition, but Icanchu's index finger, of its own accord, pointed to the spot. There he unearthed the charcoal stump that he pounded as his drum. Playing without stopping, he chanted with the dark drum's sounds. . . . At dawn on the new Day, a green shoot sprang from the coal drum and soon flowered as Firstborn Tree. . . . From its branches bloomed the forms of life that flourished in the new World. . . ." (Sullivan, 1988, p. 92)

We Westerners take the past for granted, accept human evolution as something that extends back many thousands, even millions of years. Science provides us with a long perspective on ancient times. In contrast, the story of Icanchu's drum is a classic origin myth of the cosmic fire told by the Mataco Indians from South America. Like all such accounts, the tale begins with a **primordium** (the very beginning) in which a mythic being, in this case Icanchu, works to create the familiar animals, landscape, and plants of the world, and then the human inhabitants. Icanchu, and his equivalents in a myriad of human cultures throughout the world, create order from primeval chaos, as God does in *Genesis*, Chapter 1.

Myths, and the rituals and religious rites associated with them, function to create a context for the entire symbolic life of a human society, a symbolic life that is the very cornerstone of human existence. The first human beings establish the sacred order through which life endures from one generation to the next. This kind of history, based on legend and myth, is one of symbolic existence. Creation legends tell of unions between gods and monsters, of people emerging from holes in the earth after having climbed sacred trees that link the layers of the cosmos. They create indissoluble symbolic bonds between humans and other kinds of life, such as plants, animals, and celestial beings.

The vivid and ever-present symbolic world has influenced the course of human life ever since humans first acquired the power of creative thought and reasoning. The Cro-Magnons of late Ice Age Europe depicted mythical animals and the symbolism of their lives in cave paintings more than 30,000 years ago (see Chapter 4). They modeled clay bison in dark chambers deep beneath the earth (Figure 1.1). The sculptures seemed to flicker in the light of firebrands during powerful rituals carried out by **shamans**, tribal priests with the ability to voyage into the mysterious supernatural world. So compelling was the influence of the unknown powers of the cosmos and of the gods that inhabited it that the Maya and other central American civilizations created entire ceremonial centers in the form of symbolic landscapes to commemorate their mythic universe (see Chapters 12 and 13).

Figure 1.1 Late Ice Age masterpieces: two clay bison from Le Tuc D'Audoubert, France.

Today, Western science has chronicled more than 2.5 million years of prehistory, a narrative of human endeavor that extends back through hundreds of thousands of years of unfolding time. This story is one based on scientific research, something quite different from the creation legends that people use to define their complex relationships with the natural and spiritual worlds. These legends are deeply felt, important sources of cultural identity. They foster a quite different relationship with the past than that engendered by archaeology, which seeks to understand our common biological and cultural roots, and the great diversity of humanity.

Pseudoarchaeology

Golden pharaohs, lost civilizations, buried treasure—archaeology seems like a romantic world of high adventure and exciting discovery. A century ago, archaeology was indeed a matter of exotic travel to remote places. It was still possible to find a hitherto unknown civilization with a few weeks of digging. Today, archaeology is a highly scientific discipline, concerned more with minute details of ancient life than with spectacular discoveries. But an aura of unsolved mysteries and heroic figures still surrounds the subject in many peoples' eyes—to the point of obsession.

The mysteries of the past attract many people, especially those with a taste for adventure, escapism, and science fiction. These people create elaborate adventure stories about the past—almost invariably epic journeys or voyages based on illusory data. For example, British journalist Graham Hancock has claimed that a great civilization flourished under Antarctic ice 12,000 years ago. (Of course, its magnificent cities are buried under deep ice sheets, so we cannot excavate them!) Colonists spread to all parts of the world from their Antarctic home, colonizing such well-known sites as **Tiwanaku** in the Bolivian highlands and building the Sphinx by the banks of the Nile. Hancock weaves an ingenious story, by piecing together all manner of controversial geological observations and isolated archaeological finds. He waves aside the obvious archaeologist's reaction, which asks where traces of these ancient colonies and civilizations are to be found in Egypt and other places. Hancock fervently believes in his far-fetched theory, and being a good popular writer, he has managed to piece together a best-selling book that reads like a "whodunit" written by an amateur sleuth.

Flamboyant pseudoarchaeology of the type espoused by Hancock will always appeal to people who are impatient with the deliberate pace of science and to those who believe in faint possibilities. It is as if a scientist tried to reconstruct the contents of an American house using artifacts found in Denmark, New Zealand, South Africa, Spain, and Tahiti.

Nonscientific nonsense like this comes in many forms. There are those who believe that the Lost Continent of Atlantis once lay under the waters of the Bahamas and that Atlanteans fled their sunken homeland and settled the Americas thousands of years ago. Others fantasize about fleets of ancient Egyptian boats or Roman galleys that crossed the Atlantic long before Columbus. All these bizarre manifestations of archaeology have one thing in common: They are overly simple, convenient explanations of complex events in the past, based on such archaeological data as their author cares to use.

These kinds of pseudoarchaeology belong to the realms of religious faith and science fiction. The real science of the past is based on rigorous procedures and meticulous data collection, its theorizing on constantly modified hypotheses tested against information collected in the field and laboratory—in short: archaeological, biological, and other evidence.

Prehistory, Archaeology, and World Prehistory

Human beings are among the only animals that have a skeleton adapted for standing and walking upright, which leaves our hands free for purposes other than moving around. A powerful brain capable of abstract thought controls these physical traits. The same brain allows us to communicate symbolically and orally through language and to develop highly diverse cultures—learned ways of behaving and adapting to our natural environments. The special features that make us human have evolved over hundreds of thousands of years.

The scientific study of the past is a search for answers to fundamental questions about human origins. How long ago did humans appear? When and how did they evolve? How can we account for the remarkable biological and cultural diversity of humankind? How did early humans settle the world and develop so many different societies at such different levels of complexity? Why did some societies cultivate the soil and herd cattle while others remained hunters and gatherers? Why did some peoples like, for example, the San foragers of southern Africa or the Shoshone of the Great Basin in North America live in small family bands, while the ancient Egyptians and the Aztecs of Mexico developed highly elaborate civilizations (Figure 1.2)? When did more complex human societies evolve and why? The answers to these questions are the concern of scientists studying world prehistory.

Archaeologists define **prehistory** as that portion of human history that extends back some 2.5 million years before the time of written documents and archives. In contrast, **history**, the study of human experience through documents, has a much shorter time span. Written records go back to before 5,000 years in western Asia. Writing and written

Figure 1.2 Pyramids of Giza, Egypt.

records came into use centuries later elsewhere in the world, in some parts of Africa and Asia only within the past century, when European powers annexed vast new territories and started to rule their new possessions. The study of prehistory is a multidisciplinary enterprise that involves not only archaeologists but scientists from many other disciplines, including biologists, botanists, geographers, geologists, and zoologists—to mention only a few. But archaeology is the primary source of information on human prehistory.

The archaeologist is a special type of anthropologist concerned not with living societies but with ancient cultures. **Archaeology** consists of a broad range of scientific methods and techniques for studying the past, used carefully and in a disciplined way. The archaeologist studies the human societies of the remote and recent past, using the surviving material remains of their cultures to do so. Archaeology is a highly effective way of studying human cultures in the past and the ways in which they have changed over long periods of time. It covers the entire time span of human existence, from over 2.5 million years ago right up to the study of nineteenth-century railroad stations and the garbage from modern industrial cities.

A century ago, most archaeologists worked in Europe and western Asia. They thought of human prehistory in very provincial terms and were convinced that all significant developments such as agriculture and civilization itself had originated in the area between Mesopotamia and the Nile. Today, archaeologists are at work all over the globe—in Africa, Alaska, and Australia. Thanks to universal dating methods such as radiocarbon dating, we can date and compare prehistoric developments in widely separated parts of the world. We know, for example, that agriculture began in Syria in about 10,000 B.C. and in central Africa about 2,000 years ago. We can date the first human occupation of Europe to about 500,000 years ago, and that of North America to about 15,000 years before present. This is the study of **world prehistory**, the prehistory of humankind evaluated not just from the perspective of a single region such as western Asia, but from a global viewpoint.

World prehistory developed as a result of two major developments in archaeology. The first was the development of **radiocarbon dating** by University of Chicago chemists Willard

Libby and J. R. Arnold in 1949. For the first time, archaeologists had at their disposal a dating method of potentially global application that enabled them not only to date sites in all corners of the world, but also to compare the chronology of, say, the first agriculture in southwest Asia with that in the Americas (see "Radiocarbon Dating" box in Chapter 4).

Until then, no one could make easy, direct chronological comparisons between widely separated regions, nor did they have a way of measuring the rate of cultural change through time. Within fifteen years of Libby and Arnold's remarkable discovery, radiocarbon dates from hundreds of sites allowed the construction of the first reliable global chronologies, as a population explosion of professional archaeologists occurred worldwide.

Today, archaeological expeditions are at work in every corner of the world and in every environment imaginable: in the remote wilds of Siberia, in tropical rain forests along the Amazon River in South America, on Easter Island in the Pacific, in the middle of the arid Sahara Desert, and under the world's oceans.

The second major development came in 1961, when the Cambridge University archaeologist Grahame Clark published his classic *World Prehistory* (third edition, 1977), the first synthesis of archaeology that took full account of radiocarbon chronology and global archaeological research. This ground-breaking volume helped turn archaeology intellectually from a somewhat provincial discipline into the global enterprise it is today.

Major Developments in Human Prehistory

World prehistory, as described in this book, is concerned with the broad sweep of the human past, more specifically with four major developments (Table 1.1):

- The origins of humankind some 2.5 million years ago. We describe the ancestors of the first humans, the fossil evidence for our origins, and some of the behavioral changes and innovations that accompanied the appearance of our earliest forebears.

- The evolution of archaic humans like *Homo erectus* and the origins of anatomically modern people, ourselves. These developments span a long period between about 1.8 million and 150,000 years before the present. We also describe the spread of fully modern humans through the Old World and into the Americas, a process that ended about 15,000 years ago.

- The origins of more complex forager societies, of agriculture and animal domestication, sometimes called **food production**, after about 12,000 years ago. We evaluate the different theories developed to explain greater cultural and social complexity and why humans took up farming, and describe the early beginnings and spread of agriculture in western Asia, Europe, Asia, and the Americas.

- The origins of urbanized, literate civilization (state-organized societies) in about 3100 B.C. in western Asia and the development of similar, complex societies in other parts of the world in later millennia. These major developments provide us with a broad framework for telling the story of prehistory. Central to this framework are the notions of time and space—the context of biological and cultural developments in the past. (For a brief summary of how archaeological research proceeds, see Figure 1.3 on page 10.)

TABLE 1.1 Major Developments in Human History

A.D./B.C. Years B.P.	
A.D. 1532	Spanish conquest of Peru
A.D. 600	Classic Maya civilization
A.D. 1	Roman empire
3100 B.C.	Origins of civilization
	Metallurgy
12,000 B.P.	Origins of food production
c. 15,000 B.P.	First settlement of the Americas
c. 45,000 B.P.	First settlement of Australia
c. 150,000 B.P.	Origins of modern humans
1.8 million	*Homo erectus* in Africa and Asia
2.5 million	Human origins

Cyclical and Linear Time

All human societies have an interest in the past. It is always around them, haunting, mystifying, tantalizing, sometimes offering potential lessons for the present and future. The past is important because social life unfolds through time, embedded within a framework of cultural expectations and values. In the high Arctic, Inuit preserve their traditional attitudes, skills, and coping mechanisms in some of the harshest environments on earth. They do this by incorporating the lessons of the past into the present. In many societies, the ancestors are the guardians of the land, which symbolizes present, past, and future. Westerners have an intense scientific interest in ancient times, partly born of curiosity, but also out of a need for historical identity. There are many reasons to attempt to preserve an accurate record of earlier times, and no one, least of all an archaeologist, should assume that they are uniquely privileged in their interest.

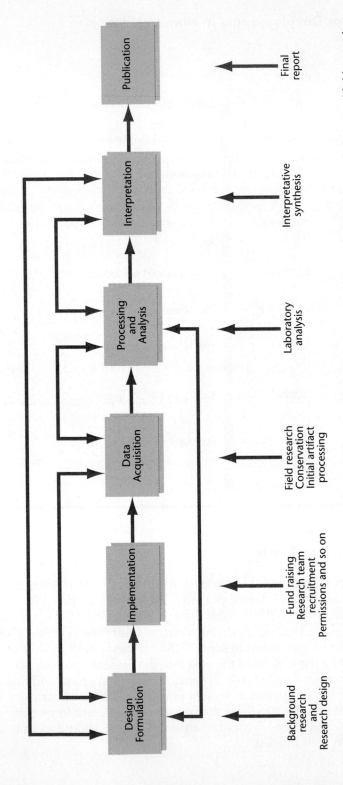

Figure 1.3 The process of archaeological research, which starts with the discovery of the site and proceeds through research design and field research to laboratory analysis, interpretation, and, finally, publication of the results.

We may all share an interest in the past, but we think of it, and use it, in different ways, just as we have different perspectives on time.

While it is true that archaeology is the only method Western science has of studying cultural change through time, that does not give archaeologists unique authority over the past. In many societies, history is a valued cultural commodity, in ways that are fundamentally different from those of the archaeologist. The transmission of knowledge about ancient times lies in the hands of respected elders, who take pains to preserve the accuracy of oral traditions. Such traditions are of vital importance, and they are carefully controlled, for they define and preserve a group's identity from one generation to the next. The past is vested not in science, but in household, community, kin groups, and territory. Among the Yolngu Aborigines of Australia's Northern Territory, for example, only the oldest clan members are repositories for the most important historical knowledge. As both Australian Aborigines and Native Americans have pointed out, there is a fundamental incompatibility between Western science and its perspectives on the past and those of other societies. In part, this incompatibility revolves around the notion of linear time.

Westerners think of the passage of the human experience along a straight, if branching, highway of time. The great nineteenth-century German statesman Otto von Bismarck called this the "stream of time," upon which all human societies ride for a time. We have a sense of linear, unraveling history that goes back through 5,000 years of recorded history to early Egypt and Mesopotamia. Ancient Egyptian civilization began in 3100 B.C.; Rome was founded in 753 B.C.; Christopher Columbus landed in the Bahamas on October 12, 1492; and the Declaration of Independence dates to July 4, 1776. These are landmarks along the ladder of historical chronology, which continues to unfold inexorably every day, month, and year, as we live our lives.

An unfolding, linear past is not the only way of conceptualizing ancient times. Many non-Western societies, ancient and modern, think of time as a cyclical phenomenon, or sometimes as a combination of the linear and the cyclical. The cyclical perspective stems from the passage of seasons and of heavenly bodies, from the close relationships between foragers and village farmers and their natural environments. It is also based on the eternal verities of human life: fertility and birth, life, growth, and death. The endlessly repeating seasons of planting and harvest, of game movements or salmon runs, and of ripening wild foods govern human existence in deeply significant ways. The ancient Maya developed an elaborate cyclical calendar of interlocking secular and religious calendars to measure the passage of the seasons and to regulate religious ceremonies (see Chapter 12).

However, we should not assume that societies with cyclical views of time did not have linear chronologies as well. The celebrated Maya "Long Count" was a linear chronology that formed an integral part of the close relationship between Maya rulers and the cosmos. The ancient Egyptians developed a linear chronology for administrative purposes. But, in general, societies develop linear chronologies only when they need them. For example, Western societies use linear time to regulate times of prayer, to control the working day, and for airline schedules. It is hard to generalize, but societies with centralized political systems tend to use the reigns of chiefs or kings as signposts along a linear time scale. For instance, the history of the rulers of the state of **Benin** in West Africa shows a significant shift in the interpretation of time. Before the fourteenth century A.D., Benin history is essentially mythological, with inaccurate chronology and a variable number of kings. But with the founding of the Yoruba dynasty, the deeds and reigns of every *oba* (king) are remembered in detail with chronological accuracy right down to modern times (see Figure 1.4 on page 12).

Figure 1.4 A bronze plaque from Benin City, Nigeria, West Africa, showing a seated *oba* (king) with kneeling attendants. These artifacts served as important historical records of royal reigns and genealogy and were stored in the royal palace.

Many non-Western societies do not perceive themselves as living in a changeless world. They make a fundamental distinction between the recent past, which lies within living memory, and the more remote past, which came before memory. For instance, the Australian Aborigine groups living in northeast Queensland distinguish between *kuma*, the span of events witnessed by living people, *anthantnama*, a long time ago, and *yilamu*, the period of the creation. Furthermore, many societies also accept that there was cultural change in the past, among them Hindu traditions of history, which tell of early people who lived without domesticated animals and plants, and the Hadza hunter-gatherers of East Africa, who speak of their homeland's first inhabitants as being giants without fire or tools. These paradigms of the past take many forms, with mythic creators of culture, usually primordial ancestors, deities, or animals establishing contemporary social customs and the familiar landscape, or a more remote, discontinuous heroic era like that of the Greeks, which allowed writers like the playwright Aeschylus to evaluate contemporary behavior.

Written Records, Oral History, and Archaeology

Most human societies of the past were nonliterate, meaning that they transmitted knowledge and history orally, by word of mouth. Written records are the most comprehensive source of information about the past, but they usually follow a strictly linear chronology. They also served as educational tools. Apart from anything else, written documents were useful as cues for people to memorize standardized historical, ritual, or mythical information. In the early civilizations, such as those of Egypt, Mesopotamia, and the Maya, scribes enjoyed considerable prestige, for they were the repositories of knowledge and information (Figure 1.5). They were considered so important that conquering Maya lords cut off the fingers of captured scribes to render them useless.

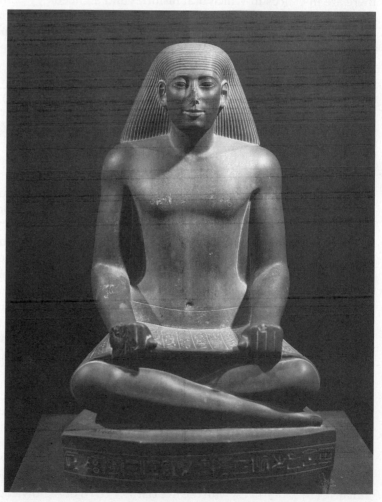

Figure 1.5 Statue of Nespekasuti, scribe of Karnak, Egypt, c. 490 B.C.

The Aztec oral histories, partially set down after the Spanish Conquest of the fifteenth century A.D., are an excellent example of history transmitted by word of mouth. They were recited according to a well-defined narrative plot, which focused on Great Men, key events (like the dedication of the Sun God Huitzilopochtli's temple in the Aztec capital in 1487), and the histories of favored groups. In these, as in other oral histories, there were formulas and themes, which formed the central ingredients of a story that varied considerably from one speaker to the next, even if the essential content was the same. Many oral histories are mixtures of factual data and parables that communicate moral and political values. But to those who hear them, they are publicly sanctioned history, performed before a critical group and subject to the critical evaluation of an audience who may have heard the same stories before.

Both written records and oral histories are subject to all kinds of bias. Neither can claim to be totally objective, any more than archaeology is. The problem for the archaeologist is to correlate data from excavations with that from oral traditions, to establish critically what is factual history and what is myth or moral exhortation. Oral traditions are hard to use since their antiquity is very difficult to establish. In some cases, in Australia for example, there are instances in which oral histories and archaeology coincide in general terms. For example, the traditions speak of the arrival of the first people from overseas, of the flooding of coastal areas, and of the hunting of giant marsupials (pouched animals like the kangaroo). So Australia's past can be said to come from two sources: archaeological data and oral traditions. In some instances, the archaeologists and indigenous people have shared interests and come together in identifying sacred places and historic places, often to ensure they are preserved. Sometimes the two groups differ drastically on the "significance" of a particular location, where the archaeologist finds no buildings or artifacts, yet the local people consider it a "sacred place."

But, all too often, the archaeologist and a local community have different interests in the past. To the archaeologist, the past is scientific data to be studied with all the rigor of modern science. To local people, the past is often highly personalized and the property of the ancestors. Such histories are valid alternative versions of history that deserve respect and understanding because they play a vital role in the creation and reaffirmation of cultural identity.

Archaeologists are not alone in considering the past of value, nor are they immune to the politics that sometimes surround the interpretation of aspects of the past. Many Westerners may consider "world prehistory" written from archaeology and many other sources the most reliable account of the human past. But we should never forget that alternative, and often compelling, accounts of ancient times exist, which play an important role in helping societies to maintain their traditional heritage as it existed before the arrival of the Westerner.

World Prehistory offers an account of 2.5 million years of human history based on the latest scientific archaeological research, but it does so with a profound respect for the cultures and histories of others with different historical perspectives.

Studying World Prehistory

The study of human prehistory extends back from modern times deep into the remote past. It is as if we are looking back into prehistoric times through the wrong end of a telescope. We can discern relatively recent cultures like those of the Aztecs or the sixteenth-century Pueblo Indians of the Southwest with relative clarity, even if our knowledge is lamentably incomplete.

Further back into the past the images become dimmer, more blurred, the scale smaller. We cannot use the lifeways of, say, modern arctic foragers or Maya farmers from Guatemala to interpret this remoter past. The first Native Americans of 15,000 years ago, the late Ice Age foragers who flourished in Europe 25,000 years ago—these peoples lived in a world that is unimaginably remote from our own. And the world of the archaic humans of earlier prehistory, of a quarter of a million years ago or more, is so far distant that it is hard for us to comprehend in realistic terms. Such, then, is the objective of world prehistory—to understand prehistoric human behavior in a past separated from our own not only by thousands of years, but by environmental and social challenges very different from those we face today.

World prehistory can be likened to a vast, branching chronological tree, whose roots ultimately extend back to the seminal moment some 5 to 6 million years ago when the remotest ancestors of humanity split off from the forebears of our closest living ape-like relatives, chimpanzees. We may think of the human past as linear, but the tree analogy is an apt one, for even the earliest hominins and their cultures diversified rapidly after the first tool-making humans appeared some 2.5 million years ago. Studying the many branches of this hypothetical tree requires use of a fundamental theoretical conception, that of culture.

Culture

As anthropologists, archaeologists study human cultures and how they have changed through time.

Culture is a concept developed by anthropologists to describe the distinctive adaptive system used by human beings. Culture can be called a society's traditional systems of belief and behavior, as understood by individuals and the members of social groups, and manifest in individual or collective behavior. It is also part of our way of adapting to our environment. Our tools and dwellings are also part of our culture. Humans are the only animals to manufacture tools for this purpose, although some other animals, among them chimpanzees, do fashion objects to use to achieve certain specific objectives.

Ordinarily, when animals die their experience perishes with them. However, human beings use the symbolic system of language to transmit ideas and their culture, their feelings and experiences, from one generation to the next. This is why oral traditions are so important in many societies. We learn culture by intentional teaching as well as by trial and error and simple imitation. People could share ideas, which in turn became behavior patterns that were repeated again and again—witness the long-lived stone hand ax, a multipurpose tool that remained in use for more than 1 million years of early prehistory (see Chapter 3). All archaeological research is based on the principle that culture is an ongoing phenomenon that changes gradually over time.

Unlike biological adaptation, culture is nongenetic and provides a much quicker way to share ideas that enable people to cope with their environment. It is the adaptiveness of culture that allows archaeologists to assume that artifacts found in archaeological sites are patterned adaptations to the environment.

A **cultural system** is a complex system comprising a set of interacting variables—tools, burial customs, ways of getting food, religious beliefs, social organization, and so on—that function to maintain a community in a state of equilibrium with its environment. When one element in the system changes, say hunting practices as a result of a prolonged drought, then reacting adjustments will occur in many other elements. It follows that no cultural system is ever static. It is always changing in big and small ways, some of which can be studied in archaeological sites. A cultural system can be broken down into all manner of subsystems: religious and ritual subsystems, economic subsystems, and so on. Each of these is linked to the others. Changes in one system, such as a shift from cattle herding to wheat growing, will cause reactions in many others. Such relationships give the archaeologist a measure of the constant changes and variations in human culture that can accumulate over long periods as cultural systems respond to external and internal stimuli. Many of the interacting components are highly perishable. So far, no one has been able to dig up a religious philosophy or an unwritten language.

Archaeologists work with the tangible remains of human activity that still survive in the ground, such as clay potsherds and the foundations of dwellings. But these surviving remains of human activity are radically affected by the intangible aspects of human culture. For instance, the **Moche** people of the Peruvian coast buried their great lords with elaborate gold and copper ornaments, with fine textiles and elaborate ceremonial regalia. Thanks to Walter Alva's excavations in the great mounds at Sipán, we know of one lord who was buried in A.D. 400 with a golden rattle that showed a Moche warrior in full regalia beating a prisoner on the head with his war club (see Chapter 14). The artistic masterpieces buried with the Lord of Sipán reflected a culture with an elaborate symbolism and complex religious beliefs that formed part of the intangible world of the Moche.

Culture History, Time and Space, and "The Myth of the Ethnographic Present"

The past extends back hundreds of thousands of years into remote prehistory, a featureless landscape that archaeologists people with cultures, each with their context in time and space. Culture history, the study of these many contexts, is a fundamental part of archaeology.

Culture history is the description of human cultures that extends back thousands of years into the past. Culture history is derived from the study of archaeological sites, and the artifacts and structures in them, within the context of time and space. By investigating groups of sites and the **artifacts** found there, it is possible to construct local and regional sequences of human cultures that extend over centuries, even millennia. The study of culture history depends on another important principle, that of context.

Context

Archaeological **context** is the position of an archaeological find in time and space, established by excavation, recording, and survey. The dimension of time combines in archaeological context with that of space—not the limitless space of the heavens, but a precisely defined location for every find made during an archaeological survey and excavation. Every archaeological find, be it a tiny pin or a large palace, has an exact location in latitude, longitude, and depth, which together identify any point in space and time absolutely and uniquely. When carrying out surface surveys or excavations, archaeologists use special methods to record the precise positions of sites, artifacts, dwellings, and other finds. They locate the position of each site on an accurate survey map so that they can use the grid coordinates on the map to define the location in precise terms. When investigating a site, they lay out recording grids made up from equal squares over the entire site, using the grids to record the exact position of every object on the surface or in the trenches, a context in time

Figure 1.6a Stratigraphy and association: two fundamental principles of archaeology. **(a)** Superposition and stratigraphy: a farming village built on virgin subsoil. After a time, the village is abandoned and the huts fall into disrepair. Their ruins are covered by accumulating soil and vegetation. **(b)** After an interval, a second village is built on the same site, with different architectural styles. This in turn is abandoned; the houses collapse into piles of rubble and are covered by accumulating soil. **(c)** Twentieth-century people park their cars on top of both village sites and drop litter and coins, which when uncovered reveal to the archaeologists that the top layer is modern. An archaeologist digging this site would find that the modern layer is underlain by two prehistoric occupation levels, that square huts were in use in the upper of the two, which is the later under the law of superposition. Round huts are stratigraphically earlier than square ones here. Therefore village I is earlier than village II, but the exact date of either, or how many years separate village I from village II, cannot be known without further data.

and space, determined by stratigraphic observation (Figure 1.6a), chronometric dating, and the law of association (Figure 1.6b, page 18).

Time

The time scale of the human past is hard to imagine. We are separated by 15,000 years from the end of the Ice Age, when great ice sheets covered much of Europe and North America. At least 150,000 years have passed since the first anatomically modern humans appeared in Africa. Fewer than a million archaic humans lived in Africa, Asia, and Europe, and the Americas were uninhabited 250,000 years ago. Two million years ago, the only humans on earth dwelt in tropical Africa. Some idea of the scale of prehistoric time can be gained by piling up 100 quarters. If the whole pile represents the entire time that humans

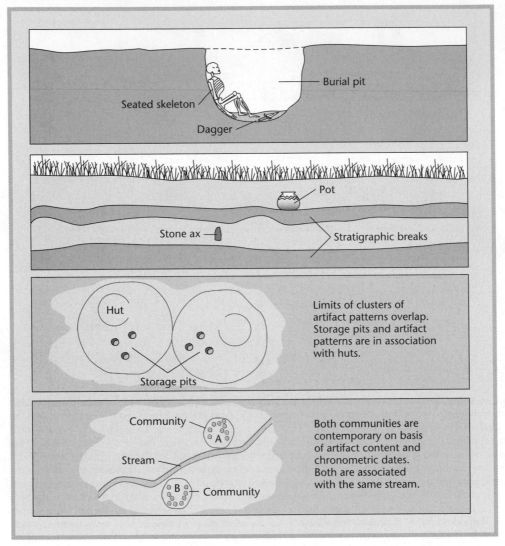

Figure 1.6b Some archaeological associations: (1) The burial pit, dug from the uppermost layer, contains not only a skeleton but also a dagger that lies close to its foot. The dagger is associated with the skeleton, and both finds are associated with the burial pit and the layer from which the grave pit was cut into the subsoil. (2) In contrast, a pot and a stone ax are found in two different layers, separated by a sterile zone, a zone with no finds. The two objects are not in association. (3) Two different household clusters with associated pits and scatters of artifacts. These are in association with one another. (4) An association of two contemporary communities.

and their culture have been on earth, the length of time covered by historical records would equal considerably less than the thickness of one quarter.

How, then, do archaeologists date the past? The chronology of world prehistory is based on observations of stratified occupation levels, and on a variety of chronometric dating methods that take us far back into the past, long before the earliest historical records appear in western Asia about 5,000 years ago (Table 1.2). Ninety-nine percent of all human existence lies in prehistoric times and can be measured only in millennia, and occasionally in centuries.

TABLE 1.2 Dating Methods and Human Prehistory

Date	Method	Major developments
Modern times (after A.D. 1)	Historical documents; dendrochronology; imported objects	Columbus in the New World; Roman Empire
2500 B.C.		Origins of cities Origins of food production Colonization of New World
40,000 B.C.	Radiocarbon dating (organic materials)	Colonization of Australia
75,000 B.C.	Uranium series dating	
100,000 B.C.	Potassium-argon dating (volcanic materials)	*Homo sapiens*
500,000 B.C.		Early humans
5,000,000 B.C.		

Space

Spatial location is indispensable to archaeologists because it enables them to establish the distances between objects or dwellings, between entire settlements, or between settlements and key vegetational zones and landmarks. Such distances may amount to only a few centimeters, or they may be found to extend for hundreds of miles as a team of fieldworkers traces the distribution of traded luxury goods in dozens of settlements. Thus, archaeologists think of space on two general scales: the distribution of artifacts within a settlement (Figure 1.7, page 20) and the **settlement pattern**, the placement of the settlements themselves over the landscape.

Context in space is closely tied to people's behavior. Archaeologists examine both an artifact itself and its association with other artifacts to gain insight into human behavior. For example, Belgian archaeologists investigated a 9,000-year-old hunting camp in a sandy clearing at **Meer** in northern Belgium. By plotting all of the stone fragments on the ancient ground surface, they were able to identify not only a camping area but an outlying scatter of stone fragments where one or two people had sat down and fashioned several flint artifacts. The spatial relationships among the stone chips enabled them to reconstruct what had happened 9,000 years ago in astounding detail. By fitting together the stone flakes, they were able to replicate the stoneworking technique and even to show that one of the workers had been left-handed!

Figure 1.7 A hypothetical ancient farming village, showing (A) houses, (B) household areas, (C) activity areas, and (D) the community.

Analogy and the "Ethnographic Present"

The study of culture history depends heavily on **ethnographic analogy**—the comparisons of the artifacts and culture of living, modern-day societies with those of the past. Of course, there are numerous, and sometimes obvious, analogies that can be made between ancient and modern hunting weapons, or, for example, between grindstones (metates) used by modern Maya Indians and their remote ancestors. But to assume that prehistoric foragers thought the same way about the environment as modern San peoples from southern Africa do, or to consider late Ice Age hunters living in arctic environments as similar in many respects to living Eskimos, is nonsensical.

One approach is **ethnoarchaeology**, sometimes called "living archaeology," the study of living societies to aid in the understanding and interpretation of the archaeological record. For example, archaeologist John Yellen lived for many months among !Kung San foragers in the Kalahari Desert in southern Africa. He went back to their campsites, recorded the scatters of abandoned artifacts, the remains of brush shelters, hearths, and sleeping places. Yellen even excavated some of the sites, gathering a valuable body of information for studying ancient foragers. For instance, most artifact patternings at !Kung sites were the result of family activities, whereas communal events such as dancing and the first distribution of meat took place in open spaces and left no traces in the archaeological record. Other such researches have been carried out among the Hadza hunter-gatherers of Tanzania in East Africa (Figure 1.8).

Everywhere in the world, archaeologists work back from the known present into the remote past, from historic Pueblo settlements in the American Southwest, from modern African villages, and contemporary Australian Aboriginal camps. These societies, be they Aztec, Inca, Pueblo, or Zulu, represent something often called the **ethnographic present**, traditional culture in its so-called pristine condition before the contaminating influence of Western civilization transformed it forever. The ethnographic present is, however, a myth, for all human societies are in a constant state of change. There was never a moment, let alone one at European contact, when any ancient culture stood still, when it was pristine.

For example, throughout North America, the American Indian societies encountered and described by Europeans had already suffered the effects of widespread Western contact. Smallpox and other diseases spread far inland and decimated indigenous populations long before anyone physically encountered a foreigner. So even the first explorers of, say, the interior of the southeastern United States interacted with Indian societies that were often a shadow of their former selves. No one could describe their decimated societies as the "ethnographic present."

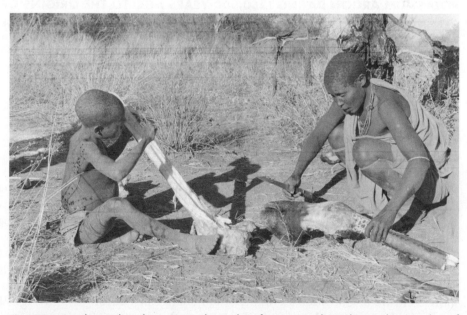

Figure 1.8 Ethnoarchaeology among the Hadza of Tanzania. Shown here is the recording of details of a hunter's kill.

SCIENCE

Dating the Past

Four major chronological methods date the 2.5 million years of the human past (see Table 1.2 on page 19):

HISTORICAL RECORDS (PRESENT DAY TO 3000 B.C.)

Historical records can be used to date the past only as far back as the beginnings of writing and written records, which first appeared in western Asia in about 3000 B.C., much later in many other parts of the world.

DENDROCHRONOLOGY (TREE-RING DATING) (PRESENT DAY TO 8000 B.C.)

The annual growth rings of long-lived trees such as sequoias, bristlecone pines, and European oaks, used for beams, posts, and other purposes by ancient people, can be used to date sites in some areas such as the American Southwest, the Mediterranean, and western Europe. Originally used on southwestern pueblos, **dendrochronology** (tree-ring dating), using sequences of growth rings, is also used to calibrate radiocarbon dates (see "Tree-Ring Dating" box in Chapter 7).

RADIOCARBON DATING (c. A.D. 1500 to 40,000 Years Ago)

Radiocarbon dating is based on the measurement of the decay rates of 14C atoms in organic samples like charcoal, shell, wood, hair, and other materials. When combined with **accelerator mass spectrometry (AMS)**, it can produce dates from tiny samples, which are then calibrated, if possible, against tree-ring dates to provide a date in calendar years. Radiocarbon chronologies date most of prehistory after about 40,000 years ago, well after modern humans appeared in Africa for the first time (see "Radiocarbon Dating" box in Chapter 4).

POTASSIUM ARGON DATING (250,000 YEARS AGO TO THE ORIGINS OF LIFE)

A chronological method used to date early prehistory, which measures the decay rate of 40K atoms in volcanic rocks (see "Potassium Argon Dating" box in Chapter 2). **Potassium argon dating** is an excellent way of dating East African hominin fossils, many of which are found in volcanic levels.

Other dating methods include obsidian hydration, paleomagnetic dating, thermoluminescence, and uranium thorium dating, but none of them can be universally applied.

Cultural Process and Past Lifeways

Cultural process refers to the changes and interactions in cultural systems. The study of cultural process provokes intense theoretical debate among archaeologists, who assume that archaeology is far more than merely a descriptive activity and that it is possible to explain how cultural change occurred in the remote past.

Every cultural system is in a constant state of change. Its various political, social, and technological subsystems adjust to changing circumstances. We ourselves live in a time of rapid cultural change in which there are measurable differences between decades, let alone centuries. Consider the many small changes in automobile design that have occurred in the past few decades. In themselves, the changes often are not very significant, but the cumulative effect of several years of steady change toward safer cars is striking—air bags, energy-absorbing bumpers, padded steering wheels, anti-lock brakes, and so on. The automobile of today is very different from that of the 1960s, and many of the changes are due to stricter government safety regulations, which in turn result from greater safety consciousness on the part of consumers. Here we see a major cumulative change in part of our enormous technological subsystem. By examining the relationships between these technological changes and the political and social subsystems, we can understand the processes through which culture has changed.

Most processes of culture change in human prehistory were cumulative, occurring slowly over a long time period. They were the result of adaptations to constantly changing external environments. Cultural systems were continually adjusting and evolving in response to internal and external feedback, including changes in the natural environment. The study of past lifeways—that is, how people have made their living in the past—involves the examination of prehistoric cultures within their environmental context. Environmental data come from many sources, including ancient plant remains, fossil pollen grains, and animal bones. Ancient subsistence patterns, and even diet, can be reconstructed from food residues such as animal bones, carbonized seeds, and fish remains. This is also descriptive archaeology, but it relates **archaeological cultures** to the complex and continually changing patterns of settlement, subsistence, and environmental influences.

The fundamental questions about prehistory revolve around culture change. How did anatomically modern humans, *Homo sapiens,* evolve their more advanced cultures? What cultural processes came into play when people began to cultivate the soil, or when complex and elaborate urban societies developed in western Asia just over 5,000 years ago? Clearly, no single element in a cultural system is the primary cause of cultural change, because a complex range of factors—rainfall, vegetation, technology, social restrictions, and population density, to mention only a few—interact with one another and react to a change in any element in the system.

The Mechanisms of Culture Change

Culture history is a sound way of describing the past, but it is of minimal use for studying variations in different prehistoric cultures, for answering fundamental questions about the nature of culture change in the past. But the archaeological record does not invariably reflect an orderly and smooth chronicle of culture change. A radically new artifact inventory may suddenly appear in contemporary occupation layers at several sites, while earlier tool kits suddenly vanish. A culture's economy may change rapidly within a century as the plow revolutionizes agricultural methods. How do such changes come about? What mechanisms of cultural change were at work to cause major and minor alterations in the archaeological record? Archaeologists use four descriptive models to characterize culture change: inevitable variation, invention, diffusion, and migration.

- ■   **Inevitable variation.** As people learn the behavior patterns of their society, inevitably some differences in learned behavior will appear from generation to generation. These, although minor in themselves, accumulate over a long period of time, especially in isolated populations. The snowball effect of such inevitable variation among isolated, thinly scattered populations can be considerable. For example, projectile point forms varied considerably between different, isolated big-game hunting groups on the North American Great Plains in 4000 B.C., even though they all pursued the same animals with much the same techniques.

- **Invention**. Humans are inquisitive, constantly innovating, having ideas. Invention is the creation or evolution of a new idea. The term invention refers to new ideas that originate in a human culture, either by accident or by design. All innovations in human society have their origin in such actions or chance occurrences, but only a very few inventions are truly unique and not introduced from outside by some other culture. It is one thing to invent something, quite another to have it accepted by society as a whole. In general, technological innovations such as, for example, the plow are more readily accepted than social or religious innovations, for they are less likely to conflict with established value systems. The genius of humanity was that it recognized opportunities when they came along and adapted to new circumstances, often in similar ways in widely separated areas, resulting in independent invention of very similar ideas such as farming.

- **Diffusion.** The spread of ideas, over short or long distances, is termed diffusion. Neither the exchange of ideas nor of technological innovations necessarily involve actual movements of people. Diffusion can result from regular trade between neighboring communities. Commerce of any kind implies a two-sided relationship, in which both parties exchange goods, services, and, of course, ideas such as new religious beliefs. For instance, brightly painted Minoan pots from Crete carried olive oil and wine through the Aegean Islands and as far afield as Egypt (Figure 1.9).

Figure 1.9 Minoan pot from Knossos, Crete.

- **Migration**. This involves movements of entire societies that deliberately decide to expand their spheres of influence. Spanish conquistadors occupied Mexico, the Polynesians deliberately voyaged from island to island across the Pacific. In each case, new land masses were found by purposeful exploration, then colonized. Smaller-scale migrations are more commonplace, such as when a group of merchants from lowland Veracruz, Mexico, moved into the highland city of **Teotihuacán** and settled in their own barrio, identified from their distinctive cream-colored pottery and dome-shaped thatched adobe houses (Figure 1.10). There are other types of migrations, too, unorganized movements of slaves and artisans and of people fleeing religious persecution.

Invention, diffusion, and migration are far too general cultural mechanisms to explain the ever-changing relationships between human cultures and their environments. The identification of these mechanisms is largely a descriptive activity, based on artifacts and other material remains. The explanation of culture change requires more sophisticated research models that reflect the interaction of human societies with the natural environment.

Figure 1.10 A reconstruction of the Veracruz enclave at Teotihuacán, Mexico.

Culture as Adaptation

In the 1950s, American anthropologists Julian Steward and Leslie White developed what they called **cultural ecology**, the study of the total way in which human populations adapt to and transform their environments. Archaeologists who study cultural ecology are concerned with how prehistoric cultures as systems interacted with other systems: with other human cultures, the biotic community (other living things around them), and their physical environment. This is what is often called the culture-as-adaptation approach to human prehistory.

Culture as adaptation—this phrase is behind most contemporary interpretations of world prehistory. Leslie White called culture "man's extrasomatic [outside the body] means of adaptation." Culture is the result of human beings' unique ability to create and infuse events and objects with meaning that can be appreciated, decoded, and understood, with, among other things, ideology. Thus, human cultures differ greatly from place to place and from time to time, resulting in variations in prehistoric material culture—the data for studying prehistory.

Under the culture-as-adaptation rubric, human behavior is an adaptation not to a single site but to environmental regions. Thus, the archaeologist has to study not individual sites but entire regions. The archaeological record is not just a system of structured sites, but a continuous pattern of artifact distribution and density over the landscape. As individuals and groups hunt, forage, or farm their way across this landscape, they leave behind material remains of their presence, a record that reflects their continual behavior within the region.

Multilinear Cultural Evolution

The culture-as-adaptation approach attempts to interpret cultural variation and adaptation on a regional basis over long periods of time. This strategy means that the archaeologist must pay close attention to the relationships between ecological and social systems. Under this theory of **multilinear cultural evolution** (evolution along multiple tracks), each human society pursues its own evolutionary course, determined by the long-term success of an adaptation, via technology and social institutions, to its natural environment. Multilinear evolution is widely used as a general framework for interpreting world prehistory, which witnessed occasional dramatic incidents of cultural change.

Some societies achieve a broad measure of equilibrium with their environment, in which adaptive changes consist of little more than some refinements in technology and the fine-tuning of organizational structures. Others become involved in cycles of change that are triggered by external environmental change or from within society. If these changes involve either greater food supplies or population growth, there can be accelerated change resulting from the need to feed more people or the deployment of an enlarged food surplus. Such was probably the case in parts of southwestern Asia in 10,000 B.C., when some communities living in favored regions began cultivating wild cereal grasses to expand their food supplies (see Chapter 6). Within generations of the first experiments with farming, many groups depended heavily on cereal crops. Major technological and social changes followed. People now settled in permanent villages under entirely different social conditions.

Every society has its growth limits imposed by the environment and available technology, and some environments, such as Egypt's Nile valley, have more potential for growth than others. Certain types of sociopolitical organization, such as centralized control of specialized

SITE

Ancient War Casualties at Thebes, Egypt

Archaeology studies not only great rulers but anonymous, ordinary people, too. Few tales of ordinary people are as vivid as the one unearthed in a remarkable discovery made by Egyptologist Herbert Winlock in a sepulcher close to the tomb of the Middle Kingdom pharaoh Mentuhotep (2061–2010 B.C.) at Thebes in 1911. Sixty soldiers killed in battle were stacked in the tomb dressed in linen shrouds. Their dried-out bodies were so well preserved that they began to decay when removed from the tomb. Winlock used biological and archaeological data to reconstruct their last battle. All the soldiers were young men in the prime of life, each with a thick mop of hair bobbed off square at the nape of the neck. All had perished in an attack on a fort, for their wounds came from arrows shot from above or from crushing blows from stones thrown down from a fortification.

Contemporary pictures show attackers sheltering under thin shields as they attempt to breach the defenses under a rain of missiles. In this case, the fire was too fierce, so the men had run out of range. A shower of arrows overtook some of them. At least one was hit in the back with an arrow that came out on the other side of his chest. He pitched forward. The slender reed shaft broke off as he fell and he bled to death. The defenders now sallied forth and mercilessly clubbed at least a dozen wounded men to death with heavy blows. Then, waiting vultures and ravens descended on the corpses and worried away the flesh with their beaks. A second attack was successful. The torn bodies were recovered and buried with honor in a special tomb next to their pharaoh. We do not know where the attack took place, but it was somewhere in Egypt, for the arrows that killed the attackers were of Egyptian design. Few discoveries make such a powerful statement about the lives of the anonymous players of the past as this one.

---

labor, are more efficient than others. Adaptive changes triggered technological innovations that led to increased food supplies and higher population densities. Multilinear evolution assumes human societies have developed along many tracks.

The widespread use of multilinear evolution as an explanatory mechanism has led a number of archaeologists to talk of two broad stages of social development in prehistory: prestate and state-organized societies. These should not be thought of as universal stages through which all societies pass, as some Victorian anthropologists once argued, but as degrees of social development that are achieved by many groups quite independently in many environments (see box on page 28).

Multilinear cultural evolution combines systems approaches to human culture and cultural ecology into a closely knit, highly flexible way of studying and explaining cultural process. The culture-as-adaptation approach requires that one look at cultural change in the context of the interrelationships among many variables. Thus, there is no one prime agent of cultural evolution that caused, say, farming in ancient Syria or Maya civilization in **Mesoamerica** (the area of Central America where prehistoric states flourished). Rather, a series of important variables, such as, for example, population growth, food shortages and a prolonged drought cycle, and intergroup competition, acted together to trigger cultural change.

When we seek to explain the major and minor events of prehistory, we have to consider the ways in which change takes place, the processes and mechanisms of change, and the social and economic stresses (population pressure, game scarcity, and so on) that trigger

SCIENCE

Ancient Social Organization

Prestate societies are small-scale societies, based on the community, band, or village. They vary greatly in their degrees of political integration and are sometimes divided into three loosely defined categories:

1. **Bands** are associations of families that may not exceed twenty-five to sixty people. They are knit together by close social ties; they were the dominant form of social organization for most of prehistory, from the earliest times up to the origins of food production some 10,000 years ago.

2. **Tribes** are clusters of bands that are linked by clans (formal kin groups). A clan is not a tribe, which contains people from many kin groups, but a group of people linked by common ancestral ties that serve as connections between widely scattered communities. Clans are important because they are a form of social linkage that gives people a sense of common identity with a wider world than their own immediate family and relatives. Many early farming societies throughout the world can be classified as tribal societies.

3. **Chiefdoms** are a controversial category, for they display great differences in organization and social complexity, making them hard to define precisely. Fundamentally, they are societies headed by individuals with unusual ritual, political, or entrepreneurial skills and are often hard to distinguish from tribes. Society is still kin-based but more hierarchical, with power concentrated in the hands of kin leaders responsible for acquiring and then redistributing food and other resources throughout the group. Chiefdoms tend to have higher population densities and vary greatly in their elaboration; they were politically very volatile, rising to power and collapsing with dramatic rapidity.

State-organized societies (Preindustrial civilizations) operated on a large scale, with centralized political and social organization. Tiny elites ruled such societies. They held monopolies over strategic resources, including food surpluses, and used force to impose authority. Their social organization can be likened to a pyramid, with a single ruler at the apex and stratified classes of nobles, priests, bureaucrats, merchants, artisans, and commoners below. Most were based in large cities, with populations that ranged upward from 5,000 people.

The state-organized society was based on intensive agricultural production, which often relied heavily on irrigation or swamp farming—carefully watered lands that yielded several bountiful crops a year. These painstakingly administered and controlled agricultural works were the means by which society supported thousands of nonfarmers: the artisans, officials, traders, and priests; also city dwellers. State economies were based on the centralized accumulation of capital and social status through tribute and taxation. Long-distance trade and the division of labor, also craft specialization, were often characteristic of early states, as were advances toward record keeping, science, and mathematics, and usually some form of written script.

these mechanisms. Such multicausal models are a far cry from speculative theories that speak of ancient Egyptian voyages across the Atlantic Ocean or brilliant, solitary inventors. They require rigorous methodologies for identifying the many factors involved, using data that consist, for the most part, of material remains such as potsherds and stone implements.

Cultural Traditions and Cultural Change

The culture-as-adaptation approach to the past is concerned primarily with identifying variations in ancient human cultures and with explaining cultural change over long periods of time. Archaeologists espousing this approach have focused on explanations for culture change, and on relationships between people and their environments, to the point that many archaeologists have complained that this perspective is more concerned with the processes of culture change than with the people behind these changes. All human societies are made up of individuals—men and women, children and adults, families, entire communities, their neighbors near and far. They spend their lives interacting with one another, agreeing, disagreeing, negotiating, quarreling, and living in peace. From these interactions stem cultural traditions, which provide guidance for coping with the environment. The same traditions can be a powerful, conservative force, one that inhibits change, or encourages innovation in times of stress.

Ecological and other external constraints can be culturally mediated, but they operate independently of human actions, which makes them susceptible to understanding in terms of evolutionary theory and other such generalizations. Cultural traditions are far more idiosyncratic and haphazard. This makes it difficult to impose evolutionary order on human history, for despite external constraints, much cultural change is contingent on ever-changing circumstances and cultural traditions. By studying individual cultural traditions, archaeologists try to explain the distinctive features of cultures in ways that evolutionists and cultural ecologists can never hope to. Increasingly, we seek to explain the past in terms of both external (environmental) and internal (social) constraints. Internal constraints include knowledge, beliefs, values, and other culturally conditioned habits, all of them different in every culture. Yet some of them are shared by cultures flourishing thousands of miles apart. For instance, two widely separated cultures may develop bronze metallurgy, which is based on a common body of technological know-how, but the cultural context of that knowledge is radically different, as it was, say, in the Shang civilization of China (Chapter 11) and the Moche culture in coastal Peru (Chapter 14). Some symbols, like the common practice of elevating chiefs or kings on a dais, or associations between rulers and the sun, have developed in many places. That does not mean, of course, that they are connected.

A new generation of archaeological research has moved beyond cultural process and ecology to take a first, cautious look at what was going on inside the early human mind. Sometimes called **cognitive archaeology**, the study of the archaeology of mind, this new approach to the past is both controversial and stimulating, since it draws on lines of evidence from many disciplines, including evolutionary psychology.

Intangibles: Ideology and Interaction

Archaeologists study the remote human past from rare fossil human remains and the surviving consequences of human behavior—artifacts, food remains, and so on. The human mind, our speech, thought processes, beliefs, and interpersonal dealings are intangibles, which do not survive in the archaeological record. Nevertheless, this same record provides dramatic evidence for evolving human behavior and much enhanced intellectual capabilities over 2.5 million years. The appearance of toolmaking in East Africa about 2.5 million years before present was one moment when major change occurred. Perhaps it was no coincidence that human brain size increased dramatically over the next million years. Another major moment came after the development of the fully modern brain, some 60,000 to 30,000 years ago, when *Homo sapiens* developed much more complex technology, art, and the earliest religious beliefs.

Herein lie many fundamental questions about the past: What happened to the human mind during these great spurts in brain size? When did language and human consciousness first arise? What was the nature of human intelligence both before and after the development of the modern brain? Our increased understanding of cultural forces and constraints, and of cognitive issues, has caused archaeologists to focus more attention on people and groups rather than on the processes of culture change. Much new research has tried to look beyond the material aspects of the archaeological record to search for the complex, intangible ideas behind ancient societies. This approach, which has generated an extraordinary outpouring of (often verbose and irrelevant) theoretical argument, is sometimes called **postprocessual archaeology**. The theoretical debate continues, but has had the effect of focusing attention on two important topics: ancient ideologies and beliefs, and the interactions between groups and individuals.

Ideology and Beliefs

The intangible ideologies and beliefs of ancient times are extremely difficult to reconstruct from material remains such as artifacts, art, and architecture. We can only guess at the beliefs and motivations behind late Ice Age cave art (Chapter 4) or the celebrated plastered human portraits from the early farming settlement at **Jericho**, Jordan (Figure 1.11). But the

Figure 1.11 Plastered skull from Jericho, Jordan.

study of ancient ideology and beliefs offers great potential when written records such as Egyptian documents or Maya glyphs can be combined with excavations. One of the best examples of such research is Linda Schele and David Freidel's remarkable work on ancient Maya iconography in ancient Mesoamerica, based on a combination of deciphered glyphs and archaeological data (Chapter 12). Their work shows how ritual life, shrines, and temple structures helped shape past lives. "The Maya believed in a past which always returned . . . in endless cycles repeating patterns already set into the fabric of time and space," they write in their book *A Forest of Kings*. "Our challenge . . . is to interpret this history, recorded in their words, images, and ruins, in a manner comprehensible to the modern mind, yet true to the Mayans' perception of themselves" (Schele and Freidel, 1990, p. 18).

Interactions

In the final analysis, it is people who share culture, groups and individuals who make decisions about daily life. Men interact with women, children with adults; a kin group quarrels within itself, pitting small faction against small faction; ethnic groups compete for access to wealth or political power—such dealings between individuals, between individuals and groups, and between groups are the forces that constrain or encourage cultural change. By its very nature, the archaeological record tends to be impersonal, its artifacts and food remains chronicling the dealings of blurred groups rather than individuals, or even categories of people, for instance, women at a given moment in time.

Only rarely can the archaeologist go beyond artifacts and food remains to study the roles of groups or individuals, the work they undertook, and the subtle ways in which they influenced the course of events. For example, at the early farming village of **Abu Hureyra** in Syria, dating to 9700 B.C., biological anthropologist Theya Molleson observed malformations of the toes, knees, and lower vertebrae in the skeletons of all the adult women, a condition due, almost certainly, to hours of grinding grain (see Figure 6.4 on page 155). Male skeletons did not display the same impairments. This is some of the earliest evidence for division of labor between men and women in human history.

Studying ancient beliefs, the intangibles of the past, can be likened to studying a series of pictures without the captions. Herein lies one of the great frustrations of archaeology. We can admire a giant bull from the 15,000-year-old frieze painted by Stone Age artists on the walls of a cave at **Lascaux** in southwestern France (Chapter 4), walk among the stone circles at **Stonehenge** in England (see Figure 1.12 on page 32), or trace the intricate engraving on a freshwater shell from the **Mississippian** culture of the southeastern United States (Chapter 7). But while we can admire the artistry behind the image, we can only rarely discern the complex beliefs and motives that resulted in these magnificent achievements. We cannot speak to the ancients, we can only seek to understand some of the brilliant, and often frustrating, complexity of their diverse societies.

British archaeologist Steven Mithen, an expert on the ancient human mind, has likened the long millennia of our past to an archaeological play with several acts, which reaches a climax with the appearance of farming a mere 12,000 years ago. In ten short millennia, humanity moves away from a simple village existence into a world of automobiles, aircraft, vast industrial cities, and an emerging global, computerized society. World prehistory performs most of this play, ending with the Spanish conquest of Mexico and Peru, with the climactic encounter between Westerners and the last of the preindustrial civilizations in the early sixteenth century A.D.

Our play begins over 2.5 million years ago.

Figure 1.12 Stonehenge in southern England.

Summary

Archaeology is the study of the ancient human past, using the material remains of past human behavior. These material remains make up the archaeological record, the archives of prehistoric times. While historians study written records, archaeologists deal with an anonymous past. Archaeology is unique among the sciences in its ability to study culture change over long periods of time. Text-aided archaeology combines the evidence of archaeology with documentary sources, while prehistoric archaeology is the study of prehistory, the period of the human past before the advent of written records. The study of world prehistory, which developed in the 1950s, is the study of human prehistory from a global perspective using archaeological data and other sources.

All human societies are interested in the past, but they think of it in different terms and use it for different purposes. Archaeologists, Westerners generally, conceive of time in a linear way, while many non-Western groups measure time by the cycles of the seasons and the movements of heavenly bodies. They use linear time only when it is of use to them. Archaeology is not the only way of approaching history, for many societies have oral histories, alternative perspectives on the past that are of vital importance in preserving traditional culture and values.

Theoretical approaches to human prehistory abound, but can be divided, in general terms, into processual and post-processual approaches. The processual (culture-as-adaptation) approach uses multilinear cultural evolution and cultural ecology to provide a viable general framework for studying world prehistory, based on the assumption that human societies evolved in many diverse ways.

Archaeologists conventionally make a distinction between prestate and state-organized societies as part of this framework. Evolutionary ecology makes use of the mechanism of natural selection and optimal foraging strategy to interpret hunter-gatherer societies in terms of energy costs and risk management. In recent years, archaeologists have distinguished between external constraints on cultural change, such as environmental factors, and internal constraints, created by the actions of individuals and groups. A new generation of research is focusing on ideologies, human interactions, gender relations, and other topics, combining processual and post-processual approaches to study both types of constraints and their influences on the past.

PART II

THE WORLD OF THE FIRST HUMANS

When yet all was in darkness, when yet no sun had shone and no dawn had broken—it is said—the gods gathered themselves together and took counsel among themselves there in Teotihuacán. They spoke, they said among themselves: "Come hither, oh gods! Who will carry the burden? Who will take it upon himself to be the sun, to bring the dawn?

FROM AN AZTEC LEGEND OF THE CREATION (Anderson and Dibble, 1963, p. 4)

2 Human Origins

| 4.5 Million | 2.5 Million | 1.0 Million | 500,000 B.P. | 100,000 B.P. | 50,000 B.P. | 15,000 B.P. | A.D. 1 | A.D. 1950 |

PROLOGUE

It was a blazing hot day at Olduvai Gorge, East Africa, in 1959. Back in camp, Louis Leakey lay in his tent, suffering from a bout of influenza. Meanwhile, Mary Leakey, sheltered by a beach umbrella, was excavating the small scatter of broken bones and crude artifacts deep in the gorge. For hours she brushed and pried away dry soil. Suddenly, she unearthed part of an upper jaw with teeth so humanlike that she took a closer look. Moments later, she jumped into her Land Rover and sped up the track to camp. "Louis, Louis," she cried, as she burst into their tent, "I've found Dear Boy at last." Louis leapt out of bed, his flu forgotten. Together, they excavated the fragmentary remains of a magnificent, robust hominin skull. The Leakeys named it *Zinjanthropus boisei* ("African human of Boise"), a Mr. Boise being one of their benefactors. With this dramatic discovery, they changed the study of human evolution from a part-time science into an international detective story.

Biologist Thomas Huxley called it "the question of questions," the nature of the exact relationship between humans and their closest living relatives such as the chimpanzee and the gorilla—the question of human origins. Ever since his day, scientists have been locked in controversy as they trace the complex evolutionary history of humanity back to its very beginnings. At first, they thought in terms of simple, ladderlike evolutionary schemes. These theories have now given way to highly tentative studies of early human evolution completed by reconstructing precise evolutionary relationships from fossil specimens, a process fraught with difficulty when bone fragments are the raw materials. It is a matter of fine and careful judgment, the comparing of anatomical details, the weighing of different characteristics, and the assessment of chronology and stratigraphy. The problem is complicated by an extremely thin fossil record between 5 million and 1 million years ago (mya), representing less than 2,000 individuals. Most of these are single teeth found in fossil-rich South African caves. Very few are skull fragments or jaws, the most valuable of all fossil finds. During this 4-million-year time period, our ancestors went through dramatic transformations, visible only through an incomplete paleontological lens. We know that many hominin forms flourished in tropical Africa during this period. Which of them, however, were direct human ancestors? We can only achieve an understanding of human evolution by getting to know as many species as we can, and this task has hardly begun. In this chapter, we examine some of the controversies that surround the biological and cultural evolution of humankind and describe what we know about the behavior and lifeways of our earliest ancestors.

The Great Ice Age (1.8 million to 15,000 years ago)

The story of humanity begins deep in geological time, during the later part of the Cenozoic Era, the age of mammals. For most of geological time, the world's climate was warmer than it is today. During the Oligocene epoch, some 35 million years ago, the first signs of glacial cooling appeared with the formation of a belt of pack ice around Antarctica. This development was followed by a major drop in world temperatures between 14 and 11 million years ago. As temperatures fell, large ice sheets formed on high ground in high latitudes. About 3.2 million years ago, large ice sheets formed on the northern continents. Then, some 2.5 million years ago, just as humans first appeared in tropical Africa, glaciation intensified even more, and the earth entered its present period of constantly fluctuating climate. These changes culminated during the **Quaternary** period or **Pleistocene** epoch, the most recent interval of earth history, which began at least 1.8 million years ago. This period is sometimes called the Age of Humanity, for it was during this epoch, the Great Ice Age, that humans first peopled most of the globe. The major climatic and environmental changes of the Ice Age form the backdrop for some of the most important stages of evolution.

   The words "Ice Age" conjure up a vision of ice-bound landscapes and frigid, subzero temperatures that gripped the earth in a prolonged deep freeze. In fact, the Pleistocene witnessed constant fluctuations between warm and intensely cold global climates. Deep sea cores lifted from the depths of the world's oceans have produced a complex picture of Ice Age climate (Table 2.1). These cores have shown that climatic fluctuations between warm and cold were relatively minor until about 800,000 years ago. Since then, periods of intense cold have recurred about every 90,000 years, with minor oscillations about 20,000 and 40,000 years apart. Many scientists believe that these changes are triggered by long-term astronomical cycles, especially in the earth's orbit around the sun, which affect the seasonal and north–south variations of solar radiation received by the earth.

TABLE 2.1 Major Events of the Ice Age

Temperature (← Lower — Higher →)	Dates (B.P.)	Periods	Epochs	Glacials	Human Evolution	Prehistory
	10,000	Holocene	Holocene	Holocene	Homo sapiens	Cities, agriculture; Settlement of New World
	118,000	Quaternary	Pleistocene — Brunhes	Würm (Wisconsin in North America)		
	128,000			Saale		
	780,000		Matuyama	Many cold episodes	Archaic Homo sapiens; Homo erectus	
		Tertiary	Pliocene — Olduvai Event			
	1,600,000				Early hominins	

Uncertain climatic detail before 130,000 years ago

There were at least nine glacial periods that mantled northern Europe and North America with great ice sheets, the last one retreating only some 15,000 years ago. Interglacial periods, with climates as warm or warmer than that of today, occurred infrequently, and the constant changes displaced plants and animals, including humans, from their original habitats. During colder cycles, plants and animals generally fared better at lower altitudes and in warmer latitudes. Populations of animals spread slowly toward more hospitable areas, mixing with populations that already lived there, and creating new communities with new combinations of organisms. For example, paleontologist Björn Kurten has estimated that no fewer than 113 of the mammalian species living in Europe and adjacent Asia evolved during the past 3 million years. This repeated mixing surely affected human evolution in many ways.

The earliest chapter of human evolution unfolded during a period of relatively minor climatic change, indeed before the Pleistocene truly began. Between 4 million and 2 million years ago, the world's climate was somewhat warmer and more stable than it was in later times. The African savanna, the probable cradle of humankind, contained many species of mammals large and small, including a great variety of the order of primates, of which we humans are a part.

Early Primate Evolution and Adaptation

The Order Primates

All of us are members of the order primates, which includes most tree-loving placental mammals. There are two suborders: **anthropoids** (apes, humans, and monkeys) and **prosimians** (lemurs, tarsiers, and other so-called pre-monkeys). The many similarities in behavior and physical characteristics between the **hominins** (primates of the family **Hominidae**, which includes modern humans, earlier human subspecies, and their direct ancestors) and the **pongidae** (our closest living nonhuman primate relatives) can be explained by identical characteristics that each group inherited millions of years ago from a common ancestor. In other words, humans and our closest nonhuman primate relatives evolved along parallel lines from a common ancestor (Table 2.2).

When did humankind separate from the nonhuman primates? Experts disagree violently about the answer. It was in Africa that humans and apes diverged from monkeys, but no one knows when this divergence took place. Several species of apes were flourishing in Africa at the beginning of the Miocene epoch, some 24 million years ago. The basic anatomical pattern of the large hominins appears in the Middle Miocene, 18 to 12 million years ago. A second radiation began in the Late Miocene, between 8 and 5 million years ago. This radiation eventually produced four lineages, at least one of which, human beings, was much modified. A similar evolutionary pattern occurs among herbivores such as elephants. In both cases, the patterns reflect changing climates and habitats—from warmer, less seasonal, more forested regimens to colder, more seasonal, and less forested conditions. They also mirror changes in the configuration of continents, mountain systems, and antarctic ice.

For the hominins, the critical period was between 10 and 5 million years ago, when the segment of the African hominin lineage radiated to produce gorillas, chimpanzees, and hominins. Unfortunately, this 5-million-year period is a black hole in our knowledge of early

TABLE 2.2 Evolution of the Primates

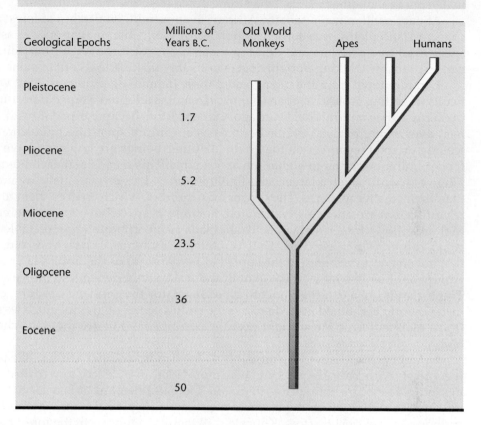

Geological Epochs	Millions of Years B.C.	Old World Monkeys	Apes	Humans
Pleistocene				
	1.7			
Pliocene				
	5.2			
Miocene				
	23.5			
Oligocene				
	36			
Eocene				
	50			

human evolution. We can only guess at the nature of the apelike animals that flourished in Africa during these millennia.

Paleoanthropologist David Pilbeam theorizes that these animals were mostly tree-living, with long arms and legs and a broad chest. They would have used all four limbs in the trees, occasionally scrambling on the ground and even standing on their rear limbs at times. About 5 million years ago, Pilbeam believes, the hominoid lineage divided into western and eastern parts. The western segment, the proto-chimpanzee, remained dependent on fruit and other tree foods, scattered resources that required a flexible social organization. Intense controversy surrounds the relationships between humans, chimpanzees, and gorillas, but many biologists agree that chimpanzees are humans' closest relatives. Using molecular time clocks, they calculate that these three primate forms last shared a common ancestor about 6 to 7 million years ago.

"Coming Down from the Trees"

A fall in world temperatures after 20 million years ago resulted in increasingly open environments in tropical latitudes. With this reduction in forested environments probably came a trend toward ground-adapted species. Many species of living and now-extinct primates, including hominins, adapted to this kind of existence some time after 10 million years ago. In other words, "they came down from the trees."

About 5 million years ago, the African savanna, with its patches of forest and extensive grassland plains, was densely populated by many mammalian species as well as by specialized tree-dwellers and other primates. Some of these were flourishing in small bands, probably walking upright, and conceivably making tools out of stone and wood.

Coming down from the trees created three immediate problems. First was the difficulty of getting around in open country. Hominins adopted a bipedal posture as a way of doing so at least 4 million years ago. Our ancestors became **bipedal** (walking on two feet) over a long period of time, perhaps as a result of spending more and more time feeding on food resources on the ground. Human beings are large and have additional food requirements due to higher metabolic rates. This means that each hominin has to range efficiently over a larger area to obtain food. Larger mammals are more mobile than their smaller relatives. They cover more ground, which enables them to subsist off resources that are unevenly distributed, not only in space but also at different seasons. Mobility allows larger mammals like humans to incorporate unpredictable, often seasonal, resources in their diets. They can tolerate extremes of heat and cold, a capacity that may have contributed to the spread of humans out of the tropics later in prehistory. Bipedal humans have sweat glands and are heavily dependent on water supplies. These glands are a direct adjunct to bipedalism, for they enhance endurance for long-distance foraging. Bipedalism displaces the body's center of gravity much less and walking is more efficient. An upright posture and bipedal gait are the most characteristic hominin physical features.

Upright posture is vital because it frees the hands for other actions, like toolmaking. It contrasts with **knuckle walking**, which provides an excellent power thrust for jumping into a tree or a short sprint (think of a football lineman). It is a specialized way of moving around in which the backs of the fingers are placed on the ground and act as main weight-bearing surfaces. Knuckle walking was adaptive in the forest because long arms and hands as well as grasping feet were still vital for climbing (Figure 2.1). Human arms are too short for us to be comfortable with this posture. Bipedalism favors endurance and the covering of long distances, important considerations in open country. It was a critical antecedent of hunting, gathering, and toolmaking.

Second, the savanna abounded in predators, making it hard for primates to sleep safely. Large hominins made home bases, where they sheltered from the hot sun and slept in safety. What form these home bases took is a matter of great debate. Lastly, high-quality plant foods, abundant in the forests, were widely dispersed over the savanna. It is striking that later foragers subsisted off a broad range of game and plant foods. As part of human evolution, their hominin ancestors expanded their food range to include more meat, perhaps during long periods of plant scarcity. Among mammals, these characteristics are associated with a trend toward larger brain size. And, as brain size increased, so, gradually, the lifeways of evolving hominins became less apelike and closer to that of human foragers, a process that took hundreds of thousands of years to unfold.

These and several other factors—such as increased longevity and brain enlargement—required much greater behavioral flexibility. This flexibility included enhanced intelligence and learning capacity, increased parental care, and new levels of social interaction.

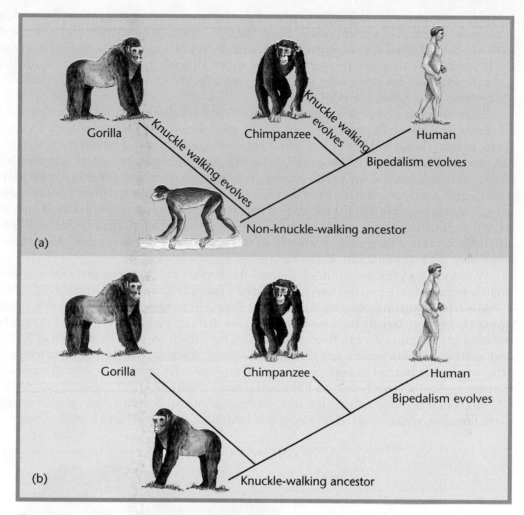

Figure 2.1 Knuckle walking and four-footed posture. Two major theories account for the evolution of bipedalism: (a) If the last common ancestor of chimpanzees, gorillas, and humans was not a knuckle walker (the body's center of gravity lies in the middle of the area bounded by legs and arms), then knuckle walking would have evolved independently in both chimpanzees and gorillas. Under this theory, the ancestral locomotion for humans was not knuckle walking. (b) If the last common ancestor for chimpanzees, gorillas, and humans was not a knuckle walker, then the ancestral condition for humans is knuckle walking.

The Fossil Evidence for Human Evolution (7 million to 1.5 million years ago)

The Earliest Hominin?

The **Toro-Menalla** region of the Djurab Desert in Chad, Central Africa, is a brutal place for paleoanthropological research. In 2001, French scholars Michel Brunet, Patrick Vignaud, and their colleagues found the chimpanzee-sized skull of a hominin dated (albeit very loosely) to between 6 and 7 million years old. The head is confusing. From the back, the skull looks like that of a chimpanzee. From the front, the facial structure and tooth layout look like that of a hominin of about 1.75 mya (million years ago) (Figure 2.2). The point at the base of the skull where the neck muscles attach suggest that this creature walked upright. Brunet and his team have named this remarkable fossil *Sahelanthropus tchadensis* ("hominin of the Sahel, of Chad").

Sahelanthropus tchadensis suggests that hominin evolution was much more complicated than was suspected a generation ago. In all probability, a wide variety of apes, some with larger brains, flourished in tropical Africa between 8 and 5 mya, of which the Chad find is but one. At this early stage in research, paleoanthropologists are uncertain whether *Sahelanthropus tchadensis*, usually called Toumaï, is a hominin or an ape. Most believe it may be a very early hominin, perhaps even an ancestor of hominins known from Ethiopia after 5 mya. It is also possible that the date when the ancestors of humans split off from apes may have to be pushed back somewhat earlier. The finders of Toumaï readily admit that they still have not dated their find accurately, so this remarkable discovery may prove to be of somewhat different antiquity in the future.

Whatever the ultimate status of Toumaï, the find shows that very early human evolution took many branches and was not a matter of simple linear development.

Most paleoanthropologists believe that East Africa was the main crucible of early human evolution, largely because this is the area that has yielded the greatest diversity of primordial hominins. Five to four million years ago, the now-desertic regions of Ethiopia and northern Kenya were open savanna grassland, teeming with herds of antelope and other mammals, hunted by both predators and our remote hominin ancestors. And it is here that the earliest known hominins have been found (Figure 2.3).

Molecular biology tells us the last common ancestral hominoid stock split into two main lineages, which evolved into apes and hominins, between 9 and 4 million years ago.

Figure 2.2 *Sahelanthropus tchadensis.*

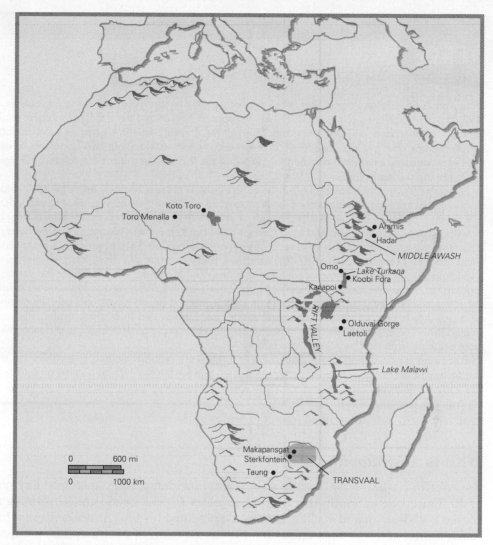

Figure 2.3 Map of archaeological sites described in Chapter 2.

The details of this split are still a complete mystery, largely because fossil beds dating to this critical period are very rare in Africa. The fossil record increases after about 5 million years ago, but is still very fragmentary and controversial.

The summary of fossil hominins that follows is certain to be outdated within a few years. (For a guide through the many taxonomic labels and a basic chronology, see Figure 2.11 on page 52.)

Between 5 and 2 million years ago, a great variety of hominins populated the East African savanna. Paleoanthropologists divide them into two broad groups: the australopithecines and *Homo.* (For dating, see box on page 44.)

SCIENCE

Potassium Argon Dating

The world's first archaeological sites are so ancient that they lie far beyond the chronological range of radiocarbon dating (Chapter 1). Potassium argon dating allows the dating of volcanic rocks between 2 billion and 100,000 years old. Many of the earliest hominin sites occur in volcanically active areas. Human tools are found in direct association with cooled lava fragments or ash from contemporary eruptions, allowing the dating of the East Turkana locations, Olduvai Gorge, and other famous early sites.

Potassium (K), an abundant element in the earth's crust, is present in nearly every mineral. Potassium in its natural form contains only a small proportion of radioactive 40K atoms. For every 100 40K atoms that decay, 11 percent become argon 40, an inert gas that can easily escape from its material by diffusion when lava and other igneous rocks are formed. As volcanic rock forms by crystallization, the argon 40 concentration drops to almost nothing, but the process of 40K decay continues, and 11 percent of every 100 40K atoms will become argon 40. Thus, it is possible, using a spectrometer, to measure the concentration of argon 40 that has accumulated since the volcanic rock formed. Recent advances in potassium argon dating involve computerized laser fusion, a variant of the method that uses a laser beam to analyze irradiated grains of volcanic ash, which give off a gas that is purified and its constituent argon atoms measured in a spectrometer. The new method draws on crystals of volcanic materials from layers associated with fossils to produce much more accurate dates for the earliest hominins.

Potassium argon dating has provided the first relatively reliable method of establishing the chronology of the earliest stages of human evolution, and for the first human cultures on earth.

What Is *Australopithecus?*

Australopithecus (Latin for "southern ape") was first identified by anatomist Raymond Dart at the Taung site in South Africa in 1925. He described a small, gracile primate that displayed both human and apelike features. Dart named his find *Australopithecus africanus*, a much lighter creature than another, more robust form of australopithecine that subsequently turned up at other South African sites and, later, in East Africa (Figures 2.4 and 2.5). The latter is known as *Australopithecus robustus*, a squat, massively built primate with a crested skull.

For years, paleoanthropologists thought that *Australopithecus africanus* was the direct ancestor of humankind, that human evolution had proceeded in a relatively linear way through time. More recent finds from East Africa have muddied the picture and revealed far earlier primates on the human line.

Ardipithecus ramidus

The earliest-known hominin was a small creature, which stood upright, with thin-enameled teeth and a skull closer to those of apes, suggesting close links with ancestral chimpanzees. We know little of this remote, small-brained ancestor, which was found by paleoanthropologist Tim White in a 4.5-million-year-old layer at **Aramis** in the arid Awash region of Ethiopia (Figure 2.6, page 46). White and his colleagues named their find *Ardipithecus*

Figure 2.4 *Australopithecus africanus.*

Figure 2.5 *Australopithecus robustus.*

ramidus, to distinguish it from later, and different, Australopithecines. Fragments of about seventeen individuals are known.

Ardipithecus ramidus apparently lived in more wooded terrain than many of its successors and must lie close to the first hominins to diverge from the African apes. At Aramis, this still little-known, probably bipedal hominin occurs in a layer stratified below two later horizons that have yielded its descendants: *Australopithecus anamensis* and *Australopithecus afarensis.*

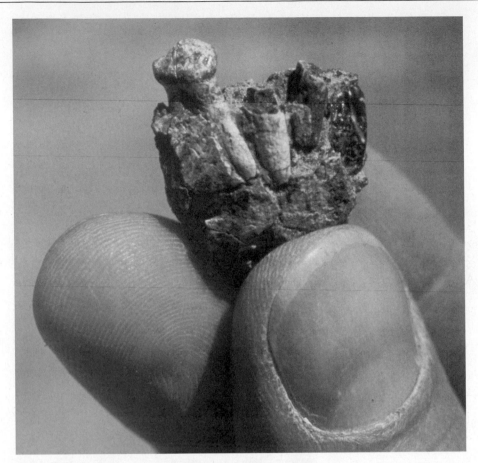

Figure 2.6 *Ardipithecus ramidus.*

From *Ardipithecus* to *Australopithecus*

Australopithecus anamensis dates to about 4.1 mya at Aramis and to about 4 mya at **Allia Bay** and **Kanapoi** on the shores of Lake Turkana, northern Kenya. The fossil fragments, found by Meave Leakey and Alan Walker and named *Australopithecus anamensis* ("anam" is "lake" in Turkana), come from a hominin with large teeth and a mosaic of what appear to be apelike and more evolved features. The hind limbs are thick enough to support the extra weight of walking on two feet, but *anamensis* was not such an efficient walker as modern humans. Measurements of the hind limb suggest the hominin weighed between 47 and 55 kilograms (104 and 121 pounds).

   Ardipithecus ramidus and *Australopithecus anamensis* were the ancestors of a much better known and somewhat later australopithecine, found at **Hadar**, about 72 kilometers (45 miles) south of Aramis, also on the Middle Awash River. It was at Hadar in northern Ethiopia that Maurice Taieb and Donald Johanson discovered a remarkably complete skeleton of a small primate (the famous "Lucy"), together with fragments of at least thirteen males, females, and children. Lucy, who dates to about 3.2 million years ago, stood just under 1.2 meters (4 feet) tall and was nineteen to twenty-one years old (Figure 2.7).

Figure 2.7 "Lucy," *Australopithecus afarensis.*

She was a powerful, heavily muscled primate, fully bipedal, with arms slightly longer for their size than those of humans. Lucy and her contemporaries had humanlike hands and brains about the size of chimpanzees. Johanson and Tim White have classified Lucy as *Australopithecus afarensis,* a direct ancestor of later australopithecines. Undoubtedly, they are correct.

The virtually complete skeleton of a 3-year-old *A. afarensis* has come from the Dikika area of northeastern Ethiopia. Inevitably named "Lucy's child," the Dikika *afarensis* dates to about 3.3 mya, walked bipedally, but has apelike shoulder blades and upper limbs, as if it spent much time in the trees. This important find confirms that all the *A. afarensis* finds made over the past 25 years are from a single australopithecine species. From other Awash discoveries, we know that *afarensis* flourished as late as 3 million years ago and displays considerable size variation. Some individuals stood 1.5 meters (5 feet) tall and probably weighed approximately 68 kilograms (150 pounds), a far cry from the small, slender Lucy.

These early australopithecines were powerful, heavily muscled individuals, thought to be as strong as chimpanzees. Like its predecessors, *A. afarensis* was an anatomical mosaic, bipedal from the waist down, arboreal in the upper part of the body. All were fully bipedal, with the robust, curved arms associated with tree climbers. The arms were slightly longer for their size than the arms of modern humans.

Even more remarkable evidence of bipedalism comes from fossil-bearing beds at **Laetoli** in Tanzania, where Mary Leakey uncovered not only hominin fossils like those at Hadar, but the actual 3.6-million-year-old footprints of big game and some fairly large bipedal primates. The footsteps are those of an adult male and female, the latter carrying a child and making deeper imprints (Figure 2.8). "The tracks indicate a rolling and probably slow-moving gait, with the hips swiveling at each step, as opposed to the freestanding gait of modern man," Mary Leakey wrote (Leakey and Harris, 1990, p. 49). Some scientists believe the Laetoli prints are from *Australopithecus afarensis,* flourishing about 1,600 kilometers (1,000 miles) south of Hadar.

The Hadar and Laetoli finds confirm that the fundamental human adaptation of bipedalism predates the first evidence of toolmaking and the expansion of the brain beyond the level found in our nearest living relatives, the African apes. Bipedalism also implies that later hominins were preadapted (had evolved sufficiently) to utilize their hands for toolmaking.

Originally, experts thought *Australopithecus afarensis* was confined to East Africa. Then Michel Brunet discovered a 3- to 3.5-million-year-old fossilized *A. afarensis* jaw with seven teeth at **Koto Toro** in Chad, in the southern reaches of the Sahara Desert. The Chad hominin flourished in a savanna-woodland environment, much wetter than the arid landscape of today. Koto Toro is the first australopithecine find west of East Africa's Rift Valley and debunks a long-held theory that the great valley formed a barrier separating ape populations and causing those in more open country to move from the trees onto the ground.

A. afarensis was a primitive form of the australopithecines, one that displayed considerable anatomical variation yet was hardy enough to adapt to harsh, changing savanna environments and survive for nearly a million years. Without question, there were several, as yet largely unknown hominin forms in eastern Africa before 3 million years ago.

Figure 2.8 Hominin footprints from Laetoli, Tanzania.

About 3 million years ago, the descendants of *afarensis* split into different lines. At this point, the evolutionary plot really thickens. One line comprises the more gracile *Australopithecus africanus,* first identified by Raymond Dart in 1925 and known entirely from South Africa, far from the putative East African cradle of humankind. The second line held at least three species of robustly built Australopithecines, somewhat later than *africanus,* which became extinct about 1 million years ago. There are probably other, still undescribed lines. With this diversification, we emerge into a more complex chapter in human evolution, marked by geographic and biological diversification and many competing theories.

All Kinds of Australopithecines (3 million to 2.5 million years ago)

Gracile Australopithecines: *Australopithecus africanus*

Australopithecus africanus was a gracile, highly mobile hominin, marked in fossil form by small, almost delicate skulls and prognathous (jutting-out) faces (see Figure 2.4 on page 45). Found entirely in South Africa, *africanus* is an evolutionary mystery, for no one has yet found this form in East Africa, where *A. afarensis* flourished, even if it ultimately evolved from this widely distributed ancestor. It could be an evolutionary experiment that went nowhere, or even have been among the first of a doomed line of robust hominins.

Robust Australopithecines: *A. aethiopicus,* *A. boisei,* and *A. robustus*

The robust australopithecines, known by several taxonomic labels, lived between 3 million and 1 million years ago. Found in both eastern and southern Africa, they are remarkable for their heavy build (see Figure 2.5 on page 45). These hominins had large teeth and small brains and were specialized for the chewing of coarse, fibrous plant foods. As a group, these squat, heavily built hominins were very diverse.

Australopithecus garhi

Working the arid washes of the Ethiopia's Awash desert, a team of forty researchers from thirteen countries have unearthed teeth and skull fragments from yet another hominin form, dating to about 2.5 million years ago. The new hominin, named *Australopithecus garhi* (garhi means "surprise" in the local dialect) stood about 1.46 meters tall (4 feet 10 inches) and had protruding features, not unlike those of a chimpanzee (Figure 2.9, page 50). The lower molars are three times the size of those of modern humans, the canines almost as large. *A. garhi*'s brain was only a third the size of that of a modern human. The legs were long and humanlike, while the arms were long and more like an ape's. The hominin was an efficient scavenger. Bones of antelope and other large animals found only a few feet away display cut marks from stone tools, the earliest known instance of hominin butchery of animals. Unfortunately, no stone tools were found close to the fossil remains, but surface finds of crude stone flakes and cobbles have come from a nearby lake bed level dating to about 2.5 mya.

Australopithecus garhi is a remarkable find, which will renew debate over the identity of the very first human toolmaker. This large-toothed, small-brained hominin with an apelike face defies classification within either the gracile or robust Australopithecine lines. That this hominin was eating meat suggests that a switch to a high-energy, high-fat meat diet was

Figure 2.9 *Australopithecus garhi.*

under way. This, in turn, may have led to an increase in brain size among some hominins, which occurred only a few hundred thousand years later. With its apparent toolmaking and meat-eating propensities, *A. garhi* could conceivably be the exclusive ancestor of the *Homo* family tree and technically the first human. No one, least of all Tim White, is prepared to make such a claim on so little fossil evidence. What we do know is that a far-from-robust Australopithecine derived from *A. afarensis* survived until at least 2.5 mya. But whether this form participated in a rapid evolutionary transition or series of transitions into an early form of *Homo* remains a complete mystery. Certainly, major changes to the hominin skull and face occurred after 2.5 mya, many of them as a direct consequence of brain enlargement. New behavior patterns connected with obtaining more meat and marrow using stone tools may have played a highly important role during what may have been a short, and highly critical period of human evolution.

Early *Homo: Homo habilis* (2.5 million to 2 million years ago)

Louis and Mary Leakey were the first to identify the first hominin that was classified as early *Homo*—at Olduvai Gorge in Tanzania in 1960. They named their fragmentary discovery *Homo habilis*, "Handy Person," a label that commemorated the assumed toolmaking abilities of these hominins. Then Richard Leakey found the famous Skull 1470 in East Turkana, a large-brained, round-headed cranium that confirmed the existence of *H. habilis* in no uncertain terms (Figure 2.10).

Figure 2.10 Skull 1470 from East Turkana, northern Kenya, a specimen of early *Homo*, sometimes called *Homo habilis*.

If you had encountered *H. habilis* 2 million years ago, you would have seen little to distinguish the new hominin from *Australopithecus*. Both were of similar height and weight, about 1.3 meters (4 feet 3 inches) tall and about 40 kilograms (88 pounds). Both were bipedal, but *H. habilis* would have looked less apelike around the face and skull. The head was higher and rounder, the face less protruding, the jaw smaller. Some of the most significant anatomical differences involved the more even and less specialized teeth. The molars were narrower; the premolars smaller; and the incisors larger and more spadelike, as if they were used for slicing. However, microscopic wear studies of the teeth have shown that both *Australopithecus* and *H. habilis* were predominantly fruit eaters, so there does not seem to have been a major shift in diet between the two. *H. habilis* had a larger brain, with a larger cranial capacity, between 600 and over 700 cubic centimeters, in contrast with those of australopithecines, which ranged between 400 and 500 cubic centimeters.

Thigh and limb bones from Koobi Fora, Kenya, and from Olduvai confirm that *H. habilis* walked upright. The hand bones are somewhat more curved and robust than those of modern humans. This was a powerful grasping hand, more like that of chimpanzees and gorillas than of humans, a hand ideal for climbing trees. An opposable thumb allowed both powerful gripping and the precise manipulation of fine objects. With the latter capacity, *H. habilis* could have made complex tools. There was probably considerable difference in size between males and females.

   H. habilis' skeletal anatomy gives a mosaic picture of both primitive and more advanced features, of a hominin that both walked bipedally and retained the generalized hominoid ability to climb trees. A telling clue comes from one of the Olduvai's specimen's upper arm bones, which, like Lucy's, are within 95 percent of the length of the thigh bone. The chimpanzee has upper arm and upper leg bones of almost equal length, whereas modern human upper arms are only 70 percent of the length of the upper leg bones. Almost certainly *H. habilis* spent a great deal of time climbing trees, an adaptation that would make them much less human in their behavior, and presumably in their social structure, than had been assumed even a few years ago.

   H. habilis, like many taxonomic labels, accommodates what may actually be two or more early human species. The resulting proliferation of hominin names reflects a concern with documenting an anatomical variation that far exceeded possible differences between males and females. For example, *H. habilis* may have lived alongside another East African form, *Homo rudolfensis* (see Figure 2.11). For clarity, we retain the generic term *H. habilis* here but stress that it disguises considerable morphological variation, especially after 2 million years ago, when new human forms were evolving in Africa and perhaps in Asia, too.

A Burst of Rapid Change?

Our scientific predecessors thought of evolution as a gradual and progressive mechanism. The early East African fossils suggest a very different scenario, coinciding with that of the current view of evolution as punctuated equilibrium—long periods of relative stability punctuated with bursts of rapid change caused by new, selective pressures resulting from altered conditions, perhaps environmental change or alterations in the organism itself.

   Such a burst of rapid change could have taken hold during the brief 500,000 years that separate *A. garhi* from *H. habilis*. Whoever was the first toolmaker, the development of stone tool technology gave its inventors a major advantage over other hominin species. Stone hammers and flakes let them exploit predator kills and shift to an energy-rich, high-fat diet, which could lead to all manner of evolutionary consequences. Major anatomical developments occurred during the millennia that separated early *Homo* (*H. habilis*) from *H. erectus,* who appeared in East Africa about 1.9 million years ago. Brain size increased from about

Figure 2.11 A highly simplified diagram showing the chronology and evolutionary status of early hominins and humans.

450 cubic centimeters in *A. afarensis* to 1,000 cubic centimeters in *H. erectus*. There were further modifications in hips and limbs for bipedal locomotion and a reduction in sexual dimorphism (size difference due to sex). The primitive body form and sexual dimorphism characteristic of earlier hominins vanished only with the emergence of the much more advanced *H. erectus* (see Chapter 3). But what caused this change of evolutionary pace remains a mystery, although climate change, especially cooler temperatures, played a role.

Who Was the First Human?

A generation ago, human evolution was thought of as a ladder through time, with an ape-like ancestor at the base and modern humans at the top. As for humans, they first appeared at the moment when toolmaking began. This was the reasoning that caused the great controversies of the 1960s as to who was the earliest toolmaker. Was it *Australopithecus,* or some closely related hominin form, like the hopefully named *Homo habilis?* As the pace of discovery accelerated, it soon became apparent that there were several hominin forms around at the time when toolmaking began, making identification of the first "human" an even more challenging task.

In recent years, four criteria have been used generally to assign a fossil to the genus *Homo:*

- An absolute brain size of 600 cubic centimeters,
- The possession of language, identified from casts of the brain patterns on the inside of the brain case,
- The possession of a modern, humanlike precision grip and an opposable thumb,
- The ability to manufacture stone tools.

There are serious problems with all of these criteria. Absolute brain capacity is of dubious biological importance. We now know that evidence of language cannot be inferred from a brain cast. Furthermore, we still do not know much about the range of precision grips found among early hominins. Stone tools are an inconclusive criterion to use, simply because, 2.6 million years ago, both early *Homo* and robust Australopithecines flourished in the same area where the earliest artifacts are found.

Hominin evolution involves a far greater level of species diversity than was previously thought. Human evolution can be seen as one or more **adaptive radiations** (a burst of evolution, in which a single species diverges to fill a number of ecological niches, the result being a variety of new forms) rather than a simple, one-way evolution of successive species. This view stems from **cladistics** (noun: clade), an analytic system for reconstructing evolutionary relationships, first proposed in the 1950s. Classical evolutionary analysis is based on morphological similarities between organisms. So is cladistics, but with a difference: Cladistic analysis concentrates not only on features that identify common ancestry but also on those that are derived independently and are unique to specific lineages. Inevitably, cladistics tends to emphasize diversity over homogeneity.

A cladistic definition considers the human genus a group of species that are more closely related to one another than to species assigned to another genus. This interpretation insists that the human genus is **monophyletic**, that is with all its members ultimately descended from a common ancestor. Wood and Collard define the human genus "as a

SITE

Olduvai Gorge, Tanzania

Olduvai Gorge is a vast gash in the game-rich Serengeti Plains of northern Tanzania, formed by an earthquake more than 100,000 years ago and called a miniature Grand Canyon by many visitors (Figure 2.12). The earth movement exposed a long series of ancient lake beds extending back as far as 2 mya, stratified in the walls of the gorge. Geologists have identified four major series of lake beds, labeled from Bed I (at the base) to Bed IV, which formed in a semi-arid environment much like that of today. Olduvai was discovered by German butterfly hunter Wilhelm Kattwinkel before World War I and was investigated by paleontologist Hans Reck in the 1920s. He found numerous fossil animal bones, including a long-extinct elephant, which he named after himself. Today, more than 150 species of extinct animals ranging in size from elephants to birds and rodents are known from Olduvai. But the gorge will always be associated with Louis and Mary Leakey, who realized the great potential of Olduvai for documenting early human evolution. Louis Leakey first found stone axes in the gorge in 1931. Between 1935 and 1959, the Leakeys surveyed and excavated numerous sites and published an important monograph on the Olduvai stone tools, in which they traced the evolution of stone artifacts from a simple technology based on lava lumps, which they named the Oldowan, to progressively more complex and better-made hand axes and flake tools (the Acheulian). Then, in 1959, they discovered *Zinjanthropus boisei* and changed the chronicle of human evolution forever. Subsequently, large-scale excavations by the Leakeys unearthed other hominin fossils, including *Homo habilis,* whom they considered the first toolmaker. Don Johanson of Lucy fame has also worked in the Gorge and recovered further *Homo habilis* fragments.

The most important Olduvai hominin fossils come from Beds I and II. Bed I lies on a volcanic bedrock, known as a tuff, which has been potassium argon dated to about 2 million years ago, an excellent baseline for the lake bed sequence above. The beds themselves were close to the shore of an extensive, shallow lake, which expanded and contracted from one season to the next. The waters covered places where hominins had paused to process and eat animal parts they had scavenged from nearby predator kills (see page 60), preserving both stone tool fragments and broken animal bones, as well as the occasional hominin fossil in situ. Excavating these land surfaces requires great patience and skill. Once a location is identified, the investigators sift the ground surrounding the original find through fine screens, looking for significant fossils. Then they excavate into the lake bed to establish the stratigraphic relationship of the ancient land surface

species, or monophylum, whose members occupy a single adaptive zone" (1999, p. 66). Using this definition, they carried out a cladistic analysis of all the known fossil *Homo* species and devised a cladogram that separates all the Australopithecine forms and *Homo habilis* into one genus, and later humans, starting with *Homo ergaster,* into another (see Figure 2.11 on page 52). Their intricate statistical analyses suggest that enough is known of body size and shape, locomotion, development, and relative size of chewing apparatus to divide fossil hominin adaptive strategies into two broad groups:

■   The Australopithecines and *Homo habilis* (also its possible relative *H. rudolfensis*) belong in a group of hominins with a relatively low body mass, a body shape better suited to a relatively closed environment, and a postcranial skeleton that combined terrestrial bipedalism with expert climbing. The teeth and jaws of these

Figure 2.12 Olduvai Gorge, Tanzania.

to the surrounding lake bed layers before exposing the scatter of artifacts and bones in the horizontal plane. This process is slow-moving and calls for meticulous excavation and recording, with each fragment, even those as small as snake fangs, being exposed in place, then its precise location recorded, before removal. The end-product after months of work is a precise 3-dimensional plan of the artifact and bone scatter, so that the relationships between stone fragments and other finds, including (hopefully) hominin fossils, are established with the greatest possible precision.

The pioneer excavation methods used by the Leakeys at Olduvai have been adopted and refined in both the Lake Turkana and Hadar regions, where archaeologists work alongside human paleontologists, geologists, geomorphologists, and other specialists in a multidisciplinary investigation of the earliest human behavior (see Figure 2.14 on page 59).

hominins are well adapted to chewing and biting a varied and mechanically demanding diet. *Australopithecus* teeth and upper leg bone studies show that the rate of development (and dependence) of young hominins in this group was closer to that of modern African apes. The tooth development of *H. habilis* and *H. rudolfensis* also appears to have been closer to that of African apes, as if their development period was also shorter than that of modern humans.

■ *Homo ergaster, Homo erectus* and contemporary and later human forms belong in a second group, marked by a larger body mass, a modern, humanlike physique that was adaptive in more open terrain, and a postcranial skeleton consistent with terrestrial bipedalism. The ability to move around in trees was very limited, teeth and jaws had similar mechanical properties to those of modern humans. Development rates were the same as our own.

This definition of *Homo* makes a clear distinction between the hominins of earlier than 1.9 million years ago, and *H. erectus* and its successors who evolved after that date. It implies that a behavioral and evolutionary chasm separates true humans from the many other hominins who flourished in Africa before 2 million years ago. Quite what caused this adaptive shift in human evolution is unknown. Did it correspond with significant climatic and environmental change, with equivalent evolutionary changes in other large mammal groups, or with specific changes in hominin culture? The answers will have to come from a new generation of research.

Hominin evolution can be thought of as a series of adaptive radiations that unfolded over at least 5 million years. The first radiation was of bipedal apes, which lived, for the most part, in the drier parts of Africa. Two later radiations gave rise to what is still called early *Homo* and the robust australopithecines, each with their own adaptive theme. In the case of early *Homo*, expanded brain size played a key role, while the robust australopithecines developed specialized teeth. Although the latter varied greatly in morphological terms, later humans radiated not so much morphologically as ecologically, spreading from Africa and creating distinct geographic populations. This flowering of hominin types is exactly what evolution is about: "an endless production of novel ways of doing things, exploring alternatives, trying out new strategies as conditions themselves shift and change all driven by natural selection" (Foley, 1995: 103). Hominins were no different from other mammals, which began as a slim stem and radiated into distinct branches. We still do not know much about the relationships between such branches.

This same pattern of adaptive radiation may have continued much later in prehistory, during the long millennia when *Homo ergaster* and *Homo erectus* flourished in Africa, Asia, and Europe, with only a small part of this evolutionary process resulting in modern humans, *Homo sapiens*, probably in Africa.

The Earliest Human Toolmakers

"Humans the toolmakers . . .": This phrase has served to distinguish the earliest toolmaking humans from all other primates of the day. Their ability to manufacture tools was a clear indication of that uniquely human attribute, culture (see Chapter 1). Other animals like chimpanzees make tools to dig for grubs or other specific purposes, but only people manufacture artifacts regularly and habitually, as well as in a much more complex fashion. We have gone considerably further in the toolmaking direction than other primates. One reason for this is that our brains allow us to plan our actions much further in advance.

The earliest human tools may well have been made of perishable wood, perhaps rudimentary clubs, digging sticks, or spears, but they have not survived. Simple stone tools, made by knocking one rock against another, appeared in East Africa about 2.6 million years ago, the conventionally agreed-upon date for the origin of human culture. These stone artifacts have been found in large numbers throughout East and southern Africa, and are associated with broken animal bones in the East Turkana region and at Olduvai Gorge. They were made from convenient pebbles, some perhaps converted into simple choppers by removing one or two flakes (Figure 2.13).

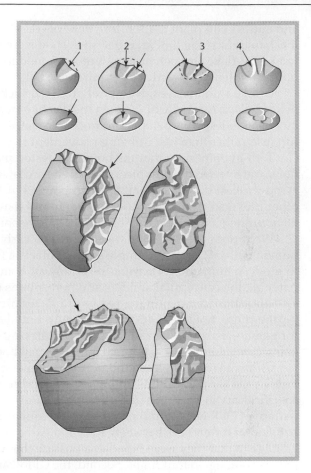

Figure 2.13 The earliest human technology, sometimes called Oldowan, after Olduvai Gorge. Many cobbles at Koobi Fora and Olduvai were used as cores to produce sharp-edged flakes. First, sharp blows were struck near the natural edge of a pebble to remove flakes. The pebble was then turned over, and more blows struck on the ridges formed by the scars of the earlier flakes. A "core" with a jagged edge, perhaps used as a chopper, resulted. Many cores were "mined" for as many flakes as possible before being discarded. The figure shows Oldowan cores from Olduvai Gorge. Arrows show flake edges. Front and side views (two-fifths actual size).

Stone tool expert Nicholas Toth has shown that the most important artifacts were not pebbles or even crude choppers, but the sharp-edged flakes removed from them. Angular flakes and lumps of lava made weapons, scrapers, and cutting tools, used to cut meat, butcher animals, and perhaps to shape wood. There are few formal tools, but Toth's controlled experiments show that the first toolmakers had a clear understanding of the potential of stone as the basis for a simple, highly effective technology that grew more complex over time. Eventually, the simple choppers evolved into crude ax-like tools, flaked on both surfaces—the hand ax used widely over a million years ago. The earliest human technology is called the Oldowan, after Olduvai Gorge, where it was first described in detail.

Nicholas Toth has replicated thousands of Oldowan artifacts and shown by experiment that sharp-edged flakes are highly effective for slitting skin and butchering game animals. By studying the working edges of the tools under microscopes, he has detected wear from three possible uses: butchery and meat cutting, sawing and scraping wood, and cutting soft plant matter. Toth believes our earliest ancestors had a good sense of the mechanics of stone tool manufacture. They were able to find the correct acute angle for removing flakes by percussion. Not even modern beginners have this capacity; it takes hours of intensive practice to acquire the skill.

Unlike chimpanzees, who rarely tote the sticks and stones they use more than a few meters, *Homo habilis* carried flakes and pebbles over considerable distances, up to 14 kilometers (9 miles). This behavior represents a simple form of curation, retaining tools for future use rather than just utilizing convenient stones, as chimpanzees do.

Toth hypothesizes that the hominins tested materials in stream beds and other locations; transported the best pieces to activity areas; and sometimes dropped them there, carrying the rest off with them. He also points out that they must have relied heavily on other raw materials, like wood and bone, and that stone artifacts do not necessarily give an accurate picture of early hominin cognitive abilities.

What does the Oldowan mean? Did the early toolmakers possess a form of "proto-human culture," with its simple stone artifacts a first step on the long evolutionary trail to modern humanity? Or were the Oldowan hominins at an apelike grade of behavior? After all, the conceptual abilities and perceptions needed to manufacture Oldowan tools also appear in ape-manufactured tools like termite-fishing tools and sleeping platforms. Furthermore, not only Oldowan hominins but also chimpanzees scavenged and hunted for game—chasing down small animals, carrying meat over considerable distances, and using convenient objects to break open animal bones and nuts.

Chimpanzees, like early hominins, use the same places again and again, pounding nuts at the same locations and carrying food to their favorite eating sites. Even if the specifics vary in some instances and the natural environments are different, the behavioral pattern of Oldowan hominins is generally similar to that of apes. There are, however, two behavioral differences between apes and early hominins. First, hominins were at an advantage in that they were bipedal, a posture that is far more efficient for carrying objects than is walking on four limbs. Second, the Oldowan humans were adapted to savanna living, where they had to organize and cover far larger territories in open country than their primate relatives in the forest. In the long term, this may have resulted in new concepts of space and spatial organization, concepts that were definitely reflected in more complex stone tool forms after a million years ago.

Early hominins with their larger brains probably would not have behaved the same way as modern apes. We can be certain that there were significant differences between nonhuman primates and hominins 2 million years ago, but these changes may not be reflected in stone artifacts. Without question, our ancestors became more and more dependent on technology. The opportunistic nature of primeval stone technology is in sharp contrast to the better designed, much more standardized stone artifacts of later humans.

Hunters or Scavengers?

Studying early hominin behavior is complicated both by poor preservation conditions and by the vast time chasm that separates us from our remotest ancestors. Two sources of information on very early human behavior survive in East Africa—the first is manufactured artifacts, the second scatters of tools and food remains found at a few locations like Koobi Fora in East Turkana, northern Kenya, and Olduvai.

Concentrations of broken animal bones and stone tools in these regions and a few others have been excavated and studied with meticulous care. The concentrations are usually only some 6 to 9 meters (20 to 30 feet) across, places that were visited and used by hominins either once or on several occasions. Later prehistoric foragers made habitual use of central places, places where they returned to sleep, cook food, and engage in a wide variety of social activities. Are we, then, to assume that the Koobi Fora and Olduvai concentrations are evidence that our earliest ancestors also used central places like their successors did? Did they hunt and kill big-game animals, or did they merely scavenge flesh from abandoned predator kills?

At Koobi Fora, a group of hominins found the carcass of a hippopotamus in a stream bed about 1.8 million years ago. They gathered around and removed bones and meat from the dead animal with small stone flakes. The sandy deposits in which the artifacts lay are so fine that we can be certain that every stone cobble was carried in to make tools at the carcass, some of them from as far as 14 kilometers (9 miles) away. The site contains abundant evidence of butchering and of tool manufacture, but we do not know if the hominins actually killed the animal.

Site FxJj50 at Koobi Fora is also in an ancient watercourse, a place where the hominins could find shade from the blazing sun, located close to water and abundant tool-making stone (Figure 2.14). The site is a cluster of stone artifacts and fragments, including

Figure 2.14 Excavations at site FxJj50, Koobi Fora, East Turkana, northern Kenya.

sharp flakes, choppers, and scraping tools. More than 2,000 bones from at least seventeen mammalian species, mostly antelope, are associated with the tools, some of which have been chewed by hyenas and other carnivores. There are clear signs that the bones were smashed and cut by hominins, for reconstructed fragments show traces of hammer blows and fine linear grooves that could have resulted only from cutting bone with stone flakes. Many of the FxJj50 bones have their articular ends chewed off by carnivores, a characteristic of bone accumulations resulting from carnivore kills. Perhaps the hominins simply chased away lions and other predators and then moved in on a fresh kill; we cannot be sure.

At Olduvai Gorge, Mary Leakey plotted artifact and bone scatters in the lowest levels of the ancient lake bed. Many artifacts and bones were concentrated in areas about 4.6 meters (15 feet) across. At one site, a pile of shattered bones and rocks lay a short distance away, the bones perhaps piled in heaps as the marrow was extracted from them. Recent microscopic studies of the Olduvai scatters have shown that many of the bones were heavily weathered. They had lain on the surface for considerable periods of time, some for perhaps as long as a decade. The bones of many different animals come from the scatters, parts of carcasses from a very ecologically diverse set of animals. Limb bones predominate, as if these body parts were repeatedly carried to the sites.

At both Koobi Fora and Olduvai, meat- and marrow-rich bones occur concentrated in small areas with stone tools. The percentage of carnivore bones is somewhat higher than in the natural environment, as if there was intense competition between hominins and other carnivores. Perhaps the presence of such predators restricted the activities of hominins at Olduvai. They may have grabbed meat from fresh carnivore kills and then taken their booty to a place where they had a collection of stone tools near water or other predictable food supplies. There they would hastily cut off meat and extract the marrow before abandoning the fresh bones to the carnivores hovering nearby. Without fire or domesticated animals, scientists believe that *Homo habilis* probably had to rely on opportunistic foraging for game meat, it being unsafe for them to camp in open watercourses or on lake shores. It is worth noting that one hominin bone found at Olduvai Gorge had been gnawed by carnivores.

Most of the bones from the Olduvai accumulations are of smaller animals that could be run down and thrown to the ground with ease. This is more of an apelike form of behavior, although apes have been observed scavenging meat. Microscopic studies of the Olduvai bones show that the hominins rarely butchered and disarticulated large animals and carried their bones back to base. They seem to have obtained meat without cutting up too many carcasses, as if they scavenged it from already dismembered predator kills. In some cases, human cutting marks overlay predator tooth marks, as if the hominins had scavenged bones from carcasses that had already been killed by other animals. In others, predators have chewed bones abandoned by *Homo*.

Archaeologist Robert Blumenschine spent several field seasons studying animal predators on the game-rich Serengeti Plains of northern Tanzania. Semi-arid grassland crossed by occasional streams lined with trees, this was the kind of environment that early hominins shared with other predators like lions and hyenas. Blumenschine observed dozens of predator kills, studying the abandoned, shattered bones and comparing them to the archaeological finds at Olduvai Gorge. As a result of these observations, he believes the hominins could take unique advantage of two scavenging opportunities. The first was near streams, because lions kill close to water in the dry season. Sometimes more than a day would elapse before hyenas moved in, ample time, Blumenschine believes, for hominins to seize their share. It is here, too, that leopards hide small antelope kills in trees, high above the ground, but not out of reach of humans. Scavenging would have been most common in the dry months, when game (and its predators) stayed near to permanent water supplies and plant foods were in short supply. During the rains, both antelope and predators would range far over the plains, where it was easy for hyenas to find lion kills. But these were the months when hominins relied on plant foods and fruit in more wooded environments. Blumenschine argues that scavenging and plant gathering went hand-in-hand, each complementing the other at different times of year. Opportunism has always been an important quality of humankind, from the earliest times. Undoubtedly, however, plants and all kinds of vegetable foods were an important, if not the most important, part of very early human diet.

The Earliest Human Mind

By 2 million years ago, there were probably several species of early *Homo,* but, for convenience, we can group them under a single toolmaking species, *Homo habilis.* What, then, were the specialized mental processes found in these earliest humans as opposed to much earlier, non-toolmaking hominins?

Some clues lie in stone tool manufacture. Chimpanzees shape termite twigs with their teeth from convenient wood fragments, removing leaves so they can poke the "artifact" down a small hole. The making of stone tools requires good hand-eye coordination, the ability to recognize acute angles in stone, and the mental processes necessary to shape one tool by using another. But the Oldowan stoneworkers were carrying out simple tasks: shaping stones so they can hold them in one hand to crack bones and striking off sharp-edged flakes. Their artifacts defy precise classification in the way that one can subdivide later stone tools into forms such as choppers, scrapers, and knives, for example. Their lumps and flakes display continuous variability, an understanding of basic fracture mechanics, not the ability to impose standardized forms, or to choose easily worked raw materials. Could chimpanzees have made such tools, as has been suggested? When Nicholas Toth tried to train a pygmy chimpanzee named Kanzi to make Oldowan tools, he found that Kanzi could make sharp flakes, but he never mastered the art of recognizing acute angles in stone, or other flaking. Archaeologist Steven Mithen argues for two possibilities: Either a more general intelligence had evolved, or some mental processes for basic stone working had appeared—intuitive physics in the mind of *Homo habilis.* Oldowan stone tools were mainly used to process animal carcasses, for skinning, cutting joints and meat, and breaking open bones. But how did *Homo habilis* interact with the natural world?

One obvious and significant difference between *Homo habilis* and chimpanzees appears in the archaeological record of 2 million years ago: a dramatic rise in meat consumption. In practice, *Homo habilis* was probably a behaviorally flexible, nonspecialized forager, whose lifeway was marked by diversity, by shifts between hunting and scavenging, and between food sharing and feeding on the move. The larger brain of *Homo habilis* would have required the consumption of more energy and a higher quality of diet. The stable basal metabolic rate was maintained by a reduction in the size of the gut, which could only become reduced as a result of a higher-meat diet, since a high-fiber diet requires more intestinal action.

Steven Mithen believes that this need for more meat required another cognitive ability as opposed to that for toolmaking—that of being able to use one's knowledge of the environment to develop ideas about where to find predator kills and high densities of animals. He argues that the presence of toolmaking stone up to 10 kilometers (6 miles) from its source is a sign that *Homo habilis* was moving not only stone but meat to different, ever-changing locations. Such ability suggests a relatively sophisticated interaction with the environment when compared with chimpanzees who only transport "tools" to fixed locations.

Homo habilis was so far confined to tropical Africa, and to a relatively narrow range of savanna and grassland environments, in contrast with later humans who adapted to every kind of climate imaginable. Many groups lived close to permanent water, tethered, as it were, to places like the shallow lake at Olduvai, where sites are "stacked" one above another over considerable periods of time. Many animal species appear in the Olduvai caches, as if our ancestors ranged widely over the surrounding landscape, but they may have transported much of their food to well-defined locations.

Homo habilis shared the ability of its earlier ancestors to "map" resources over wide areas. But it may also have possessed additional cognitive abilities: to develop ideas about where food might be found, and to use tell-tale signs such as animal droppings to find it, within a relatively narrow environmental setting. At the same time, its general intelligence was supplemented by some specialized abilities in artifact manufacture, which were to be an important foundation for environmental intelligence in later millennia.

Social intelligence may have evolved significantly. Anthropologist Robin Dunbar has studied living primates and discovered evidence for larger brain size in individuals living in larger groups, developing an equation for relating brain to group size. He then estimated the brain size of *Homo habilis,* and applied his figures to the chimpanzee equation. Chimpanzees lived in predicted group sizes of about 60 individuals. In contrast, he predicted that australopithecines lived in groups with a mean size of about 67 individuals, whereas *Homo habilis* flourished in larger groups of about 81. Group living was an essential for *Homo habilis,* which lived in an environment teeming with carnivores, often competing with them for meat with only the simplest of weaponry for protection. Large group living has dramatic advantages for hominins living in environments where resources come in large "parcels" that are irregularly distributed across the landscape. Members of a group can search for food individually or in pairs, then share it with others, allowing the group as a whole to cover a much larger area. Mithen believes the larger brain of the first humans allowed for greater social intelligence, for coping with the complexities of living in closer juxtaposition to others, where assuming that others know things is of vital importance.

The Development of Language

Cooperation, the ability to get together to solve problems of both subsistence and potential conflict, is a vital quality in human beings. We are unique in having a spoken, symbolic language that enables us to communicate our most intimate feelings to one another. But at what point did hominins acquire the ability to speak?

Our closest living relatives, the chimpanzees, communicate with gestures and many voice sounds in the wild, whereas other apes use sounds only to convey territorial information. However, chimpanzees cannot talk to us because they do not have the vocal apparatus to do so. Articulate speech was an important threshold in human evolution because it opened up whole new vistas of cooperative behavior and unlimited potential for the enrichment of life. When did hominins abandon grunts for speech? We cannot infer language from the simple artifacts made by *Homo habilis*, but there are two potential lines of research open.

Both comparative anatomy and actual fossils can be used to study differences between apes and humans. Biological anthropologist Jeffrey Laitman and others studied the position of the larynx in a wide variety of mammals, including humans. They found that all mammals except adult humans have a larynx high in the neck, a position that enables the larynx to lock into the air space at the back of the nasal cavity. Although this position allows animals like monkeys and cats to breathe and swallow at the same time, it limits the sounds they can produce. The pharynx—the air cavity part of the food pathway—can produce sounds, but animals use their mouths to modify sounds since they are anatomically incapable of producing the range of sounds needed for articulate speech.

Until they are about eighteen months to two years old, human children's larynxes are also situated high in the neck. Then the larynx begins to descend, ending up between the fourth and seventh neck vertebrae. How and why are still a mystery, but the change completely alters the way the infant breathes, speaks, and swallows. Adult humans cannot separate breathing and swallowing, so they can suffocate when food lodges in an airway. However, an enlarged pharyngeal chamber above the vocal cords enables them to modify the sounds they emit in an infinite variety of ways, which is the key to human speech.

Using sophisticated statistical analyses, Laitman and his colleagues ran tests on as many complete fossil skulls as possible. They found that the australopithecines of 4 to 1 million years ago had flat skull bases and high larynxes, whereas those of *Homo ergaster* and *Homo erectus*, dating to about 1.9 million years and later, show somewhat more curvature, suggesting that the larynx was beginning to descend to its modern position. It was only about 300,000 years ago that the skull base finally assumed a modern curvature, which would allow for fully articulate speech to evolve. *Homo habilis* probably had very limited speaking abilities.

The real value of language, apart from the stimulation it gives brain development, is that with it we can convey feelings and nuances far beyond the power of gestures or grunts to communicate. We may assume that the first humans had more to communicate with than the gestures and grunts of nonhuman primates, but it appears that articulate speech was a more recent development.

The Earliest Social Organization

The few early sites that have been excavated show that the first phase of human evolution involved shifts in the basic patterns of subsistence and locomotion as well as new ingredients—food sharing and toolmaking. These led to enhanced communication, information exchange, and economic and social insight, as well as cunning and restraint. Human anatomy was augmented with tools. Culture became an inseparable part of humanity, and social life acquired a new, and as yet little understood, complexity.

What sort of social organization did *Homo habilis* enjoy? However much we look at contemporary nonhuman primates, we cannot be sure. Most primates are intensely social and live in groups in which the mother–infant relationship forms a central bond. The period of infants' dependency on mothers found in, say, chimpanzees was probably lengthened considerably with *H. habilis.* The larger brain size would mean that infants were born with much smaller heads than adults, at an earlier stage of mental maturity. This biological reality would have had a major impact on social organization and daily habits.

Chimpanzees have flexible, matriarchal social groups. They occupy a relatively small territory, one with sufficient vegetable resources to support a considerable population density; this pattern contrasts sharply with the average hunter-gatherer band, typically a closely knit group of about twenty-five people of several families. The kind of systematic hunting such people engage in requires much larger territories and permits much lower densities per square kilometer or mile. The few sites that have been excavated suggest that *Homo habilis* tended to live in bands that were somewhat more akin to those of modern hunter-gatherers. But in all probability their social organization resembled more closely that of chimpanzees and baboons, which is very different from those of humans.

The world of *Homo habilis* was much less predictable and more demanding than that of even *Australopithecus.* What was it that was more complex? Why do we have to be so intelligent? Not for hunting animals or gathering food but for our interactions with other people. The increased complexity of our social interactions is likely to have been a powerful force in the evolution of the human brain. For *H. habilis,* the adoption of a wider-based diet with a food-sharing social group would have placed much more acute demands on the ability to cope with the complex and unpredictable. And the brilliant technological, artistic, and expressive skills of humankind may well be a consequence of the fact that our early ancestors had to be more and more socially adept.

Summary

The earliest known hominin is *Sahelanthropus tchadensis* from central Chad, dating to c. 6 to 7 mya, but its evolutionary status is uncertain. A more complete story of human evolution begins with the separation of the chimpanzee and human lines from from a common, and as yet unknown, ancestor about 5 to 6 million years ago. The first hominins were tree-living, with long arms and legs and broad chests, who eventually became bipedal, walking on two limbs. They adapted to more open country in Africa, which resulted from global cooling over 4 million years ago, by broadening their diet to include more meat, and by achieving great mobility and behavioral flexibility, A small bipedal hominin named *Ardipithecus ramidus* is the earliest known form and flourished 4.5 million years ago in Ethiopia. Its descendants were *Australopithecus anamensis* and *Australopithecus afarensis,* which flourished between about 4.1 and 3 mya. By 3 million years ago, the hominin line had radiated into many forms, among them robust and more gracile Australopithecines and the larger-brained *Homo habilis,* another hominin form. *Homo habilis* was a forager who also scavenged game meat and perhaps hunted. These hominins used a simple stone technology, had some ability to communicate, and had a very rudimentary social organization. New definitions of the genus *Homo* make a major distinction between the more ape-like hominins described in this chapter, which flourished before 2 million years ago, and the true humans, beginning with *Homo ergaster,* which evolved after 1.9 million years before present.

3 African Exodus

2.5 Million	1.0 Million	500,000 B.P.	100,000 B.P.	50,000 B.P.	15,000 B.P.	A.D. 1 A.D. 1950

PROLOGUE

Eugene Dubois was a Dutchman obsessed with the "Missing Link," the mythical human that was the evolutionary connection between apes and modern people. A surgeon by profession, in 1887, young Dubois even wangled a posting as an army physician to distant Sumatra in Southeast Asia, where, he was convinced, the Missing Link would be found. Incredible though it may seem, Dubois actually found what he claimed was such an ancestor on nearby Java in 1891. Digging into fossil-rich ash and river sediments at Trinil on the Solo River in northeastern Java, he found not only the bones of extinct animals but a human tooth, a thick-walled skull, and a human thigh bone.

Dubois named his fossil *Pithecanthropus erectus*, "ape-human which stood upright." This, he claimed, was the missing link between apes and humans, a very primitive human being. On his return to Europe in 1895, he was greeted with skepticism, then scorn. Dubois' reaction was to withdraw from the scientific arena. He is said to have kept his fossils under his bed. Modern science has vindicated Eugene Dubois, for he was the first to discover what is now known as *Homo erectus*, a direct ancestor of modern humanity.

About 1.9 million years ago, early *Homo* (*Homo habilis* and other forms) gave way to more advanced humans capable of far more complex and varied lifeways. These new human ancestors were among the first to tame fire and the first to settle outside the tropical savannas of Africa. They did so at the beginning of the last geological epoch, the Pleistocene, sometimes called the Ice Age. Chapter 3 describes the diverse archaic humans who moved out of Africa into Asia and Europe and their increasingly sophisticated adaptations to constant climatic change during the Ice Age.

Ice Age Background

The Pleistocene began about 1.8 million years ago, after an intensification of glaciation worldwide about 2.5 million years ago. By this time great mountain chains had formed in the Alps, Himalayas, and elsewhere. Land masses had been uplifted; connection between these latitudes and southern areas was reduced, lessening their heat exchange and causing greater temperature differences between them. Northern latitudes became progressively cooler after 3 million years ago, but climatic fluctuations between warmer and colder climatic regimens were still relatively minor during the first million years of the Ice Age. This was a critically important time, when a more advanced human form evolved in Africa and moved out of the tropics into Asia and Europe.

About 730,000 years ago, the earth's magnetic field changed abruptly from a reversed state it had adopted about 2.5 million years ago to a normal one (see Table 2.1 on page 37). This **Matuyama/Brunhes** boundary, named after the geologists who first discovered it, marks the beginning of constant climatic change for the remainder of the Ice Age. Deep sea cores give us a record of changing sea temperatures. They tell us that ice sheets formed gradually, but deglaciation and global warming trends took place with great rapidity. These corresponded with major sea level rises that flooded low-lying coastal areas. During glacial maxima, ice sheets covered a full third of the earth's surface, mantling Scandinavia and the Alps in Europe, as well as much of northern North America. Sea levels fell dramatically as a result, hundreds of feet below modern levels. The glaciers were about as extensive as they are today during warmer periods, the so-called interglacials, when sea levels were close to present shorelines. Much less is known about changes in tropical regions, although it is thought that the southern fringes of Africa's Sahara Desert expanded dramatically during cold periods.

Archaic, and, later, modern humans, evolved during a long period of constant climatic transition between warmer and colder regimens in northern latitudes. Experts believe that the world's climate has been in transition from one extreme to the other for over 75 percent of the past 730,000 years, with a predominance of colder climate over the period (see Table 2.1 on page 37). There were at least nine glacial episodes, a major one about 525,000 years ago, when there was ice as far south as Seattle, St. Louis, and New York in North America, and sea levels were as much as 197 meters (650 feet) below modern levels. In contrast, there were periods of more temperate conditions between 515,000 and 315,000 years ago. This was the period when human settlement outside Africa expanded, as small bands of foragers exploited the rich animal and plant resources of European and Asian river valleys and forests.

Another intensely cold cycle lasted from about 180,000 to 128,000 years ago, a cycle that coincided in general terms with the period when fully modern *Homo sapiens*, was evolving in Africa. Between 100,000 and 15,000 years ago, the last Ice Age glaciation saw the spread of *Homo sapiens* throughout the Old World and into the Americas. These constant climatic changes played an important role in the spread of early human beings throughout temperate and tropical latitudes (see Figure 3.1 on page 70).

Chronological Table A

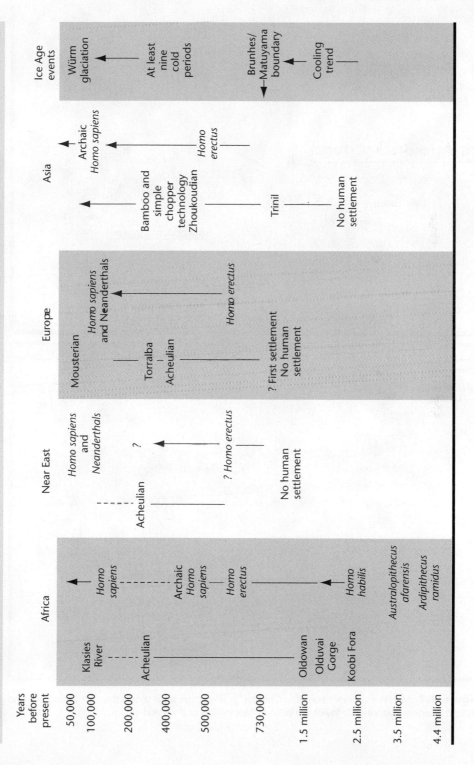

Years before present	Africa	Near East	Europe	Asia	Ice Age events
50,000	Homo sapiens ←				Würm glaciation ←
100,000	Klasies River	Homo sapiens and Neanderthals	Mousterian	Archaic Homo sapiens ←	
200,000	Acheulian -----	Acheulian -----	Homo sapiens and Neanderthals		At least nine cold periods
400,000	Archaic Homo sapiens	? ←	Torralba — Acheulian	Bamboo and simple chopper technology Zhoukoudian ←	
500,000	Homo erectus	? Homo erectus	Homo erectus ←		Brunhes/ Matuyama boundary ↓
730,000	Homo erectus ← Homo habilis ←	No human settlement	? First settlement No human settlement	Trinil	Cooling trend ←
1.5 million	Oldowan Olduvai Gorge Koobi Fora			No human settlement	
2.5 million	Homo habilis				
3.5 million	Australopithecus afarensis				
4.4 million	Ardipithecus ramidus				

69

Figure 3.1 Maps of sites mentioned in Chapter 3. The upper map shows the distribution of hand ax and chopper cultures, the lower the area of Mousterian and related cultures.

Homo ergaster in Africa
(c. 1.9 million to c. 600,000 years ago)

All paleoanthropologists agree that the successors to *H. habilis* evolved in tropical Africa. They point to the continuous record of human evolution in that continent, from *Ardipithecus ramidus* to the later australopithecines, then *Homo habilis* and then later humans. However bushlike the evolutionary tree, and it was much more complex than we know today, the best and longest fossil record comes from Africa. As we shall see later in this chapter, the same continent also may have been the cradle of modern humans, *Homo sapiens*.

Early hominin evolution followed a pattern of constant diversification, to the point that there were probably about five or six species of them at the beginning of the Ice Age some 1.6 million years ago. By a million years ago, the only known survivors were *Homo ergaster* and *Homo erectus*, larger humans with overall proportions more like those of modern people. True humans, in the sense of members of the genus *Homo*, may only have appeared about 1.9 mya, with the evolution of *Homo ergaster* in eastern Africa, a powerfully built human with massive eyebrow ridges and a large face, with a long, low skull, who flourished between about 1.8 mya and 600,000 years ago.

That the new human evolved from a *H. habilis*–like hominin seems unquestionable, but we still await the discovery of larger-brained transitional forms.

The earliest East African *H. ergaster* specimens come from the Lake Turkana region of northern Kenya, where current estimates place their appearance at about 2 mya or slightly later (Figure 3.2). Skull KNM-ER 3733 from East Turkana dates to between 1.6 and 1.5 mya.

Figure 3.2 *Homo ergaster,* represented by skull KNM-ER 3733 from East Turkana, Kenya. This individual has a larger brain and more rounded skull than the australopithecines.

This fossil, with its massive brow ridges, enlarged brain size, and high forehead, is morphologically very close to examples of *H. erectus* dating to a million years ago and earlier. We also know that *Australopithecus boisei*, the robust australopithecine best known from Olduvai Gorge, survived alongside *H. erectus* until at least 1.5 mya.

Another fossil find, this time of a twelve-year-old boy from the western shore of Lake Turkana, dates to about the same time period (Figure 3.3). From the neck down, the boy's bones are remarkably modern looking. The skull and jawbone are more primitive, with brow ridges and a brain capacity perhaps as high as 700 to 800 cubic centimeters, about half the modern size. The boy stood about 1.8 meters (5 feet 6 inches) tall, taller than most modern twelve-year-olds. The Turkana boy seems to confirm the theory that different parts of the human body evolved at different rates, the body achieving fully modern form long before the head.

Homo ergaster's brain size was only some 130 cc larger than that of *H. habilis*, and well below that of modern humans. This may have allowed them to develop new tool forms, but they and their archaic descendants made few changes to their simple technology over hundreds of thousands of years. In many respects, the new humans were radically different—flat and receding foreheads, long skulls with thick walls, with a projecting, humanlike nose in contrast to the apelike noses of the australopithecines. They were chinless people with massive, projecting jaws and large teeth, adept at chewing. *Homo ergaster* had short arms and

Figure 3.3 Lake Turkana, East Africa. A reconstruction of a young *Homo ergaster* boy, who died in a small lagoon on the western shores of Lake Turkana about 1.5 million years ago. Drawing by Ian Everard.

long legs, for these hominins lived entirely on the ground. They had barrel-like chests and narrower hips, which led to more efficient muscles for walking and running bipedally. The more constricted pelvis would have reduced the amount of brain growth before birth and led to a longer dependence on the mother, like modern humans. *H. ergaster* was an African, adapted with a long, slim body to living in hot, arid environments. These may have been the first nearly hairless, naked humans, for they could not have sweated efficiently if covered with apelike body hair. The marked sexual dimorphism of the australopithecines and perhaps *Homo habilis* has now vanished, perhaps creating social environments where males no longer competed for females and male–female relationships lasted longer.

We know that the earliest hominins could adapt to a variety of climates and habitats. Both *Australopithecus* and *Homo habilis* adjusted to plunging global temperatures during a glacial episode between about 2.7 and 2.5 million years ago. The colder conditions turned much of Africa's moist woodlands into much drier, open savanna. The hominins thrived in these conditions, as tree-dwelling primates yielded to bipedal forms better able to survive in the open. This adaptability let hominins move into new environments, where their mixed diet of meat and plant foods caused them to move over large home territories. *Homo ergaster* was just as adaptable and mobile, but was the first human to use fire, fashion more elaborate tools, and leave Africa.

Humans Radiate out of Africa

At about 1.9 mya, *Homo ergaster* is older than its close relative *Homo erectus*, known from Eugene Dubois' discoveries in southeast Asia, and from Chinese fossils (see "*Homo erectus* in Europe and Asia"), meaning that the latter may have originated in Africa before migrating to Asia (see Figure 3.1 on page 70). The African hominins have less massive faces, thinner skull walls, and other features that are either more primitive or less specialized than those of *Homo erectus*, which is why they are classified separately by most experts as *H. ergaster*, although many still classify them as *Homo erectus*, on the grounds that we have too few specimens to work with.

If potassium argon dates for *Homo erectus* fossils in Indonesia are to be believed, then archaic humans radiated out of Africa with remarkable speed, appearing on the savanna by 1.9 million years ago, and in the southeast Asian rainforest by 1.8 million years ago. But would a radiation of hunter-gatherer populations from Africa into Asia occur within such a short time frame as 100,000 years? Such a rapid spread is theoretically possible. With small bands covering large, open territories where food resources were scattered unevenly over the landscape, even an expansion of about 30 to 50 kilometers (20 to 30 miles) a year soon translates to hundreds, then thousands of kilometers, within a few generations. Unfortunately, the archaeological and fossil evidence for this extraordinary radiation is still tantalizingly incomplete.

Why did this sudden movement occur? Around two million years ago, hominins were adjusting to cyclical alterations among savanna, forest, and desert, as the Ice Age began. They did so by migrating with changing vegetational zones, as many mammals did, or by adapting to new environments, changing their dietary emphasis from meat to plant foods. Finally, they could move out of tropical latitudes altogether, into habitats that human beings had never occupied before.

Very likely *Homo ergaster* adapted to changed circumstances in all these ways, radiating out of Africa by way of the Sahara, when the desert was capable of supporting human life. Geologist Neil Roberts has likened the Sahara to a pump, sucking in population during wetter savanna phases and forcing foragers out northward to the margins of the desert during drier cycles. In radiating out of Africa, *H. ergaster* behaved just like other mammals in its ecological community.

The new humans were carnivores and plant eaters, and thus linked ecologically with other predators. There was widespread interchange of mammals between Africa and more temperate latitudes during the Pliocene and Lower Pleistocene. For example, a major change in the mammalian populations of Europe took place about 700,000 years ago. Hippopotamuses, forest elephants, and other herbivores and carnivores like the lion, leopard, and spotted hyena seem to have migrated northward from Africa at this time. Migrations by the lion, leopard, and hyena—the animals with which hominins shared many ecological characteristics—were in the same direction as that taken earlier by humans. That the first successful human settlement of tropical Asia and temperate Europe coincided with radiations of mammalian communities out of Africa seems plausible. It may also have coincided with the taming of fire.

We don't know exactly when humans domesticated fire, but it may have been as early as 1.8 mya. Early people would have been familiar with the great grass and brush fires that swept across the savanna during the dry months. Fire offered protection against predators and an easy way of hunting game, with even insects and rodents fleeing from a line of flames. Perhaps *Homo ergaster* developed the habit of conserving fire, taking advantage of long-smoldering tree stumps ignited by lightning strikes and other natural causes in order to kindle flames to light dry brush or simply to scare off predators. It may be no coincidence that the radiation of *Homo ergaster* out of tropical Africa into temperate environments in Asia and Europe occurred after the taming of fire and during a period of accelerated climatic change.

Homo erectus in Europe and Asia

While most experts agree that Asia was settled soon after 2 million years ago, the evidence for first settlement in Southwest Asia and Europe is more uncertain. To judge from the Southeast Asian dates, archaic humans moved rapidly eastward out of Africa, but settling the more northerly latitudes of Europe and Eurasia may have presented a more formidable challenge, especially during glacial cycles. Male and female skulls of *Homo erectus* have recently been discovered at **Dmanisi** southwest of Tbilisi in Georgia in association with crudely shaped choppers and flakes (see chapter opener on page 66). The crania came from river deposits dated to about 1.7 million years ago, making them the earliest humans to be unearthed in Eurasia. The earliest human inhabitants of western Europe date to about 800,000 years ago—the evidence is uncertain.

The classic *Homo erectus* fossils come from Asia, from the **Trinil** area of Java, where they date to between 1.8 million and 600,000 years ago, and from northern and southern China, dating to between 600,000 and 350,000 years ago, perhaps considerably earlier (Figure 3.4). These well-preserved specimens show that these archaic humans had a brain capacity between 775 and 1,300 cubic centimeters, showing much variation. It is probable that their vision was excellent and that they were capable of extensive reasoning. The *H. erectus* skull is more rounded than that of earlier hominins. It also has conspicuous brow ridges and a sloping forehead. *Homo erectus* had limbs and hips fully adapted to an upright posture. Males stood over 1.8 meters (5 feet 6 inches) tall and had hands fully capable of precision gripping and many kinds of toolmaking.

Figure 3.4 *Homo erectus* from Zhoukoudian, China.

During archaic humans' long history, people adapted to a far wider range of environments, ranging from tropical savannas in East Africa to forested Javanese valleys, temperate climates in North Africa and Europe, and the harsh winters of northern China and central Europe. The newcomers were certainly capable of a far more complex and varied lifeway than previous hominins. With such a wide distribution, it is hardly surprising that some variations in population occur. For example, Chinese scholars claim that the *Homo erectus* fossils from the famous **Zhoukoudian** cave near Beijing display a gradual increase in brain capacity from about 900 cubic centimeters 600,000 years ago to about 1100 cubic centimeters in 200,000-year-old individuals. In any case, *Homo erectus* was far more human than *Homo habilis*, a habitual biped, who had probably lost the thick hair covering that is characteristic of nonhuman primates.

The Lifeway of *Homo erectus*

We still know little of the world of archaic humans, beyond a certainty that, between 1.8 million and half a million years ago, they had radiated far beyond their tropical African homeland (see Figure 3.1 on page 70). Nowhere were people abundant, and the global population of archaic humans was undoubtedly minuscule. As far as is known they did not settle in extreme arctic latitudes, in what is now northern Eurasia and Siberia, nor did Asian *Homo erectus* groups cross into the Americas. Neither did they develop the watercraft needed to cross from the islands of Southeast Asia to New Guinea and Australia, land masses that remained isolated by the ocean until the late Ice Age.

Throughout an enormous area of the Old World, archaic humans developed a great variety of lifeways and local tool kits that reflected different needs. They were part of a vast animal community, and their long-term success resulted from their ability to adapt to the cyclical changes in the Ice Age environment, from temperate to much colder, then to full glacial conditions, and then, more rapidly, to warmer again. Many of these early human populations flourished in regions where dense, abundant, and predictable resources were to be found, isolated from other regions where similar conditions existed.

The climatic conditions of the Ice Age sometimes brought these isolated populations together, then separated them again, ensuring gene flow and genetic drift and continued biological and cultural evolution over the millennia. As it had been for *Homo habilis*, the key to adapting to temperate environments was mobility. Human bands could respond quickly to changes in resource distribution by moving into new areas. Theirs was a primarily opportunistic adaptation based on knowledge of where resources were to be found, rather than on deliberate planning, as was the case in much later times.

Archaic Human Lifeways

Separated as we are from these people by hundreds of thousands of years, it is difficult for us to obtain even a general impression of their simple but opportunistic lifeway. Almost invariably, the only signs of their existence are scatters of stone artifacts, most frequently discovered near lakes and in river valleys, where the most plentiful food resources were to be found. These many finds have enabled us to divide the archaic human world into two broad and still ill-defined provinces: one comprising Africa, Europe, and some parts of Asia—more open country where hunting was important and multipurpose stone axes were commonly used; and the other, a vast area of forested and wooded country in Asia where wood artifacts were all-important and stone technology tended to be more conservative. This is almost certainly a gross simplification of a very complex picture, but it provides us with a general portrait of an archaic lifeway far removed from that of more modern humans.

The simple Oldowan technology of *Homo habilis* remained in use for more than a million years before evolving slowly into a more diverse, stone technology that itself remained in use for a further half-million years. Neither *H. habilis* nor its successors relied exclusively on stone. Our remote ancestors also made use of wood, one of the most versatile raw materials known to humanity, to make spears, throwing sticks and other artifacts (see Schoningen box on pages 78–79). However, most insights into the technology of *H. erectus* come from stone tools and the by-products associated with them, because wood and other organic materials are rarely preserved.

In Africa, Europe, and some parts of Asia, archaic humans are associated with a distinctive tool kit that includes not only a variety of flake tools and sometimes choppers, but also one of the most common exhibits in the world's museums—the hand ax (Figure 3.5). Unlike the crude flakes and choppers of the Oldowan, the **Acheulian** hand ax (named after the northern French town of Saint Acheul) was an artifact with converging edges that met at a point. The maker had to envision the shape of the artifact, which was to be produced from a mere lump of stone, then fashion it, not with opportunistic blows but with carefully directed hammer strokes.

Acheulian hand axes come in every size, from elegant oval types a few inches long to heavy axes more than 0.3 meter (1 foot) long and weighing 2.3 kilograms (5 pounds) or more. They were multipurpose tools, used for woodworking, scraping skins, and especially skinning and butchering of animals. The hand ax and its near relative the cleaver, with a straight end, were ideal for butchery because the artifact could be sharpened again and again. When it became a useless lump of stone, it could be recycled into flake tools. But one can achieve effective butchery with simple flakes as well. A number of researchers have wondered whether the hand ax was not used for other purposes such as throwing at game or digging for roots.

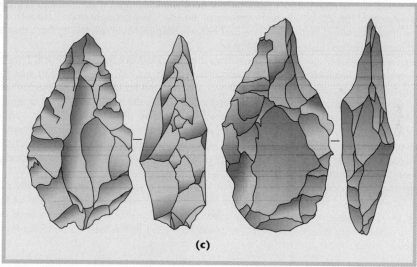

Figure 3.5 Acheulian technology. **(a)** Hand axes were multipurpose artifacts shaped symmetrically around a long axis. **(b)** A stoneworker thins the edge of a hand ax with a bone hammer. **(c)** Acheulian hand ax from **Swanscombe,** England and cleaver from **Kalambo Falls,** Zambia.

Hand axes and related artifacts occur over an enormous area of the Old World, and they underwent considerable refinement during the million years or so they were in use. But what do we know of the behavior of their makers? Without question, *Homo ergaster* and *H. erectus* hunted and foraged for food, probably in far more effective ways than *Homo habilis*. Time and time again, hand axes and other butchering artifacts have been found in association with the bones of large game animals. But did the hunters actually kill such formidable herbivores as the elephant and the rhinoceros? To do so would require social mechanisms to foster cooperation and communication abilities far beyond those of their predecessors.

SITE

Schoningen, Germany

Since 1983, Harmut Thieme has investigated a 6-square-kilometer (2.31 square mile) area within the area of an open cast coal mine at **Schoningen**, northern Germany, where mining operations cut deep into massive Pleistocene deposits. He has uncovered lake-shore sites where *Homo erectus* once camped. One location was a campsite by a lake, where the inhabitants butchered elephants and other animals, and also took birds and fish. Thieme recovered four worked branches from silver fir trees here, each with a diagonal groove cut into one end, perhaps to hold sharp stone flakes or flint tools to make a more efficient tool. The wood was carefully selected—the hard, intact roots of the boughs of rotten fir trunks.

Another location lay about 10 meters (33 feet) below the modern ground surface, where a hunt took place on the shores of a shallow, elongated lake. The area was dry and treeless, allowing the hunters to watch their prey. Here, a hunting band stalked, intercepted, killed, and butchered a complete herd of wild horses on the shore. Thieme and his colleagues have excavated more than 3,200 square meters (3,445 square ft.) of an organic mud where the artifacts lie. Plant pollens from the mud reveal a meadow and forest landscape that thrived in a cool, temperate climate. The inhabitants of the site hunted and butchered at least twenty wild horses, whose remains represent more than 90 percent of the 25,000 bone fragments at the site. They brought stone scrapers and points with them, manufacturing them elsewhere and only resharpening or reworking them on-site—there is no toolmaking debris, just refinishing flakes.

At least nine wooden spears have come from the site. Most are made of spruce, between 1.82 and 2.5 meters (5.9 and 8.2 feet) long, each made from an individual tree that was felled, the branches and bark stripped off, the tips being made from the hardest wood at the foot of the tree (Figure 3.6). The points are carefully shaped and symmetrical, the tails pointed and tapering toward the pointed, proximal end. The hunters smoothed and shaped the surfaces of their weapons with great care, the maximum thickness and weight lying a third of the way from the tip. Thieme remarks that they resemble modern hunting javelins. A replica spear tested under controlled conditions displayed excellent ballistic qualities and a range of about 60 meters (198 feet) with good penetrating power, ideal for hunting horses.

The first wooden tool from the site, found in 1994, was a spruce stick with carefully sharpened ends, 0.78 meters (2.6 feet) long, made from the stem of a small tree. Thieme believes this was a throwing stick, its shape and size like those used by Australian Aborigines to hunt birds in flight. It would have been very effective against the geese that lived in the reeds around the lake, whose bones occur in the site.

Evidence for butchery and perhaps big-game hunting comes from three remarkable sites: **Boxgrove** in southern England, where hunters drove rhinoceroses, bison, horses, and other large animals over a cliff overlooking a small lake about 500,000 years ago. At **Ambrona** and **Torralba** in central Spain, people living in a deep, swampy valley either 200,000 or 400,000 years ago (the date is controversial) butchered elephants mired in muddy water (see Figure 3.7 on page 80). But the most vivid portrait of archaic hunting skill comes from a 400,000-year-old kill site at **Schoningen** in northern Germany (see box).

Figure 3.6 One of the Schoningen spears exposed in the original excavations.

Numerous other worked wood fragments came from this large hunting camp, among them a carefully shaped and charred stick that may have been used to cook meat over a fire. Hearths lie along the western edge of the main concentration of finds, each about a meter (3 feet) apart. The nearby finds include large bison bones, the flat surfaces of which bear traces of repeated cut marks, as if people were slicing up butchered meat into strips for drying. Thieme points out that the hearths lay on dry ground, which means they were probably used in late summer or fall, when water levels were low and rainfall sparse. Then, in late autumn, the first snow covered the bones and abandoned tools with a thick layer of decaying reeds before rising waters in spring preserved the site for posterity.

Bamboo and Choppers in Tropical Forests

The eastern portions of the archaic human world lay in Asia, in an enormous region of woodland and forest with great environmental diversity. The tropical forests of east Asia are rich in animal and plant foods, but these food resources are widely dispersed over the landscape. Thus, *Homo erectus* bands were constantly on the move, carrying tools with them. Under these circumstances, it was logical for them to make use of bamboo, wood, and other

Figure 3.7 Torralba, Spain. A remarkable linear arrangement of elephant tusks and leg bones that were probably laid out by those who butchered the animals. Torralba has yielded most of the left side of an elephant, which had been cut into pieces, while Ambrona contained the remains of thirty to thirty-five dismembered elephants. Concentrations of broken bones lay all over the site, and the skulls of the elephants had been broken open to get at the brains. In one place, elephant bones had been laid out in a line, perhaps to form stepping stones in the swamp where the animals had been killed. Both sites were littered with crude hand axes, cleavers, scrapers, and cutting tools. The original scenario for the sites had hunters watching the valley floors, which may have lain astride an important game trail. At a strategic moment several bands would gather quietly, set brush fires, and drive the unsuspecting beasts into the swamps, where they would be killed and butchered at leisure. Other archaeologists challenge this scenario. They believe the hunters were actually scavenging meat from animals that had perished when they became mired in the swamps.

fibrous materials—the most convenient materials at hand. There was no need for the specialized, often complicated artifacts used in the open country of the West either for spear points or for the butchering tools used on large animals. As archaeologist Geoffrey Pope has pointed out, the distribution of the simple choppers and flakes used by many eastern populations coincides very closely with the natural distribution of bamboo, one of the most versatile materials known to humankind. Bamboo was efficient, durable, and portable. It could be used to manufacture containers, sharp knives, spears, weapon tips, ropes, and dwellings. To this day, it is widely used in Asia as scaffolding for building skyscrapers

(Figure 3.8). It is an ideal material for people subsisting not off large game but off smaller forest animals such as monkeys, rats, squirrels, lizards, and snakes, as well as plant foods. Simple stone flakes and jagged-edged choppers, the only artifacts to survive the millennia, would be ideal for working bamboo and may, indeed, have been used for this purpose for hundreds of thousands of years, long after *Homo erectus* had been superseded by more advanced human forms.

Archaics humans were eclectic and flexible hunter-gatherers, who relied on hunting, scavenging, and plant foods. They may have understood the telltale signs of the passage of seasons, the meanings of cloud formations, the timing of game and bird migrations, and the geography of their territories. They probably lived in relatively large groups at times, both to reduce the danger from carnivores and to improve the chance of finding food, especially from larger animals. Usually, band size was much smaller, especially when plant foods were more abundant and easily obtained by individuals. All of this argues for considerable social flexibility and intelligence, reflected in larger brain sizes. However, archaic humans may have been unable to integrate their social intelligence—their ability to share food and cooperate in the hunt—with other aspects of human intelligence.

Figure 3.8 Bamboo scaffolding in use to build a modern high-rise. This flexible and versatile material has been used by Asians since the earliest times.

Language

Homo erectus had a large brain with a well-developed Broca's area, the zone associated with speaking ability. Its vocal tracts were more modern, suggesting considerable potential for articulate speech. Anthropologists Leslie Aiello and Robin Dunbar have argued that the basis for language ability appeared in humans by at least 250,000 years ago. They believe it first evolved as a way to handle increasingly complex social information. As group sizes increased, so did a capacity for language, used primarily to talk about social relations. It was only later that humans developed the kind of general-purpose language we use today, which allows us to communicate freely, whatever the behavioral domain. So like us in many ways, *Homo erectus* lacked the cognitive flexibility characteristic of modern humans, yet it was from this archaic human that ultimately modern *Homo sapiens* evolved.

Archaic *Homo sapiens* (c. 600,000 to 130,000 years ago)

The all-embracing label *Homo erectus* dates from the days when scholars thought of human evolution in more linear terms. They linked anatomically primitive features such as heavy brow ridges and bun-shaped skull-caps, which are indeed common to the various archaic human fossils from Africa, Asia, and Europe. Specialized features, such as the massive faces found on Asian individuals, may in fact be evidence for geographically defined forms, only one of which evolved into anatomically modern humans. This branching view sees the various forms of archaic humans as an adaptive radiation of hominins after 1.9 million years ago, with only a small part of this evolution resulting in the emergence of *Homo sapiens*. (There are numerous local labels for different European fossils in particular, which I have ignored here for clarity. See a biological anthropology text for details.)

Between about 600,000 and 130,000 years ago, archaic humans were evolving toward more modern forms throughout the Old World. Fossil fragments from Africa, Asia, and Europe display both *erectus*-like and *sapiens*-like traits, sufficient for them to be classified under the general label archaic *Homo sapiens*. These anatomical advances take several forms. Brain capacities are larger, the sides of the skull are wider, and the rear of the cranium is now more rounded. Human skeletons become less robust and molar teeth are smaller.

These general trends occur in African fossils, such as the well-known, massive **Broken Hill** skull from **Kabwe**, Zambia, in central Africa. They are found in China, too, where both archaic and *sapiens* traits appear, traits that Chinese anthropologists also claim appear in modern populations there. In Europe, too, fossil remains dating to this long period display a mosaic of *erectus* and *sapiens* features. But the fossils from each continent differ considerably. European fossils, for example, often appear somewhat more robust than those from Asia. Everywhere, however, brain sizes increase gradually and skull shapes become rounder. In Asia and Africa, the changes seem to have a trend toward modern *sapiens*, whereas the European fossils are evolving toward an archaic-like Neanderthal form. This evolutionary trend toward more modern anatomy appears everywhere, but it was only on one continent, Africa, that archaic humans gave rise to modern *Homo sapiens*. In other words, the pattern of human evolution based on the adaptive radiation seen with the australopithecines hundreds of thousands of years earlier persisted into much later times.

The Neanderthals (c. 200,000 to 30,000 years ago)

Much of what we know about archaic *Homo sapiens*, the descendant of *Homo erectus*, comes from the Neanderthals, long-term inhabitants of Europe and Eurasia, whose anatomical features appear in archaic European populations such as those from **Atapuerca,** Spain, at least 300,000 years ago (Figure 3.9). Fragments of Neanderthal DNA from a 38,000 year-old leg bone found in Croatia suggest that the direct ancestors of the Neanderthals split from the ancestors of modern humans as early as 418,000 years ago.

The Neanderthals are still the subject of great controversy among physical anthropologists. Some people still use the word *Neanderthal* to describe dim-witted, ugly people who are like apes, an insult aimed at those they consider dumb. This stereotype and that of the shambling cave people so beloved by cartoonists come from mistaken studies of Neanderthal skeletons in the early years of this century. In fact, the Neanderthals were strong, robustly built humans with some archaic features. Their skulls display retreating foreheads, projecting faces, and sometimes eyebrow ridges, when compared with modern people. There is every reason to believe they were expert hunters and beings capable of considerable intellectual reasoning.

There are, of course, striking anatomical differences between Neanderthals and modern humans, both in the robust postcranial skeleton of the Neanderthal and in its more bun-shaped skull, sometimes with heavy brow ridges and a forward projecting face (see Figure 3.10 on page 84). These features are the reason this extinct hominin form is classified as *Homo sapiens neanderthalensis*, a subspecies of *Homo sapiens*, and not as a fully modern human.

Researchers at the University of Munich, Germany, and at Pennsylvania State University were able to extract deoxyribonucleic acid (DNA) from the first Neanderthal arm bone ever discovered in the Neander Valley near Dusseldorf, Germany, in 1856. The scientists

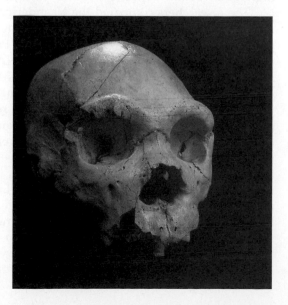

Figure 3.9 Archaic *Homo sapiens* skull from the Pit of Bones, Atapuerca, Spain.

Figure 3.10 A classic Neanderthal skull, showing the prominent brow ridge and prognathous face.

pulverized a small amount of the bone and were able to extract several small fragments of **mitochondrial DNA** (see "DNA and Archaeology" box). By overlapping the small fragments of Neanderthal DNA and using a technique known as polymerase chain reaction to make many copies of the molecules, the scientists were able to identify a sequence of 378 base pairs (chemicals that form the fundamental units of the genetic code) in a specific region of the Neanderthal DNA. This area, known as hypervariable region 1, is known to show changes over many generations. In general, the greater the dissimilarity in this region between two species, the more remote the relation is thought to be.

The researchers compared the Neanderthal DNA sequence to sequences in the same region of DNA for 994 modern human lineages, which included Africans, Asians, Australians, Europeans, Native Americans, and Pacific Islanders. The Neanderthal DNA sequence differed from all modern human DNA by either 27 or 28 base pairs. In contrast, modern human sequences in this region of DNA differ from each other on average by 8 base pairs. The difference between modern human DNA and chimpanzee DNA in this region is much greater, at about 55 base pairs. As a result, the geneticists concluded that Neanderthals and modern humans are distant relations and did not interbreed or evolve from one another. If chimpanzees and humans diverged about 4 million to 5 million years ago, then we can estimate Neanderthals may have split from early modern humans between 550,000 and 690,000 years ago.

The Neanderthals flourished in Europe, Eurasia, and part of southwestern Asia from about 200,000 years ago until around 30,000 years ago. Their anatomical pattern stabilized for more than 50 millennia before changing rapidly to essentially modern human anatomy within a brief period of 5,000 years approximately 40,000 years ago. Neanderthal populations displayed great variation, but everywhere had the same posture and manual abilities as modern people. They differed from us in having massive limb bones, often

SCIENCE
DNA and Archaeology

Ever since the identification of the ABO blood system in the early twentieth century, genetics has had a profound effect on the study of human evolutionary history. Modern molecular biological techniques have made it much easier to detect and analyze new polymorphic genes (genes present in slightly different forms in different people) that might have medical or anthropological interest. All humans carry in their genes the record of their past history. In recent years, studies of mitochondrial DNA (mtDNA), present outside the cell nuclei in small structures called mitochondria, have attracted particular attention. MtDNA is inherited through the female line and is passed from mothers to offspring virtually unaltered except for rare changes caused by mutation. Large-scale studies of human MtDNA in present-day populations from all parts of the world have shown that there is relatively little MtDNA variation throughout the globe, suggesting that there was a relatively recent branching out of human populations. The African mtDNAs were the most variable, having had more time to accumulate genetic changes, consistent with the theory that the African human lineages were the oldest ones. Molecular biologists Rebecca Cann, Mark Stoneking, and Alan Wilson proposed that all modern humanity is descended from a single anatomically modern human, who lived in tropical Africa about 200,000 years ago. This hypothesis has been widely criticized and refined, but it seems increasingly likely that *Homo sapiens* (ourselves) evolved in Africa, then spread into other parts of the Old World and eventually to the Americas. MtDNA research on American populations links them to Siberian ancestors, as one might expect. In recent years, research on the male-inherited Y chromosome has also confirmed modern human origins in tropical Africa.

The first ancient DNA sequences were reported by Swedish scientist Svaante Pääbo, who extracted and characterized DNA from the skin of a Predynastic Egyptian of about 4000 B.C. in 1985. Since then, DNA has been extracted from bones, teeth, and plant remains using a new technique called polymerase chain reaction (PCR). Pääbo used this technique on a human brain of 3000 B.C. from a hunter-gatherer site at Windover, Florida, and identified an MtDNA strain not previously observed in North America. In recent years, scientists have succeeded in extracting DNA from a Neanderthal bone over 50,000 years old and have shown that these archaic Europeans were genetically distinct from the modern humans who succeeded them. MtDNA analysis of ancient human skeletons from Easter Island in the Pacific has also shown that the ultimate origins of the Easter Islanders lies in Polynesia, for this remote land mass was colonized from the Society Islands (the Tahiti region) by A.D. 500.

Molecular biology is playing an increasingly important role in the study of ancient human populations and population movements.

---

somewhat bowed in the thigh and forearm, features that reflect their greater muscular power (see Figure 3.11 on page 86). For their height, the Neanderthals were bulky and heavily muscled, and their brain capacity was slightly larger than that of modern humans. Their antecedents are in earlier archaic *Homo sapiens* Europeans, from which they inherited their heavy build and their ability to withstand extreme cold, an adaptation so successful that it lasted for more than 100,000 years.

Figure labels:
- large and wide rib cage
- long clavicle
- wide scapula with more muscle attachments along rear edge
- large shoulder joint
- large elbow joint
- bowed and short forearm
- wide hips
- large hip joint, rotated outward
- hand with strong grip and wide fingertips
- long, thin superior pubic ramus
- rounded, curved, and thick-walled femur shaft
- large and thick patella
- short, flattened, and thick-walled tibia
- large ankle joint
- wide and strong toe bones

Neanderthal Male

Figure 3.11 The skeleton of a male Neanderthal, showing major anatomical features.

Neanderthal culture and technology was far more complex and sophisticated than that of their more archaic predecessors. Many of their artifacts were not multipurpose tools but were made for specific purposes, such as stone spear points mounted on wooden spears or curved scrapers for treating pegged-out hides (Figure 3.12). Like their predecessors, they occupied large territories, which they probably exploited on a seasonal round, returning to the same locations year after year when game migrated or plant foods came into season.

The Neanderthals were skilled hunters, especially when one realizes that they had to attack game at close quarters with spears and clubs rather than with the bow and arrow (see Figure 3.13, top, on page 88). They were not afraid to tackle such formidable animals as mammoth, bison, or wild horses. Many western European bands lived in caves and rock shelters during much of the year as a protection against arctic cold. During the brief

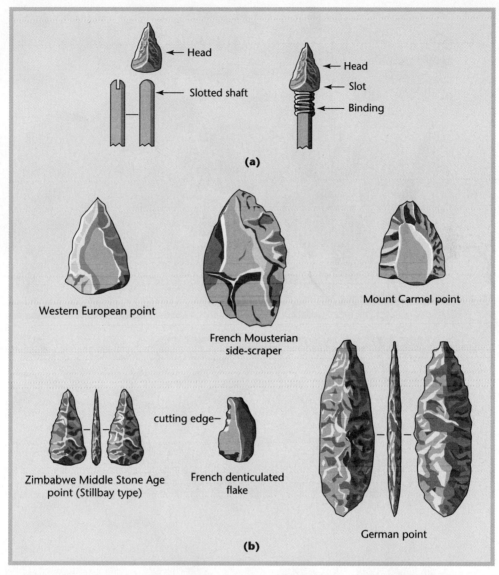

(a)

Head
Slotted shaft

Head
Slot
Binding

Western European point

French Mousterian
side-scraper

Mount Carmel point

Zimbabwe Middle Stone Age
point (Stillbay type)

cutting edge—

French denticulated
flake

German point

(b)

Figure 3.12 Composite spear points. Stone artifacts fabricated by archaic *Homo sapiens* included **(a)** composite tools that mounted stone points to the ends of wooden shafts and **(b)** a variety of spear points, also cutting and scraping tools.

summer months they may have fanned out over the open plains, living in temporary tented encampments, also exploiting plant foods (see Figure 3.13, bottom, on page 88). There can be little doubt the Neanderthals knew their local environments intimately and that they planned their lives around migration seasons and such factors as herd size and the predictability of animal movements. By this time, too, humans had learned how to store food for the lean months, maximizing the meat taken from seasonally migrating herds of reindeer and other animals.

Figure 3.13 Reconstruction of Neanderthal lifeways. (top) Hunters during the early last glaciation. (bottom) Neanderthal woman foraging for plant foods.

The resulting cultural variability is reflected in the diverse **Mousterian** tool kits of Neanderthal groups (named after the site of Le Moustier in southwestern France). Unlike the hand-ax makers, the Neanderthals made most of their artifacts of flakes, the most common being scraping tools and spear points. Some of their weapons were **composite tools,** artifacts made of more than one component—for example, a point, a shaft, and the binding that secured the head to the shaft, making a spear. Their technology was simple, highly variable, and a logical development of earlier technologies developed over hundreds of thousands of years (see Figure 3.12 on page 87). Neanderthal sites in France have yielded a great diversity of tool kits. Some levels include hand axes; others notched flakes, perhaps used for stripping meat for drying or pressing fibrous plants. Such wide variation in Mousterian tool kits is found not only in France but at other Neanderthal sites throughout Europe and Southwestern Asia and in North Africa, where other archaic *Homo sapiens* made similar tools. No one knows exactly what all these variations in tool kits mean, but they reflect the ability of the Neanderthals and other archaic *Homo sapiens* to develop tools for different, highly specific activities, perhaps at a time of rising human populations and slightly enhanced social complexity.

The Neanderthals and their archaic contemporaries elsewhere were foragers, and the world's population was still small, but life was gradually becoming more complex. We find the first signs of religious ideology, of a preoccupation with the life hereafter. Neanderthal burials have been recovered from caves and rock shelters, and from open campsites. One rock shelter, **La Ferrassie** near Les Eyzies in France, yielded the remains of two adult Neanderthals and four children buried close together in a campsite. Group sepulchers occur at other sites, too, signs that the Neanderthals, like most later foragers, believed in life after death.

We find in the Neanderthals and their increasingly sophisticated culture the first roots of our own complicated beliefs, societies, and religious sense. But the Neanderthals, like other archaic *Homo sapiens* forms, gave way to fully modern humans after 40,000 years ago, people whose awesome intellectual and physical powers created a late Ice Age world unimaginably different from that of earlier prehistory.

The Origins of Modern Humans (?c. 180,000 to 150,000 years ago)

Homo sapiens means the "wise person." We are the clever people, capable of subtlety, of manipulation, of self-understanding. What is it that separates us from earlier humans, scientists wonder. First and foremost must be our ability to speak fluently and articulately. We communicate, we tell stories, we pass on knowledge and ideas, all through the medium of language. Consciousness, cognition, self-awareness, foresight, and the ability to express oneself and one's emotions—these are direct consequences of fluent speech. They can be linked with another attribute of the fully fledged human psyche: the capacity for symbolic and spiritual thought, concerned not only with subsistence and technology but also with the boundaries of existence and the relationships among the individual, the group, and the universe.

Fluent speech, the full flowering of human creativity expressed in art and religion, expert toolmaking—these are some of the hallmarks of *Homo sapiens*. With these abilities humankind eventually colonized not just temperate and tropical environments but the entire globe. With the appearance of modern humans we begin the study of people anatomically identical to ourselves, people with the same intellectual potential as our own.

For hundreds of thousands of years, both *Homo erectus* and early *Homo sapiens* survived and evolved with the aid of multiple intelligences, separated by walls analogous to those dividing the chapels of a Medieval cathedral. As archaeologist Steven Mithen says, the thoughts in one chapel could barely be heard in another. Archaic humans lacked one vital component of the modern mind: cognitive flexibility, the ability to bridge the walls between their many intelligences. Such flexibility appears to have been the prerogative of modern humans, *Homo sapiens*. The controversies surrounding the origins of modern humanity, of ourselves, rank among the most vigorous in archaeology.

Continuity or Replacement?

Over generations of debate, two major, and diametrically opposed, hypotheses have developed to explain the origins of modern humans (Figure 3.14):

- The so-called candelabra (or multiregional) model hypothesizes that *Homo erectus* populations throughout the Old World evolved independently, first to archaic *Homo sapiens*, then to fully modern humans. This continuity model argues for multiple origins of *Homo sapiens* and no migrations later than those of *Homo erectus*. Thus, modern geographic populations have been separated from one another for a long time, perhaps for nearly 2 million years. Under this scenario, continuous gene flow within the group meant that highly adaptive, novel anatomical features spread rapidly, thereby keeping all human populations on the same fundamental evolutionary path toward anatomically modern people, even if some evolved into fully modern humans before others.

- The Out-of-Africa model takes the diametrically opposite view. According to it, *Homo sapiens* evolved in one place, then spread to all other parts of the Old World. This model, which assumes population movement from a single point of origin, implies that modern geographic populations have shallow roots and were derived from a single source in relatively recent times.

These two models represent extremes, which pit advocates of anatomical continuity against those who favor rapid replacement of archaic populations. A torrent of new discoveries has shown that archaic human populations displayed great variation and were morphologically more different from anatomically modern humans than once suspected. Advocates of the multiregional model rely heavily on anatomical traits from surviving fossils to argue their case, whereas out-of-Africa supporters make use not only of fossils but of genetics, an approach their opponents regard as highly controversial. The debate continues and is likely to continue for generations as both new discoveries and more refined genetic researches radically alter our knowledge of archaic *Homo sapiens* and its contemporaries and successors.

Molecular Biology and *Homo sapiens*

Molecular biology has played a significant role in dating earlier human evolution and is now yielding important clues to the origins of *Homo sapiens* (see box on page 85).

Researchers have zeroed in on mitochondrial DNA (mtDNA), a useful tool for calibrating mutation rates because it accumulates mutations much faster than nuclear DNA.

(a)

(b)

Figure 3.14 Theories of the origins of modern humans, each of which interprets the fossil evidence in very different ways. **(a)** The Candelabra or multiregional model, which argues for the evolution of *Homo sapiens* in many regions of the Old World. The dotted lines between different columns represent gene flow between regions. **(b)** The Out-of-Africa model, which has modern humanity evolving in Africa, then spreading to other parts of the world.

Mitochondrial DNA is inherited only through the maternal line; it does not mix and become diluted with paternal DNA. Thus, it provides a potentially reliable link with ancestral populations. When genetic researchers analyzed the mtDNA of 147 women from Africa, Asia, Europe, Australia, and New Guinea, they found that the differences among them were very small. Therefore, they argued, the five populations were all of comparatively recent origin. There were some differences, sufficient to separate two groups within the sample—a set of African individuals and another comprising individuals from all groups. The biologists concluded that all modern humans derive from a 200,000-year-old African population, from which populations migrated to the rest of the Old World with little or no interbreeding with existing, more archaic human groups.

With mitochondrial data from more than 5,000 modern individuals, there is evidence that Africans display more diverse types of mitochondrial DNA than other present-day populations elsewhere in the world, which suggests they had more time to develop such mutations. An even larger database of normal (nuclear) DNA, also of its products (blood groups and enzymes), displays a hierarchy of clusters. There was a primary split between Africans and non-Africans, then a later one between Eurasians and southeast Asians. This also implies that modern humans originated in Africa, then dispersed from there to split again in Asia. It is thought that the ancestral population lived in Africa before 100,000 years ago. This also means that, assuming a constant rate of genetic diversification, all human variation could have arisen in the past 150,000 years. Recent studies of the Y chromosome, the male equivalent of mtDNA, inherited only through males, reveals a similar diversity in African men, again strengthening the out-of-Africa theory.

Fortunately, there is some archaeological and fossil evidence that tends to confirm an early appearance of anatomically modern humans in sub-Saharan Africa. According to German physical anthropologist Günter Bräuer, there were at least three forms of *Homo sapiens* in sub-Saharan Africa. An archaic *Homo sapiens* form was distributed from southern to northeast Africa some 200,000 years ago. These archaic populations had evolved from earlier *Homo erectus* populations and had higher cranial vaults and other anatomical features akin to those of anatomically modern humans. Before and after 150,000 years ago, many Africans displayed mosaics of both archaic and modern features.

Thanks to a recent discovery at **Herto,** about 225 km (140 miles) northeast of Addis Ababa, Ethiopia, we now know that anatomically fully modern people were flourishing in northeast Africa 160,000 years ago. Paleoanthropologist Tim White and his colleagues unearthed three skulls (one of a child), as well as other human fragments, from a location where people had caught numerous fish and killed or scavenged hippopotami (Figure 3.15). The skulls are clearly from anatomically modern people, although there are

Figure 3.15 *Homo sapiens idaltu* from Herto, Ethiopia.

minor differences that mark them as more primitive, sufficient for them to be labeled *Homo sapiens idaltu* (after the local Afar name for "elder"). The adult male skull is long and rugged, with heavily worn upper teeth, also slightly larger than modern crania. Interestingly, there are signs that the skulls were defleshed with stone tools after death, while the child's skull displays a polish resulting from repeated handling. Judging from modern-day practices in New Guinea and elsewhere, the people may have preserved heads as part of some ancestor cult—the earliest evidence of any form of death ritual from the past.

The Herto finds show that the biological developments that led to the appearance of modern humans had almost run their course by 150,000 years ago, earlier than anywhere else in the world, including Europe, where archaic human forms such as the Neanderthals still flourished. *Homo sapiens* also lived in southern Africa at an early date. Archaeologists have found well-preserved footprints of an anatomically modern human preserved in a fossilized sand dune at **Langebaan Lagoon** near Cape Town, South Africa, dating to at least 117,000 years ago.

Ecology and *Homo sapiens*

Ecological anthropologist Robert Foley points out that the savanna woodland of Africa before 100,000 years ago was an ideal environment for promoting the speciation of modern humans. He has studied monkey evolution in Africa and found that the widely dispersed populations had diverged; They did not continue on a single evolutionary course. Africa experienced considerable habitat fragmentation and reformation during the constant cold and warm cycles of the Ice Age, fluctuations that enhanced the prospects of speciation among the continent's animals and plants. For example, says Foley, one monkey genus alone radiated into 16 species at about the same time as modern humans may have evolved in Africa. Foley's monkey studies have convinced him that modern humans evolved in just such a fragmented mosaic of tropical environments, developing distinctive characteristics that separated them from their archaic predecessors. There were areas where food resources were predictable and of high quality. In response to such regions, some human populations may have developed wide-ranging behavior, lived in larger social groups with considerable kin-based substructure, and been highly selective in their diet.

As part of these responses, some groups may have developed exceptional hunting skills, using a technology so effective that they could prey on animals from a distance with projectiles. With more efficient weapons, more advance planning, and better organization of foraging, our ancestors could have reduced the unpredictability of the environment in dramatic ways. Few archaeologists would be so bold as to associate ancient technologies with specific fossil forms, but we do know that tens of thousands of years later, *Homo sapiens* relied on much more sophisticated tool technology than that of their predecessors. The new tool kits were based on antler, bone, wood, and parallel-sided stone-blade manufacture. This technology was much more advanced than anything made by their predecessors, and it took many millennia to develop. There is no question but that this technology would have conferred a major advantage on its users, both in terms of hunting efficiency and energy expended in the chase (see Figure 3.16 on page 94).

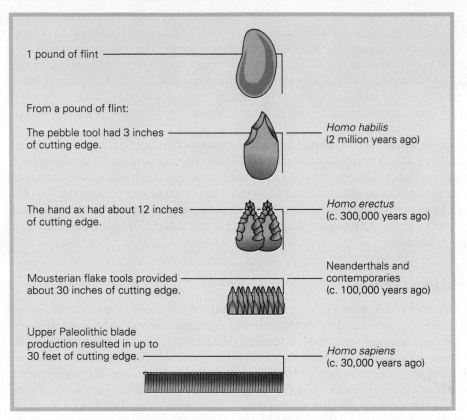

1 pound of flint

From a pound of flint:

The pebble tool had 3 inches
of cutting edge.

Homo habilis
(2 million years ago)

The hand ax had about 12 inches
of cutting edge.

Homo erectus
(c. 300,000 years ago)

Mousterian flake tools provided
about 30 inches of cutting edge.

Neanderthals and
contemporaries
(c. 100,000 years ago)

Upper Paleolithic blade
production resulted in up to
30 feet of cutting edge.

Homo sapiens
(c. 30,000 years ago)

Figure 3.16 The growing efficiency of stone technology, shown by the ability of ancient stoneworkers to produce ever-larger numbers of cutting edges from a unit of stone or other fine-grained rock. The Neanderthals were far more efficient stone artisans than were their predecessors. By the same token, *Homo sapiens* used blade and other technologies that produced up to 4.5 meters (15 feet) per kilogram of rock (see Figure 3.5 on page 77).

Interestingly enough, there are signs of technological change throughout eastern and southern Africa between 200,000 and 100,000 years ago, as age-old hand ax technology gave way to lighter tool kits that combined sharp stone flakes with wooden spear shafts, and to other more specialized artifacts used for woodworking and butchery. Such simple artifacts, made on medium-sized flakes, could have been the archaic prototypes of far more efficient tools and weapons developed by anatomically modern humans after 100,000 years ago (Figure 3.16). But again, one must emphasize that the existence of such artifacts in Africa at the time when modern humans apparently first appeared there is not necessarily proof they were developed by *Homo sapiens*.

We can now state with some confidence that modern humans originated in tropical Africa some 150,000 years ago.

Out of Tropical Africa

If tropical Africa was the cradle of modern humans, how and why did *Homo sapiens* spread into Europe and Asia? The critical period was between 100,000 and 45,000 years ago, the date by which anatomically modern people were certainly living in southwest Asia. The only major barrier to population movement between tropical Africa and the Mediterranean Basin is the Sahara desert, today some of the driest territory on earth. Bitterly cold glacial conditions in the north brought a cooler and wetter climate to the desert from before 100,000 until about 40,000 years ago. For long periods before then, the country between East Africa and the Mediterranean was passable, supporting scattered game herds and open grassland. The Nile Valley was always habitable, even during periods of great aridity in the desert. Thus, small groups of modern people could have hunted and foraged across the Sahara into the Nile Valley and southwest Asia as early as 100,000 years ago. From there, their successors may have moved into south and southeast Asia at a still unknown date, but perhaps between 80,000 and 50,000 years ago. This population movement may have been interrupted by a massive volcanic eruption of Mount Toba on the island of Sumatra, which covered much of south Asia with several meters of fine volcanic ash. One paleoanthropologist has estimated that only 10,000 modern humans survived the disaster—but research on Mount Toba is still in its infancy.

As southwest Asia became increasingly dry and less productive after 50,000 years ago, small numbers of modern people may have responded to population pressure and food shortages by moving across the wide land bridge that joined Turkey to southeastern Europe at the time, spreading into the homeland of the European Neanderthals within a few millennia.

With these still little-known population movements, the initial radiation of modern humans throughout the Old World ended, perhaps by about 40,000 years ago. As we shall see in Chapter 4, the next 30,000 years saw the greatest of all human diaspora take our ancestors into the islands of southeast Asia, to New Guinea, Australia, Siberia, and, ultimately, the Americas.

Summary

The climatic events of the Great Ice Age (the Pleistocene) between about 1.8 million and 15,000 years ago saw complex fluctuations between glacial maxima and much shorter interglacial periods that were the backdrop to the evolution not only of *Homo ergaster* and *Homo erectus*, but of also of modern humans—*Homo sapiens*—as well. *Homo erectus* had evolved from earlier *Homo* in tropical Africa by 1.9 million years ago, at about the same time that fire was tamed, then radiated into Europe and Asia as part of a general radiation of mammalian species soon afterward. The new humans used a simple technology based on hand axes and basic flake technology in the west, relying heavily on bamboo and other forest products in Southeast Asia. There was a gradual increase in brain size, perhaps beginning as early as about 0.4 million years ago, as archaic forms of *Homo sapiens* with enlarged brain capacities evolved in various parts of the Old World. The best known of these forms are the Neanderthals of Europe and Eurasia, who developed more sophisticated toolmaking technology than *Homo erectus*, were more adept hunters and foragers, and were the first humans to bury some of their dead.

Two competing theories account for the appearance of anatomically modern humans. The Out-of-Africa hypothesis argues that modern humans evolved in tropical Africa before 150,000 years ago, then spread into other parts of the world from Southwest Asia after 45,000 years ago (see Chapter 4). The Multiregional hypothesis has it that modern humans developed independently in Africa, Europe, and Asia, and that the biological diversity of contemporary humankind has very deep roots in prehistory. With the appearance of modern humans, the long prehistory of the archaic world ends.

Imagine a dinner table of a thousand guests, in which each man is sitting between his own father and his own son. (We might just as well imagine a ladies' banquet . . .) At one end of the table there might be a French Nobel laureate in a white tie and tails and with the legion of Honor on his breast, and at the other end a Cro-Magnon dressed in animal skins and with a necklace of cave-bear teeth. Yet each would be able to converse with his neighbors to his left and right, who would either be his father or his son. So the distance from then to now is not really very great.

ATTRIBUTED TO AXEL KLINCKOWSTRÖM, QUOTED BY BJORN KÜRTEN (1986, p. 61)

4 Diaspora

| 4.5 Million | 2.5 Million | 1.0 Million | 500,000 B.P. | 100,000 B.P. | 50,000 B.P. | 15,000 B.P. | A.D. 1 | A.D. 1950 |

PROLOGUE

Spanish landowner Marcellino de Sautuola had a casual interest in archaeology. He had visited an exhibit in Paris of some of the fine stone tools from French caves. In 1875, he decided to dig for some artifacts of his own in the caverns of Altamira on his estate. Sautuola's five-year-old daughter, Maria, begged for the chance to dig with him, so he good-naturedly agreed. Maria soon tired of the muddy work and wandered off with a flickering lantern into a low side chamber of the cave. Suddenly, he heard cries of "Toros! Toros!" ("Bulls! Bulls!"). Maria pointed excitedly at brightly painted figures of bison and a charging boar on the low ceiling. Daughter and father marveled at the dynamic paintings, arranged so cleverly around bulges in the rock that they seemed to move in the flickering light.

Sautuola was convinced the paintings had been executed by the same people who had dropped stone tools in the cave. But the experts laughed at him and accused the marquis of smuggling an artist into Altamira to forge the bison. It was not until 1904 that the long-dead Spaniard was vindicated, when some paintings with strong stylistic links to Altamira came to light in a French cave that had been sealed since the prehistoric artists had worked there. Clearly, whoever had painted on the cave walls at Altamira was a far cry from *Homo habilis,* the earliest known toolmaker.

Something dramatic happened to humanity about 50,000 to 60,000 years ago. Suddenly, the pace of human life, of cultural evolution, accelerated rapidly. Some scientists have called these changes a "cultural explosion," but a better term is probably a series of "sparks," where there was rapid cultural change in one area, but not in others. One such spark was the development of new stone technologies in Southwest Asia by 50,000 years ago, another the first appearance of art in Europe about 40,000 years ago, a third the first settlement of Australia by 45,000 years before present. Only after about 30,000 years ago, during the late Ice Age, did rapid cultural change take hold in all parts of the world. This chapter describes the rapidly changing late Ice Age world of about 50,000 to 15,000 years ago. We show how humans first adapted to extreme arctic climates and developed highly specialized forager cultures that subsisted off cold-loving animals such as the mammoth and steppe bison. We discuss, also, the radiation of *Homo sapiens* throughout the Old World, and then turn to one of the most controversial subjects in modern archaeology—the first settlement of the Americas (Figure 4.1).

Archaeologist Steven Mithen believes that the new types of behavior associated with the cultural explosion resulted from the development of full cognitive fluidity. Some 50,000 years ago, perhaps as a result of a fortuitous mutation that promoted the fully human brain, people developed new connections between previously isolated mental domains—environmental, technical, and social intelligence, knocking down the walls between the chapels of the metaphorical medieval cathedral referred to in Chapter 3. One consequence was much more sophisticated social relations; another was visual symbolism, the development of art as a means of expression and communication. As the great cave paintings of western France show (described on pages 109–112), humankind now had the ability to bring the natural and social worlds together in a seamless synthesis that is characteristic of many human societies, whether hunter-gatherers or farmers, to this day. The evolution of cognitive fluidity gave *Homo sapiens*, spreading throughout the world after 45,000 years

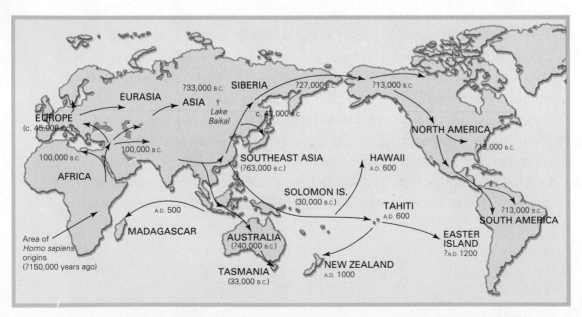

Figure 4.1 Map showing the settlement of the world by modern humans.

ago, perhaps earlier, a competitive edge over resident earlier human populations. With their superior intellectual capabilities, they pushed earlier populations into extinction, perhaps occasionally interbreeding with them. Once the move toward cognitive fluidity began, there was no stopping the process. By 30,000 years ago, the final step on the path to full modernity had been taken everywhere.

The Late Ice Age World (50,000 to 15,000 years ago)

For most of the past 45,000 years, the world was very different from that of today. At the height of the last Ice Age glaciation, some 18,000 years ago, vast ice sheets mantled Scandinavia and the Alps, leaving a chilly corridor of open tundra between them. Sea levels were more than 90 meters (300 feet) lower than today. Britain was joined to the European continent, the North Sea was under ice, and the Baltic Sea did not exist. One could walk from Turkey to Bulgaria dry-shod (Figure 4.2). Vast, treeless plains stretched north and east from central Europe to the frontiers of Siberia and beyond, a landscape of rolling scrub country dissected by occasional broad river valleys. The only signs of life were occasional large herds of big-game animals like the mammoth, bison, and reindeer, and they were

Figure 4.2 Generalized vegetation map of Europe during the late Ice Age.

often confined to river valleys. For humans to survive in these exposed landscapes required not only effective hunting methods and weaponry, but well-insulated winter dwellings and layered, tailored clothing that could keep people warm in sub-zero temperatures.

In more temperate and tropical latitudes, the effects of the last glaciation are harder to detect in geological strata. Tropical regions were often drier, many rain forests shrank, and there were more open grasslands and woodlands. In Africa, the Sahara Desert was as dry as, if not drier than, today, as cold polar air flowed south of the Mediterranean. Much lower sea levels exposed enormous areas of continental shelf in Southeast Asia. Many offshore islands became part of the Asian mainland. Great rivers meandered over what were then exposed coastal plains, across another sunken Ice Age continent known to scholars as **Sunda.** Offshore lay two large land masses—**Wallacea,** made up of the present islands of Sulawesi and Timor, and **Sahul,** a combination of New Guinea, Australia, and the low-lying and now flooded shelf between them (Figure 4.3).

Let us now look at how late Ice Age humans peopled this diverse, often harsh, world.

The Peopling of Southeast Asia and Australia (45,000 to 15,000 years ago)

Homo sapiens had appeared in Southeast Asia, including Indonesia and the Philippines, by at least 50,000 years ago. At the time, sea levels were much lower than today, so human settlement on Sunda, the exposed continental shelf, may have been concentrated in river

Figure 4.3 Sunda and Sahul during the late Ice Age.

Exotic Islanders:
Homo floresiensis

The earliest known occupation of Sunda comes from the island of Flores, where *Homo erectus* fragments have been fission-track-dated to between 900,000 and 800,000 years ago, but these dates remain controversial.

One would reasonably expect this remote island to have been settled once efficient watercraft came into use, but this was not the case. Excavations in **Liang Bua cave** on Flores yielded a remarkable series of diminutive human skeletons dating to before 38,000 and 13,000 years ago, associated with stone flakes and other artifacts, also the bones of a now-extinct, elephant-like animal known as a stegodon. These people were only about a meter (3.2 feet) tall (Figure 4.4). Their bones display a unique mixture of primitive and more advanced characteristics. Their brains are the same size as those of chimpanzees (c. 380cc), the skull displaying prominent brow ridges and a low brain case. However, the face is small and delicate like that of modern humans, being tucked under the brain, like that of *Homo sapiens*. The teeth also are entirely modern, whereas the legs are slight, the hips like those of an australopithecine.

Michael Morwood and his colleagues have named these hominins *Homo floresiensis*, but their evolutionary status is a puzzle. Are these a remnant *Homo erectus* population or are they modern humans, who crossed to Flores before 40,000 years ago, then developed their unique anatomical characteristics and small stature as a result of isolation that led, among other things, to endemic dwarfing? Or did they descend from a much earlier, still unknown, small brained hominin? At this early stage in research, we do not know. Certainly the artifacts, and evidence for use of fire, suggest fully human behavior.

Figure 4.4 An artist's impression of *Homo floresiensis*.

valleys, along lake shores, and on the coasts. If there were technological changes associated with *Homo sapiens,* they probably involved more efficient ways of exploiting the rich and highly varied environments of the mainland and offshore islands. The coastlines that faced offshore were relatively benign waters that probably offered a bounty of fish and shellfish to supplement game and wild plant foods. Perhaps coastal peoples constructed

SCIENCE

Radiocarbon Dating

Radiocarbon dating is the primary dating method used between about 40,000 years ago and the past 2,000 years. The method is based on the knowledge that living organisms build up their own organic matter by photosynthesis and by using atmospheric carbon dioxide. The percentage of radiocarbon in the organism is equal to that in the atmosphere. When the organism dies, the carbon 14 (14C) atoms disintegrate at a known rate, with a half-life of 5,730 years. It is possible then to calculate the date of an organic object by measuring the amount of 14C left in the sample. The initial quantity in the sample is low, therefore the limit of detectability is soon reached, so the oldest reliable radiocarbon dates are about 40,000 years old.

Radiocarbon dates can be obtained from many types of organic material, including charcoal, shell, wood, and hair. The beta particle decay rate is conventionally measured with a proportional counter, but the use of accelerator mass spectrometry has refined the procedure dramatically. Every radiocarbon date arrives with a statistical error, a standard deviation. For example, a date of 2,200 ± 200 years, means that the date has a probable range of 200 years, with a two-out-of-three chance that the date lies between the span of one standard deviation (2,400 and 2,000 years). Unfortunately, the concentration of radiocarbon in the atmosphere has varied considerably over time, as a result of alterations in solar activity and changes in the strength of the earth's magnetic field. It is possible to correct dates by calibrating them against accurate dates from tree rings, by radiocarbon dating rings and developing a master correction curve. Dates as far back as nearly 9000 B.C. can be calibrated with tree rings, earlier dates with coral growth rings from tropical seas. (See also box on AMS Radiocarbon Dating in Chapter 5.)

---

simple rafts for fishing in shallows or used rudimentary dugout canoes for bottom fishing. At some point, some of these people crossed open water to Wallacea and Sahul. Sahul was a landscape of dramatic contrasts, of rugged mountain chains and highland valleys in the north, and rolling semi-arid lowlands over much of what is now Australia. Colonizing Sahul meant an open-water downwind passage of at least 98 kilometers (62 miles), an entirely feasible proposition in simple watercraft in warm tropical waters and smooth seas.

The earliest documented human settlement of New Guinea comes from the **Huon Peninsula** in the southeastern corner of the island, where some 40,000-year-old **ground stone** axes came to light. The Huon Peninsula faces New Britain Island, 48 kilometers (30 miles) offshore. Fishermen were living in caves on the island by at least 32,000 years ago. Some 4,000 years later, people had sailed southward between 130 to 180 kilometers (81 to 112 miles) to settle on Buka Island in the northern Solomons (Figure 4.3, page 102). From Buka it would have been an easy matter to colonize the remainder of the Solomon chain, for the islands are separated by but short distances. All these data point to a rapid spread of late Ice Age foragers through Sahul by at least 40,000 years ago, using some form of quite effective watercraft.

Human occupation in what is now Australia is well documented by 35,000 years ago, but may extend back 10,000 to 15,000 years earlier—the evidence is highly controversial. The **Willandra Lakes** region has yielded shell middens and campsites dating from perhaps as early as 37,000 to about 26,000 years ago. They include the skulls and limb bones of robustly built, anatomically modern people, the earliest human remains found in Australia. Recently, more than 450 footprints of a group of 22,000-year-old hunters, some as tall as 1.98 meters

(6 feet, 6 inches), have come to light in a dried mud level covered by sand dunes (Figure 4.5). By 33,000 years ago, human beings had crossed the low-lying strait that joined the island of Tasmania to the Australian mainland in the far south, to colonize the most southerly region of the earth settled by Ice Age people. At the height of the glacial maximum, people lived in the rugged landscape of the Tasmanian interior, hunting red wallabies and ranging over a wide area for many centuries.

The ancient Australians adapted to a remarkable variety of late Ice Age environments, as did people living in northern China, Japan, and on coastlines bordering chilly Ice Age seas. We do not have the space to cover all the diverse societies of the late Ice Age world, but, on the other side of the globe from Australia, the hunter-gatherer societies of Europe and Eurasia offer insights into the remarkable adaptive and opportunistic skills of the inhabitants of this long-vanished world.

Late Ice Age Europe: The Cro-Magnons (c. 43,000 to 15,000 years ago)

The first fully modern Europeans are known to biological anthropologists as the **Cro-Magnons**, named after a rock shelter near the village of Les Eyzies in southwestern France. Anatomically, the Cro-Magnons are indistinguishable from ourselves, strongly built, large-headed people,

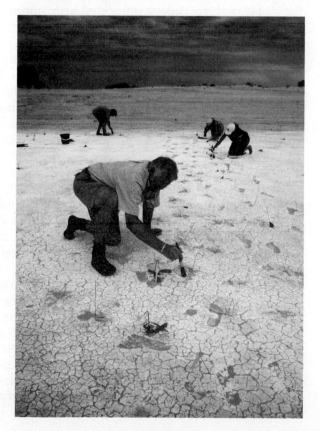

Figure 4.5 Excavating 22,000-year-old Aboriginal footprints at Willandra Lakes, Australia.

whose appearance contrasts dramatically with that of their Neanderthal predecessors. The Cro-Magnons had settled in Southeast and Central Europe by at least 43,000 years ago, apparently near Neanderthal groups. Some of them had penetrated into the sheltered, deep river valleys of southwestern France by 40,000 years ago (see Figure 4.2, page 101). By 35,000 years ago, the Neanderthals had vanished and the density of Cro-Magnon settlement intensified considerably. (Some isolated bands may have survived as late as 24,000 years ago in Gibraltar at the southern tip of Spain.)

Subsistence

The Cro-Magnons entered Europe during a brief period of more temperate climate. Even then, climatic conditions and seasonal contrasts may have been such as to require new artifacts and much more sophisticated hunting and foraging skills. These adaptations developed rapidly, indeed spectacularly, after 35,000 years ago. It was during these millennia that *Homo sapiens* finally mastered winter, for it was in northern latitudes that human ingenuity and endurance were tested to the fullest. The Cro-Magnons of western and central Europe developed elaborate and sophisticated hunting cultures during this period. Their cultures were marked not only by many technological innovations, but by a flowering of religious and social life, reflected in one of the earliest art traditions in the world.

The center of these activities was away from the open plains, in the river valleys of southwestern France and northern Spain, and in parts of central Europe like the Danube Basin. Here, deep valleys supported lush summer meadows and a mix of open steppe and forest where cold-tolerant animals ranging in size from the mammoth and bison to the wild horse and boar flourished. High cliffs often provided caves and rock shelters warmed by the winter sun. The area lay astride reindeer migration routes in spring and fall, while salmon ran up the fast-running rivers. The Cro-Magnons may have migrated to open country during the short summer months, concentrating in more sheltered river valleys from fall through spring. They hunted not only big game, but smaller animals such as arctic fox, beaver, rabbits, wolves, and many birds; they also gathered plant foods. After about 16,000 years ago, they also fished for salmon, trout, perch, and eels from rivers and streams.

The Cro-Magnons survived in a harsh and unpredictable environment not only because they were expert hunters and foragers, but because they had effective ways of keeping warm outside in the depth of winter and the ability to store large amounts of meat and other foods to tide them over lean periods. Above all, anyone living in late Ice Age Europe had to be adaptable, capable of cooperating with others, and ready to grab opportunities to obtain food when they arose. Survival depended on diversification, on never concentrating on one or two animals to the exclusion of others.

For most of the year, the Cro-Magnons lived in small groups, subsisting off a wide range of game and stored foods. The times when they came together in larger groups may have been in spring, summer, and early fall, when reindeer, and in later times, salmon, were abundant. This period of coming together was an important annual occasion, when social life was at its most intense. It was then that people arranged marriages, conducted initiation rites, and bartered raw materials, artifacts, and other commodities with one another. Then, as winter closed in, the groups would disperse through the sheltered river valleys, returning to their stored foods and the small herds of game animals that also took refuge from the bitter winds.

Reindeer were vital to survival. At the **Abri Pataud** rock shelter near Les Eyzies in France's Dordogne, reindeer provided up to 30 percent of all prey for more than 10,000 years (Figure 4.6). The hunters located their camps close to shallow river crossings where they knew migrating reindeer were likely to pass. This complex rhythm of reindeer hunting was but a part of a constant pattern of group movements that persisted over many thousands of years. It survived for thousands of years from at least 32,000 years ago right up to the end of the Ice Age, when the glaciers finally melted and dense forest spread over the open plains and deep valleys of central and western Europe. Not that life stayed exactly the same through these many millennia, for climatic conditions changed constantly. The Cro-Magnons had an efficient and highly versatile tool kit and a wide range of food resources to choose from, so they could readily adjust to changing circumstances.

Cro-Magnon Technology

Cro-Magnon technology was versatile, yet fundamentally very simple. It depended on four interrelated foundations:

- Careful selection of fine-grained rock such as chert, flint, or obsidian for blade cores;
- The production of relatively standardized, parallel-sided artifact blanks from these cores that could be used to make more specialized cutting, piercing, and scraping tools;
- The refinement of the burin (engraving tool), which enabled people to work antler and bone efficiently;
- The use of the so-called **groove-and-splinter technique** for working antler and bone.

Figure 4.6 Excavations at the Abri Pataud rock shelter, Les Eyzies, France.

These technological innovations had a profound impact on the future course of human history, for they were the material means by which humans adapted to the climatic extremes of Eurasia and Siberia. Late Ice Age stoneworkers everywhere were highly selective in their use of flint and other fine-grained rock. The Cro-Magnons' primary objective was to produce **blades,** long, parallel-sided artifact blanks that could then be turned into a wide spectrum of specialized artifacts for hunting, for butchery and processing skins, for woodworking and clothing manufacture, and for the production of the raw materials needed to create specialized antler and bone tools in treeless environments. So great was Cro-Magnon concern for good toolmaking stone that they bartered it with neighbors over considerable distances. Once procured, the precious raw materials were turned into carefully prepared blade cores that were carried around from one camp to the next. The cores were a kind of savings bank, an account of toolmaking stone used to produce tool blanks whenever they were needed. Thus, Cro-Magnon people were able to respond at a moment's notice to an opportunity to butcher an animal or to cut long slivers from fresh reindeer antlers.

The closest analogies in our own technology are the Leatherman and Swiss Army knife (or "snap-on" mechanics' tools) (Figure 4.7). Both are multipurpose artifacts built on a strong

Figure 4.7 Blade core technology acts like a Swiss Army knife, producing blanks for making many specialized artifacts for working antler and bone.

chassis with a special spring system that enables the user to call on a wide variety of different tools, everything from a pair of scissors to pliers. The late Ice Age equivalents were the cores and the blades that came from them.

One important Cro-Magnon artifact was the **burin,** a delicate chisel for carving fine lines. The burin was used for woodworking; for cutting grooves in animal hides; for engraving designs on antler, bone, and cave walls; and, above all, for cutting the long antler blanks for making artifacts of antler, bone, and ivory (see Figure 4.7). Many of these were specialized tools like barbed points, mounted with foreshafts that snapped off when the spear entered its quarry. Some were important innovations, especially the eyed needle, essential for making tailored winter clothes, and the **spear-thrower,** a hooked and sometimes weighted device that extended the range and accuracy of hunting weapons. It is said that a spear propelled by a spear-thrower can hit its target with greater velocity than a bow and arrow. The same technology of fine-barbed antler head spears and stone-barbed weapons could be used for hunting big game, as well as for taking salmon in shallow water, for dispatching rabbits, even for developing bows and arrows, which appeared some time during the late Ice Age.

The archaeological record reflects many refinements in Cro-Magnon technology over more than 15,000 years. In the early years of the twentieth century, French archaeologist Henri Breuil classified the late Ice Age cultures of southwestern France into four basic cultural traditions that culminated in the celebrated **Magdalenian culture** of about 18,000 to 12,000 years ago. The Magdalenian, named after **La Madeleine** rock shelter on the Vezère River, was not only a technologically sophisticated culture, but one with a new concern for artistic expression and body ornamentation.

The World's First Art

The symbolic and ceremonial life of the Cro-Magnons was probably no more elaborate than that of their contemporaries known to have been painting in southern Africa and Australia at much the same time. However, it is the best known and most thoroughly explored. Fortunately, much has survived, for Cro-Magnon artists used cave walls as their canvas and durable antler and ivory, not wood and skins, as palettes.

The first appearance of cave art coincides with a new concern with body ornamentation, especially perforated carnivore teeth and sea shells. This explosion in body ornamentation probably coincided with realizations that such adornments could define and communicate social roles—gender, group affiliation, and so on. Late Ice Age people mastered the ability to think in specific visual images, using them as well as chants, recitations, and songs to share and communicate images and ideas. This resulted in complex and diverse art traditions that lasted for more than 25,000 years.

The surviving Cro-Magnon art of Europe and Eurasia is but a minor proportion of their artistic output, for the artists almost certainly used many perishable materials—clay, wood, fiber, bark, hides, and bird feathers. Without question, too, they used red ocher and other pigments as body paint, for decoration. The surviving art occurs over a vast area from North Africa to Siberia, with major concentrations in northern Spain, southwestern France, and Central and Eastern Europe. On cave walls, the artists engraved and painted animals and occasional humans, also schematic patterns: lines, elaborate panels, and complex shapes. The same artists engraved antler, bone, and ivory with consummate skill. They created animals in the round, engraved bison with delicate strokes that etched in every detail of eyes, manes, and hair. There are figurines of animals and humans in ivory, soft stone, and baked clay, such as the celebrated Venus figurines that depict women of all ages (Figure 4.8a).

Cro-Magnon art is full of compelling images, many of them concentrated at major sites such as Lascaux and **Trois Frères** in southwestern France, and **Altamira** in northern Spain (Figure 4.8; see also Figure 1.1 on page 5). These may have been places of unusual religious and symbolic importance. They were ritual shrines, not only for local groups, but for people from far wider areas, too. Other locations were sacred places used occasionally for major ceremonies. These are illustrated dramatically by **Le Tuc d'Audoubert** Cave in Ariège, France, where two carefully modeled clay bison lie in a remote, low-ceilinged chamber far from the entrance, placed against a rock (see Figure 1.1 on page 5). The bison are about one-sixth the full size, shaped with a skilled artist's fingers and a spatula, the eyes, nostrils, and other features marked with a pointed object. Ancient human heel marks can be seen around the figures in this remote and dark chamber. In many other caves, paintings and engravings are far from daylight (see box on pages 112–113). There are several instances in which the footprints of both adults and children are preserved in damp clay, perhaps left by small parties of initiates who attended ceremonies in remote subterranean chambers. Some caves may also have been chosen for their echoes and other resonant effects.

(a)

(b)

(c)

Figure 4.8 Cro-Magnon art. **(a)** Venus figurine from Dolni Vestonice, Moravia, central Europe. **(b)** Wild bull from Lascaux, France. **(c)** Bison painted on a natural bulge of a chamber in Altamira cave, northern Spain. All three works date to the period 25,000 to 12,000 B.C.

Upper Paleolithic art defies easy interpretation, for the symbolic messages it communicates come from a world that is remote from our own. Yet the paintings and engravings still seem to come alive and appear larger than life when seen by modern candlelight flickering in the intense darkness. Did the artists paint art for art's sake, as some art historians and archaeologists allege? Or were they symbolically killing their prey before setting out on the chase? Such explanations are too simplistic, for we can be sure that the motivations for the art extended far beyond mere environmental and subsistence concerns.

Today, we know a great deal more about symbolic behavior and the art that goes with it, and much more about how forager societies function. In such societies, visual forms are manipulated to structure and give meaning to existence. For Cro-Magnon artists, there were clearly continuities between animal and human life and with their social world. Thus, their art was a symbolic depiction of these continuities. Shamans, priests or spirit mediums (the word comes from the Siberian Tungus word *saman*, meaning "priest"), are important members of forager and subsistence farming societies all over the world. They are individuals perceived as having unusual spiritual powers, the ability to cross over into the world of the gods and ancestors. Through trance and chant, they would intercede with the ancestors and define the order of the world and the creation—the relationship between the living and the forces of the environment. Perhaps, argue some experts, much of the cave art was involved with shamanistic rituals, the animal figures being images of spirit creatures or the life force for the shamans.

Some of the art may also have been associated with initiation rites, the journey through dark passages adding to the disorienting ordeal of initiation. Almost certainly, the art was a way of transmitting environmental and other knowledge from one generation to the next. Australian Aborigines, for example, commit to memory vast quantities of information about their territory that is closely tied to the mythical and symbolic world of their ancestors. Much of this data is vital to survival, constantly imparted to the young in ceremonies and rituals.

Hunter-Gatherers in Eurasia (45,000 to 15,000 years ago)

The open steppe-tundra plains that stretched from the Atlantic to Siberia were a far harsher environment than the sheltered valleys of southwestern Europe. To live there permanently, late Ice Age people had to find sheltered winter base camps and have both the technology to make tailored, layered clothing with needle and thongs and the ability to build substantial dwellings in a treeless environment. Only a handful of big-game hunting groups lived in the shallow valleys that dissected these plains before the glacial maximum 18,000 years ago. Thereafter, the human population rose comparatively rapidly, each group centered on a river valley where game was most plentiful, and where plant foods and fish could be found during the short summers. It was here that the most elaborate winter base camps lay. One such base camp lay at **Mezhirich** on the Dneipr River, a complex of well-built, dome-shaped houses fashioned of intricate patterns of mammoth bones. The outer retaining walls were made of patterned mammoth skulls, jaws, and limb bones. The completed oval-shaped dwellings were about 4.8 meters (16 feet) across, roofed with hides and sod, and entered through subterranean tunnels. The use of mammoth bone for houses was a logical strategy in a largely treeless environment. American archaeologist Olga Soffer has calculated that it would have taken some fifteen workers about ten days to build a Mezhirich dwelling, much more effort than would have gone into a simpler base camp or hunting settlement.

SITE

Grotte de Chauvet, France

On December 18, 1994, three French cave explorers with an interest in archaeology crawled into a narrow opening in the Cirque de Estre gorge in the Ardèche region of southeastern France. They felt a draft flowing from a blocked duct, pulled out some boulders and lowered themselves into a network of chambers adorned with exquisite calcite columns. To their astonishment, their lights shone on human hand imprints, then paintings of mammoths, cave lions, and other animals. The three explorers were "seized by a strange feeling. Everything was so beautiful, so fresh, almost too much so. Time was abolished, as if the tens of thousands of years that separated us from the producers of these paintings no longer existed." (Chauvet, Deschamps, and Hillaire, 1996, p. 42).

The **Grotte de Chauvet** is a series of painted and engraved chambers undisturbed since the late Ice Age. Hearths on the floor looked as if they had been extinguished the day before. Flaming torches had been rubbed against the wall to remove the charcoal so they would flare anew. More than 300 paintings adorn the walls (Figure 4.9). They include a frieze of black horses, wild oxen with twisted horns, and two rhinoceroses facing one another. The horses have half-open muzzles; the eyes are depicted in detail. There are lions, stags, and engravings of an owl, animals never before seen in painted caves, covering an area of more than 10 meters (30 feet). A little farther on in the chamber lies a slab that has fallen from the ceiling. A bear skull has been set atop it. The remains of a small fire lie behind it. More than thirty calcite-covered, and intentionally placed, bear skulls surround the slab. A 10-meter (30-foot) frieze of black figures dominated by lions or lionesses (without manes), rhinoceros, bison, and mammoth lies in an end chamber, a human figure with a bison head standing to its right. The discoverers wrote that it "seemed to us a sorcerer supervising this immense frieze" (Chauvet, Deschamps, and Hillaire, 1996, p. 110).

The artists were masters of perspective, overlapping the heads of animals to give the effect of movement and numbers. They even scraped some of the walls before painting them to make the figures stand out better. They would spread the paint with their hands over the rock, obtaining values that showed dimension and color tonality.

Accelerator mass spectrometry (AMS) radiocarbon dates (see box on AMS Radiocarbon Dating in Chapter 5) from two rhinoceroses and a large bison point to a 1,300-year period around 34,000 B.C., making these paintings the earliest securely dated art in the world. Two more dates from torch smears on the walls are around 24,500 B.C., while two charcoal samples on the floor gave readings of about 22,500 B.C., suggesting that humans visited Chauvet on several occasions over at least 10,000 years. Whether they painted over that long period is still unknown, but AMS dates will ultimately produce some answers.

Soffer believes that these base camps were occupied by groups of about thirty to sixty people for about six months of the year. Mezhirich was but one of several important base camp locations in the Ukraine, sites that contain the bones of a greater variety of game animals than smaller, more specialized settlements (see Figure 4.10 on page 114). The mammoth bone dwellings also yielded many bones from fur-bearing animals like the beaver, and exotic materials and ornaments such as shiny amber from near Kiev and shells from the Black Sea, far to the south. The items from afar exchanged between neighboring communities were predominantly nonutilitarian, luxury goods that had social and political significance. Much of the trade may have been ceremonial, a means of validating important ideologies, of ensuring exchange of information and cooperation in daily life, just as it was elsewhere in the late Ice Age world at the time.

Figure 4.9 Wild horses, oxen, and rhinoceroses painted by late Ice Age Cro-Magnon people on the walls of the Grotte de Chauvet, Southwestern France, c. 36,000 to 24,000 years ago.

Grotte de Chauvet was a bear cave, a place where these powerful animals hibernated. Interestingly, many of the animals on the cave walls represent dangerous members of the late Ice Age bestiary: the bear and the lion, the mammoth, rhinoceros, and bison, even, occasionally the nimble and ferocious aurochs. Perhaps human visitors to the cave, with its claw marks, hollows, prints, and scattered bones, came to the chambers to acquire the potency of the great beast, whose smell probably lingered in the darkness.

Late Ice Age groups settled much of the steppe-tundra as far east as Lake Baikal in Siberia, not through a deliberate process of migration, but as a result of the natural dynamics of forager life. The tundra hunters lived in small, highly flexible bands. As the generations passed, one band would coalesce into another, sons and their families would move away into a neighboring, and empty, valley. And, in time, a sparse human population would occupy thousands of square kilometers of steppe-tundra, concentrated for the most part in river valleys, at times venturing out onto the broad plains, and always on the move. It was through these natural dynamics of constant movement, of extreme social flexibility and opportunism, that people first settled the outer reaches of Siberia and crossed into the Americas.

North and east of Lake Baikal, the steppe-tundra extends all the way to the Pacific, the home of more late Ice Age hunting groups that are known from a handful of settlements

Figure 4.10 Artist's reconstruction of two mammoth bone houses at Mezhirich, Ukraine.

along lake shores and in river valleys. They are part of a widespread late Ice Age cultural tradition that reflects a varied adaptation by *Homo sapiens* to an enormous area of central Asia and southern Siberia from well west of Lake Baikal to the Pacific coast. But where did these Siberian hunters come from? Did they originate in the west, or were their cultural roots in China to the south? These questions have a direct bearing on one of the most debated questions of world prehistory—the date of the first Americans.

East Asia (35,000 to 15,000 years ago)

We know enough about prehistoric Asia to realize that this was not a backward, peripheral region of the late Ice Age world. We cannot just argue that big-game hunters from the Ukraine and the western steppe-tundra migrated steadily northeastward into Siberia and then into the Americas. Rather, the spread of modern humans into Central Asia, northern China, and the extreme northeast was a complex process that began at least 40,000 years ago.

Many biological anthropologists assume that *Homo erectus*, originally a tropical and subtropical animal, settled in the warmer southern parts of China first, then radiated northward into more temperate environments. But how far north? It is not until just before 35,000 years ago that a few signs of human settlement appear along the banks of the Huang Ho River in the arid grasslands of Mongolia. Open landscapes such as this and the neighboring steppe-tundra could support only the sparsest of forager populations, people who placed a high premium on mobility and portable tool kits. They were some of the first of the late–Ice Age people to develop diminutive microliths.

The **microlith** (a term derived from the Greek *micros:* "small" and *lithos:* "stone") is a highly distinctive artifact, manufactured from carefully prepared wedge-shaped, conical, or cylindrical cores (Figure 4.11). By their very size, microliths were designed to be mounted in antler, bone, or wooden shafts to serve as spear barbs, arrow points, or small knives and scraper blades. Such diminutive artifacts came into use almost everywhere in the post–Ice Age world, for they were highly adaptive when used with slender wooden arrow shafts or with stout wooden handles. They first appear in a crude form in northern China at least 30,000 years ago, were in widespread use by 25,000 to 20,000 years ago, and soon became

Figure 4.11 Microlith technology. **(a)** Siberian microblade artifacts were made by striking small blades of a wedge-shaped core, which produced fine, sharp artifacts that could be mounted on spears or in bone heads. **(b)** Later microliths used after the Ice Age were made by notching and snapping blades.

popular in the arid open country of the steppe-tundra, an area where high mobility and portable tool kits were at a premium. A somewhat similar microblade technology developed in Siberia late in the Ice Age. We do not know, however, whether the first human inhabitants of northeast Asia were people with such diminutive tool kits, or whether they used a heavier weaponry that included stone-tipped spears with sharp projectile points. Unfortunately, the archaeology of northern China, northeastern Siberia, and Alaska is little known because harsh environmental conditions make fieldwork possible for a mere two months or so a year in many places. We can only guess at a possible scenario for first settlement of this vast area, and of the Americas.

Sinodonty and Sundadonty

That the first Americans came from Siberia is unquestionable, but their ultimate ancestry is a matter of much debate. Christy Turner of Arizona State University has long studied the dental characteristics of native American populations and compared them to other groups in the Old World. He has shown that the crowns and roots of human teeth give clues to the degree of relationship between prehistoric populations. These tooth features are more stable than most evolutionary traits, with a high resistance to the effects of environmental differences, sexual distinctions, and age variations. In particular, he has focused on a pattern of specialized tooth features he calls **Sinodonty**.

Sinodont hallmarks include incisor shoveling (the scooped-out shape on the inside of the tooth), double-shoveling (scooping out on both sides), single-rooted upper first premolars, and three-rooted lower first molars. Sinodonty is characteristic of all Native Americans. They share this feature with northern Asians, including northern Chinese. The morphological difference between Sinodonts and the other Mongoloid populations, whom Turner labels **Sundadonts,** is so great that he believes Siberia and the Americas were settled by Sinodont populations from northern Asia. It was in China, he believes, that Sinodonty evolved, at least 40,000 years ago. The problem is to find the archaeological sites to confirm his theory.

Early Human Settlement of Northeast Siberia (?before 25,000 to 15,000 years ago)

If the ancestry of the first Americans lies in Siberia, what, then, is the earliest evidence for human settlement in extreme Northeast Asia? The earliest known settlement is on the Yana River, only 140 kilometers (87 miles) from the Arctic Ocean. Here people hunted mammoth, wild horse, and other animals as early as 25,000 to 2,700 years ago, during a period of slightly warmer conditions than the extreme cold snap of the late Ice Age, when far northeast Asia was probably depopulated.

Some of the earliest evidence of later human settlement comes from the **Diuktai Cave** in the Middle Aldan Valley. There, Russian archaeologist Yuri Mochanov found 14,000- to 12,000-year-old mammoth and musk ox bones associated with flaked-stone spear points, burins, microblades, and other Upper Paleolithic tools. The best dated Diuktai-like site is **Verkhene-Trotiskaya,** also on the Aldan River, which has been radiocarbon dated to about 18,000 years ago. Subsequently, microblades and characteristic wedge-shaped cores have been found over a wide area of northeast Asia, across the Bering Strait in Alaska, and as far south as British Columbia. The first widespread occupation of the extreme northeast was much later, perhaps no earlier than about 13,500 B.C.

With its microblades and wedge-shaped cores, the Diuktai culture has plausible links with widespread microblade cultures to the south, in China. A case can be made, then, for linking Diuktai cultural traditions with northern China, where Sinodonts have been found, as well as with microblade finds in Alaska and British Columbia. Were the Diuktai people thus the first Americans? Almost certainly not, for recent discoveries in Alaska have shown that foragers without microlithic tool kits flourished in the far north of North America just after the end of the Ice Age. Diuktai-style microliths appear late, by about 9000 B.C.

When Diuktai people or even earlier settlers first crossed the windy, steppe-tundra-covered land bridge that joined Alaska to Siberia remains a mystery. We do not even know how they subsisted, except for a likelihood that they preyed on all kinds of arctic game. They may also have hunted sea mammals, taken ocean fish, and traveled by canoe. Unfortunately, their settlements are deep beneath the waters of the Bering Strait.

The First Americans (?before 15,000 years ago to 11,000 B.C.)

During all of the last glaciation, the Bering Land Bridge joined extreme northeast Siberia and Alaska. During warmer intervals, it was little more than a narrow isthmus; during the glacial maximum, a broad plain. Thus, it was theoretically possible for humans without canoes to cross into North America from the Old World dry shod for all of the past 100,000 years. Therein lies one of the great questions of world prehistory. When and how did the first human beings settle the Americas?

The controversies that surround the first Americans are still unresolved. Most authorities agree that the first Americans were anatomically modern humans. This is a strong argument in favor of first settlement during the past 45,000 years, especially since recent mitochondrial DNA research suggests there were as many as four mtDNA lineages for the Americas, with a considerable, as yet undefined, time depth. The chronology of first settlement divides archaeologists into two camps. Some scientists argue passionately for a late–Ice Age occupation before 30,000 years ago, perhaps as much as 15,000 years earlier. Their theories pit them against most American archaeologists, who believe humans first crossed into Alaska at the very end of the Ice Age, perhaps as the land bridge flooded, after 15,000 years ago. We must examine these two viewpoints more closely.

Settlement before 30,000 Years Ago?

The case for early settlement rests on a handful of sites, most of them in South America, none of them yielding much more than a scatter of alleged stone artifacts and sometimes animal bones. Therein lies the controversy, for what one archaeologist claims as a stone tool is rejected out of hand by another. Unfortunately, most of the claims for early settlement are based not on fine-grained, scientific examination of the artifacts and their context in the surrounding deposits, but on an individual archaeologist's subjective belief that a handful of chipped stones are humanly manufactured rather than of natural origin. For example, if one finds 35,000-year-old "stone artifacts" deep in a hypothetical Peruvian cave, it is not sufficient to state they are of human manufacture. One must prove beyond all measure of reasonable scientific doubt that they were made by prehistoric people, and not formed, for example, by stones falling from a cliff face or by pebbles being knocked together in a stream that once ran through the cave. Such research is extremely time-consuming and very difficult. Such inquiries have not yet been carried out at most of the sites where early settlement has been claimed.

Further south, in northern Chile, Tom Dillehay has uncovered a remarkable settlement on the edge of a stream. **Monte Verde** was occupied by foragers living in simple wooden dwellings between 11,800 and 12,000 B.C. (see box on page 118). A 31,000-year-old lower level is said to contain split pebble and wood fragments, but excavations in these levels have been relatively limited, insufficient to document the proven presence of human occupation at such an early date.

There is no theoretical reason why *Homo sapiens* could not have moved south from the Bering Strait area well before 25,000 years ago, but we still lack credible proof of such early human settlement in Siberia, let alone the Americas. Whether this is because the Americas were still uninhabited, or because the human population was so mobile and tiny that little or no material survived, continues to be hotly debated. As an outside observer, African

Monte Verde, Chile

Monte Verde lies in a small river valley in southern Chile, a streamside settlement covered by a peat bog, so that not only stone and bone but also wooden artifacts survive (Figure 4.12). The site has been excavated very thoroughly by Tom Dillehay and has been radiocarbon dated to between 11,800 to 12,000 B.C. Thus far, only a portion of the site has been excavated, revealing two parallel rows of what are said to be rectangular houses, joined by connecting walls. The skin-covered houses were 3 to 4 meters (9 to 13 feet) square, with log and crude-plank foundations and a wooden framework. Clay-lined hearths, wooden mortars, and large quantities of vegetable foods were found in the houses. A short distance away lay a wishbone-shaped structure associated with chewed bolo-plant leaves (used today to make a form of medicinal tea), mastodon bones, and other work debris. This may have been a work area.

The Monte Verde people exploited a very wide range of vegetable foods, including wild potatoes; they also hunted small game and perhaps mammals such as extinct camels and mastodons (it is possible that they scavenged such meat, however). Monte Verde was in a forest, with abundant vegetable foods year-round. The site was almost certainly a long-term campsite. What is fascinating is that 90 percent of the stone artifacts are crude river cobbles. It is clear that wood was the most important raw material. It was certainly used for spears and digging sticks and for hafting stone scrapers, three of which have survived in their wooden handles. Sites yielding simple flaked-stone artifacts like those from Monte Verde have been found elsewhere in South America, as far south as Patagonia, but this is the first place that anyone has been able to make more complete discoveries.

Figure 4.12 Excavations at the Monte Verde site, Chile, showing a wishbone-shaped structure.

archaeologist Nicholas Toth has made the important observation that it is pointless to place too much reliance on isolated finds. Rather, we should be searching for patterns of very early human settlement, characteristic distributions of artifacts and human activity that occur over wide areas, that indeed reflect widespread early occupation. Such patterns document the very earliest human occupation on earth. So far, consistent distributions of human settlement in the New World date to after the Ice Age, to after 15,000 years ago. But we stress again that there is no reason why earlier settlement might not be found one day. So far, however, the evidence is unconvincing.

Another scenario places first settlement during a brief warmer spell of the last glaciation, between 30,000 and 20,000 years ago. This would be shortly before the late–Ice Age maximum cutoff movement south of Alaska until after about 13,000 years ago.

Settlement after 15,000 Years Ago?

Most American archaeologists consider first settlement a much later phenomenon. Under the late scenario, a few families may have moved into Alaska during the very late Ice Age, perhaps before 15,000 years ago. At that time, vast ice sheets mantled much of northern North America, effectively blocking access to the midcontinent. After 14,000 years ago, these ice sheets retreated rapidly, allowing a trickle of human settlers to move onto the plains and into a new continent.

This hypothesis is based on the late dates of first settlement in northeastern Siberia and on earliest indisputable archaeological evidence for human settlement in North America, which dates to between 14,000 and 12,000 years ago. A handful of sites, among them **Meadowcroft Rock Shelter** in Pennsylvania, and **Fort Rock Cave,** Oregon, may belong in this time frame. So do scattered sites from Central and South America, among them **Valsequillo** in Mexico, **Taima Taima** in Venezuela, and Monte Verde in northern Chile. All these sites have yielded small scatters of stone artifacts, occasionally a projectile point. After about 9200 B.C. the trickle of archaeological sites turns into a flood. There are now traces of **Paleo-Indian** (Greek *paleos:* "old") settlement between the southern margins of the ice sheets in the north and the Straits of Magellan in the far south. (The term Paleo-Indian is conventionally used to refer to the prehistoric inhabitants of the Americas from earliest settlement up to the beginning of the **Archaic** period in about 6000 B.C.)

How, then, did Paleo-Indians travel southward from the arctic to the heart of North America? (See Figure 4.13 on page 120.) Were they big-game hunters who followed small herds of animals southward through a widening corridor between the two great North American ice sheets to the east of the Rockies as the ice sheets melted? Or were the first Americans expert sea-mammal hunters and fisherfolk, who crossed from Siberia along low-lying coasts in canoes while fishing and sea-mammal hunting? Did their successors then travel southward along the Pacific coast into more temperate waters? Again, fierce controversy surrounds what is virtually nonexistent archaeological evidence. Perhaps both coastal settlement and terrestrial occupation took hold in the rapidly changing world of the late Ice Age. We simply do not know, partly because the coastal sites of the day are buried many meters below modern sea levels.

At present, the consensus of archaeological opinion favors a relatively late human occupation of the Americas at the very end of the Ice Age, but it is entirely possible that this scenario will change dramatically as a result of future research.

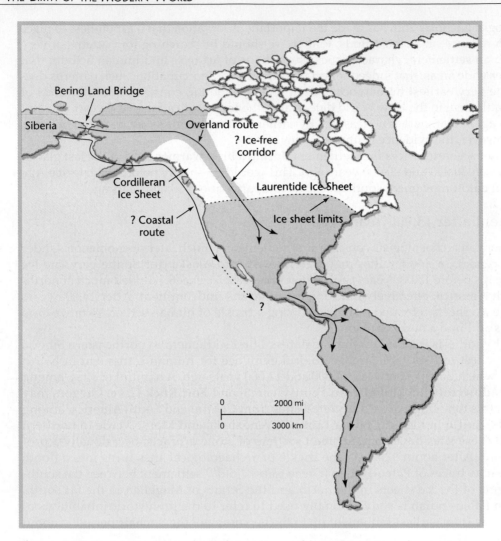

Figure 4.13 Hypothesized routes for the first settlement of the Americas. Coastal routes are now buried under the higher sea levels of modern times.

But why did first settlement take place? In all probability, the first Americans were probably behaving in the same way as other animal predators. They spent their days tracking the game herds, and perhaps sea mammals, that formed an important part of their subsistence, and when Siberian game herds moved onto the Bering Land Bridge during the coldest millennia of the last glaciation, their human predators followed. The higher ground to the east—Alaska—formed part of the same hunting grounds.

The Clovis People (c. 11,200 to 11,000 B.C.)

The earliest well-documented Paleo-Indian settlement is associated with the distinctive **Clovis** fluted point (Figure 4.14). The Clovis tradition, named after a town in New Mexico, once flourished in various forms over much of North and Central America from about

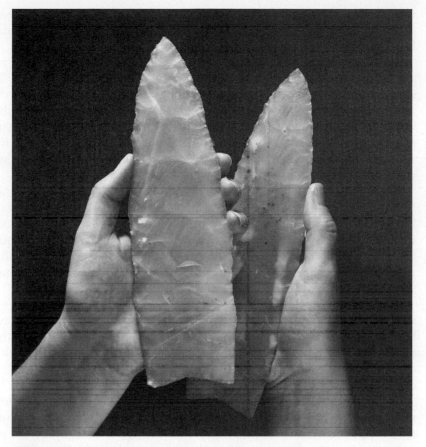

Figure 4.14 Two magnificent Clovis points from an artifact cache on the Great Plains.

11,200 to 11,000 B.C. Clovis may be an indigenous North American cultural tradition, but its roots lie in northern forager cultures such as flourished in Alaska at such locations as the **Hidden Mammoth** and **Mesa** sites as early as 11,800 B.C., where foragers used simple bifacial spear points in the chase. These locations, little more than tiny scatters of bones, hearths, and stone artifacts, are the earliest evidence for human settlement in Alaska and have no direct equivalents in earlier traditions such as Diuktai in Siberia.

Clovis is best, and misleadingly, known from occasional mammoth and bison kills on the Northern American plains. These plains expanded at the end of the Ice Age, their short grasses providing ample feed for all kinds of big game, including bison, mammoth, and other ruminants. Clovis bands on the plains preyed on these and many other game species, large and small. They were constantly on the move, often camping along rivers and streams and close to permanent waterholes. Here they killed their prey, camping near where the carcass lay.

It would be a mistake, however, to think of the Clovis people as purely big-game hunters. They settled not only on open grasslands, but in woodlands, tundra, deserts, and along sea coasts. In some areas, wild plant foods were probably as important as, if not more important than, game. Fish and sea-mammal hunting may also have assumed great local importance, especially along rising coastlines. But wherever Clovis people and their contemporaries settled, large game was of some importance, simply because it was a relatively abundant meat source.

Nowhere were Clovis populations large. Their tool kit was highly portable, based on an expert stone-flaking technology that produced fine, **fluted** points. The hunters mounted these on long wooden shafts, sometimes attaching the head to a detachable foreshaft that acted as a hinge. When the spear penetrated an animal, the foreshaft would snap off, ensuring that the lethally sharp point stayed in the wound. Like other later Paleo-Indian groups, and like Ice Age hunters in the Old World, the Clovis people hunted their prey on foot, relying on their stalking skill and the accuracy of their throwing sticks (**atlatls**) to dispatch their quarry.

The origins of the Clovis people remain a complete mystery. However, most experts believe their ultimate origins were among late–Ice Age forager populations in Alaska and Northeast Asia. If the first Americans crossed into the New World about 15,000 years ago, then the peopling of the uninhabited continent took place remarkably quickly. By 10,000 B.C., Stone Age foragers occupied every corner of the Americas. The overall human population probably numbered no more than a few tens of thousands, but they had adapted to every form of local environment imaginable.

By this time, the last glaciation was long over and the great ice sheets of the north were in rapid retreat. Climatic conditions were warming up rapidly, and many species of Ice Age big game vanished. The descendants of the first Americans adapted to these new circumstances in very diverse ways, along trajectories of cultural change that led, ultimately, to the brilliant array of Native American societies encountered by Europeans in the late fifteenth century A.D.

With the first settlement of the Americas, the great radiation of *Homo sapiens*, the wise person, was nearly complete. This was the second great radiation of humanity, the climactic development of world prehistory. From it stemmed not only the great biological and cultural diversity of modern humankind, but food production, village life, urban civilization, and the settlement of the Pacific Islands—the very roots of our own diverse and complex world.

Summary

This chapter documents the spread of *Homo sapiens* into Europe and Eurasia from Africa and Southwest Asia after 45,000 years ago, during the late Ice Age. By this time, there was increasing specialization and flexibility in human hunting and foraging, as anatomically modern humans replaced Neanderthal groups by 35,000 B.C. The sheer diversity of the late–Ice Age environment gave the Cro-Magnon people of western Europe great flexibility. They developed more complex societies and developed elaborate bone and antler technology, as well as an intricate symbolic life reflected in their artistic traditions. These cultures reached their apogee in the Magdalenian culture, which flourished after 16,000 B.C., and for about 5,000 years. Late–Ice Age hunter-gatherers also spread slowly onto the Russian plains, relying heavily on game of all kinds. Far to the northeast, Siberia was settled at least as early as 25,000 years ago, but the extreme northeast was probably abandoned during the last cold of the late Ice Age, then reoccupied around 15,000 years ago.

The first humans to settle the Americas crossed from northeast Asia, probably across, or along the coasts of, the Bering Land Bridge (central Beringia), but the date of their arrival is highly controversial. Some scientists claim that archaeological evidence from South America proves that Native Americans were flourishing in the Americas as early as 40,000 years ago. Most experts believe that first settlement occurred much later, perhaps at the very end of the Ice Age, as early as 15,000 years ago. There is evidence for human occupation in Chile by 11,800 B.C., while the Clovis people of North America flourished between 11,200 and 10,900 B.C.

5 The Origins of Food Production

2.5 Million   1.0 Million   500,000 B.P.   100,000 B.P.   50,000 B.P.   15,000 B.P.   A.D. 1   A.D. 1950

PROLOGUE

The men climb high above the ground, lopping off small branches with their stone-bladed axes. The women and children gather up the foliage and pile it around the bare tree trunks. It is hard, backbreaking work that goes on for days on end, as the farmers watch the brazen sky for thunderclouds and signs of rain. A few spits of rain and building clouds bring hope of imminent showers. The people fire the tinder-dry brush, which burns fiercely. The sky fills with dense brown smoke as far as the eye can see, as the women turn over the fresh ash into the cleared soil and plant their precious seed. Then everyone waits for the life-giving rains to conjure bright green shoots from the soil.

It's hard for us to imagine, buying our food from supermarkets, that for more than 99 percent of our existence as humans we were hunters and gatherers, tied to the seasons of plant foods, the movements of game, and the ebb and flow of aquatic resources. Food production, the deliberate cultivation of cereal grasses and edible root plants, is a phenomenon of the last 12,000 years of human existence. Agriculture and animal domestication ("food production") were a major turning point in human history, the foundation for all early civilizations and, ultimately, for our own modern industrial world. Before describing the development and spread of farming, we must examine some of the major theories that explain this development and review some of its consequences. Also, we must describe the intensification of hunter-gatherer societies that came immediately after the Ice Age (see Figure 5.1 on page 128).

Serious discussion of the origins of food production began in the 1930s. Australian-born archaeologist Vere Gordon Childe was an eccentric genius, who regarded artifacts and archaeological sites as the equivalent of historical documents and actual characters on the ancient world stage. Childe's main claims to fame were an encyclopedic knowledge of the clay and metal tools of Europe and southwestern Asia, and a priceless ability to write popular accounts of the prehistoric past. To Childe, southwestern Asia, from Turkey to the Nile Valley and Mesopotamia, was the cradle of both farming and early civilization. In his famous syntheses of the origins of civilization, he wrote of two great revolutions in the early human past. An **Agricultural** (or **Neolithic** [New Stone Age]) **Revolution** resulted from the development of village farming, followed a few thousand years later by an **Urban Revolution** and the beginnings of cities, writing, metallurgy, and literate civilization.

The notion of an Agricultural and Urban Revolution appealed to historians like George Trevelyan and Will and Ariel Durant, who adopted Gordon Childe's revolutions for the early chapters of their widely read world histories. The revolutions were convenient labels, just like the Industrial and Information Revolutions we talk about today. To archaeologists, the Agricultural Revolution is a simplistic designation, long outdated by a flood of new field data unavailable in Childe's day. However, the term does have merit in the sense that it draws attention to a catalytic development in the human past and, above all, to its consequences. Animal and plant domestication had important outcomes for humankind—new economies and great interdependence, permanent settlement, and more complex social organization, accelerating population growth, and increasing social inequality—to mention only a few.

The Holocene (after 10,000 B.C.)

Some 15,000 years ago, the great ice sheets began to retreat, at times very rapidly, ushering in postglacial times, often called the **Holocene** (Greek *Holos*: "recent"). At the same time, world sea levels rose dramatically, if irregularly, from their previous lows up to 90 meters (300 feet) below modern levels, leading to major changes in world geography. The chilly waters of the Bering Sea flooded central Beringia and separated Siberia and Alaska by 11,000 B.C. Sunda in Southeast Asia became an enormous archipelago. Britain became an island and the North Sea and Baltic assumed their modern configurations. The most striking climatic and vegetational transformations took place in northern latitudes, in areas like western and central Europe and in regions of North America contiguous to the great ice sheets. Only 9,000 years after the Scandinavian ice sheet began retreating, forests covered much of Europe. There were major vegetational changes in warmer latitudes, too. Rainfall patterns changed at the end of the Ice Age, bringing large, shallow lakes and short grasslands to the

Chronological Table B

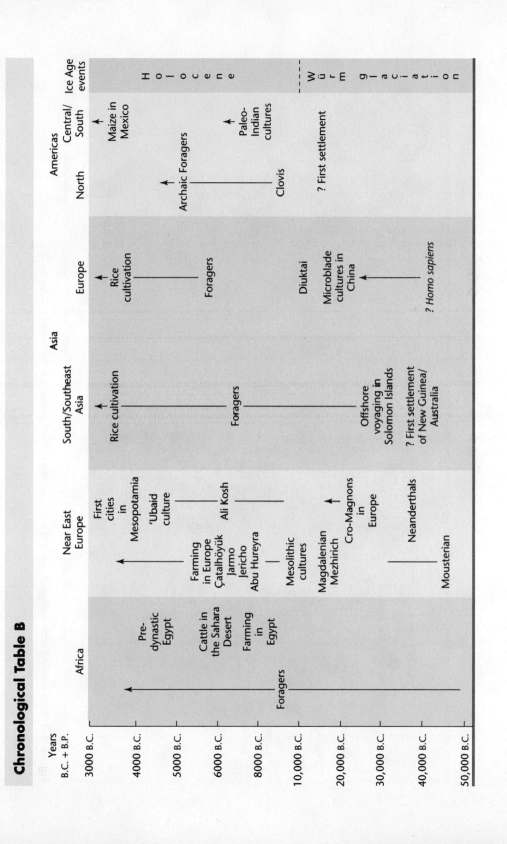

Years B.C. + B.P.	Africa	Near East Europe	South/Southeast Asia	Asia Europe	Americas North	Americas Central/South	Ice Age events
3000 B.C.							Holocene
4000 B.C.	Pre-dynastic Egypt	First cities in Mesopotamia				Maize in Mexico	
5000 B.C.		'Ubaid culture	Rice cultivation	Rice cultivation			
6000 B.C.	Cattle in the Sahara Desert	Ali Kosh					
	Farming in Egypt	Farming in Europe / Çatalhöyük / Jarmo / Jericho / Abu Hureyra					
8000 B.C.					Archaic Foragers		
10,000 B.C.		Mesolithic cultures	Foragers	Foragers		Paleo-Indian cultures	
	Foragers	Magdalenian / Mezhirich			Clovis		
20,000 B.C.		Cro-Magnons in Europe		Diuktai / Microblade cultures in China	? First settlement		Würm glaciation
30,000 B.C.		Neanderthals	Offshore voyaging in Solomon Islands				
40,000 B.C.		Mousterian	? First settlement of New Guinea/Australia	? Homo sapiens			
50,000 B.C.							

127

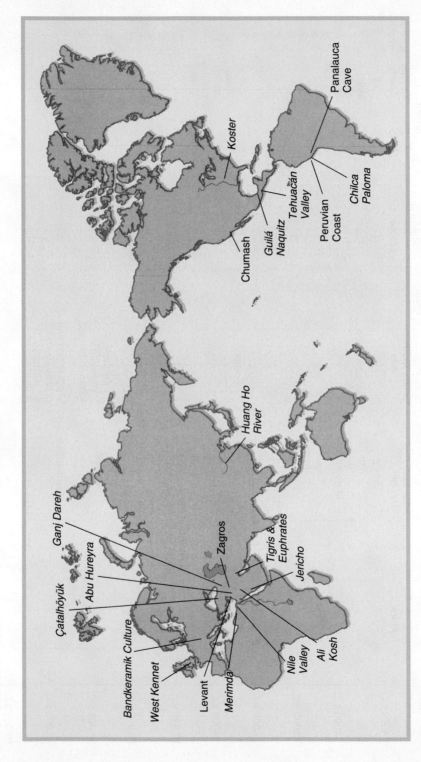

Figure 5.1 Map showing archaeological sites and major centers of food production mentioned in Chapter 5.

Koster

Panalauca
Cave

Chumash

Guilá
Naquitz

Tehuacán
Valley

Chilca
Paloma

Peruvian
Coast

Huang Ho
River

Ganj Dareh

Çatalhöyük

Abu Hureyra

Zagros

Tigris &
Euphrates

Bandkeramik Culture

Jericho

West Kennet

Levant

Merimda

Nile
Valley

Ali
Kosh

Sahara. As late as 6000 B.C., hunter-gatherer populations flourished in the desert, in areas that are now arid wilderness.

In southwestern Asia, warmer conditions saw the immigration of new plant species into highland areas such as the Zagros mountains in Iran, among them wild cereal grasses. Their distribution expanded dramatically, to the point that wild wheat and barley became important staples for hunter-gatherer groups in the highlands and fertile river valleys like the Euphrates. Far away, in Mexico, rising temperatures brought a rich forest of cacti and legume trees to mountain valleys of the central highlands. This thorn-scrub-cactus forest included many wild ancestors of domesticated plants, among them the maguey, squash, bean, and teosinte, the wild grass that was probably the ancestor of wild maize, the crop that was to become one of the staples of Native American life.

Changes in Hunter-Gatherer Societies

These and other Holocene climatic changes had profound effects on hunter-gatherer societies throughout the world, especially on the intensity of the food quest and the complexity of their societies. So did natural population growth. By 15,000 years ago, the world's population was probably approaching about 10 million people. Except in the most favored areas, like southwestern France or the Nile valley, late-Ice Age environments were incapable of supporting anything but the sparsest of human population densities—well under one person per square kilometer. As a result, in early Holocene times, after 10,000 B.C., still-rising human populations began to match the ability of the world's environment to support them as hunter-gatherers. It was no longer possible to solve a subsistence problem simply by moving elsewhere. People began to exploit a wider range of food resources with greater efficiency, both to avert starvation and to protect themselves from food shortages caused by short-term droughts and other unpredictable changes. In time, hunter-gatherer societies underwent profound changes and in some areas acquired greater complexity.

Nowhere can these changes be seen more clearly than in the Americas, settled by Stone Age hunter-gatherers either during, or immediately after, the Ice Age. By 11,000 B.C., the big game that formed a staple part of their diet was extinct. The Paleo-Indians responded to changed circumstances by developing ever more intensive and specialized ways of exploiting local environments. The change is especially marked in areas of exceptional resource diversity like parts of the West Coast, the Peruvian coast, and the fertile river valleys of the southern Midwest and southeastern United States. In all these areas, hunter-gatherer populations became more sedentary; developed specialized technologies for hunting, foraging, and fishing; and in the process, developed some form of social ranking.

The famous **Koster** site in the Illinois River valley provides a chronicle of this process of intensification taking place over many thousands of years, from about 7500 B.C. until A.D. 1200 (see Figure 5.2 on page 130). The first visitors were Paleo-Indian hunters who camped on the edge of the valley. About 6500 B.C., some later inhabitants founded a base camp that covered about 0.1 hectare (0.75 acre). An extended family group of about twenty-five people returned repeatedly to the same location, perhaps to exploit the rich fall hickory nut harvests in the area. Between 5600 and 5000 B.C., there were substantial settlements of permanent mud and brush houses that were occupied for most of the year, if not all of it. During spring and summer the inhabitants took thousands of fish, gathering mussels and hickory nuts in fall and migratory birds in spring. Even when hunting deer on the nearby uplands, the people could find most of their food resources within 5 kilometers (3 miles).

Figure 5.2 Excavations at Koster, Illinois.

After 2500 B.C., Koster's population had risen to the point at which the people were exploiting a much wider range of food resources, including acorns, which require much more preparation than hickory nuts. Eventually, they experimented with the deliberate planting of wild native grasses like goosefoot, simply to increase supplies of wild plant foods. The Koster excavations document several long-term trends in many early Holocene hunter-gatherer societies, trends toward more sedentary settlement, intensive exploitation of locally abundant and predictable food resources such as salmon or nuts, and carefully organized mass processing and storage of staple foods.

Such intensive exploitation, processing, and storage was adaptive in environments where seasonal phenomena such as salmon runs, caribou migrations, or hickory nut harvests required not only efficient harvesting of quantities of food in a short time, but also their processing and storage for later use. By using storage, and by careful seasonal exploitation of game, plant, and aquatic resources like fish and waterfowl, Holocene hunter-gatherers compensated for periodic food shortages caused by short-term climatic change and seasonal fluctuations. For example, Native American societies developed a remarkable expertise with wild plant foods. They also evolved an array of simple pestles, grinders, and other tools to process seeds and other wild plant foods. Later, it was an easy matter to adapt these tool kits to new, specialized tasks such as farming.

More restricted territories, less mobility, rising population densities, unpredictable environmental variations, and seasonal flood fluctuations were problems common to early Holocene hunter-gatherers throughout the world. A few of these societies, especially those in areas with rich and diverse food resources that included fish and sea mammals, achieved a greater complexity than any Ice Age society, with some signs of social ranking.

Social Complexity among Hunter-Gatherers

Complex hunter-gatherer societies did not appear everywhere, but they developed in a remarkable variety of environments, from fertile river valleys to coastal deserts. Everywhere, however, certain general conditions were necessary. First, population movements had to be limited by either geography or the presence of neighbors. Second, resources had to be abundant and predictable in their seasonal appearance. Such resources included fish, shellfish, nuts, and seeds, species that are abundant and seldom exhausted. Third, population growth might reach a point at which food shortages occur and there is an imbalance between people and their food supply. Again, a solution was to intensify the food quest, an intensification that might result in a more complex society, or, as we shall see, in food production.

Social complexity was most common in areas where freshwater or marine fish, shellfish, or sea mammals were abundant. The full potential of marine and freshwater resources was realized only in a relatively few areas like northern Europe, Peru, and western North America. Here, higher than normal population densities were concentrated in restricted territories circumscribed by geography or neighbors. These populations acquired a more varied diet by using more specialized tool kits and sophisticated food storage systems and preservation techniques. These groups often lived in sedentary, large base camps ruled by important kin leaders who monopolized trade with neighboring groups. For example, the Chumash Indians of the southern California coast were skilled navigators, fishers, and sea-mammal hunters. Some Chumash communities numbered as many as 1,000 people, living under hereditary chiefs (*wots*). There was a small elite of ceremonial officeholders, shamans, and such experts as canoe builders. Chumash culture was a maritime adaptation made possible by a specialized fishing technology that included planked canoes about 7.6 meters (25 feet) long (see Figure 5.3 on page 132). A flourishing canoe-borne trade in acorn meal and sea shell beads flourished between the offshore islands and the mainland, controlled by powerful chiefs and canoe skippers. Each community maintained exchange contacts with other coastal communities and with people living far in the interior.

Chumash culture achieved a degree of social elaboration that represents about the limit of such complexity possible without adopting agriculture. Why did such social complexity develop? Some scholars see the ocean as a kind of Garden of Eden, an environment sometimes so productive that hunter-gatherers could maintain permanent, sedentary settlements and maintain high population densities. Perhaps people turned to fish, shellfish, and sea mammals in a period of rapid environmental change, like that at the end of the Ice Age. Unfortunately, however, we do not know how decisive marine or riverine resources were in allowing dense populations and sedentary living, both essential prerequisites for social complexity.

Away from coasts, rivers, and lake shores, and especially among groups living at the edges of several ecological zones, people living in more or less permanent settlements in rich inland environments turned to another strategy. They experimented with the planting of wild plant staples to supplement food resources in short supply. The cultural changes forced upon them by Holocene climate change made it easier for their descendants to adopt radically new economic strategies such as deliberate cultivation of the soil and animal domestication—food production.

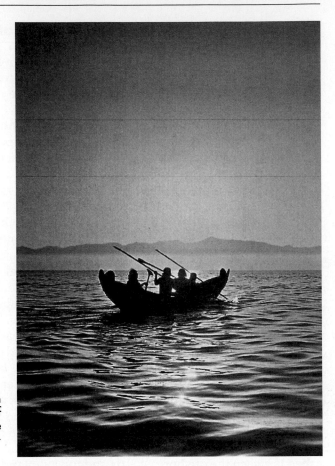

Figure 5.3 Reconstruction of a Chumash Indian *tomol* (canoe), used on the waters of the Santa Barbara Channel, California. The Chumash were among the most sophisticated hunter-gatherer societies on earth.

Theories of Farming Origins

Victorian scientists believed agriculture was a brilliant invention, fostered by a rare genius. One day, went the scenario, a solitary forager was carrying home a bundle of edible grasses when she stumbled, spilling some of her load on damp ground. A few days later, she passed the same way and noticed small green shoots sprouting from the soil. With startling insight, the woman realized the potential of her new invention, planted more seeds near her hut, and fed her family off the bountiful harvest. Other families soon copied her example and agriculture was born.

Such captivating scenarios offer simple explanations, but have no foundation in scientific fact. First, no one ever "invented" agriculture, because all hunter-gatherers knew that grasses germinated each year. You can propagate root crops like the African yam simply by cutting off the top and placing it in the soil. Hunter-gatherers living on the fringes of the African rainforest as early as 40,000 years ago may have planted yams in that way, but such practices are a far cry from the cultivation of cereal grasses, which began in the Old World and New after the Ice Age. Reality was more complex than mere invention and is still little understood.

Nor did a single society "invent" agriculture, for farming appeared at widely different times in many parts of the world. Farmers in southeastern Turkey and in southwestern Asia's Euphrates and Jordan River Valleys cultivated wheat and barley by about 10,000 B.C. Central American cultivators grew domesticated squashes by about the same date. Chinese villagers harvested rice by 6000 B.C., perhaps much earlier. Most scientists believe that a set of complex cultural and environmental factors combined with population growth to cause societies in widely separated parts of the world to shift from foraging to food production, usually within a relatively short time, sometimes a few generations.

At the end of the Ice Age, hunter-gatherers in drought-prone subtropical zones such as southwestern Asia and highland Mesoamerica were exploiting potentially domesticable wild grasses and root plants with greater intensity. Dependence on such foods probably came earlier in these regions, where there were only a few forageable plant foods. Such dependence was essential to long-term survival and led almost inevitably to experimentation with deliberate planting of wild cereals and ultimately to cultivation. In contrast, populations in more humid, plant-rich tropical regions, like the African and Amazonian rainforests, probably did little more than plant a few wild species to minimize risk of starvation in lean years long after farming appeared in more temperate regions. Cereal agriculture came to tropical Africa only within the past 3,000 years, and it spread widely after the introduction of iron technology some centuries later.

During the 1920s, University of Chicago Egyptologist Henry Breasted popularized the term **Fertile Crescent** to describe the cradle of agriculture and civilization in southwestern Asia. The Crescent has its arms in Mesopotamia and the Nile Valley, joined by a great arch across the Jordan Valley and Zagros Mountains of Iran. The label has fallen into disuse in recent years, but is apt in the sense that it spans the vast arc of contrasting terrain where agriculture, and urban civilization, first began. Most speculation about agricultural origins has surrounded the Fertile Crescent.

Early Theories: Oases and Hilly Flanks

Gordon Childe's Agricultural Revolution offers a good starting point, for it was the first modern attempt to explain agricultural origins. Drought conditions formed the core of his revolution thesis. He speculated that after the Ice Age the southwestern Asian climate became increasingly dry, forcing both animals and humans to concentrate in areas like the Jordan Valley, where permanent water supplies were available and plant foods perennially abundant. The arid conditions brought animals, humans, and plants into a close symbiosis (Greek: "life together"), creating favorable conditions for hunter-gatherers to experiment with cereal grasses and with herding wild goats and sheep. These experiments revolutionized human existence and spread rapidly throughout southwestern Asia and further afield.

Childe proposed the Agricultural Revolution long before pollen analysis, deep sea cores, and other highly sophisticated tools for climatic reconstruction were applied to Asian sites. The theory was simple, but unproven. During the 1950s, University of Chicago archaeologist Robert Braidwood took a multidisciplinary team of botanists, geologists, and zoologists on a major field expedition to the Zagros Mountains, what he called the "hilly flanks" of southwestern Asia. He recovered the first climatic data for Holocene times and found evidence of increased forest cover and high rainfall after the Ice Age. He also excavated early farming settlements high above the fertile lowlands, which, at the time, were considered exceptionally early, as they radiocarbon dated to about 6000 B.C.

Braidwood rejected Childe's oasis theory and argued that agriculture and animal domestication began in the mountainous terrain at the periphery of fertile lands. Higher rainfall meant more wild food supplies and denser game populations in the lowlands. Highland peoples were not so fortunate and adopted agriculture to increase food supplies in the face of rising populations. In other words, agriculture began on the flanks, not in the center.

The Recovery Revolution

Braidwood and Childe theorized at a time when multidisciplinary research was still in its infancy. Since the 1950s, archaeology has gone through what one may call a "recovery revolution," a dramatic refinement of field and laboratory methods that has produced infinitely more fine-grained data. The recovery revolution has taken place alongside other important developments:

- Multidisciplinary studies of Holocene climatic change, which combine pollen samples from lakes and marshes with deep-sea and tree-ring data to produce a chronicle of large- and small-scale climatic change since 10,000 B.C. These data allow archaeologists to place early farming sites within much more precise environmental contexts.

- New botanical data acquired through systematic use of **flotation** methods (see box) that allow the recovery of large samples of wild and domesticated seeds from occupation levels.

- Major advances in zooarchaeology, the study of animal bones, have provided a wealth of new information on the domestication of cattle, goats, pigs, sheep, and other animals.

- Accelerator mass spectrometry (AMS) radiocarbon dating (see "AMS Radiocarbon Dating" box on pages 136–137) permits the dating of individual seeds, root fragments, or maize cobs. For the first time, we can date early farming with high precision, as opposed to merely dating layers in which tiny seeds are found (and into which they may have fallen from higher levels).

The past twenty years have seen the development of more sophisticated ecological interpretations of the origins of food production, which result in large part from much larger data bases of archaeological and environmental data.

Multicausal Theories

The recovery revolution has spawned complex, multivariate models, which take into account the emerging realization that many early Holocene hunter-gatherer societies were more complex and well preadapted to food production before anyone started planting wild cereal grasses or penning animals. For example, as recently as the eighteenth century A.D., the Kumeyaay Indians of southern California reduced the risk of starvation by "domesticating" their landscape. They lived in semiarid valleys, encouraging the growth of wild

SCIENCE

Flotation and Botanical Remains

Until the 1960s, archaeologists knew little of early domesticated plants. They lacked a recovery technology to excavate more than a few handfuls of carbonized seeds preserved in storage pits or hearths. Flotation methods, first developed in the North American Midwest, revolutionized our knowledge of ancient farming. By passing soil samples through water or chemicals, today's excavators can recover thousands of seeds, as they float to the surface while the heavier soil matrix sinks to the bottom of the screen. Elaborate flotation machines can process dozens of samples an hour. The sample is poured into a screened container and agitated by water pouring into the screen (Figure 5.4). The light plant materials float on the water and are carried out of the container by a sluiceway that leads to fine mesh screens, where the seeds are trapped and wrapped in fine cloth for further study.

Flotation is rewriting the early history of both foraging and farming. Botanist Gordon Hillman has reconstructed the foraging habits of 16,000-year-old hunter-gatherers living alongside the Nile River during the late Ice Age. His studies of the environment at Abu Hureyra, Syria, described in Chapter 6, document how tree cover receded from the site as drought became endemic. The inhabitants responded by gathering wild grasses, then cultivating them to amplify their food supply. Flotation has also been used extensively in eastern North America, the Southwest, and the Andean area, with similarly dramatic results.

Figure 5.4 An elaborate flotation machine, used to process large numbers of soil samples, developed for use at the early farming village of Abu Hureyra, Syria.

SCIENCE

Accelerator Mass Spectrometry (AMS) Radiocarbon Dating

Until about twenty years ago, dating the rate of decay (beta counts) from different radio-carbon samples had a calculated ratio that gave only approximations. Using carbon 14 (C14) and carbon 12 (C12), scientists could detect and count individual decay events with radiocarbon. They would observe the emission of beta particles to determine the rate of radioactive breakdown and so estimate the number of C14 atoms remaining in the sample. Since only a small number of C14 atoms break down over the many hours of the sample count, the samples had to be large enough to provide an adequate number of beta counts.

Back in the 1960s, archaeologists collected handfuls of charcoal from hearths in plastic bags, the rule being, the larger the sample, the better. Scientists could not date small objects like maize cobs or tiny wood fragments embedded in the sockets of prehistoric bronze spear-heads. Furthermore, minute samples such as seeds can easily move upward or downward into other occupation layers, either through human agencies such as trampling, or through natural phenomena such as burrowing animals. The development of a new radiocarbon method based on accelerator mass spectrometry (AMS) in 1983 revolutionized radiocarbon chronologies and the study of early food production.

An accelerator mass spectrometer can date the age of sample material by counting the number of C14 atoms present. Rather than counting decay events (beta counts), researchers estimate the remaining C14 by directly counting C14 atoms. By doing this, they can date samples 1,000 times smaller than the handful of charcoal used a generation ago.

The development of small, high-energy mass spectrometers solved a major problem, that of background noise from ions or molecules of a similar mass to the C14 masking their presence (Figure 5.5). The new instruments filter out background, as a proportion of the sample's atoms are propelled through an accelerator toward a detector. Ionized carbon atoms from the

grasses by burning of harvested stands, then broadcasting some of the seed over the burnt ground. They created groves of oaks and pines by planting edible nuts at high elevations and planted agave and other desert plants in suitable habitats. In this way they flourished by means of a complex mosaic of manipulated wild plants.

Population and Resources Theories

All of us take risks in our lives and try to protect ourselves against the dangers of a sudden catastrophe. This is why wise investors diversify their holdings, and why parents carry life insurance policies. This is known as risk management. In the case of prehistoric people, it meant minimizing anything that would threaten long-term survival. All environments, however favorable, involve some form of risk for foraging societies—drought cycles, long, cold winters, and unpredictable floods, to mention only a few. Often people respond to these risks by moving away or by developing new storage and food preservation technologies.

Figure 5.5 Accelerator Mass Spectrometry (AMS) Radiocarbon Dating.

sample are pulled in beam form toward the accelerator. A magnet bends the beam, so lighter atoms turn more sharply than heavier ones and move to the inside of the diverging beam. A filter blocks the passage of all charged particles except those of atomic mass 14. The accelerator pushes the stripped beam through a second beam-bending magnet filtering out any last non-C14 particles. A magnetic lens focuses the beam as a C14 detector counts the number of remaining ions, allowing the calculation of the sample age.

One logical and straightforward solution to rising populations, resulting food shortages, or risk factors may be to go one step further, to cultivate familiar plants and domesticate common prey so that people can draw on familiar stored food during scarce periods. In other words, food production arose as a result of risk management, as a way of increasing food supplies.

Ecological Theories

Proponents of ecological models talk of so-called opportunities for the introduction of food production, of people turning to superior local resources when the moment arrived. In this kind of scenario, some resources, say wild wheat or barley or wild oats, are seen as attractive. People use them more and more, to the extent that they eventually become domesticated. Ecological theories are founded on the assumption that human societies are cultural systems operating within much larger environmental systems.

The classic exposition of this point of view is that of University of Michigan archaeologist Kent Flannery, who works in Mexico's southern highlands. He discovered that between 8000 and 4000 B.C. the local people relied on five basic food sources—deer, rabbits, maguey, legumes, and prickly pears—for their sustenance. By careful prediction of the seasons of each food, they could schedule their hunting and gathering at periods of abundance and before animals gained access to the ripe plants. Flannery assumed that the southern highlands and their inhabitants were part of a large, open environmental system consisting of many subsystems—economic, botanical, social, and so on—that interacted with one another. Then something happened to jolt the food procurement system toward the deliberate growing of wild grasses.

Flannery's excavations at dry caves dating to between 5000 and 2000 B.C. showed maize cobs slowly increasing in size, as well as other signs of genetic change. Thus, he suggested that the people began to experiment with the deliberate planting of maize and other crops, intentionally expanding the areas where they would grow. After a long period, these intentional deviations in the food procurement system caused the importance of wild grass collecting to increase at the expense of other collecting activities until it became the dominant one. Eventually, the people created a self-perpetuating food procurement system, with its own vital scheduling demands of planting and harvesting that competed with earlier systems and won out because it was more durable. By 2000 B.C., the highly nutritious bean and corn diet of the highland people was well established.

The crux of all these theoretical approaches is to identify the processes that caused people to shift to deliberate cultivation and domestication. For example, were there new cost-benefit realities that favored farming? What about such factors as the nutritive value and seasonal availability of different foods? Did genetic changes in plants and animals play a role? Unfortunately, it is difficult to link complex theoretical models with actual field data, largely because the factors involved in such profound cultural change (the reasons why people make the changeover) do not lend themselves to easy documentation.

Many variables must be understood before we can reconstruct the conditions under which agriculture was first regarded as a profitable activity. We are searching for sets of conditions in which population pressure, the distribution of plants, the rate at which the environment was changing, and even the techniques of harvesting wild grasses all played their part in making agriculture work. Then there are variations among the potentially domesticable plants and animals, some of which resisted domestication because of their long life span or because parts of their lives took place outside human control. The seasonal distribution of wild vegetable foods or game may also have prevented experiments in domestication, when the seasons during which these wild foods were exploited coincided with the times of year when it was important that experimenting farmers stay near their growing crops. Under these circumstances, people would tend to pursue their traditional food-getting habits.

The Consequences of Food Production

Once successful, food production spread rapidly, partly because population growth after the fact prevented people from reverting to hunting and gathering. Food production spread to all corners of the world except where an environment with extreme aridity or heat or cold rendered agriculture or herding impossible or where people chose to remain hunters and gatherers. In some places, food production was the economic base for urbanization and literate civilization; but most human societies did not go further than subsistence-level food production until the industrial power of nineteenth- and twentieth-century Europe led them into the machine age.

Differing Dates and Why

As we shall see in Chapter 6, food production began at very different times in various parts of the world, being well established in Southwest Asia by 10,000 B.C., in China by at least 6,000 B.C. and probably earlier, in Mesoamerica by 5000 B.C., but much later in tropical Africa—by about 1000 B.C., and then only in some locations. What were the local variations that accounted for this time lag? We know that hunter-gatherers in subtropical zones such as Southwest Asia and highland Mesoamerica were beginning to manipulate potential domesticates among wild grasses and root species at the end of the Ice Age. Dependence on such foods probably came earlier in these regions, where there were only a few forageable species. Such dependence was essential to long-term survival. In contrast, populations in more humid tropical regions, like the African and Amazonian rain forests, probably did little more than manipulate a few wild species to minimize risk in lean years. Many African agricultural peoples still turn to hunting and gathering in lean years to this day. Agriculture was established considerably earlier in subtropical Southwest Asia, Middle and South America, Southeast Asia, and India than it was in humid, tropical zones, undoubtedly because these were rich in game and wild vegetable foods. Furthermore, domesticated crops and animals were more susceptible to irregular rainfall, locusts and other insect attacks, and endemic stock diseases. A strong and sustained incentive to obtain food must have been a prerequisite for a lasting shift from foraging to agriculture.

An interesting question remains: Why did food production not take hold much earlier in prehistory? Surely, there were many previous occasions during the Ice Age when conditions were favorable for people to start cultivating plants. Here, population models for prehistory offer some clues. We know there was gradual population growth during the Stone Age. The constant, cyclic changes of the past 700,000 years must have led to conditions in some areas that presented human societies with the challenge of constant environmental change and population shifts. However, it was not until the end of the Ice Age that global populations rose sufficiently to limit mobility, and the easiest strategy for people faced with food shortages is to move away. There was initially a slow and then a rapidly accelerating intensification of hunter-gatherer lifeways during and after the last glacial maximum, especially during Holocene times. This intensification preadapted many societies to food production for the first time.

Changes in Human Life

Food production resulted, ultimately, in much higher population densities in many locations, for the domestication of plants and animals can lead to an economic strategy that increases and stabilizes available food supplies, although more energy is used to produce them (see Figure 5.6 on page 140). Farmers use concentrated tracts of territory for agriculture and for grazing cattle and small stock if they practice mixed farming. Their territory is much smaller than that of hunter-gatherers (although pastoralists need huge areas of grazing land for seasonal pasture). Permanent villages replaced the temporary camps of earlier times. New

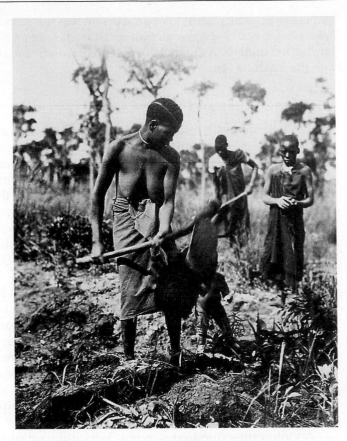

Figure 5.6 Bemba women from Central Africa hoeing a freshly burnt and cleared field.

social units came into being as more lasting home bases were developed; these social links reflected ownership and inheritance of land and led to much larger settlements that brought hitherto scattered populations into closer and more regular contact. Within a smaller area of farming land, property lines are carefully delineated as individual ownership and problems of inheritance arise. Shortages of land can lead to disputes and to the founding of new village settlements on previously uncultivated soil.

The technological consequences of food production were, in their way, as important as the new economies. A more settled way of life and some decline in hunting and gathering led to long-occupied villages, lasting agricultural styles, and more substantial housing. As they had done for millennia, people built their permanent homes with the raw materials most abundant in their environment. The early farmers of Southwest Asia worked dried mud into small houses with flat roofs; these were cool in summer and warm in winter. At night during the hot season, people may have slept on the flat roofs. Some less substantial houses had reed roofs. In the more temperate zones of Europe, with wetter climates, timber was used to build thatched-roof houses of various shapes and sizes. Early African farmers often built huts of grass, sticks, and anthill clay (Figure 5.7). Nomadic pastoralists of the northern steppes had no concern with a permanent and durable

Figure 5.7 A mud-and-pole dwelling hut typical of the Middle Zambezi Valley, Central Africa (left). Such dwellings, often occupied fifteen years or more, are more lasting than the windbreak or tent of the hunter-gatherer. At right is a grain storage bin from an African village, used for cereal crops. Storing food is a critical activity of many hunter-gatherers and farmers.

home, yet they, too, took advantage of the related benefits of having a domestic food supply: They used animal skins to make clothing, as well as tents to shelter them during the icy winters.

Agriculture is a seasonal activity, with long periods of the year in which the fields are lying fallow or are supporting growing crops. Any farmer is confronted with the problem of keeping food in ways the hunter-gatherer never has to ponder. Thus, a new technology of storage came into being. Grain bins, jars, or clay-lined pits became an essential part of the agricultural economy for stockpiling food for the lean months and against periods of famine. The bins may have been made of wattle and daub, clay, or timber (Figure 5.7). Basket and clay-lined silos protected valuable grain against rodents.

Hunter-gatherers use skins, wood containers, gut pouches, and sometimes baskets to carry vegetable foods back to base. Farmers face far more formidable transport problems: They must carry their harvest back to the village, keep ready-for-use supplies of foods in the house as opposed to storage bins, and store water. Early farmers began to use gourds as water carriers and, in some areas and somewhat later, to make clay vessels that were both waterproof and capable of carrying and cooking food (see Figure 5.8 on page 142). They made pots by coiling rolls of clay or building up the walls of vessels from a lump and firing them in simple hearths. Clay vessels were much more durable than skin or leather receptacles. Some pots were used for several decades before being broken and abandoned.

For tens of thousands of years, people dug up wild edible roots with simple wooden sticks, sometimes made more effective with the aid of a stone weight. The first farmers

Figure 5.8 A Pueblo woman from the American Southwest making pottery using the coil method.

continued to use the digging stick to plant crops a few inches below the surface, probably in readily cultivable soils. They also used wooden or stone-bladed hoes (and much later, iron hoes) to break up the soft soil. These they fitted with short or long handles, depending on cultural preferences. European and Southwest Asian farmers made use of the ox-drawn plow in later millennia, at first with a blade tipped with wood, then with bronze, and later with iron. The plow was an important innovation, for it enabled people to turn the soil over to a much greater depth than ever before. Every farmer has to clear wild vegetation and weeds from the fields, and it is hardly surprising to find a new emphasis on the ax and the adze. In Southwest Asia, metal axes replaced the simpler stone tools of earlier farmers by 2500 B.C. Present-day experiments in Denmark and New Guinea have shown that the ground and polished edges of stone axes are remarkably effective in clearing woodland and felling trees. In later millennia, the alloying of copper and bronze and, still later, the development of iron cutting edges made forest clearance even easier.

New tools meant new technologies to produce tougher working edges. At first, the farmers used ground and polished stone, placing a high premium on suitable rocks, which were traded from quarry sites over enormous distances. Perhaps the most famous ax quarries are in western Europe, where ax blanks were traded the length of the British Isles, and Grand Pressigny flint from France was prized over thousands of square miles. In Southwest Asia and Mexico, one valuable toolmaking material, not for axes but for knives and sickles, was **obsidian**, a volcanic rock prized for its easy working properties, sharp edges, and ornamental appearance. Early obsidian trade routes carried tools and ornaments hundreds of miles from their places of origin. By using spectrographic techniques to identify distinctive trace elements in different obsidians, scientists have been able to match obsidian fragments in distant villages in the eastern Mediterranean to such places of origin as Lipari Island off Italy and Lake Van in Turkey.

All these technological developments made people more and more dependent on exotic raw materials, many of which were unobtainable in their own territory. We see the beginnings of widespread long-distance trading networks, which were to burgeon even more rapidly with the emergence of the first urban civilizations.

Food production led to changed attitudes toward the environment. Cereal crops were such that people could store their food for winter (see Figure 5.7 on page 141). The hunter-gatherers exploited game, fish, and vegetable foods, but the farmers did more; they altered the environment by the very nature of their exploitation. Expansion of agriculture meant felling trees and burning vegetation to clear the ground for planting. The same fields were then abandoned after a few years to lie fallow, and more woodland was cleared. The original vegetation began to regenerate, but it might have been cleared again before reaching its original state. This shifting pattern of farming is called slash-and-burn, or swidden, agriculture (see Figure 5.6 on page 140). Voracious domesticated animals stripped pastures of their grass cover; then heavy rainfalls denuded the hills of valuable soil, and the pastures were never the same again. However elementary the agricultural technology, the farmer changed the environment, if only with fires lit to clear scrub from gardens and to fertilize the soil with wood ash. In a sense, shifting slash-and-burn agriculture is merely an extension of the age-old use of fire to encourage regeneration of vegetation.

Food production resulted in high population densities, but disease, available food supplies, water supplies, and particularly famine controlled population growth. Also, early agricultural methods depended heavily on careful selection of the soil. The technology of the first farmers was hardly effective enough for extensive clearing of the dense woodland under which many good soils lay, so potentially cultivable land could only be that which was accessible. Gardens probably were scattered over a much wider territory than is necessary today. One authority estimates that even with advanced shifting agriculture, only 40 percent of moderately fertile soil in Africa is available for such cultivation. This figure must have been lower in the early days of agriculture, with the simpler stone tools and fewer crops.

In regions of seasonal rainfall, such as southwestern Asia, sub-Saharan Africa, and parts of Asia, periods of prolonged drought are common. Famine was a real possibility as population densities rose. Many early agriculturalists must have worriedly watched the sky and had frequent crop failures in times of drought. Their small stores of grain from the previous season would not have carried them through another year, especially if they had been careless with their surplus. Farmers were forced to shift their economic strategy in such times.

We know that the earliest farmers availed themselves of game and wild vegetable foods to supplement their agriculture, just as today some farmers are obliged to rely heavily on wild vegetable foods and hunting to survive in bad years. Many hunter-gatherer bands collect intensively just a few species of edible plants in their large territories. Aware of many other edible vegetables, they fall back on these only in times of stress; the less-favored foods can carry a comparatively small population through to the next rains. A larger agricultural population is not so flexible and quickly exhausts wild vegetables and game in the much smaller territory used for farming and grazing. If the drought lasts for years, famine, death, and reduced population can follow.

Nutrition and Early Food Production

Was food production a real improvement in human lifeways? For generations archaeologists thought that human health improved dramatically as a result of agriculture, because people worked less and lived on more reliable food supplies. But the economist Esther Boserup and others have argued that in fact agriculture brought diminishing returns in relation to labor expended in the new systems that were adopted to feed many more people. Richard Lee's studies of the !Kung San of the Kalahari Desert tend to support her views. They show that these hunter-gatherers, and presumably others, had abundant leisure and worked less than farmers. Some nutritionists point out that hunter-gatherers may have had better-balanced diets than many farmers, who relied heavily on root or cereal crops. Further, farmers, with their sedentary settlements and higher population densities, were much more vulnerable to famine than their hunter-gatherer predecessors. They would also have been more vulnerable to gastrointestinal infections and epidemics because of crowded village populations.

Nutrition studies based on the skeletons of early farmers suggest some incidence of anemia and slow growth resulting from malnutrition. Regional studies of prehistoric populations have suggested a decline in mean age life expectancy in agricultural populations, which contradicts the commonly held perception. Taken as a whole, paleopathological studies hint at a general decline in the quality, and perhaps the length, of human life with the advent of food production. However, there are many unknowns involved, among them changes in fertility and population growth rates, which caused the world's population to rise even if general health standards and life expectancy fell.

What impact these studies will have on population-pressure theories about the origins of agriculture is still uncertain. Certainly, any shift to food production caused by increasing population pressure could be reflected in a decline in the overall health and nutrition displayed by prehistoric skeletons.

In the final analysis, some people probably turned to food production only when other alternatives were no longer practicable. The classic example is the Aborigines of extreme northern Australia, who were well aware that their neighbors in New Guinea were engaged in intensive agriculture. They, too, knew how to plant the top of the wild yam so that it regerminated, but they never adopted food production simply because they had no need to become dependent on a lifeway that would reduce their leisure time and produce more food than they required. We should never forget that humans have always been opportunistic, and the planting of food crops and the first taming of animals may have been the simple result of pure opportunism.

Chapter 6 describes the beginnings of food production throughout the world.

Summary

Many late-Ice Age and early Holocene hunter-gatherer societies were preadapted to food production, as they were already exploiting some food resources intensively and living more sedentary lifeways. Most of these societies were in regions where food resources were diverse and seasonally predictable. In contrast to early theories that food production was a revolutionary development, modern hypotheses invoke social relations, population growth, and ecological factors as multivariate causes of food production. Its development was a gradual process, one that saw increasing reliance on food crops, especially in areas with constant and unpredictable environmental change. Food production resulted in more sedentary human settlement, more substantial housing, elaborate storage technologies, and special implements for agricultural tasks. All these technological developments led to greater interdependence and to more long-distance exchange of raw materials, as well as increasing human social complexity.

6 The Earliest Farmers

2.5 Million   1.0 Million   500,000 B.P.   100,000 B.P. 50,000 B.P. 15,000 B.P.   A.D. 1 A.D. 1950

PROLOGUE

It was the final day of the 1953 excavation season at Jericho. For weeks, the top of a human skull had projected from the side of the trench dug deep into one of the earliest farming communities in the world. Excavator Kathleen Kenyon had given strict instructions that it was not to be disturbed until the stratigraphic layers in the trench wall had been drawn and photographed. Then the excavators recovered a complete cranium, with facial features carefully modeled in clay, the eyes inset with shells (see Figure 1.11 on page 30). Kenyon looked closely at the small hole in the wall. She could see two more plastered skulls within. They were removed. Three more now appeared behind them, then a final seventh head. It took five days to extract the nest of skulls from the wall, for the crushed bones were packed tightly with stones and hard earth. They formed the earliest portrait gallery in the world, each head modeled with individual features—nose, mouth, ears, and eyebrows molded with delicacy. Kenyon believed she had found the heads of revered ancestors, who were critical intermediaries between the living and the spiritual world, linking people closely to the land that brought forth their crops.

Whatever the complex factors that led to agriculture and animal domestication, the new food-producing economies proved dramatically successful. In 10,000 B.C., virtually everybody in the world lived by hunting and gathering. By A.D. 1, the time of Christ, most people were farmers or herders, and only a minority were still hunter-gatherers, most of them living in environments where extreme cold or aridity prevented the growth of domesticated crops. The spread of food production throughout the world took only about 8,000 years.

As we saw in Chapter 5, hunter-gatherers everywhere had a profound knowledge of the food resources in their local environments. Nevertheless, many fewer animals and wild vegetable foods were domesticated than foraged over the millennia. In the Old World, early farmers tamed wheat, barley, and other cereals that grow wild over much of Asia and Europe. In the New World, Native Americans developed a remarkable expertise with plants of all kinds—indigenous cereal grasses, root species, and many varieties of nuts. From this proficiency came the staples of American farming: Indian corn (*Zea mays*), the only important wild grass to be domesticated, beans, squashes, and many minor crops. Root plants such as manioc and sweet potatoes, chili peppers, tobacco, and various forms of potato were vital parts of Indian life.

Potentially tamable animal species like the wild ox, goat, pig, and sheep were widely distributed in the Old World during the late Ice Age. Native American farmers domesticated only such animals as the llama, the guinea pig, and the turkey, and then only under special conditions and within narrow geographic limits.

This chapter examines the archaeological evidence for the origins and initial spread of farming in the Old and New Worlds, a process that was the foundation for subsequent, more complex human societies and the early civilizations.

Domesticating Animals

Having one's own herds of domesticated mammals ensured a regular meat supply. The advantages to having a major source of meat under one's control are obvious. Later, domesticated animals provided by-products such as milk, cheese, and butter, as well as skins for clothes and tent coverings and materials for leather shields and armor. In later millennia, people learned how to breed animals for specialized tasks such as plowing, transportation, and traction.

Domestication implies a genetic selection emphasizing special features of continuing use to the domesticator. Wild sheep have no wool, wild cows produce milk only for their offspring, and undomesticated chickens do not lay surplus eggs. Changes in wool bearing, lactation, or egg production could be achieved by isolating wild populations for selective breeding under human care. Isolating species from a larger gene pool produced domestic sheep with thick, woolly coats and domestic goats providing regular supplies of milk, which formed a staple in the diet of many human populations.

No one knows exactly how domestication of animals began. Three elements are vital to domestication: constraining the movement of the target populations, regulating their breeding, and controlling their feeding to shape future generations. At the end of the Ice Age, hunters in southwestern Asia were concentrating on gazelles (a small desert antelope) and other steppe animals. Wild sheep and goats were intensively hunted on the southern shores of the Caspian Sea. Gregarious, highly social animals like goats and sheep are the most easily domesticated beasts because they follow the lead of a dominant herd member or all move together; also, they tolerate feeding and breeding in a confined environment.

Hunters often fed off the same herd for a long time, sometimes deliberately sparing young females and immature beasts to keep the source of food alive. Young animals captured alive in the chase might be taken back to the camp to grow dependent on those who caged them, thus becoming partially tamed. A hunter could grasp the possibility of gaining control of the movements of a few key members of a herd, who would be followed by the others. Once the experience of keeping pets or of restricting game movements had suggested a new way of life, people might experiment with different species. As part of domestication, animals and humans increased their mutual interdependence.

The process of animal domestication undoubtedly was prolonged, developing in several areas of southwestern Asia at approximately the same time. Although animal bones are scarce and often unsatisfactory as evidence of early domestication, most authorities now agree that the first species to be domesticated in southwestern Asia were goats and sheep, by about 9500 B.C. Goats and sheep are small animals that live in herds, whose carcasses yield much meat for their size. They can readily be penned and isolated to develop a symbiotic relationship with people.

Cattle are much more formidable to domesticate, for their prototype was *Bos primigenius*, the wild ox much hunted by Stone Age people (Figure 6.1). South African archaeologist Andrew Smith, an expert on herding, believes that the first domesticated animals came from better disciplined wild herds in arid environments, where it was easier to control the movements of animals. Such conditions may have persisted over much of southwestern Asia and the Sahara Desert as the climate became drier after 7000 B.C.

Some animals, such as sea mammals, resist domestication because much of their lives are spent out of the range of human influence. Most early successes with domestication took place with gregarious animals. They can be thought of as a food reserve, as "grain on the hoof."

Figure 6.1 The aurochs, *Bos primigenius*, the prototype for domesticated cattle as depicted by S. Von Herbenstain in 1549.

Domesticating Wheat and Barley

The qualities of wild wheat, barley, and similar crops are quite different from those of their domestic equivalents. In the wild, these grains occur in dense stands. They can be harvested by tapping the stem with the hands and gathering the seeds in a basket as they fall off or by uprooting the plant. The tapping technique is effective because the wild grain is attached to the stem by a brittle joint, or **rachis**. When the grass is tapped, the weak rachis breaks and the seed falls into the basket.

The first cultivated wheat and barley crops were of the wild, brittle-rachised type, and the resulting crops would probably have been large enough to generate domestic-type mutants in the first two to five years. Selection for the semitough rachised forms was an unconscious process during the earliest stages of domestication, perhaps accelerated by the use of sickles or uprooting of individual plants to harvest ripe seeds rather than merely tapping them into waiting baskets (Figure 6.2). Computer simulations have shown that domestic, semitough rachised forms may have been rare at first, but they would have been fully domesticated within twenty to thirty generations—for these cereals, between twenty and thirty years. DNA fingerprinting studies on einkorn in southeastern Turkey confirm this brief time frame. There, alterations in just one or two genes transformed wild wheat into a useful crop with a tough rachis.

Archaeobotanist Gordon Hillman of London University believes that the farmers would have started conscious selection as soon as the domesticates became sufficiently common to be recognized, perhaps 1 to 5 percent of the crop. From then on, domestication would have been completed in three or four years.

Although the broad outlines of the process of domestication can be reconstructed through controlled experimentation and computer simulation, it is most unlikely that anyone will ever find "transitional" grains in southwestern Asian sites that will document the actual process underway. The changeover from wild to domesticated strains was so rapid that we are more likely to find wild seeds in one level and domesticated ones in the next. DNA researches pinpoint southeastern Turkey as the most likely place for the earliest cereal domestication. Currently, the best archaeological evidence comes from sites such as Abu Hureyra in Syria, where farming appears about 10,000 B.C. (see the discussion that follows). We know, however, that figs were cultivated in the Jordan Valley as early as 9400 B.C.

Southwest Asian Farmers (c. 10,000 to 5000 B.C.)

The universal global warming at the end of the Ice Age had dramatic effects on temperate regions of Asia, Europe, and North America. Ice sheets retreated, sea levels rose. The climatic changes in southwestern Asia were more subtle, in that they involved shifts in mountain snow lines, rainfall patterns, and vegetational cover. However, these same cycles of change had momentous impacts on the sparse human populations of the region. At the end of the Ice Age, no more than a few thousand foragers lived along the eastern Mediterranean coast, in the Jordan and Euphrates Valleys. Within 2,000 years, the human population of the region numbered in the tens of thousands, all as a result of village life and farming. Thanks to new environmental and archaeological discoveries, we now know something about this remarkable change in local life.

Ripe spikelets disarticulating (and falling to ground) as the ripening rachis breaks into its constituent segments

Ripe spikelets remain in ear

Near-ripe spikelets still attached in ear

Ear shatters only when threshed

The basal few spikelets, which generally fail to disarticulate

Dense ear due to shorter rachis segments

1 cm

1 cm

A more or less ripe ear in the process of shattering and thereby shedding its spikelets. The ear ripens from the top downward.

A fully ripe ear. The ear will shatter only when threshed.

(a)

(b)

Figure 6.2 Wild and domesticated einkorn, showing brittle and tough rachis. **(a)** Wild einkorn showing its brittle-rachised ear and arrow-shaped spikelets adapted for penetrating surface litter and cracks on the ground. **(b)** Domestic einkorn, showing its semitough rachised ear and its plumper spikelets, which have lost some key features necessary for self-implantation.

Pollen samples from freshwater lakes in Syria and elsewhere tell us forest cover expanded rapidly at the end of the Ice Age, for the southwestern Asian climate was still cooler and considerably wetter than today. Many areas were richer in animal and plant species than they are now, making them highly favorable for human occupation. About 10,000 B.C., most human settlements lay in the Levant (the area along the Mediterranean coast) and in the Zagros mountains of Iran and their foothills (see Figure 5.1 on page 128). Some local areas like the Jordan River valley, the Middle Euphrates valley, and some Zagros valleys were more densely populated than elsewhere. Here more sedentary and more complex societies flourished. These people exploited the landscape intensively, foraging on hill slopes for wild cereal grasses and nuts, while hunting gazelle and other game on grassy lowlands and in river valleys. Their settlements contain exotic objects such as sea shells, stone bowls, and artifacts made of obsidian (volcanic glass), all traded from afar. This considerable volume of intercommunity exchange brought a degree of social complexity in its wake.

Thanks to extremely fine-grained excavation and extensive use of flotation methods, we know a great deal about the foraging practices of the inhabitants of Abu Hureyra in Syria's Euphrates Valley (Figure 6.3). Abu Hureyra was founded about 11,500 B.C., a small village settlement of cramped pit dwellings (houses dug partially in the soil) with reed roofs supported by wooden uprights. For the next 1,500 years, its inhabitants enjoyed a somewhat warmer and damper climate than today, living in a well-wooded steppe area where wild cereal grasses were abundant. They subsisted off spring migrations of Persian gazelles from the south. With such a favorable location, about 300 to 400 people lived in a

Figure 6.3 Abu Hureyra, Syria. Excavations in the earlier settlement, showing interconnecting pits that were roofed with poles, branches, and reeds to form small huts. Part of a later rectangular house can be seen at a higher level (top right).

sizable, permanent settlement. They were no longer a series of small bands, but lived in a large community with more elaborate social organization, probably grouped into clans of people of common descent. The flotation samples from the excavations allowed botanist Gordon Hillman to study changing plant-collecting habits, as if he were looking through a telescope at a changing landscape. Hundreds of tiny plant remains show how they exploited nut harvests in nearby pistachio and oak forests. However, as the climate dried up, the forests retreated from the vicinity of the settlement. The inhabitants turned to wild cereal grasses instead, collecting them by the thousands, while percentages of nuts fell. By 10,200 B.C., drought conditions were so severe that the people abandoned their long-established settlement, perhaps dispersing into smaller camps. There are signs that they experimented with growing rye, but not permanently.

Five centuries later, about 9700 B.C., a new village rose on the mound. At first, the inhabitants still hunted gazelle intensively. Then, about 9000 B.C., within the space of a few generations, they switched abruptly to herding domesticated goats and sheep and to growing einkorn, pulses, and other cereal grasses. Abu Hureyra grew rapidly until it covered nearly 12 hectares (30 acres). It was a close-knit community of rectangular, one-story, mud-brick houses, joined by narrow lanes and courtyards, finally abandoned about 6000 B.C. (see box on pages 154–155).

Many complex factors led to the adoption of the new economies, not only at Abu Hureyra, but at many other locations such as **'Ain Ghazal**, also in Syria, where goat toe bones showing the telltale marks of abrasion caused by foot tethering (hobbling) testify to early herding of domestic stock. Most settlements lay on low ground, near well-watered, easily cultivable land. Their inhabitants usually lived in small, densely clustered villages of circular or oval one-room houses. The most famous of these many settlements is at the base of the Biblical city of Jericho, famous for the siege in which Joshua collapsed the city walls with the blast of trumpets.

A small camp flourished at the bubbling Jericho spring by at least 10,500 B.C., but a more permanent farming settlement quickly followed. Soon the inhabitants built massive stone walls complete with towers and a rock-cut ditch more than 2.7 meters (9 feet) deep and 3 meters (10 feet) wide around their settlement. Their beehive-shaped huts clustered inside the walls. The communal labor of wall and ditch building required both political and economic resources on a scale unheard of a few thousand years earlier. Why the walls were needed remains a mystery, but they may have been flood works or for defense, resulting from competition from neighboring groups for scarce food resources. Jericho also yielded compelling evidence of ancestor worship in the form of human skulls with plastered faces, a clear sign that people enjoyed a close link with the supernatural and the land, guarded traditionally by the dead. (See Figure 1.11 on page 30.)

The population of the Levant increased considerably between 8000 and 6000 B.C., scattered in permanent villages as far east as the more arid Syrian plateau. Emmer wheat, barley, lentils, and peas were grown in small fields, crops were rotated with pulses to sustain soil fertility. Some communities like Jericho became important trading centers. The farmers were using obsidian from Turkey, turquoise from Sinai, and sea shell ornaments from the Mediterranean and the Red Sea. The volume of trade was such that many villages used small clay spheres, cones, and disks to keep track of commodities traded. These tokens may represent a simple recording system that later evolved into written script (see Chapter 8).

What is now southeastern Turkey was a diverse, favorable highland and lowland environment for human settlement from early in the Holocene. Food production probably began in this region at about the same time as it did in the Euphrates Valley.

SITE

Men's and Women's Work at Abu Hureyra, Syria

In earlier times, many people spent most of their lives working at specific tasks, labor that left telltale signs on their bones. For instance, people who squat habitually develop specific anatomical conditions of their hips, knees, and ankles.

Biological anthropologist Theya Molleson of London's Natural History Museum examined the fragmentary skeletons of about 162 people from the early farming village at Abu Hureyra in Syria. She found ample evidence of repetitive tasks. Some people's neck bones displayed enlarged upper vertebrae, the result of carrying heavy loads on their heads. Others displayed the characteristic facets at the forward side of the ankles that are found in people who squat habitually from an early age. This condition occurred in men, women, and children.

Many Abu Hureyra skeletons from people in otherwise good health displayed collapsed lower vertebrae, grossly arthritic big toes, and muscular arms and legs (as revealed by prominent muscle attachments).

The toe bones were very revealing: Older individuals displayed a degenerative condition of the metatarsals, and even younger people showed changes in the big toe and second toe joints that had resulted from kneeling with the toes tucked under the foot. This position was used by people who spent long periods of time laboring at household tasks such as grinding grain. When Molleson examined pictures from ancient Egyptian and Assyrian tombs, she found just such a position being used by grain grinders, metalworkers, and other artisans.

At Abu Hureyra, a community without metal, the inhabitants must have been grinding grain on shallow querns. The weight of the body was used to grind the grain, the toes being used as a base for applying force to the grinding motion. This was a very painful and tiring activity indeed, hard on the arms as well as the toe (Figure 6.4). The Abu Hureyra skeletons displayed well-marked attachments for the deltoid muscles on the upper arms, which probably resulted from the movement at the end of the pushing stroke during grinding.

Theya Molleson measured the first metatarsal bone of the feet bones in her sample. She found the larger ones belonged to males, the smaller to females. On the latter, the arthritic condition as-

---

The upper reaches of the Euphrates and Tigris rivers drain the tableland of the Urfa region of southeastern Turkey. This is a place of arid, limestone hills, where the summers are hot and dry, the winters wet, with diverse soils that supported natural stands of wild cereals, and eventually became ideal for farming. DNA researches have pinpointed the Karacadag Mountains in this area as the original homeland of domesticated einkorn.

Was the Urfa, then, the area where farming began, as opposed to the Euphrates and Jordan Valleys to the south? The answer must be that we do not yet know, but there are some fascinating archaeological sites that chronicle sophisticated ritual observances that coincide, in general terms, with the changeover from hunting and gathering to food production. For the first time, we find evidence for communal structures, for public areas where more elaborate structures served as a focus for the settlement (see box on pages 156–157).

What are we to make of these extraordinary sites, which apparently straddle the changeover from hunting and gathering to food production? They hint that elaborate rituals and more complex social organization predated agriculture in this region. Steven Mithen, an expert on human cognition, believes that the religious beliefs behind these early carvings not only predated farming, but also may have led to it. The elaborate construction and ritual activities at

Figure 6.4 Deformed toe bones of an Abu Hureyra woman, Syria, c. 9000 B.C.

sociated with grinding was found. The constant, daily use of saddle querns (saddle-shaped grinding stones) caused this condition to develop in the knees and the lower back of many Abu Hureyra individuals. Grinding with such a quern is very laborious; it involves pushing a rubbing stone over a slightly tilted quern set as close to the knees as possible. Many passes are needed to produce flour for baking, a grinding method placing severe stress on knees, wrists, and lower back, reflected in the bones of those who carried out this constant daily work—the women of the community.

The Abu Hureyra people had heavily abraded teeth, resulting from eating coarse grain. But they may have sifted grain through fiber baskets: Some of the teeth display the characteristic grooving resulting from chewing basket fiber to soften it.

these sites would have required dozens, if not hundreds, of people. Feeding them would have required large quantities of wild grain, some of which would have fallen on the ground, germinated, and been gathered again—a form of domestication. In time, some of this quality Karacadag grain would have been carried back home, and, eventually been traded, like obsidian and sea shells, to communities many kilometers away, perhaps even as far as Jericho. This theory offers a speculative alternative to the common view that persistent drought was a major contributor to the changeover—the unresolved debate continues. But whatever the cause of early food production in this region, we can be sure that it resulted in major adjustments not only to society, but to its complex relationship to the cosmos and the environment.

In the Zagros highlands of Iran, the herding of goats and sheep probably began somewhat earlier than in the lowlands. Here, open steppe was ideal country both for intensive hunting of wild goats and sheep and, after about 10,000 B.C., for herding them as well. At the village of **Ganj Dareh** near Kermanshah in Iran, foragers occupied a seasonal hunting camp in about 10,500 B.C. About 1,500 years later, a small farming village of rectangular mud-brick houses stood on the same spot, a settlement based on goat and sheep herding and cereal horticulture. One of the best-known prehistoric farming villages in the Zagros is **Jarmo** in

SITE

Ritual Buildings in Southeastern Turkey

Communal buildings, open spaces, monoliths, and sometimes human remains—convincing evidence for ritual comes from several early villages in southeast Turkey. At **Çayönü Tepesi** in southeastern Turkey, occupied from about 8600 to 7000 B.C., the settlement lay on a terrace above a small river, the rectangular houses standing at right angles to the river. They form an arc, with a large open space at the center. Three quite distinct buildings once stood in this plaza. One of them was continually rebuilt, with three stone-built cells crammed with human bones under one end of the structure. One contained a pile of over forty human skulls. This "House of the Dead" also yielded a flat stone slab bearing traces of animal and human blood, as if some of the dead were sacrificial victims. Were the dead part of ancestor rituals, or were they war captives sacrificed after their capture? We don't know. The remains of at least 400 people lay in the cells. Another of the public buildings was virtually square with a floor made of small stones pressed into plaster, and tall, stone monoliths set into the floor.

Nearby **Göbekli Tepe** lies on the summit of a hill with a fine view over the surrounding landscape. In about 9600 B.C., at least four circular structures were cut partially into the limestone bedrock, so they are semisubterranean, almost cryptlike. Two huge stone pillars stood in the center of each crypt, with as many as eight other ones around the edges of each (Figure 6.5a). Rectangular, with flat cross-sections, they are up to 2.4 meters (8 feet) high and weigh as much as 7 tons. Stone-cut benches lie between the pillars. The pillars bore carvings of game animals like wild boar, gazelle, and aurochs, also snakes and birds—no domesticated animals or humans (Figure 6.5b). One pillar bears a human arm, as if the columns were partially anthropomorphic. The pillars came from a quarry 91 meters (300 feet) away, where at least one still in place would have been 6 meters (20 feet) long and weighed 50 tons.

Contemporary with Göbekli Tepe, nearby **Nevali Çori** yielded twenty-nine limestone and mud houses, some of them cult buildings set slightly into a slope so that the visitor stepped down into the interior, which was surrounded by a stone bench. Monolithic stone pillars interrupted the bench, as did a niche, out of sight of the entrance. Some of the pillars were carved; the same religious beliefs persisted over several rebuildings. Sculptures interred in a later cult

northern Iraq, little more than a cluster of twenty-five mud houses, forming an irregular huddle separated by small alleyways and courtyards. Jarmo was in its heyday in about 6000 B.C., by which time more than 80 percent of the villagers' food came from their fields or herds.

Below, on the lowlands, farming began along the eastern edge of the flat Mesopotamian plain as early as it did in the Levant. The village of **Ali Kosh** on the plains of Khuzistan, north of where the Tigris and Euphrates become one river, started off life as a small settlement of rectangular mud-brick houses as early as 9000 B.C. As time went on, the houses became larger, separated one from another by lanes or courtyards. The people drove their herds of goats and sheep to the highlands during the hot summer months, bringing them back to lush lowland pastures in fall. These same seasonal herding practices continue to this day. Ali Kosh documents more than 2,000 years of farming and herding on the lowlands, a period that saw the development of improved cereal strains and the development of irrigation as a means of intensifying agricultural production.

Only 5,000 years after food production first appeared, people in the Levant and Mesopotamia were living in cities with thousands of inhabitants.

(a)

(b)

Figure 6.5 (a) A large subterranean building at Göbekli Tepe, Turkey, showing the tops of two central T-shaped monoliths and other ones embedded in the dry stone walls at the edge of the building, where a bench is emerging from the excavation. **(b)** A T-shaped monolith from the site, with low-relief sculpture.

building include an intriguing figure with a human head and the body of a bird. In others, a bird perches on the head of a human; symmetrical human figures stand back-to-back. Perhaps the connections between bird and human heads reflect the soul of a person or a connection with the other world.

Early Egyptian and African Farmers (earlier than 7000 to 1000 B.C.)

The same dynamics of growing populations crowded into restricted territories developed in the Nile valley as a result of Holocene climatic change. During the late Ice Age, the valley was a rich, diverse habitat, abounding in game, fish, and wild plant foods. Wild cereal grasses were important in the human diet from at least 15,000 years ago.

The Nile valley is unusual in that its water supplies depend not on local rains but on floods from rainfall gathered far upstream in Ethiopia. The fluctuations in these yearly inundations had a profound effect on the pattern of human settlement downstream. The irregular cycles of higher and lower rainfall may have caused people to manage wild food resources very carefully. Like their southwest Asian counterparts, they turned to the deliberate cultivation of wild barley and wheat well before 7000 B.C.

By 6000 B.C., dozens of farming villages flourished in the Nile valley, settlements that are now buried beneath deep layers of sand and gravel laid down by thousands of years of river floods. Only 1,500 years later, the inhabitants of the valley were subsisting almost entirely off agriculture, living in small villages like **Merimda Beni Salama** near the Nile valley. Merimda was a cluster of oval houses and shelters, built half underground and roofed with mud and sticks. The farmers planted barley and wheat as the annual floods receded, while their animals grazed in flat river grasslands. Population densities were still low, so the average Nile flood allowed early Egyptian farmers to harvest grain over perhaps two-thirds of the river floodplain (Figure 6.6). Thus, there was no need for irrigation works, which first appear in about 3000 B.C., when Egypt became a unified state (see Chapter 10).

After 6000 B.C., cattle herders ranged widely over the semi-arid grasslands of what is now the Sahara Desert. These nomads left superb wall paintings of their beasts in the caves and rock shelters of the Saharan highlands, grazing their herds along the shores of shallow lakes like a much larger Lake Chad on the southern edge of the desert. The Sahara dried up rapidly after 6000 B.C., forcing its cattle-herding population into permanent oases or to the fringes of the desert. But it was not until much later, around 1000 B.C., that herders moved into sub-Saharan East Africa, and that West Africans domesticated such tropical cereals as sorghum and millet.

Figure 6.6 An ancient Egyptian tomb painting shows a noble's estate workers cultivating the soil. The roots of ancient Egyptian agriculture date back to at least 7000 B.C.

European Farmers (c. 6500 to 3000 B.C.)

The new economies were so successful that they spread rapidly from southwestern Asia into contiguous areas, especially as forager populations rose and natural food supplies were no longer sufficient to support increasingly sedentary forager groups. Many of them turned to food production to supplement their age-old game, plant, and fish diet. By using a mosaic of key sites and radiocarbon dates, we can trace the spread of farming over wide areas of Europe and southern Asia.

Agriculture and animal domestication spread rapidly through Turkey after 10,000 B.C., and from there into Greece, the Balkans, and temperate Europe. Between 9500 and 6000 B.C., long-distance exchange, especially of obsidian for ornaments and toolmaking, became a major factor in daily life. From Turkey's Lake Van it traveled to the Levant and as far afield as the Persian Gulf. A few settlements like **Çatalhöyük** prospered by controlling the trade. In about 7000 B.C., Çatalhöyük covered 13 hectares (32 acres), a settlement of numerous small mud-brick houses backed onto one another, the outside walls serving as a convenient defense wall. But the large village never became a full-fledged city. There were no powerful leaders who monopolized trade and production. It was a community of individual households and families that lacked the elaborate, centralized organization of a city (Figure 6.7).

Figure 6.7 Schematic reconstruction of a cluster of flat-roofed, mud-brick houses from Level VI at Çatalhöyük, Turkey. The inhabitants entered through the roof, the outside walls forming natural protection against intruders.

SITE

Easton Down and the Avebury Landscape, England

The great earthworks and megalithic monuments of western Europe did not stand alone. For example, the famous sacred circles at **Avebury** and Stonehenge in southern England (Figure 6.8) lay at the center of vast, long-vanished sacred landscapes, which were marked by burial mounds, enclosures, charnel houses, and other sites for commemorating the ancestors. Avebury, north of Stonehenge and less well known, was built in about 2550 B.C., in a natural amphitheater ideal for a large stone circle. In its final form, its earthwork and ditch dug into the underlying white chalk encompassed 11.5 hectares (28.5 acres) and measured about 350 meters (1,150 feet) across. Four causewayed entrances divide the monument into four unequal arcs. Ninety-eight standing stones set up inside the ditch once adorned the interior, some of them up to 14 meters (46 feet) high. Two inner circles stood within the outer circle. This staggering construction was built by farming communities with no wheeled carts and only the simplest levers and rollers, and stone, antler, and wooden tools. When new, the white earthworks with their exposed subsurface chalk must have stood out for kilometers.

Generations of archaeologists have excavated Avebury, but only recently have they paid close attention to its now-invisible landscape, very different from the rolling farmland of today. Obtaining evidence of ancient landscapes requires careful excavation and sample collection, most often of the original land surfaces under burial mounds and earthworks. When archaeologist Alisdair Whittle excavated some test trenches into a long burial mound at Easton Down in southern England, he exposed the original land surface, also the core of stacked turves, chalk, and topsoil under the mound, which gave him an unusual opportunity to obtain a portrait of the local vegetation in about 3200 B.C.

First, he turned to pollen analysis. Small amounts of pollen grains from the land surface were predominantly from grasses, showing that no woodland grew close to the tumulus when it was built. A well-sealed section of the pre-mound soil yielded eleven mollusk samples, which chronicled a dramatic change from woodland to open grassland forms over a short period of time. Whittle located an ancient tree hollow under the mound, which, hardly surprisingly, contained woodland mollusks. A sudden increase in open-country mollusks followed, a change so rapid that human clearance of the land seems the only logical explanation. Interestingly, soil scientists found signs of lateral movement of the soil below the mound, which can have resulted only from cultivation before the mound was built.

Excavations such as Easton Down can only give us snapshots of the complex mosaic of cleared and uncleared land that characterizes any agricultural landscape. For example, mollusks and soil samples under nearby Avebury itself tell us that the great temple of 2550 B.C. rose

---

At the time Çatalhöyük was a bustling village, farming had begun on the Aegean Islands, in Greece, and in parts of southeastern Europe. Since the end of the Ice Age, Europe had been the home of numerous, scattered forager groups who lived off forest game, plant foods, and sea and freshwater fish and mollusks. As in Asia, these populations were preadapted to cultivation and animal domestication, especially in areas where short-term population shifts and local environmental change may have required new subsistence strategies.

Domesticated animals and grains were probably introduced into southeast Europe from Asia by local bartering. The plants were cereals like emmer and bread wheat, which were

Figure 6.8 Avebury, Wiltshire, England. A celebrated Stone Age shrine built c. 2500 B.C.

on long-established, but little-grazed natural grassland close to a forest that had generated after being cleared for farming.

This kind of environmental archaeology is now so precise that we can fix the exact seasons when monuments were built or buildings erected. For example, soil samples from carefully cut sod laid under the original ground surface of 40-meter (130-foot) Silbury Hill, built in about 2200 B.C., also close to Easton Down, show that the builders started work in the late summer, most likely after the harvest when people had time for construction work. We know this because the well-preserved sods contain ants and anthills. The ants were beginning to grow wings and fly away from their anthills, as they do in late summer.

As environmental and landscape studies continue, we will learn a surprising amount about the setting, and perhaps the meaning, of major religious sites like Avebury and Stonehenge.

demanding crops that extracted large quantities of nutrients from the soil. The farmers had to husband their land carefully, rotating cereals with nitrogen-fixing legumes and revitalizing their fields with animal manure. Thus was born the European farming system that carefully integrated cultivation and animal rearing into a close-knit subsistence strategy based on individual households supplying their own food needs. Temperate Europe has year-round rainfall and marked contrasts between summer and winter seasons. With plentiful wood and cooler temperatures, timber and thatch therefore replaced the mud-brick architecture of southwestern Asia.

Figure 6.9 Reconstruction of a European Bandlkeramik settlement.

livestock pen possibly for sheep

wattle and daub

gate

rubbish pit

wattle fence

arable land

gate

cattle pasture

gate

wattle fence

arable fields with wattle enclosures

thatch

doorway

wattle and daub

rubbish pit

split logs

postholes

The expansion of farming society into central and western Europe coincided with a cycle of higher rainfall and warmer winters around 5500 B.C., at a time when the rising Mediterranean Sea breached a natural earthen berm and flooded into the vast Euxine Lake, turning it within a few weeks into the Black Sea. This natural cataclysm probably caused many farming communities along the lake to move inland, up river valleys and into the Danube Basin.

Within a thousand years, farming based on cattle herding combined with spring-sown crops developed over an enormous area of continental Europe. As farming groups spread across lighter soils, clearing forest for fields and grazing their animals in once-forested lands, many indigenous forager bands adopted the new economies. The best-known early European farming culture is named the **Bandkeramik complex** after its distinctive, line-decorated pottery. It first appeared in the Middle Danube valley in about 5300 B.C., then spread rapidly along sheltered river valleys far west to southern Holland and east into parts of the Ukraine. Bandkeramik (Danubian) communities were well spaced, each with territories of some 202 hectares (500 acres). The people lived in long, rectangular timber-and-thatch houses, from 5.4 to 14 meters (18 to 46 feet) long, presumably sheltering families, their grain, and their animals (Figure 6.9). Between forty and sixty people lived in Bandkeramik villages.

As the centuries passed, the population rose rapidly and the gaps between individual settlements filled in. In time, village territories became more circumscribed, their settlements protected by earthen enclosures. This was a time when communal tombs came into fashion, among them the celebrated **megaliths** (Greek *mega-lithos:* "big stone") of western Europe. These were sepulchers fashioned from large boulders and buried under earthen mounds (Figure 6.10). Such corporate burial places may have been locations where revered kin leaders were buried; people with genealogical ties with the ancestors were of paramount importance to a group of farming communities with strong attachments to their

Figure 6.10 West Kennet long barrow, Wiltshire, England. A megalithic tomb buried under an earthen mound, the side chambers filled with burials.

fertile lands. Judging from modern analogies, the ancestors were seen as the guardians of the land, the links between the living and the forces of the spiritual world that control human destiny.

Somewhat later, between about 2800 and 2300 B.C., individual graves as well as communal sepulchers appeared. These may have been the burial sites of individual leaders, prominent men who were laid to rest with their elaborate regalia of rank. They may have been the sole male ancestor of the group, the source of authority over land ownership. Chieftainship, inheritance of land and wealth, was now legitimized, as the character of European agriculture changed rapidly, partly as a result of the introduction of the plow by about 2800 B.C.

Early Agriculture in Asia (before 6000 B.C.)

A second major center of plant domestication developed in eastern Asia, where food production began almost as early as it did in southwestern Asia.

Rice Cultivation in Southern China

Rice was the staple of ancient agriculture over an enormous area of southern and southeastern Asia, and southern China. Today, rice accounts for half the food eaten by 1.7 billion people and 21 percent of the total calories consumed by humankind. Unfortunately, we still know almost nothing about the origins of this most important of domesticated crops, but DNA researchers hint that today's two major rice types were domesticated in India, Myanmar, and Thailand, and in areas of southern China.

Rice was one of the earliest plants to be domesticated in the northern parts of Southeast Asia and southern China. Botanists believe that the rices and Asian millets ancestral to the present domesticated species radiated from perennial ancestors around the eastern borders of the Himalaya Mountains at the end of the Ice Age. The initial cultivation of wild rice is thought to have taken place in an alluvial swamp area, where there was plenty of water to stimulate cereal growth. The first form to be domesticated may have flourished in shallow water, where seasonal flooding dispersed the seed on the border zone between permanently dry and permanently inundated lands. Perhaps this cultivation occurred under conditions in which seasonal flooding made field preparation a far from burdensome task. Such conditions could have been found on the Ganges Plain in India and along the rich coastal habitats of Southeast Asia and southern China with their dense mangrove swamps.

Perhaps the first efforts to cultivate rice resulted from deliberate efforts to expand seasonally inundated habitats by constructing encircling dams to trap runoff. The dams could then be breached, flooding dry land that could be used for rice planting, thereby creating additional stands of wild rice. From there, it was a short step to sowing and harvesting in wet fields (paddies). Most likely, a sedentary lifeway based on the gathering of wild rice developed in low-lying, seasonally flooded areas at the beginning of the Holocene. Systematic cultivation resulted from a response to population growth, climatic change, or some other stress.

During the early Holocene, warmer conditions may have allowed wild rice to colonize the lakes and marshes of the middle and lower Yangtze Valley of southern China, when hunter-gatherer societies throughout China were exploiting a broad spectrum of animal and plant resources. An international team of researchers led by Richard MacNeish and

Yan Wenming have excavated the important **Xianrendong** and **Wangdong** cave sites, where they identify four phases of occupation going back deep into the late Ice Age, when the inhabitants ate wild rice. Between 9200 and 7550 B.C., the inhabitants may have begun cultivating rice since a wider range of artifacts possibly used for cultivation appear, as well as **phytoliths** (minute particles of silica from plant cells) of domesticated rice. They also made some of the earliest pottery in the world. Climatic data reveals a long period of warming conditions, followed by a cooler interval, during which rice cultivation may have begun, just as food production took hold in northern China during the same cooler interval.

By 3000 B.C., much more sophisticated agricultural societies flourished along the Yangtze River and farther afield. The archaeology of these traditions is known primarily from cemetery excavations that show slow changes in grave goods. The earliest graves indicate few social differentiations, but later sepulchers show not only a much wider variety of artifacts—pottery, bone and stone tools, jade objects, and other ornaments—but also an increase in the number of elaborately adorned burials. China specialist Richard Pearson, who has analyzed several cemeteries, argues that they demonstrate an increase in the concentration of wealth, a trend toward ranked societies, and a shift in the relative importance of males at the expense of females; the last trend may be associated with the development of more intensive agriculture, an activity in which males are valued for their major roles in cultivation.

First Farmers in Northern China

A second great center of early Chinese agriculture lies nearly 650 kilometers (400 miles) north of the Yangtze, where the Huang Ho River flows out of mountainous terrain into the low-lying plains of northern China. Northern Chinese agriculture was based on millet, whereas the southern staple was rice. The first northern agricultural communities were sited in the central regions of the Huang Ho River Valley. The area is a small basin, forming a border between the wooded western highlands and the swampy lowlands to the east. As in the south, the early Holocene saw a warming trend, followed by a cooler interval, then a more prolonged period of climatic amelioration. It was during the colder period, dating to after 6500 B.C., that the first sedentary farming villages appear in the Huang Ho Valley.

The fine, soft-textured earth of the valley was both homogeneous and porous and could be tilled by simple digging sticks. Because of the concentrated summer rainfall, cereal crops, the key to agriculture in this region, could be grown successfully. The indigenous plants available for domestication included the wild ancestors of foxtail millet, broom-corn millet, sorghum, hemp, and the mulberry. Many villages lay near small streams on lower river terraces, along foothills and plains. Ancient Chinese farmers developed their own cultivation techniques, which persisted for thousands of years. By far the best known of China's early farming cultures is the **Yangshao,** which flourished over much of the Huang Ho River Basin, an area as large as the early centers of agriculture in Egypt or Mesopotamia, from before 4800 B.C. to about 3200 B.C.

Each Yangshao village was a self-contained community, usually built on a terrace overlooking fertile river valleys, situated to avoid flooding or to allow maximal use of floodplain soils (see Figure 6.11 on page 166). Using hoes and digging sticks, the farmers cultivated foxtail millet as a staple, mainly in riverside gardens that were flooded every spring. By 3000 B.C., Yangshao was a characteristic, and thoroughly Chinese, culture, with its own naturalistic art style and expert potters who made cooking pots for steaming food, the technique

Figure 6.11 Reconstruction of Yangshao houses, northern China.

that forms the basis of much Chinese cuisine to this day. The Chinese language may have its roots in Yangshao as well. Many regional variations of peasant farming culture developed throughout China. Agriculture developed over wide areas at about the same time, with people adapting their crops and farming techniques to local conditions. In time, the success of the new economies led to local population increases, more complex cultures, and the concentration of wealth in privileged hands.

Early American Agriculture (8000 B.C. onward)

Food production developed independently, also, in the Americas. For thousands of years after first settlement, the native Americans subsisted off hunting and gathering, developing an increasing expertise with wild plant foods of all kinds. In some regions, they exploited such resources intensively, especially in the Midwest and Southeast, where some groups were able to occupy more or less permanent settlements for many generations. In time, however, they also started planting wild grasses as a means of supplementing wild plant resources. In time, too, this led to agriculture, especially in areas where wild grasses were plentiful.

By the time of Columbus, the ancient Americans had developed a truly remarkable expertise with all kinds of native plants, using them not only for food but for medicinal and many other purposes. The most important staple crop was maize, the only significant wild grass in the New World to be fully domesticated. It remains the most important food crop in the Americas, used in more than 150 varieties as both food and cattle fodder. Root crops formed another substantial food source, especially in South America, and included manioc, sweet potatoes, and many varieties of the potato. Chili peppers were grown as hot seasoning. Amaranth, sunflowers, cacao, peanuts, and several types of beans were also significant crops. In contrast to Old World farmers, the Indians had few domesticated animals. Among them were the llama of the Andes and alpacas, which provided wool. The dog, the guinea pig, the raucous turkey, and the muscovy duck were also tamed.

Most archaeologists now agree there were at least three major centers of native plant domestication in the Americas: highland and lowland Central America for maize, beans, squash, and sweet potatoes; the highlands of the central Andes for root crops like potatoes and manioc; and the southeastern United States for pepo squash, sunflowers, and other local plants. There were also four areas of later cultivation activity: tropical (northern) South America, the Andean area, Mesoamerica, and southwestern and eastern North America.

Mesoamerica: Guilá Naquitz and Early Cultivation

The process of plant domestication is still little understood. Archaeologist Kent Flannery bases his arguments on ecological considerations (see Chapter 5). He believes plant cultivation began as a result of strategies designed to cope with continuous short-term climatic fluctuations and constant population shifts. Flannery bases his arguments on his own excavations at the **Guilá Naquitz** rock shelter in the Valley of Oaxaca. Guilá Naquitz was occupied about six times over a 2,000-year period between 8750 and 6670 B.C. The tiny forager groups who visited the cave faced unpredictable climatic fluctuations due to periodic droughts in an area that could support very few people per square mile.

The Guilá Naquitz people foraged eleven different edible plant species over the year. In wet years, they experimented with deliberate planting of beans. Bean cultivation near the cave allowed people to collect more food and travel less. At first the experiments were confined to wet years, but as time went on and they gained more confidence, plant yields rose and they relied more heavily on their own cultivation as opposed to foraging. In time, the Guilá Naquitz people simply added squashes, beans, and a simple form of maize to a much earlier foraging adaptation. Recent AMS radiocarbon dating of samples date squash cultivation at the cave to about 8000 B.C., as early as cereal agriculture in southwestern Asia. Flannery believes that this kind of changeover occurred in many areas of Mesoamerica.

Maize

The wild ancestor of maize was a perennial grass named teosinte, which still grows in Central America today. The process of domestication may have started as an unintentional by-product of gathering wild teosinte. What may have happened was that the foragers favored the most harvestable of teosinte grasses, those whose seeds scattered less easily when ripe. In time, this favored type of teosinte would become established near campsites and in abandoned rubbish dumps. In time, too, people would remove weeds from these teosinte stands, then start deliberately planting the more useful types. Eventually, the grass became dependent on human intervention. A genetic revolution followed, which led to maize (see Figure 6.12 on page 168).

Most experts believe maize was first domesticated in Mesoamerica, the earliest known coming from the Río Balsas region of southwestern Mexico, where it dates to before 4000 B.C. Maize from Guilá Naquitz in the Valley of Oaxaca dates to about 3400 B.C. *Zea mays* may have been domesticated in Panama as early as 5000 B.C., but the evidence does not include actual maize cobs.

Figure 6.12 The various stages in the transition from teosinte to maize. **(a)** is the earliest teosinte; **(b)** the stabilized maize phenotype. The harvesting process increased condensation of teosinte branches and led to the husks becoming the enclosures for corn ears.

The most complete archaeological evidence for early maize cultivation comes from the dry caves and open sites of the dry, highland **Tehuacán Valley** in southern Mexico (Figure 6.13). Archaeologist Richard MacNeish found that the earliest Tehuacán people lived mainly by hunting deer and other mammals and also by collecting wild vegetable foods. MacNeish estimated that in 10,000 B.C. 50 to 60 percent of the people's food came from game. After 8000 B.C., the game population declined, and the people turned more and more to wild plant foods. By at least 4500 B.C., about 90 percent of the Tehuacano diet consisted of tropical grasses, and such plants as cacti and maguey. So much grain was necessary that some form of cultivation or domestication of native plants may have been essential by this time. AMS radiocarbon dates on early maize cobs from San Marcos Cave date this staple to at least 3600 B.C.

More than 24,000 maize specimens have come from the caves of the Tehuacán Valley. They document a long sequence of maize evolution, beginning with seventy-one small cobs from the lowest levels of San Marcos Cave and from deep in the **Coxcatlán Cave** (see Figure 6.13). The cobs are less than 20 millimeters (2 inches) long, and lack the ability to disperse their kernels naturally, a clear sign of full domestication. We do not know how many centuries earlier teosinte was transformed into maize, but archaeologist Bruce Smith believes that one place where the process unfolded lay more than 250 kilometers (150 miles) west of Tehuacán, in river valleys that flow from the highlands into the Pacific—areas where the wild teosinte that is most biochemically similar to maize still grows today.

Maize was domesticated in Mesoamerica long before the Pyramids of Giza were built along the Nile River (see Chapter 10). Corn was probably also domesticated in the tropical lowlands, perhaps even earlier than in the highlands, but the evidence is still sketchy.

The primitive form of domesticated eight-rowed maize (*Maiz de ocho*) represented at Tehuacán was the common ancestral corn that spread thousands of miles from its original homeland. Subsequent derivatives of this basic maize developed elsewhere throughout the Americas. If Kent Flannery's hypothesis is correct, plant domestication in Mesoamerica was not so much an invention in one small area as a shift in ecological adaptation deliberately chosen by peoples living where economic strategies necessitated intensive exploitation of plant foods. It appears that the evidence from both Tehuacán and Guilá Naquitz bears out this hypothesis.

Andean Farmers

The story of plant domestication in Mexico shows how it was a deliberate shift in ecological adaptation. The same shift occurred in two areas of the Andean region: in the mountain highlands and along the low-lying, arid Pacific coast.

Figure 6.13 Excavations at Coxcatlán Cave, Tehuacán Valley, Mexico.

The great eighteenth-century German naturalist Alexander von Humboldt was the first European scientist to explore the high Andes. He marveled at the great variety of wild plants and animals that thrived in the harsh and varied landscape of high peaks and mountain valleys. Only a handful of these many species had been tamed by the farmers living in the foothills of the great mountains. Five important Andean species were of vital importance to highland economies: the llama, alpaca, and guinea pig, also the potato and a grain crop, quinoa. Llamas were perhaps domesticated alongside quinoa, perhaps as early as 2500 B.C. (Figure 6.14). Llama herding was widespread throughout the highlands and along the north coast of Peru by 900 B.C. Guinea pigs, an important wild food for many thousands of years, may have been domesticated in high mountain valleys at about the same time.

At the time of European contact in the fifteenth century A.D., Andean farmers used hundreds of potato varieties. Four major strains were domesticated in the highlands, of which one, *Solanum tuberosum*, is now grown all over the world. Wild potatoes were an important food for highland Andean foragers from the time of earliest settlement. Well-documented potato tubers come from midden sites dating to about 2000 B.C. at the mouth of the Casma Valley on the Peruvian coast, but earlier specimens will undoubtedly come to light in the south-central highlands, where other animal and plant species, including lima beans, were domesticated between 3000 and 2000 B.C.

The Peruvian coast forms a narrow shelf at the foot of the Andes, an arid desert strip dissected by river valleys with deep, rich soils and plentiful water for some of the year. For thousands of years, coastal communities lived off the incredible bounty of the Pacific and

Figure 6.14 Panalauca Cave near Lake Jumin, Peru. Excavations here have yielded evidence of early quinoa cultivation and llama domestication by 2500 B.C.

gathered wild plants in summer. Fishing may have assumed greater importance after 5000 B.C., when the climate was warmer and drier than today. By this time the people were also cultivating some plant species like squash, peppers, and tuberous begonias.

At large, more or less permanent coastal settlements like **Chilca** and **Paloma,** fish and mollusks were staples, but the inhabitants also ground up wild grass seeds into flour and grew squashes. By 3800 B.C., the Chilca people were growing several types of beans, including the ubiquitous lima, and squashes. They lived in circular matting and reed huts erected on frameworks of canes or occasionally whale bones. The succeeding millennia saw many permanent settlements established near the Pacific, the people combining agriculture with fishing and mollusk gathering. But fish and sea mammals were so abundant that agriculture remained a secondary activity much later than it did in Mesoamerica.

Within a remarkably short time, more-complex farming societies developed out of the simple village communities of earlier centuries. In some regions, these developments led rapidly to the emergence of state-organized societies, the world's first civilizations. In others, egalitarian farming cultures became elaborate chiefdoms, in remarkably effective adaptations to challenging environments. Chapter 7 examines some of these remarkable societies and the issue of greater cultural complexity in farming societies.

Summary

Southwest Asia was cool and dry immediately after the Ice Age, with dry steppe over much of the interior. Farming began in eastern Turkey and at Abu Hureyra on the Euphrates River in about 10,000 B.C., and sheep and goats replaced gazelle hunting abruptly at the same site and other settlements after 9000 B.C. Herding was well established somewhat earlier in the Zagros highlands, while Anatolia was inhabited by farming communities linked by long-distance exchange routes by at least 9500 B.C.

Agriculture and animal husbandry developed in southeastern Europe because of a local shift to the more intensive exploitation of cereals and wild sheep, and also because of a "drift" of domestic animals and cereals across from Southwest Asia. The flooding of the Euxine Lake may also have contributed to the spread. The widely distributed Bandkeramik complex documents the first settlement of southeastern European farmers in the Middle Danube Valley and on the light **loess** soils of central Europe around 5000 B.C. During the next millennium, food production spread widely throughout Europe, largely in the hands of indigenous foragers, who adopted sheep, pottery, and cereals, which they considered of immediate advantage to them.

Food production was probably introduced into Egypt's Nile Valley at a time of drought, by 7000 B.C. As the Sahara Desert dried up after 3000 B.C., pastoralists with cereal crops moved south of the desert, introducing cattle herding as far south as the East African highlands. In southern China, rice was apparently cultivated as early as 9500 B.C. Widespread rice agriculture was well established by 6500 B.C. The staple in the Haung Ho Valley of northern China was millet, cultivated at least as early as 6500 B.C., and perhaps much earlier.

There were at least three centers of early cultivation in the Americas, the Andes, Central America, and southeastern North America. Maize was the most important cereal, domesticated from a Central American native grass named teosinte as early as 4000 B.C. Maize agriculture spread from southern Mexico and Guatemala thousands of miles to the north and south. There were farmers in the highland Andes and in coastal Peru by 3000 B.C., but maize did not become a vital cultivated staple until about a thousand years later.

2.5 Million   1.0 Million   500,000 B.P.   100,000 B.P.   50,000 B.P.   15,000 B.P.   A.D. 1   A.D. 1950

PROLOGUE

In 1879, Frank Cushing, a young anthropologist from the Smithsonian Institution, arrived at Zuñi pueblo on a mule. A pall of wood smoke covered the town as the sun set behind the settlement. The mud-brick walls melted into the landscape. He wrote: "It seemed still a little island of mesas, one upon the other, reared from a sea of sand, in mock rivalry of the surrounding grander mesas of Nature's rearing." A pioneer of the anthropological method known as participant observation, Cushing lived among the Zuñi for four-and-a-half years, learning their language and recording their traditional life in great detail.

After three years, the Zuñi initiated him into the secret Priesthood of the Bow. Cushing now dressed in Indian clothing. He spent many hours sitting in kivas watching "the blazes of the splinter-lit fire on the stone altar, sometimes licking the very ladder-poles in their flight upward toward the skyhole, which served at once as doorway, chimney, and window." He listened to "the shrill calls of the rapidly coming and departing dancers, their wild songs, and the din of the great drum, which fairly jarred the ancient, smoke-blackened rafters" (quotations from Cushing, 1979, pp. 48 and 112).

Frank Cushing enjoyed the confidence of the Zuñi, but unfortunately he died before he could set down his account of their culture. Cushing's observations have been of priceless value to archaeologists, as they work back from the present into the remote past in the American Southwest. Food production was the foundation of the world's earliest civilizations, but agriculture did not lead, invariably, to state-organized societies or cities. As we saw in Chapter 1, the archaeologists of a century ago often thought in linear, evolutionary terms, of an inevitable ladder of human progress from simple hunting and gathering to civilization. This linear approach, with its overtones of cultural superiority and racism, was intellectually bankrupt by 1910. Multilinear evolution, developed a half century later and a common model for studying the past, likens human cultural evolution to a complex tree with many branches leading cultures in many different environments in bewilderingly diverse ways. The branching model argues that no single society, however simple or complex, is superior to another. In other words, civilization, for all its variety as well as social and technological complexity, is only one way of adapting to the world's many environments.

A generation ago, the anthropologist Elman Service made a fundamental distinction between prestate and state-organized societies, dividing the former into bands, tribes, and chiefdoms (see "Ancient Social Organization" box in Chapter 1, page 28). Ferocious academic debates about the nature of tribes and chiefdoms have erupted in recent years, many of them revolving around the relative complexity of chiefdoms both in the ancient and modern worlds. At issue here is not so much stages of social complexity, but the whole issue of complexity itself. This chapter describes several examples of emerging social complexity in the ancient world that did not result in literate civilizations. The chiefdoms surveyed here, from the Pacific Islands and the American Southwest and Southeast, represent a wide range of complexity, which resulted from diverse environmental and cultural circumstances.

Inevitably, multilinear cultural evolution has acquired a somewhat step-like association. Some scholars choose to consider "evolution" a racist and pejorative creation of Western science, ignoring in the process the branchlike model, which allows for many forms of equally successful human society without recourse to ethnocentric or racist assumptions.

Reciprocity and "Big Men"

As we saw in Chapter 1, precise definitions of chiefdoms, or of cultural complexity, are virtually impossible to formulate. There is no question, however, that all more-complex human societies depend heavily on ties of kin and reciprocity for their long-term viability. And all the world's more-intricate ancient societies, whether foragers or farmers, were based on permanent, or at least semipermanent, settlements.

While a considerable degree of cultural complexity arose in some hunter-gatherer societies, like, for example, those of the Chumash of southern California or the Pacific Northwest, the most profound changes in human society arose after the advent of farming. Perhaps the greatest changes in the new farming societies were social and political rather than economic. They stemmed in large part from the necessity for farmers to live in compact, permanent settlements, to adopt sedentary lifeways, and to maintain very close ties to their lands.

Early agricultural villages like Abu Hureyra or Merimda in western Asia, or permanent farming settlements in Mexico's Tehuacán valley, brought households into much closer juxtaposition than ever before. The members of a small forager band could always move away when factional disputes threatened to disrupt the band. Farmers, anchored to their land, did not have such a luxury. As a result, kinship ties, not only of immediate family, but of more distant kin, assumed much greater importance in daily life. Subsistence farming households produce their own food needs, but their survival depends both on cultivating a diversity of soil types and on reciprocal obligations with fellow kin. Reciprocity was vital to survival, for it created networks of obligation between near and more distant kin. These allowed people to ask for help when their crops failed, knowing that one day their kin would need help in turn, and assistance would be given without question.

The ties of kinship, of membership in hereditary clans and lineages, with all their reciprocal obligations, provided not only institutions that allowed for the settlement of domestic disputes, but also mechanisms for the ownership and inheritance of farming and grazing land. The ownership of land was vested not in individual hands, but in a clan or lineage founded by a powerful ancestor. Thus, the relationship between people and their land was closely related to their links to their ancestors, who were the guardians of the soil. It is probably for this reason that early farmers in the Levant and Turkey maintained figurines or the plastered skulls of their forebears (see chapter opener, page 172, Figure 1.11, page 30).

Trade and exchange played an important role in the development of more-complex societies. Everywhere the new farming economies developed, farmers relied increasingly on their neighbors. While late–Ice Age hunter-gatherers traded fine-grained rock and exotic objects over long distances, the more sedentary agriculturalist was forced to obtain many more commodities from elsewhere. These include foodstuffs, game meat and hides, hut poles, obsidian, and other vital materials, to say nothing of ornaments and other rare objects from afar. Complicated exchange networks linked village with village and household with household, narrow trails that carried visitors from one community to the next brought objects bartered from hand to hand over enormous distances. It was such networks that brought Gulf Coast seashells deep into the North American Midwest and obsidian from Turkey to the distant Jordan Valley. The individuals who controlled such exchange networks, or the supplies of key commodities and exotic luxuries, became natural leaders of newly complex village societies.

The earliest farming villages were egalitarian communities, for signs of social ranking do not appear in burials until long after food production took hold. In time, however, this egalitarian form of village life often gave way to new, more complex agricultural societies headed by powerful kin leaders. These were individuals, often shamans or people with extraordinary supernatural powers, linked to their followers by close kin ties and by their ability to reward loyalty with gifts of food and exotic commodities and goods obtained from afar. Anthropologist Marshall Sahlins, who has studied modern-day Pacific Island societies, calls such people "Big Men." They are clever entrepreneurs, whose power is based strictly on their above-average abilities and the loyalty they command from their followers. This loyalty is but transitory, for it does not pass from one generation to the next. This makes for volatile, ever-changing political, economic, and social orders. In time, some Big Men acquired such power that they were able to create hereditary dynasties, which passed chiefly authority from one generation to the next.

Prestate societies of this greater complexity developed in almost every part of the ancient world, in late prehistoric Europe, in sub-Saharan Africa, Polynesia, and parts of North America. Everywhere chieftainships of this type evolved, they were exceptionally volatile, as the reins of political and economic power passed from one chiefly family to another, from one center to the next. None of these elaborate prestate societies was able to maintain tight political, economic, and social control over little more than a local area. It was state-organized societies that achieved such larger-scale integration, which often transcended local ecological zones. Some complex prestate societies, notably those in western Europe, eventually came under the sway of expanding civilizations like that of Rome. Others, like those of Africa, Polynesia, and North America, survived into historic times, until the arrival of European explorers during the Age of Discovery, which began in the fifteenth century A.D.

We cannot hope to describe all the more complex prestate farming societies that developed throughout the world, so we shall confine our discussion to the first settlement of the Pacific and to the emergence of chiefdoms in North America.

Chiefs and Navigators in the Pacific (2000 B.C. to modern times)

By the end of the Ice Age some 15,000 years ago, *Homo sapiens* had settled in most areas of the Old and New Worlds. Only two areas remained uncolonized by human beings. One was Antarctica, not even visited until the eighteenth century A.D., the other the remote islands of Melanesia and Polynesia in the Pacific (Figure 7.1). In Chapter 4, we

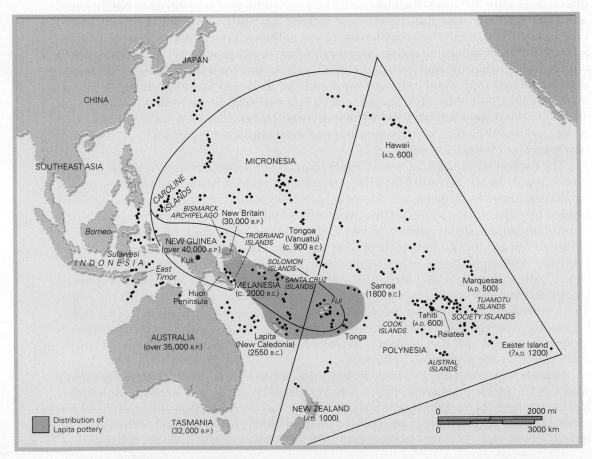

Figure 7.1 Human settlement of the Pacific Islands.

saw how late–Ice Age foragers voyaged across open straits to colonize Sahul and the Solomon Islands. Small groups of them had settled on the islands close to New Guinea, in the Bismarck Archipelago of the southwestern Pacific, by at least 32,000 years ago. Here colonization paused for many thousands of years. The successful settlement of islands even further offshore depended on the development of large offshore sailing craft and the ability to navigate far out of sight of land. It also hinged on the successful cultivation of root crops like taro and yam, and also on small, portable animals like chickens and pigs that could be penned and transported in canoes. These conditions were met by 2000 B.C.

The first settlement of offshore Melanesia and Polynesia was closely connected to the cultivation of yams and taro, which enabled people to live on islands far from the mainland, land masses too isolated for animals or plants to migrate to. The maritime expansion to the more distant Melanesian islands took place after 2000 B.C. and covered 5,000 kilometers (3,100 miles) of island chains and open ocean during a period of six centuries. The voyages took place in ocean-going, double-hulled canoes capable of carrying heavy loads (Figure 7.2). They are associated with the so-called **Lapita culture**, named after a site on New Caledonia Island in the southwestern Pacific. The Lapita people originated in the Bismarck Archipelago region of western Melanesia some millennia earlier. Their canoes carried obsidian, foodstuffs, and other commodities from island to island over long distances. Lapita trade networks were part of a chain of such contacts that extended from Malaysia in the east to coastal New Guinea and offshore.

The rapid expansion to more remote islands occurred among people who lived in an island environment where short inter-island passages were an integral part of daily life. But the journeys to off-lying islands like Fiji and Tonga involved much longer passages, some as many as about 1,000 kilometers (600 miles). Here, one-way journeys may have been rare and trade was at best sporadic. Navigation out of sight of land required expert skills. Canoe navigators became a respected and close-knit group, who passed their knowledge down from generation to generation by word of mouth. Young apprentices acquired their skills over many years of sailing under expert supervision. They learned the angles of rising and setting stars, the trends of ocean swells, the telltale and often inconspicuous phenomena that indicate the general direction and distance of islands.

Figure 7.2 Double-hulled canoes pass in review off Tahiti, as depicted by the eighteenth-century artist Sydney Parkinson, who sailed with Captain James Cook.

From Melanesia, canoes voyaged from island to island through western Polynesia, taking the plants and domesticated animals of their homelands with them. Melanesians voyaged to Micronesia and Polynesia about 2,000 years ago. After a lengthy period of adaptation in western Polynesia, small groups began to settle the more remote islands. The Marquesas were colonized by 200 B.C. and the Society Islands and Tahiti by A.D. 600. The first canoes arrived in Hawaii some 1,350 years ago and on Easter Island by A.D. 1200. New Zealand, the largest and among the most remote of all Pacific islands, has a temperate climate, not the tropical warmth of Polynesia. Despite this ecological difference, New Zealand was first settled by Polynesian ancestors of the Maori people, who voyaged southward, perhaps as early as A.D. 1000. New Zealand's temperate North Island made the cultivation of yams and other tropical island crops difficult, so the early settlers relied heavily on hunting, fishing, and foraging.

Technologically, Micronesia and Polynesia had no metals and relied heavily on stone axes and an elaborate array of bone and shellfish hooks. The crops people planted varied from island to island, but breadfruit, taro, coconut, yams, and bananas were the staples. By combining fish with simple agriculture, the islanders were able to accumulate significant food surpluses that were the basis of powerful chiefdoms. In Polynesia, as elsewhere in the world, agricultural surpluses generated on the larger islands were used as a form of wealth. This wealth, in turn, concentrated political power in the hands of a relatively few people. When European explorers visited Tahiti in the mid-eighteenth century, they chanced on a center of a vigorous eastern Polynesian society (Figure 7.3). The islands were ruled by a powerful hierarchy of warlike chiefs and nobles, descendants of the canoe crews who had

Figure 7.3 A Tahitian temple (*marae*), as drawn by eighteenth-century artist William Watson.

first settled the archipelago. The chiefs acquired prestige by controlling and redistributing wealth and food supplies just as they did in Europe, North America, and elsewhere in the prehistoric world. Their formidable religious and social powers led, inevitably, to intense competition, to warfare, and to ever more ambitious agricultural projects.

Tahitian society was riddled with factionalism and vicious infighting, as were the chiefdoms that developed far to the north, in the Hawaiian Islands, at about the same time. Polynesian chiefdoms were highly volatile and politically unstable. This volatility is well documented in New Zealand, where the introduction of the sweet potato in about A.D. 1400 made a dramatic difference to local life. The population of North Island grew rapidly as agricultural surpluses created new wealth and greater social complexity. Soon, overcrowding on the best sweet potato lands led to intense competition between neighboring chieftains. When Europeans arrived in 1769, they found the Maori people living in fortified villages and engaged in constant warfare (Figure 7.4). Their military campaigns on land and sea were short and violent, often launched from elaborately carved war canoes up to 24.3 meters (80 feet) in length. By this time, warfare was a key element in Maori society, to the extent that it was institutionalized and an important factor in maintaining cohesion and leadership.

The chiefdoms of Polynesia were fully as elaborate and hierarchical as those elsewhere in the ancient world. They were based on kin ties and on communal ownership of land. These were societies in which leadership, even when inherited, depended heavily on the personal qualities of leaders and on their ability to retain the loyalty of their followers. Their chieftains were not despotic monarchs, exercising supreme political, religious, and

Figure 7.4 Maori *pa,* a fortified village, as drawn by nineteenth-century artist Augustus Earle.

economic authority, but people who ruled because of their inborn abilities and because of their close ties to their people. As we shall see in the case of North America, some of these prestate societies achieved remarkable levels of elaboration, but they were very different from the tightly controlled, socially stratified states of western Asia, China, or the Americas, described in Chapters 9 to 14.

The transformation in Maori society that resulted from the introduction of the sweet potato can be mirrored by the history of maize in North America. Both in the Southwest and in the South and Southeast, the arrival of corn led to major changes in indigenous society, but these changes varied greatly from one region to the next. In each area, highly variable ecological factors and social realities led to the development of complex farming societies.

The American Southwest (300 B.C. to modern times)

Chapter 6 describes how maize was domesticated from an indigenous grass called teosinte in southern Mexico before 5000 B.C. and was in common use a millennium later. Maize originated in Mexico and was widely grown by 2500 B.C. The new staple did not, however, spread northward across the Rio Grande into the North American Southwest until some centuries later.

Human occupation of the Southwest dates back to before 9000 B.C. For thousands of years, the descendants of these early southwesterners gathered many plant foods, including yucca seeds, cacti, and sunflower seeds, adapting skillfully to the harsh realities of desert living. They developed a remarkable expertise with all kinds of plant foods, which preadapted them for maize agriculture. Maize, beans, and squash agriculture came to the Southwest from northern Mexico, after generations of sporadic contacts between desert foragers and settled farmers. Knowledge of domesticated plants, even gifts of seeds or seedlings, passed from south to north.

Climatic data from tree rings tells us that between about 2500 and 100 B.C. the southwestern climate was relatively stable, perhaps somewhat wetter than today (see box on pages 182–183). However, it was a semi-arid environment where hunting and gathering were high-risk occupations, mainly because rainfall was always unpredictable.

Domesticated plants like maize and beans might have low yields in these dry environments, but they had one major advantage: They were predictable food sources. Cultivators of the new crops could control their location and their availability at different seasons by storing them carefully. The people living in the southern deserts of the Southwest may have adopted maize and beans as supplementary foods, not because they wanted to become farmers, but so they could become more effective foragers and maximize the potential of their environment.

Maize first entered the Southwest during a period of higher rainfall between 2000 and 1500 B.C. The new crop spread rapidly through the region, especially when combined with beans after 500 B.C. Beans helped return vital nitrogen to the soil, maintaining fertility for longer periods of time. Maize farming in the dry Southwest was never easy, for the farmers were working close to the limits of corn's range. They selected moisture-retaining soils very carefully, used north- and east-facing slopes that received little direct sun, planted near canyon mouths and diverted water from streams and springs. They did everything they could to minimize risk, dispersing their gardens to reduce the danger of local drought or flood. The appearance of maize did not trigger a dramatic revolution in southwestern life. The earlier corns were not very productive, but more bountiful local forms soon became a vital staple to many southwestern groups who were now living in permanent hamlets and much smaller territories. They also led to more complex southwestern societies that adjusted to changing climatic conditions with remarkable flexibility.

Hohokam, Mogollon, and Ancestral Pueblo

By 300 B.C., many centuries of experimentation had produced much more productive domestic crops and a greater dependence on farming. The cultural changes of these centuries culminated in the great southwestern ancestral cultural traditions: Hohokam, Mogollon, and Ancestral Pueblo.

Hohokam people occupied much of what is now lower Arizona. They were desert farmers, who grew not only maize and beans, but cotton, which flourishes in hot environments. Where they could, they practiced irrigation from flowing streams; otherwise they cultivated floodplains and caught runoff from local storms with dams, terraces, and other devices. For centuries, much Hohokam life and trading activity centered around **Snaketown**, a large settlement and ceremonial center near the Gila River (Figure 7.5). The inhabitants maintained trading relationships not only with other parts of the Southwest and with the Pacific coast to the west, but also with Mexico. The Hohokam obtained tropical bird feathers, copper artifacts, and other exotic objects from the south, but scholars are sharply divided on the amount of Mexican influence on Hohokam culture and religious beliefs. The Hohokam vanished after A.D. 1500, its cultural heirs the O'odham people of today.

Figure 7.5 The Hohokam settlement at Snaketown, Arizona, during 1965 excavations, showing circular kivas and dwellings.

SCIENCE

Dendrochronology (Tree-Ring Dating)

Everyone is familiar with tree rings—concentric circles, each circle representing annual growth— visible on the cross section of a felled tree's trunk. These rings are formed by all trees, but especially where seasonal changes in weather are marked, with either a wet and dry season or a definite alternation of summer and winter temperatures. As a rule, trees produce growth rings each year, formed by the cambium, or growth layer, lying between the wood and the bark. When the growing season starts, large cells are added to the wood. These cells develop thicker walls and become smaller as the growing season progresses; by the end of the growth season, cell production has ceased altogether. This process occurs every growing year, and a distinct line is formed between the wood of the previous season, with its small cells, and the wood of the next, with its new, large cells. The thickness of each ring may vary according to the tree's age and annual climatic variations; thick rings are characteristic of good growth years.

Weather variations within a circumscribed area tend to run in cycles. A decade of wet years may be followed by five dry decades. One season may break a forty-year rainfall record. These cycles of climate are reflected in patterns of thicker or thinner tree rings, which are repeated from tree to tree within a limited area. Dendrochronologists have invented sophisticated methods of correlating rings from different trees so they can build up long master sequences of rings from a number of trunks that may extend over many centuries.

Samples are normally collected by cutting a full cross section from an old beam no longer in a structure, by using a special core borer to obtain samples from beams still in a building, or by V-cutting exceptionally large logs. Once in the laboratory, the surface of the sample is leveled to a precise plane. Analyzing tree rings consists of recording individual ring series and then comparing them against other series. Comparisons can be made by eye or by plotting the rings on a uniform scale so that one series can be compared with another. The series so plotted can then be computer-matched with the master tree-ring chronology for the region (Figure 7.6).

Extremely accurate chronologies for southwestern sites come from correlating a master tree-ring sequence from felled trees and dated structures with beams from Indian pueblos. The beams in many such structures have been used again and again, and thus some are very much older than the houses in which they were most recently used for support. The earliest tree rings obtained from such settlements date to the first century B.C., but most timbers were in use between A.D. 1000 and historic times.

Dendrochronology was once confined to the American Southwest, but is now widely used in many other parts of the world, including Alaska, Canada, parts of the eastern United States, England, Ireland, and continental Europe, and also the Aegean Islands and eastern Mediterranean. The Europeans have worked with oak trees with ages of 150 years or more to develop master chronologies for recent times. Using visual and statistical comparisons, they have managed to link living trees to dead specimens serving as church and farmhouse beams and others found well-preserved in bogs and waterlogged peats or prehistoric sites. The resulting tree-ring sequences go back at least 10,021 years in Germany and 7,289 years in Ireland. The Aegean Dendrochronology Project has developed a tree-ring sequence covering 6,000 of the last 8,500 years, which is leading to much more precise dates for the Minoan and Mycenaean civilizations than those suggested by

Mogollon was a more highland cultural tradition, which flourished mainly in what is now New Mexico from about 300 B.C. to between A.D. 850 and 1150. Mogollon farmers relied on direct rainfall and used little irrigation, living in small villages of pit dwellings with timber frames and mat or brush roofs. In only a few areas did more elaborate settlements develop, but by this time Mogollon was becoming part of the western pueblo Ancestral

Figure 7.6 Dendrochronology. Building a tree-ring chronology: (A) a boring taken from a living tree after the 1939 growing season; (B–J) specimens taken from old houses and progressively older ruins. The ring patterns match and overlap back into prehistoric times.

cross-dating or radiocarbon readings. So precise are the master sequences in many areas that an expert can date even short ring cycles to within a handful of years.

Tree-ring chronologies provide records of short-term climatic change in areas such as the American Southwest, where cycles of wetter and drier weather can cause radical changes in settlement patterns. Southwestern chronologies are accurate to within a year, a level of accuracy rarely achieved with archaeological chronologies anywhere. In recent years, the Laboratory of Tree Ring Research at the University of Arizona has undertaken a massive dendroclimatic study that has yielded a reconstruction of relative climatic variability in the Southwest from A.D. 680 to 1970. This enables them to study such phenomena as the "Great Drought" of A.D. 1276 to 1299, which caused many ancestral pueblo peoples to abandon their large pueblos. In 1276, the beginnings of the drought appeared in tree rings in the Northwest. During the next 10 years, very dry conditions expanded over the entire Southwest before improved rainfall arrived after 1299.

Pueblo tradition. **Ancestral Pueblo** (formerly called **Anasazi**) developed out of indigenous forager roots and was centered on the Four Corners area, where Utah, Arizona, Colorado, and New Mexico meet. Ancestral Pueblo people made heavy use of wild plant foods, even after they took up serious maize farming after A.D. 400. Most of their farming depended on seasonal rainfall, although they used irrigation where practicable.

At first the Ancestral Pueblo lived in small pithouse villages, but after A.D. 900 much of the population congregated in above-ground settlements of adjoining rooms. These became the famous pueblos, often clustered in small arcs to make them equidistant from the subterranean ceremonial rooms, the **kivas**, in the middle of the settlement (Figure 7.7). The largest and most spectacular pueblos were located in densely populated areas like Chaco Canyon in New Mexico and Mesa Verde in Arizona. It was in areas like these that Pueblo society sometimes achieved a higher degree of complexity, with larger, densely populated towns that controlled large exchange networks.

Chaco Canyon, with its dramatic cliffs, was the center of a remarkable flowering of Ancestral Pueblo culture that lasted for two centuries after A.D. 900. During this time, the **Chaco phenomenon,** as it is sometimes called, expanded from its canyon homeland to encompass an area of 64,750 square kilometers (25,000 square miles) of the San Juan Basin and adjacent uplands. The people constructed large, well-planned towns, extensive road and water control systems, and outlying sites linked to the canyon at least symbolically by ceremonial roadways and visual communication systems. The "great houses," large pueblos of Chaco Canyon such as **Pueblo Bonito,** contained luxury items, including turquoise from near Santa Fe, seashells, copper bells, even the skeletons of macaws, colorful birds from the lowland rainforests of Mesoamerica much prized for their bright feathers (Figure 7.8).

When Chaco was in its heyday between A.D. 1075 and 1115, the canyon was an important ceremonial center for dozens of outlying settlements. Chaco flourished during a

Figure 7.7 Casa Rinconada in Chaco Canyon, one of the largest kivas known. The roof is, of course, missing.

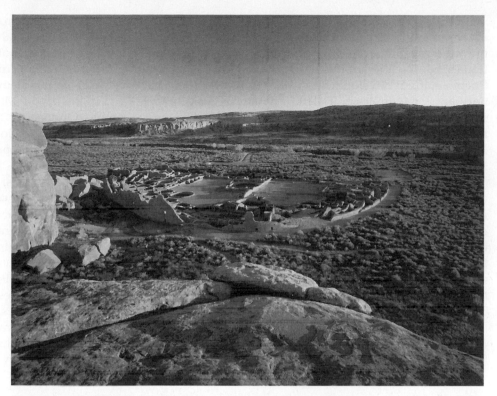

Figure 7.8 Pueblo Bonito, a Chaco Canyon "Great House," dated to between A.D. 850 and 1130. The round structures are kivas.

period of uncertain rainfall, and the local farming land could never have supported more than about 2,000 people, although population estimates for the pueblos rise as high as 5,600. Thus, archaeologists argue, Chaco may have had a relatively small permanent population and been a place where much food was stored and where large crowds of Ancestral Pueblo congregated for major ceremonial observances.

What, then, was Chaco? Was it a highly centralized chieftainship, controlled by a small, but powerful elite of chiefs and nobles, who had a monopoly over trade and important spiritual powers? Or was it what archaeologist Gwinn Vivian calls an egalitarian enterprise, a cooperative mechanism developed by dozens of communities living in a harsh and unpredictable environment? We do not know, but elaborately decorated burials were discovered at Pueblo Bonito by early archaeologists. The Ancestral Pueblo lived in a society where kin ties were all important, where everyone had complex obligations to fulfill both to his own community and to the clan. Without such obligations, it would have been impossible to carry large quantities of food to Chaco's storerooms, or to transport the more than 200,000 wooden beams needed to build its large pueblos and kivas. Perhaps the Chaco phenomenon was an adaptive mechanism whereby local kin leaders regulated and maintained long-distance exchange networks and ceremonial life as a means of supporting far more people than the environment would normally carry. They used economic, social, and ritual ties among a scattered rural population to encourage cooperation between isolated communities in times of need.

The Chaco phenomenon reached its peak between A.D. 1100 and 1130, when a prolonged drought and environmental degradation caused the system to collapse. The Ancestral Pueblo moved away into more dispersed settlements, maintained alliances with one another, or flourished in scattered, independent pueblos. Perhaps the most famous of all Ancestral Pueblo cultural developments is that centered on the Mesa Verde canyon system in the northern San Juan Basin. By 1100, as many as 30,000 people lived in the nearby Montezuma valley, mainly concentrated in villages of 1,000 people or more. Only about 2,500 of them lived in **Mesa Verde.** Between A.D. 1200 and 1300, people moved from open locations into crowded pueblos. **Cliff Palace,** which was the largest settlement, had 220 rooms and 23 kivas (Figure 7.9).

Both in Mesa Verde itself and in the surrounding countryside, large villages, almost towns, were homes for between 1,000 and 2,500 people, living in room clusters associated with kivas and other ceremonial buildings. Everywhere in Mesa Verde, the emphasis was on individual communities. Judging from the numerous kivas, there was considerable cooperative and ritual activity, and there were numerous occasions when inhabitants of different communities organized large labor parties to carry out sophisticated water control works and other communal projects. This Ancestral Pueblo tradition was quite similar to Chaco Canyon, with its intricate mechanisms for integrating dispersed communities, or the chiefdoms of the South and Southeast with their large centers and satellite villages.

The twelfth and thirteenth centuries saw the culmination of four centuries of rapid social and political development in the Mesa Verde region. About 1300, however, the entire San Juan drainage, including Mesa Verde, was abandoned by Pueblan peoples. They moved

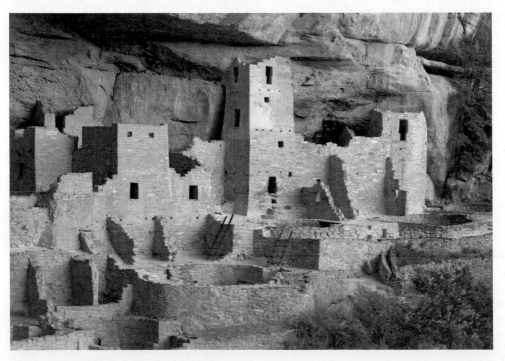

Figure 7.9 Cliff Palace, Mesa Verde, Colorado.

in scattered groups south and southeastward into the lands of the historic Hopi, Zuñi, and Rio Grande pueblos, where their ultimate descendants live to this day. Following the abandonment of large areas of the Southwest in the late thirteenth and early fourteenth centuries, large settlements formed in previously sparsely inhabited areas. Some of these pueblos are recognized as those of direct ancestors of modern communities.

Southwestern pueblo society never achieved the cultural complexity found in eastern North America or among the Hawaiians or Tahitians, but it achieved the limits of regional integration possible for a region where rainfall was irregular and the climate harsh. Perhaps the best way to describe much southwestern organization is as a theocracy, a government that regulated religious and secular affairs through both individuals, like chiefs, and kin groups or associations (societies) that cut across kin lines. The basic social and economic unit was the extended family, but for hundreds of years southwestern peoples fostered a sense of community and undertook communal labors like irrigation works using wider social institutions that worked for the common good.

Moundbuilders in Eastern North America (2000 B.C. to A.D. 1650)

No one knows exactly when maize spread across the southern plains into the eastern woodlands of North America, but at least sporadic corn cultivation may have diffused to the Mississippi River and beyond in the early first millennium A.D. Like all ancient native Americans, eastern groups had developed a great expertise with native plants of every kind soon after first settlement before 3000 B.C. The densest populations gathered by lakes and estuaries, and in the fertile river valleys of the Midwest and Southeast. By 2000 B.C., local river valley populations in some areas had increased to the point that group mobility was restricted, and there were periodic food shortages. Under these circumstances, it was almost inevitable that some groups turned to the deliberate cultivation of native food plants like goosefoot and marsh elder to supplement wild cereal grass yields. At the same time, the first signs of social ranking appear in local burials. We find, also, an increasing preoccupation with burial and life after death. For the first time, individual communities and groups maintained cemeteries on the edges of their territories, which may have served to validate territorial boundaries. As the centuries passed, the funeral rites associated with death and the passage from the world of the living to that of the ancestors became ever more elaborate and important. This elaboration was associated not only with increasing social complexity and an explosion in long-distance exchange, but with the building of ceremonial earthworks as well.

Adena and Hopewell

Thousands of years of long-distance exchange between neighboring communities had given certain raw materials and exotic artifacts high prestige value in eastern North American society. Scarce and hard to come by, such imports were important gifts exchanged between kin leaders and chiefs. They assumed great social value and significance in societies that placed a high premium on prestige. Hammered copper artifacts, conch shells from the Atlantic and Gulf coasts, certain types of stone axes—these became status symbols, buried with their powerful owners at death. By 500 B.C., the individuals who controlled these exchange networks were influential not only in life but in death, for they were buried under large burial mounds.

The **Adena culture,** which flourished in the Ohio Valley between 500 B.C. and about A.D. 400, was one of the first to build extensive earthworks. Adena earthworks follow the contours of flat-topped hills and form circles, squares, and other shapes, enclosing areas as much as 107 meters (350 feet) across. These were ceremonial enclosures rather than defensive works, sometimes built to surround burial mounds, other times standing alone. The most important people were buried in log-lined tombs under burial mounds, their corpses smeared with red ocher or graphite. Nearby lie soapstone pipes and tablets engraved with curving designs or birds of prey. Some prestigious kin leaders were buried inside enclosures or death huts that were burned down as part of the funeral ceremony. Occasionally the burial chamber was left open so that other bodies could be added later.

The building of these mounds was invariably a communal effort, probably involving fellow kin from several settlements who piled up basketfuls of earth. The earthworks grew slowly as generations of new bodies were added. Apparently, only the most important people were interred in the mounds. Most Adena folk were cremated and their ashes placed in the communal burial place.

Between 200 B.C. and A.D. 400, the **Hopewell tradition,** an elaboration of Adena with a distinctive religious ideology, appeared in Ohio. Hopewell burial practices were such a success that they spread rapidly from their heartland as far afield as upper Wisconsin and Louisiana and deep into Illinois and New York State. The Midwest experienced a dramatic flowering of artistic traditions and of long-distance trade that brought copper from the Great Lakes region, obsidian from Yellowstone, and mica from southern Appalachia. The Hopewell people themselves dwelt in relatively small settlements and used only the simplest of artifacts in daily life. They wore leather and woven clothes of pliable fabrics. All the wealth and creative skill of society was lavished on relatively few individuals and their life after death.

At first glance, Hopewell exotic artifacts and ritual traditions seem completely alien to the simple indigenous culture of the area, but they are deeply rooted in local life. The cult objects buried with the dead tell us something of the social interactions of communities and kin groups. Some of the exotic grave goods, such as pipe bowls or ceremonial axes, were buried as gifts from living clan members to a dead leader. Others were personal possessions, cherished weapons, or sometimes symbols of status or wealth. Hopewell graves contain soapstone pipe bowls in the form of beavers, frogs, birds, bears, and even humans. Skilled artisans fashioned thin copper and mica sheets into head and breast ornaments that bear elaborate animal and human motifs (Figure 7.10). There were copper axes and arrowheads, and trinkets and beads fashioned from native copper nuggets, not smelted.

A few specialists manufactured most of these artifacts, perhaps in workshops within large earthwork complexes, themselves close to major sources of raw materials. Ceremonial objects of all kinds were traded from hand to hand throughout Hopewell territory along the same trade routes that carried foodstuffs and everyday objects from hamlet to hamlet. However, the prized manufactures may have passed from one person to another in a vast network of gift-giving transactions that linked different kin leaders with lasting, important obligations to one another. The closest, but very far-fetched, modern analogy to such an arrangement is the famous *kula* ring exchange system of the Trobriand Islands of the southwestern Pacific. There, distinctive types of shell ornaments pass in perennial circles among individuals, linking them in lasting ritual and trading partnerships, in ties of reciprocal obligation. This kind of environment encourages individual initiative and competition, as kin leaders and their followers vie with one another for prestige and social status that is as transitory as life itself. Perhaps somewhat similar practices were commonplace in Hopewell

Figure 7.10 Hopewell sheet-mica ornament in the form of a human hand.

times. Once dead and buried with their prized possessions, the deceased were no longer political players, for their mantles did not necessarily pass to their children or relatives.

Hopewell burial mounds are much more elaborate than those of their Adena forebears (see Figure 7.11 on page 190). Some Hopewell mounds rise 12 meters (40 feet) high and are more than 30 meters (100 feet) across. Often, the builders would deposit a large number of bodies on an earthen platform, burying them over a period of years before erecting a large mound over the dead. Hopewell burial complexes reached imposing sizes. The twenty-four burial mounds at **Mound City,** Ohio, lie inside an earthen enclosure covering 5.26 hectares (13 acres).

The Mississippian Tradition

The center of religious and political power shifted southward after A.D. 400, as the Hopewell tradition declined. It was then that the people of the densely populated and lush Mississippi flood plain may have realized the great potential of maize as a high-yielding food staple. Much of the local diet always came from game, fish, nuts, and wild or cultivated native plants, but maize added a new, and valuable, supplement to the diet; it was demanding to grow, but eventually maize became a vital staple, especially when combined with beans in the late first millennium A.D. Beans had the advantage of a high protein value but also the asset of compensating for the nutritional deficiencies of corn. The new crops assumed greater importance as rising populations, and, perhaps, the insatiable demands of a small but powerful elite, were causing considerable economic and social stress.

Figure 7.11 Circular Hopewell mounds at Mound City national monument, Ohio. Each covers a charnel house where the cremated dead were deposited.

Maize and beans may have been planted initially as supplementary foods, but they differ from native plants such as goosefoot in that they demand more start-up labor to clear land. Within a short time, the river valley landscape was transformed in such a way that hunting and fishing provided less food for energy expended than farming. Major social and political changes and an entirely new economic pattern followed, changing eastern North American society beyond recognition. Thus was born the **Mississippian tradition,** the most elaborate prehistoric cultural tradition to flourish in North America.

Regional Mississippian societies developed in river valleys over much of the Midwest and Southeast and interacted with one another for centuries. Many Mississippian populations lived in fertile river valleys with lakes and swamps. They lived by hunting, fishing, and exploiting migrating waterfowl. Every family harvested nuts and grew maize, beans, squashes, and other crops. The cultivation of native plants like goosefoot and marsh elder, as well as sunflowers—to mention only a few species—was of vital importance. Theirs was a complex adaptation to highly varied local environments. Some groups flourished in small, dispersed homesteads, while others lived in compact villages, some so large they might be called small towns; thousands of people lived near locations like Cahokia, on the banks of the Mississippi opposite the modern city of St. Louis.

Cahokia flourished on the so-called American Bottom, an extremely bountiful flood plain area with a great diversity of food resources and fertile soils. The greatest of all Mississippian centers, Cahokia presided over a population of several thousand people in its heyday after A.D. 1000. The great mounds and plazas of its ceremonial precincts dominated the countryside for miles. Monk's Mound at the center of Cahokia rises 31 meters (102 feet) above the Mississippi floodplain and covers 6.5 hectares (16 acres) (Figure 7.12). On the summit stood a thatched temple at the east end of an enormous plaza. Around the plaza rose other mounds, temples, warehouses, administrative buildings, and the homes of the elite.

Figure 7.12 An artist's reconstruction of the central precincts of Cahokia in its heyday, c. A.D. 1100. Painting by Lloyd K. Townsend.

The entire ceremonial complex of mounds and plazas covered more than 80 hectares (200 acres) and depicted the ancient cosmos of the eastern woodlands, divided into four opposing segments and oriented toward the cardinal points.

Why did Cahokia achieve such political and religious importance? The great center lay at a strategic point close to the Mississippi River and near its confluence with the Missouri, in a region where northern and southern trade routes met. The ruling families of Cahokia achieved enormous political and spiritual power within a few generations, perhaps by virtue of their supernatural abilities as mediators between the spiritual and living worlds, between those on earth and the ancestors. At the same time, they must have been adept traders, with economic and political connections over a wide area. Their political power was sufficient to command the loyalty and labor of satellite settlements and religious centers throughout the American Bottom, to the point that elite families may have lived in subordinate centers, where they presided over critical rituals such as the annual Green Corn festival, which celebrated the new harvest. Sacred figurines and distinctive clay vessels bear motifs that are familiar in later native American religious belief and have deep roots in more ancient cultures.

Although Cahokia was the most elaborate of all Mississippian chiefdoms, its core territory was minuscule by, say, ancient Egyptian standards. Politically volatile, based on ancient religious beliefs, its power and prosperity depended heavily on the authority, charisma, and ability of a handful of rulers. The great center was destined, inevitably, for collapse, which came in about A.D. 1250, when other polities to the south and east rose to a prominence that, however, never rivaled that of the Mississippian's greatest chiefdom.

Cahokia was in the north of Mississippian lands. A major center now developed to the south, at **Moundville** in Alabama (see box on pages 192–193). Dozens of small centers and towns sprang up between the two. More than just sacred places for annual planting and harvest ceremonies, all Mississippian centers were markets and focal points of powerful chiefdoms. For example, Cahokia owed some of its importance to the manufacture and trading of local salt, and chert, a fine-grained rock used to make hoes and other tools.

Moundville, Alabama

Moundville lies by the Black Warrior River in west-central Alabama and flourished between A.D. 1250 and 1500. The site with its twenty-nine or more earthen mounds covers more than 75 hectares (185 acres). The larger mounds delineate a quadrilateral plaza of about 32 hectares (79 acres), some supporting public buildings or residences for important individuals. A few are associated with skull caches, while a sweat house and charnel structure for exposing the dead lie just outside the southern side of the plaza, which is oriented on the cardinal directions. The three sides of the site away from the river were protected by a bastioned and much rebuilt palisade during some of Moundville's history. As at Cahokia, hundreds of people lived within the general site area, perhaps as many as 1,000 souls. Over 3,000 burials have been excavated at Moundville, with the highest-status interments lying in the mounds.

In A.D. 900, a relatively small number of Woodland people lived in the Moundville area at a time of considerable political and economic unrest and increasingly circumscribed territory. The local people relied on nut harvests and other wild foods, until maize production intensified between A.D. 950 to 1000. They dwelt in relatively small settlements, which seem to have grown in size as a response to higher agricultural production, increased production of freshwater shell beads, and warfare.

Between A.D. 1050 and 1250, the first platform mounds appear at Moundville. This was a time when maize and bean agriculture assumed increasing importance, providing as much as 40 percent of the diet. The Black Warrior valley became an important maize farming area as the population dispersed into smaller agricultural communities—some little more than farmsteads, some probably much larger. The Moundville site became an important ceremonial center, the only one in the valley.

In about 1250, the site changed completely in character from a dispersed settlement to a compact, highly formalized and fortified town (Figure 7.13). The inhabitants laid out a quadrilateral plaza with accompanying earthworks arranged in their proper order. They imposed a symbolic landscape on the natural one. Moundville now had an east-west symmetry, a pairing of residential mounds with mortuary temple mounds, and a well-defined ranking of social spaces within the site. By now, Moundville resembled a compact, fortified town inhabited by about 1,000 people living in compact groupings of square pole-and-mud houses. Moundville had expanded from an important ceremonial center to the capital of a single kingdom ruled by a paramount chief, supported by tribute, and engaged in long-distance exchange. The formal layout of public architecture in the heart of the site probably reflected the status relationships of different kin groups set in the context of a sacred landscape. And the paramount chief derived his power both from his supernatural authority and the power conferred on him by the sacred landscape.

For a century and a half after 1300, Moundville was ruled by a firmly entrenched chiefly dynasty, reflected in a series of lavishly adorned burials in its burial mounds. The dynasty's increasing power isolated them both symbolically and practically from their subjects, as the population moved out of the hitherto compact town into the surrounding countryside. Only the elite and their

We know little about how Mississippian society functioned, but each major population center was probably ruled as a series of powerful chiefdoms by an elite group of priests and rulers who lived somewhat separated from the rest of the population. Unlike their recent predecessors, these individuals may have inherited political and economic power, also social position, as the offices of the elite were passed from one generation to the next. The chieftains controlled long-distance trade and were the intermediaries between the living, the ancestors, and the gods.

Figure 7.13 Moundville, Alabama.

retainers seem to have remained at the now unprotected site. No one knows why the people dispersed. It may have been as a result of administrative decision, an adjustment to soil exhaustion, or simply lessened danger of attack. Whatever the cause, Moundville now became a sparsely inhabited ceremonial center and a necropolis, with cemeteries occupying former residential areas. Many of the burials within them came from outlying communities. At the same time, the wide distribution of distinctive cult motifs on clay vessels seems to suggest that more people had access to the religious symbolism of chieftainship than ever before.

Moundville went into decline after 1450, a century before Spanish contact. Elite burial ceased, although a nominal chief may have presided over the site. Perhaps chronic factionalism and resistance to authority among lesser leaders led to the collapse of the once rigid Mississippian hierarchical system, resulting in a patchwork of local chiefdoms, who may have shown some allegiance to a hereditary chief still living among the mounds of his ancestors. Some people still lived at Moundville when Spanish conquistador Hernando de Soto passed through the area in 1540, but we do not know whether a still shadowy chiefdom still existed.

As in the Hopewell culture, high-ranking individuals went to the next world in richly decorated graves, with clusters of ritual objects of different styles that symbolized various clans and tribes. Excavations at Cahokia's burial mound 72 revealed at least six different burial events that involved 261 people, including four mutilated men and 118 women, who were probably retainers sacrificed to accompany a chief in the afterlife. One such chief lay on a layer of thousands of shell beads, accompanied by grave offerings from as far afield as Wisconsin and Tennessee. Cahokia and most other larger Mississippian communities had more or less standardized layouts. The inhabitants built platformlike mounds and capped them with temples and the houses of important individuals. These mounds were grouped around an open plaza, while most people lived in thatched dwellings clustered nearby. As we shall see in Chapter 12, somewhat similar architectural groupings are typical of Mesoamerican ceremonial centers and cities, tempting many earlier scholars to argue that Mississippian chiefs were under strong cultural influence from Mexico, claims now discounted.

Mississippian graves and mound centers contain finely made pottery and other artifacts that bear elaborate designs and distinctive artistic motifs. These artifacts include stone axes with handle and head carved from a single piece of stone, copper pendants adorned with circles and weeping eyes, shell disks carved with woodpeckers and rattlesnakes, elaborately decorated clay pots, and engraved shell cups adorned with male figures in ceremonial dress (Figure 7.14). The themes and motifs on these objects have many common features throughout the South and Southeast and as far afield as the borders of the Ohio valley. At first, experts thought that these ceremonial artifacts represented a **Southern Cult,** that its ideology and motifs like a weeping eye had arrived in North America in the hands of Mexican artisans and priests. But a closer look at indigenous art traditions show that such motifs were commonly used by many North American groups. Many Mississippian ceremonial artifacts served as badges of rank and status, and as clan symbols. They were traded from hand to hand over long distances as symbolic gifts between widely separated chieftains who shared many common religious beliefs.

Figure 7.14 A Mississippian shaman cavorts on a shell gorget (neck ornament). He carries a death's head in one hand and a ceremonial mace in the other. Diameter: 10 centimeters (4 inches).

The Mississippian was an entirely indigenous cultural tradition, the climax of millennia of steady cultural evolution in eastern North America with some significant Mesoamerican influences. Cahokia, Moundville, and other great Mississippian centers were past the height of their powers by the time European explorers reached the Mississippi valley in the sixteenth century. But numerous chiefdoms still flourished in the mid-South and Southeast right up to the time of European contact and beyond. It is interesting to speculate what trajectory the successors of Mississippian society would have taken if Europeans had not arrived. Would they have evolved into a full-fledged, state-organized society, to rival that of the Maya and Aztec to the south? Experts believe they would not have, simply because the growing seasons for maize and beans in North America are too short and the climate too harsh to support either intensive agriculture or high urban population densities under preindustrial conditions. It would have been difficult for any chieftain to accumulate the food surpluses necessary to maintain authority over more than a relatively limited area. In sum, the most important cultural consequences of food production were a long-term trend toward greater political elaboration, a degree of social ranking, and greater interdependency in a wide range of village farming societies.

The trends toward complexity that developed in eastern North America and the Pacific also unfolded in temperate Europe and in sub-Saharan Africa (see Chapter 10). In Europe, the most able of village kin leaders eventually became warrior chieftains and even hereditary leaders ruling from small towns. One catalyst for such development was an explosion in long-distance exchange that coincided with the widespread use of bronze, and later iron—metallurgy that linked even isolated communities together in larger economic, and later political, units. Roman general Julius Caesar's legions found the Iron Age people of western Europe a tough enemy to conquer. Centuries later, the descendants of these people were to shatter Rome's reputation as an invincible power. However, the most momentous consequences of food production were those that led to the emergence of the state-organized society, the urban civilizations that developed in many parts of the world after 3000 B.C., described in Part 4.

Summary

Chiefdoms are hard to define, but were based on ties of kin and reciprocal obligations. The relationships between people and their land were closely linked to kin groups and kin ancestors. In time the egalitarian form of village life gave way to new, more complex agricultural societies headed by powerful kin leaders with charisma or extraordinary supernatural powers. Some of these "Big Men" were able to acquire such power that their chiefdoms became hereditary. Others were based on individual ability and personal loyalties, which perished with their owner's death. Chiefdoms of varying complexity developed in many parts of the ancient world.

Both simple and complex chiefdoms developed on the Pacific islands. Simple root horticulture had been established in highland New Guinea by 6000 B.C. The people of the Lapita cultural complex traded widely through the southwestern Pacific after 1600 B.C., but it was not until the past 2,000 years that offshore outrigger canoes settled Micronesia and Polynesia, and New Zealand was colonized between A.D. 1000 and 1200. Thereafter, increasingly complex chiefdoms developed in island groups like Hawaii and the Society Islands of Polynesia.

More complex societies also developed in the North American Southwest and the eastern Woodlands. Maize agriculture reached the Southwest by about 1500 to 2000 B.C. By 300 B.C., sedentary villages and a much greater dependence on farming were characteristic of the Southwest, leading to the emergence of the Hohokam, Mogollon, and Ancestral Pueblo cultural traditions, among which the ultimate ancestry of modern pueblo peoples lie.

Many groups in eastern North America turned to the deliberate planting of native plants as food supplements after 2000 B.C., but maize and bean agriculture did not arrive from the Southwest until the first millennium B.C. After 1000 B.C., a series of powerful chiefdoms arose in the Southeast and the Midwest, peoples among whom elaborate burial customs and the building of burial mounds and earthworks were commonplace. The Adena tradition appeared in about 700 B.C. and was overlapped by the Hopewell in approximately A.D. 100. About A.D. 800, the focus of economic, religious, and political power shifted to the Mississippi Valley and the Southeast with the rise of the Mississippian tradition. This tradition, with its powerful religious and secular leaders, survived in a modified form until European contact in the sixteenth century A.D.

PART IV   EARLY CIVILIZATIONS

When Enlil, lord of all the lands, had given the kingship of the Land to Lugalzagezi, had directed to him the eyes [of all the people] of the Land from east to west, had prostrated [all the people] for him . . . from the lower sea, along the Tigris [and] Euphrates to the upper sea . . . from east to west, Enlil gave him no rival . . . The Land rejoiced under his rule; all chieftains of Sumer [and lords] of foreign lands bowed down before him.

SUMERIAN VASE COMMEMORATING KING LUGALZAGEZI OF MESOPOTAMIA'S RULE OVER THE ANCIENT WORLD (Kramer, 1963, p. 323)

8 State-Organized Societies

PROLOGUE

Paul Émile Botta was appointed the French consul in Mosul in northern Iraq in 1840, with one official objective: to dig the nearby mounds of biblical Nineveh. Botta had no archaeological qualifications whatsoever, except that he was an experienced traveler who spoke several western Asian languages. At first, he dug fruitlessly into Nineveh, finding nothing but inscribed bricks. Then, one of his workers told him of similar bricks that formed the chimney of his house at a village named Khorsabad, 23 kilometers (14 miles) away. To get rid of the man, he sent two of his laborers to investigate. A week later, they returned with stories of richly carved walls adorned with strange animals. Botta leaped on his horse and rode to Khorsabad, where he gasped at the curious bas-reliefs in the walls of the small pit—of bearded men in long gowns, winged animals, and wild beasts. He moved his excavations to Khorsabad. Within a few weeks, he had uncovered room after room of sculpted limestone slabs, the wall decorations of a magnificent, exotic royal palace. "I believe myself to be the first who had discovered sculptures which with some reason can be referred to the period when Nineveh was flourishing," he wrote excitedly of the palace (Fagan, 1979, p. 127).

We know now that Botta had uncovered not Nineveh but Assyrian King Sargon's palace, constructed at great expense in the eighth century B.C. Even so, Botta's remarkable discoveries ushered in a classical era of nineteenth-century archaeology—which revealed to an astonished world not only the Assyrians but, in addition, the Sumerians, the Maya, the Minoans, the Mycenaeans, and other hitherto-unknown civilizations.

Today, there are no more unknown civilizations to be unearthed, but archaeologists are still striving to understand the origins and workings of the world's earliest states. We know that in about 3100 B.C., the first **state-organized societies** appeared in Egypt and Mesopotamia, ushering in a new chapter in human history (Figure 8.1). The development of the world's first states was a complex process that took many centuries. This chapter defines a state-organized society and discusses some of the factors that contributed to the development of early civilizations. We also examine some of the theories surrounding their origins.

What Is a State-Organized Society?

Everyone who has studied the prehistory of human society agrees that the emergence of civilization in different parts of the world was a major event in human adaptation. The word **civilization** has a ready, everyday meaning. It implies "civility," a measure of decency in the behavior of the individual in a civilization. Such definitions inevitably reflect ethnocentrism or value judgments because what is "civilized" behavior in one civilization might be antisocial or baffling in another. These simplistic understandings are of no use to students of early civilizations seeking basic definitions and cultural processes.

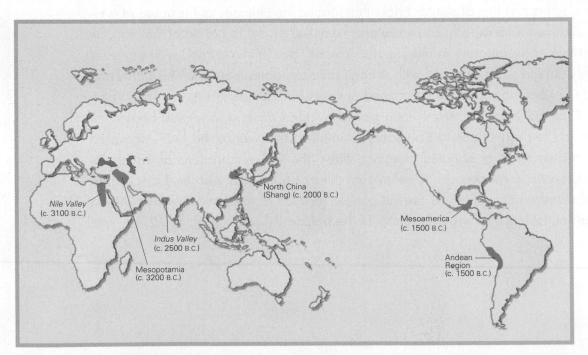

Figure 8.1 Areas of early state formation.

Chronological Table C

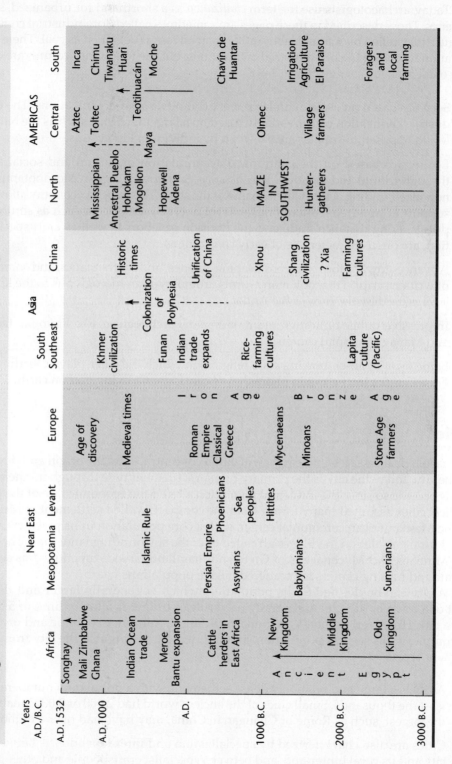

Years A.D./B.C.	Africa	Near East			Europe	Asia			AMERICAS		
		Mesopotamia	Levant			South Southeast	Asia	China	North	Central	South
A.D.1532	Songhay Mali Zimbabwe Ghana				Age of discovery				Mississippian Ancestral Pueblo Hohokam Mogollon	Aztec Toltec	Inca Chimu Tiwanaku Huari
A.D.1000	Indian Ocean trade	Islamic Rule			Medieval times	Khmer civilization	Colonization of Polynesia	Historic times			Teotihuacán Moche
A.D.	Meroe Bantu expansion	Persian Empire Assyrians	Phoenicians Sea peoples Hittites	Iron Age	Roman Empire Classical Greece	Funan Indian trade expands		Unification of China	Hopewell Adena	Maya	Chavín de Huantar
1000 B.C.	Cattle herders in East Africa New Kingdom	Babylonians		Bronze Age	Mycenaeans Minoans	Rice-farming cultures		Xhou Shang civilization	MAIZE IN SOUTHWEST Hunter-gatherers	Olmec	Irrigation Agriculture El Paraiso
2000 B.C.	Ancient Egypt Middle Kingdom Old Kingdom	Sumerians		Age	Stone Age farmers	Lapita culture (Pacific)		? Xia Farming cultures		Village farmers	
3000 B.C.									Foragers and local farming		

201

Today, archaeologists use the term *civilization* as a shorthand for urbanized, state-level societies. Those described in these pages are sometimes called "preindustrial civilizations," because they relied on manual labor rather than on fossil fuels such as coal. There are many variations between the preindustrial civilizations, but the following features are characteristic of all of them:

- Societies based on cities, with large, very complex social organizations. The preindustrial civilization was invariably based on a larger territory, such as the Nile Valley, as opposed to smaller areas owned by individual kin groups.

- Economies based on the centralized accumulation of capital and social status through tribute and taxation. For instance, Sumerian kings in Mesopotamia monopolized trading activity in the name of the state. This type of economy allows the support of hundreds, often thousands, of nonfood producers such as smiths and priests. Long-distance trade and the division of labor, as well as craft specialization, are often characteristic of early civilizations.

- Advances toward formal record keeping, science, and mathematics, and some form of written script. This took many forms, from Egyptian hieroglyphs to the knotted strings used by the Inca of the Andes.

- Impressive public buildings and monumental architecture, like Egyptian temples and Maya ceremonial centers.

- Some form of all-embracing state religion, in which the ruler plays a leading role. For example, the Egyptian pharaoh was considered a living god on earth.

Cities

Archaeological research into early civilization concentrates on the origin and development of the city. Today the city is the primary human settlement type throughout the world, and it has become so since the industrial revolution altered the economic face of the globe. The earliest cities assumed many forms, from the compact, walled settlement of Mesopotamia to the Mesoamerican ceremonial center, with a core population in its precincts and a scattered rural population in villages arranged over the surrounding landscape. The palaces of the Minoans and Mycenaeans of Crete and mainland Greece functioned as secular economic and trading centers for scattered village populations nearby.

A city can be defined by its population, which is generally larger and denser than that of a town or village. A generally used rule of thumb is a lower limit of 5,000 people for a city. However, numbers are not a sufficient definition. Economic and organizational complexity as well as population size and density distinguish the city from other settlement types:

- A city is a large and relatively dense settlement, with a population numbered in at least the thousands. Small cities of the ancient world had 2,000 or 3,000 inhabitants; the largest, such as Rome or Changan in China, may have had over a million.

- Cities are also characterized by specialization and interdependence, between the city and its rural hinterland, and between specialist craftspeople and other groups within the city. The city is a central place in its region, providing services for the villages of the surrounding area, at the same time depending on those villages for food. Most cities, for example, had a marketplace where agricultural produce could be exchanged.

■ Cities also have a degree of organizational complexity well beyond that of small farming communities. There are centralized institutions to regulate internal affairs and ensure security. These usually find expression in monumental architecture such as temples or palaces, or sometimes a city wall. Here we must recognize an overlap between the concept of the city and the concept of the state. States, too, are characterized by centralized institutions. It may be possible to have states without cities, but it is hard to envisage a city that was not embedded within a state.

An ancient city site will usually be obvious to archaeologists, from both its size and the scale of its remains. The state is more difficult to define. It is a political unit governed by a central authority whose power cross-cuts bonds of kinship. Kin groups do not disappear, of course, but their power is reduced, and a new axis of control emerges based on allegiance to a ruling elite.

Theories of the Origins of States

Few developments in world prehistory have generated as much theoretical debate as the origins of states. Modern hypotheses build on theories developed as early as the 1930s.

The "Urban Revolution"

The Victorians, like the Greeks and Romans before them, assumed that civilization had originated along the Nile, in the "Land of the Pharaohs." Eventually, early theorizing used a broader canvas, embracing all of the Fertile Crescent.

The first relatively sophisticated theories about the origins of civilization were formulated by Vere Gordon Childe of "Neolithic Revolution" fame. He wrote of a later "Urban Revolution," which saw the development of metallurgy and the appearance of a new social class of full-time artisans and specialists, who lived in much larger settlements: cities. However, the artisans' products had to be distributed, and raw materials obtained, often from long distances away. Both needs reduced the self-sufficiency of peasant communities, Childe argued. Agricultural techniques became more sophisticated as a higher yield of food per capita was needed to support a growing nonagricultural population. Irrigation increased productivity, leading to centralization of food supplies, production, and distribution. Taxation and tribute led to the accumulation of capital. Ultimately, said Childe, a new class-stratified society came into being, based on economic classes rather than traditional ties of kin. Writing was essential for keeping records and for developing exact and predictive sciences. Transportation by land and water was part of the new order. A unifying religious force dominated urban life as priest kings and despots rose to power. Monumental architecture testified to their activities. Gordon Childe considered technology and the development of craft specialization in the hands of full-time artisans a cornerstone of the Urban Revolution.

Early Ecological Models

With much more data to work with, modern scholars now agree that three elements of Gordon Childe's "Urban Revolution" were of great importance in the development of all the world's early civilizations: large food surpluses, diversified farming economies, and irrigation agriculture.

The Fertile Crescent model assumed that the exceptional fertility of the Mesopotamian flood plain and the Nile valley was the primary cause for the appearance of cities and states in these regions. Larger grain surpluses resulted from increased agricultural efficiency, as well as social and cultural changes. Some scholars, among them the economist Esther Boserup, took the opposite tack. They believed that population growth, not food surplus, was the incentive for intensified agriculture and eventually more-complex societies. But, though important, dense populations did not characterize all state-organized societies, as the Mycenaean or Inca civilizations show.

The same theorists pointed out how the ecological diversity of local environments varied greatly from one area to another. Diversified agricultural economies tended to focus on fewer, more productive crops, but the ultimate subsistence base remained wide. For instance, the Egyptians farmed wheat and barley on a large scale, but also raised large herds of cattle and goats. The highland Andean states relied heavily on their lowland neighbors for fish meal, cotton, and other resources. The resulting diversity of food resources protected the people against famine and stimulated trade and exchange for food and other products, as well as the growth of distributive organizations that encouraged centralized authority.

The adoption of irrigation agriculture was also considered a major factor in the rise of civilization since it supported far higher population densities. Early ecological theories were closely tied to the apparent widespread use of irrigation agriculture by early states to enhance agricultural output. Anthropologist Julian Steward and historian Karl Wittfogel argued during the 1950s that irrigation lay behind the development of socially stratified societies in Egypt, Mesopotamia, and elsewhere, which Wittfogel famously called "hydraulic civilizations." In areas where irrigation was practiced, both scholars argued, the relationship between the environment, food production, and social institutions was identical. Wittfogel was a China specialist, who believed that early Asian civilizations became "mighty hydraulic bureaucracies," which owed their despotic control over densely populated areas like China, Egypt, and India to the technological and environmental demands required by large-scale water control projects in areas of scant rainfall. Thus, the social requirements of irrigation led to the development of states and urban societies in several parts of the Old World. And the same requirements led to remarkable similarities in their economic and social structure.

A mass of new data, including large-scale landscape surveys, has sharpened our perceptions of early irrigation. For example, archaeologist Robert Adams carried out major field surveys of ancient irrigation works in Mesopotamia in the 1960s. Adams found that early Mesopotamian irrigation consisted of cleaning natural river channels and building just a few smaller feeder canals. Most settlements lay near major rivers and made the most of the natural hydrology of the waterways. Each community controlled its own small-scale irrigation works. Only centuries later did a highly centralized state government organize irrigation schemes on a massive scale. The same was true of Egypt, where the greatest irrigation works were undertaken during the New Kingdom, using thousands of laborers fulfilling tax obligations to the state. In contrast, early Egyptian agriculture relied on natural basins to hold back Nile water: a village-level, small-scale operation requiring no official supervision.

While some form of irrigation was a necessary precondition for the settlement of the southern Mesopotamian plains, where the world's first cities arose, large-scale irrigation does not everywhere appear to have been a factor in the rise of early civilization. By the same token, modern researchers have shown that ecology was only one component in a mosaic of many changes that led to state-organized societies.

Technology and Trade

The origins and evolution of complex societies have long been linked to technological innovation and to growing trade in raw materials like obsidian, copper, and luxuries of all kinds. Gordon Childe considered metallurgy an important component in the Urban Revolution, but, in fact, copper and other exotic materials were at first used in southwest Asia for small-scale production of cult objects and jewelry. In many cases the technological innovations that did appear, like the wheel in Mesopotamia and the sailing ship in Egypt, were of more benefit in transportation than production. Not until several centuries after civilization started were copper and bronze more abundant as demands for transportation and military needs burgeoned. Technology did evolve, but only in response to developing markets, new demands, and the expanded needs of a tiny segment of the population—the elite.

Any form of trade involves two elements, both the goods and commodities being exchanged and the people doing the exchanging. People make trade connections when they need to acquire goods and services that are not available to them within their local area. This trade (more conventionally called "exchange") can be gift-giving, the exchange of gifts that reinforce a social relationship between both individuals and groups as a whole. The gifts serve as gestures that place obligations on both parties and are often a preliminary to bartering for all manner of commodities. This kind of preliminary gift exchange is commonplace in New Guinea and the Pacific and was widespread in Africa during the past 2,000 years. Bartering, the exchange of commodities or goods, was another basic trading mechanism for many thousands of years, often sporadic, and usually based on notions of reciprocity, the mutual exchange of commodities or objects between individuals or groups. Redistribution of these goods through society lay in the hands of chiefs, religious leaders, or kin groups. As we have seen, such redistribution was a basic element in chiefdoms. The change from redistribution to impersonal market economy trade, often based on regulated commerce, involving, perhaps, fixed prices, even currency, was a change closely tied to growing political and social complexity, and hence, to the development of the state.

In the 1970s, a number of archaeologists gave trade a primary role in the rise of states. In the Aegean area, British archaeologist Colin Renfrew attributed the dramatic flowering of Minoan civilization on Crete and through the Aegean to intensified trading contacts and to the impact of olive and vine cultivation on local communities. As agricultural economies became more diversified and local food supplies could be purchased both locally and over longer distances, a far-reaching economic interdependence resulted. Eventually, this led to redistribution systems for luxuries and basic commodities, systems that were organized and controlled by Minoan palaces and elsewhere in the Aegean where there were major centers of olive production.

SCIENCE

Obsidian Sourcing

Scientists studied the sources of toolmaking stone long before the advent of spectrographic analysis, relying both on petrology and on distinctive rocks, like the butter-colored and easily recognized Grand Pressigny flint, widely used in France by Stone Age farmers. High-tech analytical methods have revolutionized sourcing since the 1960s, when British archaeologist Colin Renfrew and others used spectrographic analysis to identify no fewer than twelve early farming villages that had obtained obsidian (volcanic glass) from the Ciftlik area of central Turkey (Figure 8.2).

This pioneer study showed that 80 percent of the chipped stone in villages within 300 kilometers (186 miles) of Ciftlik was obsidian. Outside this "supply zone," the percentages of obsidian dropped away sharply with distance, to 5 percent in a Syrian village and 0.1 percent in the Jordan valley (Figure 8.2). If these calculations were correct, each village was passing about half its

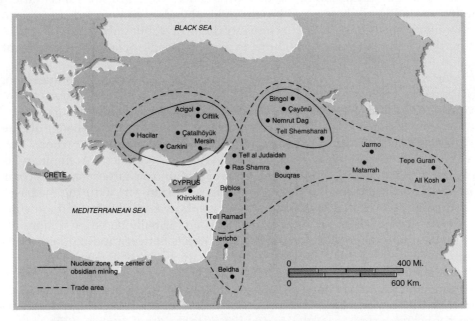

Figure 8.2 Obsidian trade in the Mediterranean region. Sourcing studies reveal that early farming communities in Cyprus, Anatolia (Turkey), and the Levant obtained their obsidian from two sources in central Anatolia. Meanwhile, villages such as Jarmo in the Zagros mountains and Ali Kosh far to the southeast relied on sources in Armenia. Settlements such as Çatalhöyük in Anatolia were so close to obsidian sources that they probably collected their own supplies. More than 80 percent of their stone artifacts are made of the material, while obsidian tools are much rarer down the line, the further the line travels from the source.

imported obsidian further down the line. Renfrew and his colleagues identified no fewer than nine obsidian "interaction zones" between Sardinia and Mesopotamia, each of them linked to well-defined sources of supply, each yielding obsidian with its own distinctive trace elements identifiable spectrographically.

Obsidian sourcing is now a commonplace method of tracing ancient exchange, and it has been applied successfully in many parts of the world, among them California and Mesoamerica (Figure 8.3).

Figure 8.3 Obsidian mirror from Mesoamerica.

Now that we know much more about ancient exchange and commerce, we know that trade can never be looked upon as a unifying factor or as a primary cause of ancient civilization, simply because no one aspect of it was an overriding cause of cultural change or evolution in trading practices. Extensive long-distance trade, like large-scale irrigation, was a consequence rather than a cause of civilization.

Warfare

In the 1970s, anthropologist Robert Carneiro used the archaeology of coastal valleys in Peru to argue that warfare played a key role in state formation. His "coercive theory" of state origins argued that the amount of agricultural land in these valleys was limited and surrounded by desert. So a series of predictable events led to the development of states. At first, autonomous farming villages flourished in the valley landscape. But as the population grew and more land was taken up, the communities started fighting over land and raided each others' fields as they competed for limited acreage. Some of the village leaders emerged as successful warlords, became chieftains, and presided over large tribal polities. The valley population continued to grow, and warfare intensified until the entire region fell under the sway of a single, successful warrior, who presided over a single state centered on the valley. Then this ambitious ruler and his successors start raiding neighboring valleys. Eventually a multivalley state developed, creating a much larger civilization.

Carneiro's theory is hard to test in the field, but an attempt to do so in Peru's Santa valley showed no sign of autonomous villages. Rather, it depicted a much more complex, evolving settlement pattern over many centuries. Archaeologist David Wilson points out that the only "coercive" processes came about in about A.D. 400, when the Moche people carved out a multivalley state by military conquest of neighboring valleys (Chapter 14). The conquest took place long after complex irrigation-based societies flourished in the Santa valley. As with irrigation hypotheses, reality is more complex than the straightforward Carneiro scenario.

Warfare also can be rejected as a primary cause of civilization on other grounds. In earlier times, the diffuse social organization of village communities had not yet led to the institutional warfare that resulted from the concentration of wealth and power in a few hands. There was raiding and violent conflict between kingdoms almost everywhere before state formation, which may have had a profound effect on peoples' lives, but other powerful factors were simultaneously at play. Only when absolute and despotic monarchs came into power did warfare become endemic, with standing armies to control important resources, solve political questions, and ensure social inequality. This type of warfare presupposes authority and is a consequence of civilization.

Cultural Systems and Civilization

Most archaeologists agree that urban life and preindustrial civilization came into existence gradually, during a period of major social and economic change. Everyone agrees, also, that linear explanations invoking irrigation, trade, or warfare are inadequate. Recent theories of the rise of states invoke multiple, and often intricate, causes and are frequently based on systems models.

In the 1960s, Robert Adams, an expert on ancient Mesopotamia, introduced a new generation of complex theories when he argued that irrigation agriculture, increased warfare, and "local resource variability" were three factors vital in newly appearing urban civilizations. Each affected society and the other factors with positive feedback, helping to reinforce each other. The creation of food surpluses and the emergence of a stratified society were critical developments. Irrigation agriculture could feed a bigger population. Larger populations, an increase in permanent settlement, and trade with regular centers for redistributing goods were all pressures for greater production and increased surpluses, actively fostered by dominant groups in society. The greatly enlarged surpluses enabled those who controlled them to employ larger numbers of artisans and other specialists who did not themselves grow crops.

Adams argued that some societies were better able to transform themselves into states because of the favorable variety of resources on which they could draw. Higher populations led to monopolies over strategic resources. These communities eventually were more powerful than their neighbors, expanding their territories by military campaigns and efficiently exploiting their advantages over other peoples. Such cities became early centers of major religious activities, of technological and artistic innovations, and of writing. Literacy, a skill confined to a few people, became an important source of power.

Archaeologists like Kent Flannery, who works in Mesoamerica, now saw the state as a very complicated "living" system, the complexity of which could be measured by the internal differentiation and intricacy of its subsystems, such as those for agriculture, technology, or religious beliefs. The way these subsystems were linked, and the controls that society imposed on the system, were vital. This model seemed to work well with Mesoamerican states, where pervasive religious beliefs formed close links between public architecture, the economy, and other subsystems of civilization.

The management of a state is a far more elaborate and central undertaking than that of a small-scale society. Indeed, the most striking difference between states and less-complicated societies is the degree of complexity in civilizations' ways of reaching decisions and in their hierarchic organization, not necessarily in their subsistence activities. Systems models of early states are bound to be complex, for they have to distinguish between mechanisms and processes of cultural change, and the socioenvironmental pressures by which we have sought to explain the origins of civilization. Religion and control of information now appear to be key elements in the regulation of environmental and economic variables in early civilizations, and, indeed in any human society.

Environmental Change

Ecologically based theories, which also rely heavily on systems approaches, have enjoyed a relatively long life compared with many other hypotheses. For example, in a classic study of the Valley of Mexico, William Sanders and a group of archaeologists showed how the Aztec state created and organized huge agricultural systems that spread over the shallow waters of the lakes that once filled the valley. The variability of the local environment meant that the Aztecs had to exploit every environmental opportunity afforded them. Thus, Sanders argues, the state organized large-scale agriculture to support a population of up to 250,000 in and close to the Aztec capital, Tenochtitlán. Environmental factors were decisive in each area where civilization began, he believes. Another important factor was centralized leadership.

The ecological approach has serious problems. How, for example, does one tell which environments would foster state formation? Fertile flood plains like those in Mesopotamia and Egypt? Coastal river valleys like those in Peru? Highland plateaus like those of Mesoamerica? Or areas where land is in short supply (also coastal Peru)? States have arisen in regions where there are few geographical constraints, like the Maya lowlands of Mesoamerica. Further, preindustrial civilizations have developed without any sign of rapid population growth, in Iran and other parts of Southwest Asia. But there can be no doubt that environmental factors were major players in a very complex process of cultural change and response.

Social Approaches: Power in Three Domains

In recent years, archaeology has shifted away from systems-ecological approaches toward a greater concern with individuals and groups. The former theories have often been somewhat impersonal, treating states as rather mechanical entities that operated according to complex processes of cultural change. A new generation of researchers is carrying social approaches and the study of power in new directions, arguing that all human societies consist, ultimately, of individuals and groups interacting with one another, and each pursuing their own agendas.

Archaeologically, one can look at power in three domains: economic power, social and ideological power, and political power. The combination of economic productivity, control over sources and distribution of food and wealth, the development and maintenance of the stratified social system and its ideology, and the ability to maintain control by force were the vital ingredients of early states. Each of these domains was closely linked to the others, but they can be studied separately in the archaeological record.

Economic power depends on the ability to organize more-specialized production and the diverse tasks of food storage and food distribution. In time, stored wealth in food and goods develops into relationships of dependency between those who produce or acquire the wealth and those who control and distribute it. A state comprises elites (the noble class), officials (the managers), and dependents (the commoners). The land-owning class and the estate—whether owned by a temple, the ruler, or a private individual—provided security for the estate's dependents. All early states developed from foundations where agricultural production became more intensified and diverse. At the same time, early states moved away from purely kin-based organization into centralized structures that crosscut or overrode kinship ties.

Economic power also rested in trade and long-distance exchange networks, which provided access to commodities that were not available locally. Sumer obtained its metal from Anatolia, Iran, and the Persian Gulf. Egypt acquired gold and ivory from Nubia (the modern-day Sudan). Highland Andean civilizations imported fish meal from the Pacific coast. The acquisition of exotic commodities or goods on any scale required organization, record keeping, and supervision. The archaeological record shows that the extent of state supervision of trade and traders varied considerably from civilization to civilization.

Social power means ideological power, and comes from the creation or modification of certain symbols of cultural and political commonality. Such common ideology, expressed in public and private ceremonies, in art and architecture, and in literature, served to link individuals and communities with common ties that transcend those of kin. Those who create and perpetuate these ideologies are held in high honor and enjoy considerable prestige, for they are often perceived as interceding with the spiritual world and the deities, and sometimes even seen as flesh and blood divines themselves. The guardians of ideology are privileged individuals, for their spiritual powers give them special social status and allow them to perpetuate social inequality.

So important was ideology that one can speak of the Mesopotamian or Maya areas not in a political sense, for they were made up of patchworks of city-states, but in an ideological one. Many great cities of the past, like the Maya city at Tikal in Guatemala, were a combination of the spiritual and the secular. They all boasted powerful priesthoods and religious institutions, which owed their wealth to their ability to manage the spiritual affairs of the state and to legitimize rulers as upholders of the cosmic order. The temples and public buildings they erected formed imposing settings for elaborate public ceremonies that ensured the continuity of human life and the universe (Figure 8.4).

Political power rested in the ruler's ability to impose authority throughout society by both administrative and military means. Those who held positions of authority within either the bureaucracy or the army did not come from within the kin system, but were recruited outside it. This political power lay in foreign relations and in defense and making war. It also operated at a statewide level, dealing with the resolution of major disputes between different factions. But a great deal of power lay outside the political estate, in the hands of community and kin leaders who handled many legal matters revolving around such issues as land ownership and family law.

Archaeologist Norman Yoffee believes that the interplay between these three sources of power led to the development of new, societywide institutions—to supreme rulers and the state. There was, he says, no one moment when civilization came into being, for social evolution did not end with the rise of the state. Preindustrial states functioned in an

Figure 8.4 The central precincts of Tikal, Guatemala, once a symbolic depiction of the Maya spiritual world.

atmosphere of continual change and constant disputation. Some collapsed, others survived for many centuries.

This approach to the origin of states argues for many trajectories for the development of social complexity. Many societies operated under significant constraints; they may have lacked, say, dependable crops or domesticated animals or the ability to store large amounts of food. Constraints like these took human societies along very different evolutionary paths than those of the state. That some societies did not become civilizations does not mean that they were stuck in a backward "stage," but simply that constraints on growth prevented the interplay of the major factors that led to state formation elsewhere. Thus, the chiefdom is an alternative trajectory to the state. In the chiefdom, social inequality came from within the kin system; in the state, inequality was based on access to resources and the power this control provided.

Factionalism and Ideology

Every early civilization had a pervasive set of religious beliefs and philosophies that reached out to every corner of society. Such ideologies shaped society and ensured the conformity of its members, but to study such intangibles is a formidable task. Ideologies come down to us in distinctive art styles, like those of the Egyptians, or the Moche art style of the Andes (Figure 8.5). Such styles are visual reminders of a state's ideology, reinforcing the power of supreme rulers and their special relationships to the gods and the spiritual world. In societies where only a minority, those with power, are literate (or have scribes in their employ), art and public architecture have powerful roles to play in shaping society and reinforcing ideology.

The Maya elite lived in cities like Copán and Tikal, which were depictions in stone, wood, and stucco of a symbolic landscape of sacred hills, caves, and forests. Here, great lords appeared before the people atop high pyramids in elaborate public ceremonies (see Figure 8.4 on page 211). Through ritual bloodletting and shamanistic trance, they entered the realm of the Otherworld, the world of the deities and ancestors. These sacred rituals validated the world of the Maya, and linked noble and commoner, ruler and humble village farmer in a complex social contract. The leaders were the intermediaries, the people who interceded with the gods to guarantee plentiful crops and ensure the continued existence of human life. The ceremonial centers, with their pyramids, plazas, and temples, were reassuring settings where the drama of life and death, of planting and harvest were played out against a backdrop of ever-changing seasons. These ceremonies justified social inequality, the great distinctions between the ruler and the ruled.

Ancient ideologies were as complex as our own, and they defy ready archaeological analysis by their very complexity and nonmaterial nature. The recent decipherment of Maya script has shown just how important and pervasive ideologies were in ancient civilizations. Until decipherment, most authorities assumed Maya rulers were peaceful priest-kings, who used their power as astronomers to preside over small city-states. But Maya glyphs reveal an intricate and complex pantheon of deities, and religious beliefs that often defy modern analysis. Each day in the Maya calendar possessed a combination of qualities; every compass direction had colors and characteristics; each deity had many roles and moods. Nothing in Maya society occurred without acquiring symbolic and often ideological meaning. In Egypt, too, the ancient precedents of the pharaohs' rule and the teachings of the gods permeated all society and governed even the collection of taxes and the distribution of rations.

Figure 8.5 Artifacts as ideological statements. A Moche ceramic vessel from coastal Peru, c. A.D. 400, depicts a man, probably a shaman, dressed as a deer and carrying a ceremonial mace.

With ideology comes factionalism. As we have seen, ancient societies were as diverse as modern ones, especially when their rulers traded with neighbors near and far. The state functioned for the benefit of a minority—privileged rulers and nobles to whom all wealth and power flowed. A ruler governed his domains by deputing governance to relatives and loyal followers who became provincial governors. But, inevitably, some individuals were more ambitious than others, rebelling against authority, plotting to gain supreme power. Competing factions within local groups and in different regions triggered further social inequality and changing patterns of leadership, increased specialization, and the development of states. And once civilizations came into being, they would challenge royal successions, even trigger civil war when a ruler was perceived as weak or indecisive. Competition and emerging factionalism were powerful catalysts in the development of many early states. One can imagine the maneuvering and plotting at an Egyptian pharaoh's court, at a time when life expectancies were short and sudden death possible at any time. Everyone wanted to be in a favorable position when a successor came to the throne.

In an era when archaeological research has become increasingly specialized, it is probably futile to search for a theory of state formation that can be applied to all civilizations. There are some common questions, however, that revolve around the implications of ecological variables in societies about to become states: How is ecological opportunity or necessity translated into political change? What were the larger goals of the political actors who were pursuing their individual goals while states were coming into being? Which ecological variables were obstacles? Which were opportunities? The answers to these questions will come from sophisticated researches that combine systems-ecological approaches with careful research into what British archaeologist Colin Renfrew has called "the archaeology of mind," the elusive intangibles behind the material record of the past.

People as Agents of Change

For all our talk of "cultural processes," we must never forget that it is people—individuals and groups—who are the agents of political and other cultural change. History is made by peoples with individuals of exceptional ability and leadership qualities. No question, such people also came to positions of great power in the early civilizations, but many of them remain anonymous because written records are very incomplete. In some cases, for example Egypt, we know the names of seminal rulers like the early pharaoh Narmer, but they are little more than shadowy personages on the stage of history. More modern examples include the Zulu King Shaka, who set up the Zulu state in South Africa in the early nineteenth century, King Kamehameha of Hawaii, and others. All of them, whether ancient or more modern, were individuals who were products of their times, whose personal abilities made the most of unusual circumstances, accidental situations, and other moments where they could further their political and military goals. The result was, invariably, a process of historical change.

Distinctive qualities marked Shaka and other modern agents of change that were shared by the chiefs of unusual ability who created the first civilizations. They were members of an elite, people with aggressive and authoritarian personalities, with outstanding military abilities that gave them upward social mobility. They usurped the position of chief by fair means or foul, then conquered their immediate neighbors, while seeking a competitive advantage over more distant rivals (this could be technological, a matter of military strategy, and so on). They used this advantage to expand into more distant lands, while using forced labor to intensify agricultural production, as a means of keeping one's subjects content and of provisioning armies. If they could not intensify their food production, they acquired additional resources by raiding. Finally, they solidified their position by power-sharing, even if it was nothing more than a nominal gesture. This was definitely not democracy, for the earliest states were ruled by strong, able rulers who governed autocratically, even if they had nominal councils of advisers.

Much depends on ideology, too, for invariably the preindustrial states were held together by a powerful and distinctive ideology. The famous *Epic of Gilgamesh* gives us a flavor of Mesopotamian ideology. The pharaohs ruled as the living personification of the sun god. Maya lords were shamans and intermediaries between the people and the ancestors. These ideologies were reflected in sacred places, where lavish ceremonies and public appearances by the ruler were important symbols of continuity and stability, where the ruler's subjects directed their loyalty to the central figure at the pinnacle of the state. Ideology never caused states to come into being, but were an invariable and important part of their fabric once they were established.

Both processes and individual agents played vital roles in the formation of states. Aggressive individuals of great ambition have been members of human societies since the beginning, but, until about 6,000 years ago, they never lived at a time when conditions of social inequality and chiefly competition were endemic in areas like Mesopotamia and the Nile valley, or later in Mesoamerica and the Andes. Then, competitive advantage, military prowess, and other circumstances turned a very few of them from powerful chiefs into authoritarian kings, soon supported by compelling new ideologies developed from earlier and less complex world views.

The Collapse of Civilizations

Many historians have written about cycles of history, the rise of civilizations, their brilliant apogees, and their sudden declines. Eventually one civilization falls and another rises to take its place, which in turn goes through the same cycle of rise and fall. The record of early civilizations could easily be written in cyclical terms, for states have risen and then collapsed with bewildering rapidity in all parts of the world within the past 5,000 years. In the Mexican highlands, for example, the great city of Teotihuacán flourished between about 200 B.C. and A.D. 700. In A.D. 600, it had a population of more than 125,000 people. For 600 years, more than 85 percent of the population of the Valley of Mexico lived in or close to Teotihuacán (Figure 8.6). Then the city collapsed in the eighth century A.D. Within half a century, the population shrank to a quarter of its former size.

Figure 8.6 The Pyramid of the Sun at Teotihuacán, Mexico, a vast edifice erected as a sacred mountain to mirror the peak behind it, which was still a sacred place 800 years after the city collapsed, c. A.D. 750.

When a complex society collapses, it suddenly becomes smaller, simpler, and much more egalitarian. Population densities fall; trade and economic activity dries up; information flow declines; and the known world shrinks for the survivors. Joseph Tainter, one of the few archaeologists to have made a comparative study of collapse, points out that an initial investment by a society in growing complexity is a rational way of trying to solve the needs of the moment. At first the strategy works. Agricultural production increases through more intensive farming methods; an emerging bureaucracy works well; expanding trade networks bring wealth to a new elite, who use their authority and economic clout to undertake great public works, such as pyramids and temples, which validate their spiritual authority and divine associations.

As the most costly solutions to society's needs are exhausted, so does it become imperative that new organizational and economic answers be found, which may have much lower yields and cost a great deal more. As these stresses develop, argues Tainter, a complex society such as that of the Maya is increasingly vulnerable to collapse. There are few reserves to carry society through droughts, famines, floods, or other natural disasters. Eventually, collapse ensues, especially when important segments of society perceive that centralization and social complexity simply do not work any more and that they are better off on their own. The trend toward decentralization, toward collapse, becomes compelling. Collapse is not a catastrophe but a rational process that occurs when increasing stress requires some organizational change. The population decline and other catastrophic effects that just preceded, accompanied, or followed collapse may have been traumatic at the time, but they can be looked at as part of what one might call an economizing process.

There is, of course, more to collapse than merely an economizing process. Complete collapse can occur only under circumstances in which there is a power vacuum. In many cases, there may be a powerful neighbor waiting in the wings. In early times, numerous city-states traded and competed with one another within a small area. Sumerian cities, Minoan and Mycenaean palace-kingdoms in Greece and the Aegean, the Maya in Mesoamerica—all lived in close interdependence within their culture areas, in a state of constant "peer-polity interaction." They traded, fought, and engaged in constant diplomacy. Under these circumstances, to collapse is an invitation to be dominated by one's competitors. There is only loss of complexity when every polity in the interacting cluster collapses at the same time.

The collapse of early civilizations may, then, be closely connected to declining returns from social complexity, and to the normal political processes of factionalism, social unrest, succession disputes, even civil war.

Summary

Chapter 8 contrasts the historical and anthropological approaches to the origins of states and summarizes the main theories developed by archaeologists. Gordon Childe's "Urban Revolution" theory centered on the development of the city. Another group of theories involved the intensification of agriculture and irrigation. Exchange networks and warfare have also been espoused as potential causes of civilization. Many modern theories revolve around systems-evolutionary hypotheses and explanations involving environmental change. A new generation of social approaches, on the other hand, argues that religious and informational factors, epitomized by centralized authority, have been key elements in the regulation of environmental and economic variables in early civilization. Such theories also stress that the social structure of a society ultimately determined its transformation, so the search for the causes of civilization focuses on ecological variables and the opportunities they present to individuals pursuing political goals in different societies—individual agents of change. In other words, how is ecological opportunity or necessity translated into political change? Recent researches are now focusing on factionalism, ideology, and gender as promising areas of inquiry.

| 2.5 Million | 1.0 Million | 500,000 B.P. | 100,000 B.P. | 50,000 B.P. | 15,000 B.P. | A.D. 1 | A.D. 1950 |

PROLOGUE

In 1872, George Smith, an earnest banknote-engraver-turned-clay-tablet-expert, was sorting through the dusty fragments of Assyrian king Assurbanipal's royal library in the British Museum. Suddenly, he came across a tablet bearing a reference to a large ship grounded on a mountain. Immediately, he realized he had found an account of a flood that bore a remarkable resemblance to the biblical story of the Flood in Genesis. A prophet named Hasisadra is warned of the gods' intention to destroy all of sinful humankind. He builds a large ship, loads it with his family, "the beast of the field, the animal of the field." The flood destroys "all [other] life from the face of the earth." The ship goes aground on a mountain. Hasisadra sends out a dove, which returns. Eventually, a raven is dispatched and never returns. Hasisadra releases the animals, becomes a god, and lives happily ever after.

George Smith's discovery caused a public sensation at a time when people believed in the literal historical truth of the Scriptures. Seventeen lines of the story were missing, so the London *Daily Telegraph* paid Smith's way to Nineveh to find the missing fragments. Incredible though it may seem, Smith found them within five days. The tablets can be seen on display in the British Museum, duly labeled "DT," for *Daily Telegraph*.

The Victorians thought of Mesopotamia (Greek for "land between the rivers"), now southern Iraq, as the location of the biblical Garden of Eden. Today, it is a far from paradisal place, for the delta regions and flood plain between the Tigris and Euphrates rivers form a hot, low-lying environment, much of it inhospitable sand, swamp, and dry mud flats. Yet this now-inhospitable region was the cradle of the world's earliest urban civilization. From north to south, Mesopotamia is approximately 965 kilometers (600 miles) long and 400 kilometers (250 miles) wide, extending from the uplands of Iran to the east to the Arabian and Syrian deserts in the west. The plains are subject to long, intensely hot summers and harsh, cold winters and would be desert but for the Euphrates and Tigris rivers. There are few permanent water supplies away from these great rivers and their tributaries. Rainfall is slight and not dependable and is insufficient for growing crops. However, with irrigation, the alluvial soils of the lower plain can be farmed and their natural fertility unlocked. Farmers can achieve high crop yields from relatively limited areas of land, sufficient to feed relatively dense populations. By 6000 B.C. and perhaps earlier, village farmers were diverting the waters of the rivers. Within 3,000 years the urban civilization of the Sumerians was flourishing in Mesopotamia. Chapter 9 describes this, the earliest of the world's civilizations, and the complex western Asian societies that developed out of the first Mesopotamian states (Figure 9.1).

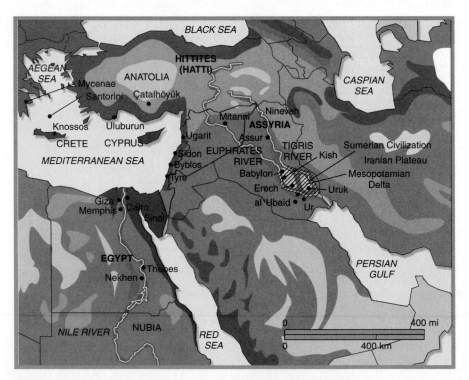

Figure 9.1 Map showing archaeological sites in Chapters 9 and 10.

Origins (5500 to 3000 B.C.)

Controversy surrounds the first settlement of the land between the rivers. Intensely hot in summer, bitterly cold in winter, the plains were far from a hospitable environment for village farmers. We know that by 5800 B.C. hundreds of small farming villages dotted the rolling plains of northern Mesopotamia upstream, settlements connected by long-distance trade routes that carried obsidian, finely painted pottery, and other goods over hundreds of kilometers, from Turkey as far as southern Iraq. By this time, much of the trade, especially in pottery, was concentrated in the hands of a small elite, living in key centers along water routes. However, we do not know whether the uninhabited plains were settled by village farmers from the north around 6000 B.C., as many scholars believe, or whether much earlier indigenous hunter-gatherers adopted farming along the shores of the Persian Gulf at this time, or even earlier.

No one knows when hunter-gatherers first settled on the shores of the Persian Gulf, which, during the late Ice Age, was a large river estuary. One school of thought believes that, as sea levels rose after 15,000 years ago, the Gulf spread far up into what is now southern Iraq, perhaps creating coastal and riverside marshlands rich in fish and plant foods. The ancient coastlines of the early and middle Holocene now lie below many feet of river alluvium and sand, as does the archaeological record of potential early occupation. As the climate dried up during the Holocene, goes this argument, forager populations tended to concentrate in more resource-rich areas. As elsewhere in western Asia, it may have been in such locations that people first experimented with growing cereal grains. Within a few thousand years, farming villages clustered along river banks and better-watered areas of the desert.

Whatever their origins, the earliest farmers developed methods of cultivation using canals and natural waterways, which allowed higher crop yields. The first known farming communities date to around 5800 B.C., small communities located in clusters along the Euphrates river channels. As early as 5500 B.C., a few farming communities were diverting flood waters from the Euphrates and Tigris onto their fields, then draining them away to prevent salt buildup in the soil. The largest of these clusters consisted of small rural communities located around a larger town that covered about 11.3 hectares (28 acres) and housed between 2,500 and 4,000 people. Some of their small irrigation canals extended out about 5 kilometers (3 miles) from the river. From the very beginning some of these 'Ubaid culture settlements (named after a village near ancient Ur) boasted of substantial buildings, alleyways, and courtyards. Others consisted of little more than humble mud-brick and reed huts. Each cluster was a group of villages linked by kin ties, with a clan leader living in one larger settlement overseeing village affairs and, probably, the irrigation schemes that connected them.

We do not know anything about how the first inhabitants of the Mesopotamian flood plain acquired or developed the skills needed to survive in their harsh environment. Interdependence among members of the community was essential because raw materials suitable for building houses had to be improvised from the plentiful sand, clay, palm trees, and reeds between the rivers. Digging even the smallest canal required at least a little political and social leadership. The annual backbreaking task of clearing silt from clogged river courses and canals could only have been achieved by communal efforts. Distinctive social changes came from the more-efficient systems for producing food that were essential in the delta. As food surpluses grew and the specialized agricultural economies of these 'Ubaid villages became successful, the trend toward sedentary settlement and higher population densities increased.

SITE

The Temple at Eridu, Iraq

Sumerian legends called Eridu the earliest city of all, the dwelling place of Enki, God of the Abyss, the fountain of human wisdom. "All lands were the sea, then Eridu was made," proclaims a much later Mesopotamian creation legend. Sumerians considered Enki's word to have created order from the chaos of the primordial waters. Eridu itself once lay in the heart of a fertile riverside landscape. Today, harsh desert surrounds the ancient city. Its ruined temple platform stands at one end of the great city mounds, a low, flat mass of clay and sand with a dune forming downwind of the crumbling mound. For generations, the desolate site defied some of the best archaeologists in the world, who lacked the expertise to distinguish sun-dried mud-brick from the surrounding soil. British archaeologist Richard Campbell-Thompson dug into Eridu in 1918 and complained that he found nothing but loose sand. Thirty years later, Iraqi archaeologist Fuad Safar and his British colleague Seton Lloyd returned to the city with a large labor force and a small mining railroad, which enabled them to move enormous amounts of sand. They also had an expertise with mud-brick structures, using methods developed by German archaeologists at the great city of Babylon just before World War I, which used picks to "feel" different soil textures. To this simple technique, they added brushes and compressed air, which proved an excellent way to clear mud-brick. The two excavators removed enough sand to expose a small complex of mud-brick public buildings still standing about 2.4 meters (8 feet) high. Then they embarked on a long-term project to decipher the history of the great shrine that had once stood at the heart of the city.

Safar and Lloyd soon found a solid brickwork platform extending from the base of the much later ruined *ziggurat* ("temple"). They spent two weeks piecing together scattered brick and reconstructed the foundations of a small, rectangular building surrounded by concentric brickwork triangles. After days of puzzlement, they realized they were looking at a temple platform that had been extended again and again by the simple expedient of building another layer of brickwork around the shrine to build ever-larger, brilliantly decorated shrines, culminating in the great ziggurat that adorned the city before it was abandoned (Figure 9.2). At least five temples had stood atop the one exposed by Safar and Lloyd. They dismantled the rectangular structure and penetrated deep toward bedrock, uncovering no less than ten earlier shrines, each built atop its predecessors. Temple XVI, dated to c. 4500 B.C., lay on clean sand, a small mud-brick shrine 14 meters (45 feet) square, with one entrance, an altar, and an offering table. Hundreds of fish bones, including the complete skeleton of a sea perch, still lay on the offering temple. Sea perch live in brackish water, like the shallow estuaries that were once close to Eridu.

Expanded trade networks and the redistribution of surpluses and trade goods also affected society, with dominant groups of 'Ubaid people becoming more active in producing surpluses, which eventually supported more and more people who were not farmers.

As Mesopotamian society grew rapidly in complexity in the centuries that followed, so did the need for social, political, and religious institutions that would provide some form of centralized authority. In time, the small village ceremonial centers grew. **Eridu,** a rapidly growing town, consisted of a mud-brick temple with fairly substantial mud-brick houses around it, often with a rectangular floor plan. The craftsworkers lived a short distance from the elite clustered around the temple (see box), and still farther away were the dwellings of the farmers who grew the crops that supported everyone. By 4500 B.C., the Eridu temple had grown large, containing altars and offering places and a central room

Figure 9.2 Artist's reconstruction of the final stage of the ziggurat at Eridu, Iraq, one of the earliest temples in the region.

Five hundred years later, Eridu's temple platform lay inside a sacred enclosure at least 180 meters (200 yards) square. A magnificent stepped ziggurat now rose in the center of the city, its facade adorned with brightly colored fired bricks. Crowded residential quarters and markets crowded on the sacred enclosure, while the ziggurat was visible for kilometers around. Thanks to months of sophisticated and painstaking mud-brick excavation, we know that this imposing shrine was the descendant of much humbler temples that had commemorated the same sacred place.

bounded by rows of smaller compartments. The population of Eridu was as high as 5,000 at this time, but exact computations are impossible. Places like Eridu assumed great importance after 4500 B.C., among them Uruk, the world's first city.

The First Cities: Uruk

Uruk began life as a small town and soon became a growing city, quickly absorbing the populations of nearby villages. During the fourth millennium B.C., Uruk grew to cover an estimated 250 hectares (617 acres). Satellite villages extended out at least 10 kilometers (6 miles), each with their own irrigation systems. All provided grain, fish, or meat for the growing urban population. The city itself was a densely packed agglomeration of houses, narrow alleyways, and courtyards, probably divided into distinct quarters where different kin groups or artisans such as potters, sculptors, and painters lived. Everything was overshadowed by the stepped temple pyramid, the ziggurat that towered over the lowlands for miles around. The ziggurat complex and its satellite temples were the center of Uruk life. Not only were these temple complexes places of worship, but storehouses, workshops, and centers of government (see Figure 9.2 on page 223).

The ruler of Uruk and the keeper of the temple was both a secular and spiritual ruler. His wishes were carried out by his priests and by a complex hierarchy of minor officials, wealthy landowners, and merchants. Tradespeople and artisans were a more lowly segment of society. Under them were thousands of fisherfolk, farmers, sailors, and slaves that formed the bulk of Uruk, and other cities' burgeoning populations. By 3500 B.C., the Mesopotamian city had developed an elaborate system of management. This system organized and regulated society, meted out reward and punishment, and made policy decisions for the thousands of people who lived under it.

Writing and Metallurgy

Two innovations appeared as Uruk and other cities grew rapidly. The first was writing, the second metallurgy. The origins of written records go back thousands of years before the Sumerians, to a time soon after the adoption of food production when the volume of inter-village trade demanded some means of tracking shipments. Its beginnings are still little understood. One popular theory has villagers using carefully shaped clay tokens as records, which they carried around on strings as early as 8000 B.C. By 5000 B.C., commercial transactions of all kinds were so complex that there were endless possibilities for thievery and accounting errors. Some clever officials made small clay tablets and scratched them with incised signs that depicted familiar objects such as pots or animals. From there it was a short step to simplified, more conventionalized, **cuneiform** signs (Figure 9.3).

At first, specially trained scribes dealt almost entirely with administrative matters, compiling lists and inventories. Eventually, the more creative among them explored the limitless opportunities afforded by the ability to express themselves in writing. Kings used tablets to trumpet their victories. Fathers chided their errant sons, lawyers recorded complicated transactions. Sumerian literature includes great epics, love stories, hymns to the gods, and tragic laments.

The Sumerians' homeland had no metals, so they imported copper, gold, and other ores from the Iranian highlands and elsewhere as early as 3500 B.C. At first these shiny metals had high prestige value, but the advent of lead and tin alloying after 2000 B.C. led to widespread use of bronze artifacts for farming tools and weapons of war. Bronze technology produced tougher-edged, more durable artifacts that could be used for more arduous, day-to-day tasks. One resulting innovation was the metal- and wood-tipped plow, an implement dragged by oxen that was capable of digging a far deeper furrow than the simple hoes and digging sticks of earlier times. The plow, which incidentally was never developed in the Americas, was developed as irrigation agriculture assumed greater importance in Sumer, and the combined innovations increased agricultural yields dramatically. These yields not only supported larger urban and rural populations but also provided a means for the rulers of city-states both in Sumer and farther afield to exercise more control over food surpluses and over the wealth obtained by long-distance exchange.

The adoption of bronze-edged weapons had momentous consequences for Sumerian life, for their appearance in local armies can be linked directly to a rising penchant for

Figure 9.3 Cuneiform tablet of c. 2500 B.C. This tablet records transactions between different temple herds. The vertical line divides into two columns; each horizontal line then begins with marks that indicate a number (e.g., six in the third line of the right-hand column) or with the name of a god (e.g., the third line on the left, with the name of the god Shuruppak).

using war as a means of attaining political ends. Cities like Eridu and Uruk were not isolated from other centers. Indeed they were only too aware of their neighbors. For example, the city-states of Lagash and Umma were uneasy neighbors and engaged in a tendentious border dispute that dragged on for three or four centuries. Cities soon had walls, a sure sign that they needed protection against marauders. Sumerian seals bear scenes with prisoners of war. By this time, too, there were southern Mesopotamian "colonies" in what is now northern Iraq, at Susa across the Tigris, in the Zagros, and elsewhere on the northern and northeastern peripheries of the lowlands. Some of these colonies were entire transplanted communities; others are represented by characteristic Uruk-style artifacts far from their homelands. Artifacts and artistic styles characteristic of Uruk have come from the Nile Valley during centuries when long-distance caravan trade was expanding rapidly in Egypt and across the Sinai. It's important to realize that the trend toward more complex societies, toward states and cities took hold over an enormous area, not just in southern Mesopotamia.

Sumerian Civilization (c. 3100 to 2334 B.C.)

With the emergence of the Sumerian civilization in about 3100 B.C., a new era in human experience begins, one in which the economic, political, and social mechanisms created by humans begin to affect the lives of cities, towns, and villages located hundreds, if not

VOICES

The Sumerians

"When Enlil, like a big bull, set his foot on the earth,
To make the good day thrive in abundance,
To make the fair night flourish in luxuriance,
To make grow tall the plants, to spread wide the grains . . ."

Sumerian literature is the earliest in the world, rich in poetry and prose, and also comprised of more prosaic documents. "Why do you idle about? Go to school, stand before your 'school-father,' recite your assignment, open your schoolbag, write your tablet . . ." The voices of the ancient Sumerians speak to us over the millennia. The delinquent student, the love song, the agricultural directory and the stirring epic—Sumerian literature vibrates with energy and perception. A bride sings to her royal bridegroom, Shu-Sin:

"Bridegroom, dear to my heart,
Goodly is your beauty, sweetheart,
Lion, dear to my heart,
Goodly is your beauty, honeysweet."

A farming handbook giving pragmatic advice from a father to his son fills 180 lines of tightly packed cuneiform. The author guides his heir through the yearly agricultural cycle, starting with the inundation of the fields by the great rivers in May and June. "Plow eight furrows to each strip of land about 6 meters [20 feet] wide." "Keep an eye on the man who puts in the barley seed that he make the seed fall two fingers uniformly." "On the day when the seed breaks through the ground," one should say a prayer to Ninkilim, goddess of field mice and vermin, so they do not harm the growing crop. The handbook contains precise instructions on watering, adjuring the young farmer to "let your tools hum with activity."

The Epic of Gilgamesh, still performed on the stage to this day, is the most famous of all Sumerian literary works, the story of a man who loves and hates, weeps and rejoices, hopes and despairs. Gilgamesh is King of Erech, a restless hero famous for his tyrannical arrogance. His subjects complain to the gods, who send Enkidu, who has lived among the beasts, to tame Gilgamesh. The two heroes fight, then become fast friends and kill the formidable Bull of Heaven. Enkidu is sentenced to an early death by the gods. The grieving Gilgamesh now seeks immortality. Eventually, he fails in his quest and returns weary and disappointed to Erech to live out his days. The *Epic* as we know it is a mixture of literary borrowings, but it is a masterpiece. Witness:

"Gilgamesh says to Enkidu:
'If now you will descend to the nether world,
A word I will speak to you, take my word,
Instruction I offer you, take my instruction
Do not put on clean clothes,
Lest like an enemy [the nether world] stewards will come forth.
Do not anoint yourself with the good oil of the bur-vessel,
Lest at its smell they will crowd about you . . .'"

But the most vivid Sumerian voices are those of common folk, expressed in proverbs of the day: "We are doomed to die, let us spend; We will live long, let us save." "Friendship lasts a day, kinship endures for ever." Or "You can have a lord, you can have a king, but the man to fear is the tax collector" (quotes from Kramer, 1981, pp. 304, 15, 246, 67–68, 196–197, 118, 121, 123).

thousands, of miles apart. No human society has ever flourished in complete isolation, but the real launching point in long-distance exchange and organized trade took place during the fourth millennium B.C., the first millennium when the history of an individual society can be understood only against a background of much broader regional developments. In a real sense, a rapidly evolving economic system linked hundreds of Southwest Asian societies all the way from eastern Iran and the Indus valley in Pakistan to Mesopotamia, the eastern Mediterranean, Anatolia, and the Nile valley with ever-changing cultural tentacles. By the third millennium B.C. this system not only embraced Southwest Asia but also extended to Cyprus, the Aegean, and mainland Greece.

This nascent economic system developed as a result of insatiable demands for nonlocal raw materials in different ecological regions where societies were developing along very similar general evolutionary tracks toward greater complexity. The broad, and apparently linear, cultural sequence in southern Mesopotamia just described can be matched by equivalent developments in northern Mesopotamia and east of the Tigris. In each area, these developments and many technological innovations were triggered not only by basic economic needs but also by the competitive instincts of newly urbanized elites, who used lavish display and exotic luxuries to reaffirm their social prestige and authority. Sumerian civilization is a mirror of this developing regional interdependence.

Sumerian civilization came into being as a result of a combination of environmental and social factors. The Sumerians lived in a treeless, lowland environment with fertile soils, but no metal, little timber, and no semiprecious stones. They obtained these commodities by trading with areas where such items were in abundance. Sumerian rulers controlled not only large grain surpluses that could be moved in river craft but also a flourishing industry in textiles and other luxuries. The trade moved up and down the great rivers, especially the placid Euphrates. Ancient overland trade routes linked the Tigris and Euphrates with the distant Levant cities and ports. Even as early as Sumerian times, caravans of pack animals joined Anatolia to the Euphrates, the Levant to Mesopotamia, and Mesopotamia to isolated towns on the distant Iranian highlands to the east.

By 3250 B.C., expanding trade networks linked dozens of cities and towns from the Mediterranean to the Persian Gulf and from Turkey to the Nile valley. By this time, states small and large flourished not only in Egypt and Mesopotamia, but also in the coastal Levant and in highland Iran. Each of them depended on the others for critical raw materials such as metal ore or soapstone vessels, for timber or even grain. In northern Mesopotamia, east of the Tigris, and in the Levant, expanding trade and a host of important technological innovations resulted not only from basic economic needs, but also from the competitive instincts of a new elite. All, however bitter their enmity, depended on their neighbors and more distant trading partners.

The broad, and apparently linear, cultural sequence in southern Mesopotamia just described can be matched by equivalent developments in northern Mesopotamia and east of the Tigris. Sumerian civilization is a mirror of developing regional interdependence. Writing and metallurgy were symbols of this rapidly changing western Asian world.

An intricate and ever-changing system of political alliances and individual obligations of friendship linked community with community and city-state with city-state. In time, financial and logistical checks and balances were maintained by an administrative system based in the temples to bring order to what had begun as informal bartering. Specialized merchants began to handle such commodities as copper and lapis lazuli. There was wholesaling and contracting, loans were floated, and individual profit was a prime motivation. Increasingly, every city-state, and indeed entire civilizations, came to depend on what we have called a nascent world system, not so much for political stability but for survival. Reliable, long-term interdependency became a vital factor in the history of southwest Asian states by 3000 B.C.

By 2800 B.C., Mesopotamia was home to several important city-states, states that were in contact with the Levant and the Iranian Plateau, even, sporadically, with the pharaohs of Egypt. As the Mesopotamian delta became an environment increasingly controlled by human activities and the volume of long-distance trade increased dramatically, so competition over resources intensified. Both clay tablets and archaeological finds tell of warfare and constant bickering between neighbors. Each state raised an army to defend its water rights, trade routes, and city walls. The onerous tasks of defense and military organization passed to despotic kings supposedly appointed by the gods. Such city-states as **Erech, Kish,** and **Ur** had periods of political strength and prosperity when they dominated their neighbors (Figure 9.4). Then, just as swiftly, the tide of their fortunes would change and they would sink into obscurity. There was a constant threat from nomadic peoples of the surrounding mountains and deserts, who encroached on settled Sumerian lands. At times, they disrupted city life so completely that any form of travel became an impossibility. In a real sense, city-states were the settings for economic and social strife in early Mesopotamia.

Figure 9.4 The reconstructed Sumerian ziggurat at Ur, Iraq, originally built in about 2300 B.C.

Some Sumerian cities nurtured powerful and wealthy leaders. When British archaeologist Sir Leonard Woolley excavated a royal cemetery at Ur, he found the remains of a series of kings and queens who had been buried in huge graves with their entire retinue of courtiers. One tomb contained the remains of fifty-nine people. Each wore his or her official dress and regalia and had laid down to die in the correct order of precedence, after taking a fatal dose of poison (Figure 9.5).

Inevitably, the ambitions of some of these proud Sumerian leaders led them to entertain bolder visions than merely the control of a few city-states in the lowlands. They were well aware that the control of lucrative sources of raw materials and trade routes was the secret of vast political power. In about 2400 B.C., a monarch named Lugalzagesi boasted of overseeing the entire area from the Persian Gulf to the Mediterranean. This boast was probably false. It is likely that Sumerian cities dominated the overland routes that linked Mesopotamia, Turkey, and the Levant, but their influence was never permanent, their control probably illusory. Lugalzagesi and others were characteristic of a tradition of Mesopotamian civilization: the combination of trade, conquest, ruthless administration, and tribute to create large, poorly integrated, and highly volatile empires. Each sought to control an enormous territory between the Mediterranean and the Persian Gulf.

The tenuous and sometimes more regular contacts maintained by Mesopotamia with dozens of city-states in Anatolia and along the eastern Mediterranean coast foreshadow the constant political and economic rivalry that was to dominate Southwest Asian history during the second millennium B.C.—rivalry over control of Mediterranean coastal ports. Here two oceans and three continents meet. The eastern Mediterranean coast had no natural harbors, so the control of its overland routes was the key to dominating a vast area of the

Figure 9.5 Reconstruction of a royal funeral at Sumerian Ur, as recorded by Sir Leonard Woolley.

known world, resource-rich Anatolia and grain-rich Egypt. The history of this region was bound inextricably to the fortunes of the larger powers that surrounded it.

Akkadians and Babylonians (2334 to 1650 B.C.)

While Sumerian civilization prospered, urban centers waxed and waned in neighboring areas. In these regions, too, lived rulers with wider ambitions, who had a vision of a larger role. By 2500 B.C., Akkadian cities to the north of Sumer were competing with lowland cities for trade and prestige. In approximately 2334 B.C., a Semitic-speaking leader, Sargon, founded a ruling dynasty at the town of Agade, south of **Babylon.** By skillful commercial ventures and judicious military campaigns, his northern dynasty soon established its rule over a much larger kingdom that included both Sumer and northern Mesopotamia. After a short period of economic prosperity, northern Mesopotamia went through a catastrophic drought that lasted some 300 years. Starving farmers thronged to the rich southern cities. Violent clashes followed and the Akkadian kingdom collapsed.

Fifty years of political instability ensued before King Ur-Nammu of Ur took control of Sumer and Akkad in 2112 B.C. and created an empire that extended far to the north. Sargon had forged an empire by military conquest but had never followed up his victories with proper administrative governance. Tablets from royal archives tell us that Ur-Nammu and his successors of Ur's Third Dynasty were a new breed of ruler, who placed great emphasis on consolidating their new empire into a powerful and well-organized bureaucracy.

Ur in turn gave way to Babylon and its Semitic rulers by 1990 B.C. Babylon's early greatness culminated in the reign of the great king Hammurabi in 1792 B.C., famous for his law code. He integrated the smaller kingdoms of Mesopotamia for a short period, but his empire declined after his death as Babylonian trade to the Persian Gulf collapsed and trade ties to Assur in the north and for Mediterranean copper in the west were strengthened.

Hittites and Sea Traders (1650 to 1200 B.C.)

All these developments came from ever-closer economic ties between different regions of southwest Asia. These ties were a sign of an economic interdependency that persisted regardless of political change or war. The desert caravans of pack animals and the ships that plied Mediterranean waters resulted from a more durable world system that transcended the boundaries of local societies and even entire civilizations. At the center of this world system lay the strategic eastern Mediterranean coast.

During the second millennium B.C. a network of small and prosperous states controlled the eastern Mediterranean coastlands. They lived in the shadow of the great kingdoms that lay inland: Egypt to the south (see Chapter 10), **Mitanni** to the east of the Euphrates, and **Hatti** (the kingdom of the **Hittites**) in Anatolia. Each of these three kingdoms controlled a large area of territory surrounded by a hinterland that lay more or less under their influence (see Figure 9.1 on page 220). The three states competed directly in the coastal zone, and they had complex dealings on all frontiers. Mitanni, for example, tried to prevent the city-state of Assur in northern Mesopotamia from going its own way, and the famous Amarna tablets, an archive of Egyptian diplomatic correspondence, tell of shifting allegiances among the city-states of the coast. By this time, the eastern Mediterranean shore was a land of many cities, a regular military and diplomatic battlefield for its powerful neighbors.

The Hittites

The Hittites were the newest, and perhaps the most able, diplomatic players. Originally the rulers of **Kanesh,** they expanded their domains and seized control of the rest of Anatolia just before 1650 B.C. Hittite kings exercised enormous political influence in southwest Asia from their capital at **Boghazkoy,** with its 6.4 kilometers (4 miles) of city walls (Figure 9.6). In the fifteenth century B.C., Syria had been a province of the Egyptian empire. The Hittites pressed hard on the Egyptians on both diplomatic and military fronts, until the Great King of Hatti, Suppiluliumas I (1375–1335 B.C.), could claim Lebanon as his frontier. Diplomatic archives in Akkadian cuneiform contain records of a peace treaty of about 1269 B.C. between the Hittite and Egyptian kings, which confined Egyptian interests to southern Palestine. The grandiloquent public architecture of the period commonly depicted Egyptians and Hittites locked in battle with state-of-the-art weaponry. This included light, two-wheeled chariots manned by archers and new siege machinery for use against the many walled cities in the disputed areas.

By 1200 B.C., Hatti was in trouble. The Hittites had prospered by virtue of their well-organized, professional army, long a stabilizing influence in the eastern Mediterranean. They were expert diplomats, who controlled what is now northern Syria through their rule over two great cities—Carchemish on the Euphrates and Alalakh of Mukish in the west. There were also treaty relationships with other powerful neighbors, including **Ugarit** (Ras

Figure 9.6 The Royal Gate, flanked by lions, at Boghazkoy (Hattusas), the Hittite royal capital.

Shamra) on the northern Levant coast. Ugarit was a cosmopolitan city ruled by a monarch who was almost like a merchant-prince. He controlled vast supplies of gold and a fleet of more than 150 ships, some of considerable size. These ventured as far afield as Cyprus and the Nile, the former being a center of exchange with the Aegean. Ugarit was vital to the Hittites, who had never become a maritime power, for they depended on its ships.

Both the lack of maritime power and a rigid feudal system contributed to Hatti's undoing. About 1200 B.C., repeated migrations of foreigners flowed into Anatolia from the northwest, at a time when severe drought was impacting much of the eastern Mediterranean world from the Aegean to the Nile, including Hatti. The central Hittite government collapsed, partly because of attacks from outside but also because powerful vassals threw off their allegiance to the king. Anatolia dissolved into the homeland of dozens of small city-states, each striving to maintain its independence.

Uluburun and Maritime Trade

All this diplomatic and military activity on the part of the great kingdoms was aimed at control of the lucrative gold, copper, and pottery trade of the eastern Mediterranean. This trade, in the hands of eastern Mediterranean and Mycenaean traders, is vividly illustrated by the investigations of a Bronze Age shipwreck off the southern Turkish coast.

The advantage of shipwrecks from the archaeological point of view is that they provide sealed capsules of maritime trade frozen at a moment in time. The famous **Uluburun** ship, excavated by Çemal Pulak from the waters near Kas off southern Turkey, was shipwrecked in about 1310 B.C. The ship carried over 350 copper ingots, each weighing about 27 kilograms (60 pounds), a load of 10 tons, enough to equip a small army with weapons and armor (Figure 9.7). A ton of resin traveled in two-handled jars made by people living in the Syria region; it was used, so Egyptian records tell us, as incense for Egyptian rituals. There were dozens of blue glass disks, ingots being sent to Egypt from Tyre. The cargo also included hardwood, Baltic amber, tortoise shells, elephant tusks and hippopotamus teeth, ostrich eggs, jars of olives, and even large jars holding stacked Canaanite and Mycenaean pottery.

The Uluburun ship's cargo contains items from Africa, Egypt, the eastern Mediterranean coast, the Greek mainland and the Aegean, Cyprus, and even copper from Sardinia. It is a dramatic reflection of the truly international nature of eastern Mediterranean trade in the second millennium B.C., when the Hittites were at the height of their power. It is hardly surprising that the great powers of the day competed savagely for control of the eastern Mediterranean shore, for it lay at the very center of an interlocking maze of trade routes that spanned the entire civilized world.

Iron Technology

Maritime trade played a major role in the diffusion of iron tools and weapons over the eastern Mediterranean. Iron is thought to have been first smelted in the middle of the second millennium B.C., perhaps in the highlands immediately south of the Black Sea. The new metal had many advantages, for its tough, sharp edges were invaluable for military tasks and for farming and carpentry. Iron was plentiful, unlike the tin used to alloy bronze. Iron tools soon became commonplace over a wide area of Europe and southwest Asia, although it was some time before domestic artifacts such as axes and hoes were invariably made with the new technology.

Figure 9.7 Excavations on the Uluburun shipwreck, Turkey.

Minoans and Mycenaeans (1900 to 1200 B.C.)

Eastern Mediterranean trade extended far west of Greece, to Sardinia, North Africa, and Spain. But the main western frontier lay in the Aegean Islands and on the Greek islands, where the Minoan and Mycenaean civilizations flourished during the second millennium B.C.

The Aegean abounds in sheltered bays and many straits, allowing even primitive, heavily laden seagoing vessels to take shelter and sail from island to island. The interisland trade expanded rapidly, not only in metal objects but in olive oil and wine carried in fine pots and also in marble vessels and figurines. A constant flow of new products and ideas flowed across the region. By 2500 B.C., numerous small towns housed farmers, traders, and skilled artisans on the mainland and the islands. The beginnings of town life fostered considerable cultural diversity in the Aegean, a diversity nurtured by constant trading connections and increasingly complex political and social organization.

Minoan Civilization (1900 to 1400 B.C.)

Minoan civilization developed out of earlier indigenous farming cultures by 1900 B.C. It is best documented at the famous Palace of Minos at **Knossos,** near Heraklion on the north coast, a site first settled as early as 6000 B.C. at about the same time that Çatalhöyük flourished in Anatolia. Parts of the Greek mainland and Aegean Islands were settled by farming peoples as early as 6500 B.C., but it was not until considerably later that village communities sprang up throughout the region. This development coincided with the cultivation not only of cereals, but of olives and vines. By 3500 B.C., the inhabitants of the Aegean and Greece were exploiting local ores to make fine metal tools and precious ornaments. The Knossos farmers lived in sun-dried mud and brick huts of a rectangular ground plan that provided for storage bins and sleeping platforms. By 3730 B.C., signs of long-distance trading increased in the form of exotic imports such as stone bowls. The first palace at Knossos was built by about 1930 B.C.; it was a large building with many rooms grouped around a rectangular central court.

In about 1700 B.C., the first royal residence on the site was destroyed by an earthquake, just as Minoan civilization reached the height of its powers. The palace that rose in its place was an imposing structure that rambled around a central courtyard (Figure 9.8). Some buildings had two stories; the plastered walls and floors were painted with brightly colored geometric designs, with landscapes, dolphins, and other sea creatures (Figure 9.9). The most remarkable art depicted dances and religious ceremonies, including acrobats leaping vigorously along the backs of prancing bulls. Part shrine, part royal residence, part storehouse, and part workshop, the Palace of Minos at Knossos was the hub of a predominantly rural civilization centered on large country houses and chieftains' residences.

The dramatic flowering of Minoan civilization resulted from intensified trading contacts throughout the Aegean and as far afield as Egypt and the Levant. The Minoans were expert seafarers and middlemen in international trade. Their ships handled all manner of cargos. But this time, olive and vine cultivation had added welcome diversity to local village farming economies, as well as providing valuable export commodities. This led to the development

Figure 9.8 General view of the Palace of Minos at Knossos, Crete.

Figure 9.9 The throne room at Knossos, with stone throne and frieze depicting mythical birds. This chamber was used for formal appearances of priests or priestesses costumed as deities.

of distribution systems organized and controlled by important leaders, who controlled ships, shipping lanes, and marketplaces, and lived in palaces large and small. Minoan society developed from entirely local roots, which was an adaptation to a mountainous environment where population densities were never high and much wealth came from the export trade.

A massive volcanic explosion devastated the island of **Santorini,** a Minoan outpost 113 kilometers (70 miles) north of Crete, in about 1620 B.C. (The date is much disputed and may be as much as a century-and-three-quarters later.) This cataclysmic eruption caused massive tidal waves and ash falls that mantled many Minoan fields, but Knossos continued to flourish long afterward. In about 1400 B.C., the great palace was destroyed by earthquake and fire. By this time, the center of the Aegean world had shifted west to the Greek mainland, where Mycenae reached the height of its power.

Mycenaean Civilization (1600 to 1200 B.C.)

Mycenaean civilization, centered on the fertile plain of Argos in southern Greece, developed in about 1600 B.C. The chieftains who ruled over the walled fortress of **Mycenae** gained their wealth and economic power not only from their warrior skills, but from wide trading contacts in the Aegean and further afield (see Figure 9.10 on page 236). Mycenaean kings were expert charioteers and horsemen, whose material culture and lifeways are immortalized in Homer's epic poems, the *Iliad* and the *Odyssey*. These epics were written many centuries after the Mycenaeans themselves had become folk memories. However, they give a splendid impression of the wealth and glitter of Bronze Age Greek life. So do Mycenaean graves. Mycenae's rulers and their relatives took their wealth with them to the next world.

Figure 9.10 Aerial view of Mycenae, Greece.

They were buried in spectacular shaft graves wearing fine gold face masks modeled in the likeness of their owners and weapons adorned with copper, gold, and silver (Figure 9.11).

Mycenaean commerce took over where Minoan trade left off. Much of the rulers' prestige was based on their contacts in the metal trade. Minerals, especially tin for alloying bronze, were in constant demand in eastern Mediterranean markets. Both copper and tin were abundant in Turkey and central Cyprus, so Mycenaean traders became middlemen, developing the necessary contacts in both areas and in the Aegean to obtain regular supplies. So complex did their trading relationships become that the Mycenaeans found it necessary to establish their own writing system. They refined a simple pictographic script known to archaeologists as Linear A, which had been used by the Minoans, and wrote it in the Greek language, creating what scholars call Linear B. Large numbers of clay tablets from a Mycenaean palace at **Pylos** in western Greece show that the script was used for inventories and records of commercial transactions, ration issues, and so on, for the daily affairs of estate administration.

Like Minoan civilization, Mycenaean society was based on small towns and palaces where the elite lived, and where trade, centralized food storage, and major religious ceremonies took place. Mycenae itself was a formidable citadel ringed with a defense wall of large boulders. The main entrance passed under a portico carved with two seated lions and led up the hill to the stone palace with its magnificent views of the Plain of Argos. Everything was set up for storage and defense. There was a water cistern within the defense walls, and rows of clay storage jars held large quantities of olive oil, with storerooms for many foodstuffs and the wealth of the palace. The rulers and their immediate relatives were buried in a circular enclosure to the west of the gate, but the Mycenaeans also used beehivelike communal burial chambers outside the citadel for many of their dead.

Figure 9.11 Golden funerary mask of a Mycenaean lord from a shaft grave at Mycenae, Greece.

Mycenae continued to dominate seaborne eastern Mediterranean trade routes until about 1200 B.C., when its power was destroyed, perhaps as a result of serious droughts and incursions from the north. In the same century, other northern barbarian raids impacted the Hittite kingdom in Turkey. These incursions, the result of unsettled political conditions and overpopulation in Europe, together with repeated crop failures from drought, threw the eastern Mediterranean world into confusion.

Sea Peoples and Phoenicians (1200 to 800 B.C.)

The Hittite civilization collapsed during a period of political upheaval, persistent drought, and, apparently, frequent earthquakes, but the trade routes that joined states large and small continued to link every corner of the Mediterranean world. The imperial powers and petty kingships that had made up much of the economic world of 1200 B.C. were governed by highly centralized palace bureaucracies. These bureaucracies controlled specialized activities such as trade in glass ingots and ivory ornaments, which allowed significant economies of operation and dense population concentrations.

When the Hittite and Mycenaean civilizations came apart in an almost dominolike effect and Egypt declined at the same time, centralized bureaucracies lost their power over economic activities. The infrastructure for controlled, specialized trade came apart and the power of urban elites declined. For 300 years, there was a political vacuum, a period of widespread suffering and piracy, much of it at the hands of warlike bands known to archaeologists as the **Sea Peoples.** In the Levant, many rural groups moved to the highlands, loosening their dependence on trading cities like Ugarit, and became herders and farmers. Some of them formed loose federations of towns, villages, and nomadic bands to preserve their sovereignty in the face of new and aggressive outside powers like the Assyrians of northern Mesopotamia. One such federation became the state of Israel, which acquired its own monarchy after 1000 B.C. and protected itself with a network of walled cities. By this time, eastern Mediterranean trade was recovering and the hillside federation expanded into the lowlands, hemmed in by the sea and the desert and by still-powerful Egyptian and Mesopotamian civilizations on either side.

A slow economic recovery during the first millennium B.C. came at the hands of the **Phoenicians.** At first, they acted as middlemen in the Cyprus and Aegean trade. Their ships were soon carrying Lebanese cedarwood to Cyprus and the Nile, copper and iron to the Aegean. Powerful cities like Byblos, Sidon, and Tyre extended their trading as far as the copper and tin mines of Spain. Phoenician merchants made enormous profits from purple dye extracted from seashells and much used for expensive fabrics. By 800 B.C., Phoenician merchants were everywhere in the Mediterranean as Assyria became the dominant power in the Levant. Their need for a highly accurate record-keeping system played a significant part in the development of the Western alphabet.

Assyrians and Babylonians (900 to 539 B.C.)

The city of **Assur** on the Tigris River in northern Mesopotamia had been a major force in the eastern Mediterranean world since Sumerian times. The merchants of Assur controlled strategic desert and river trade routes and commerce downstream to Babylon and beyond. The Assyrian empire expanded dramatically in the ninth century B.C., when a series of despotic, grandiose kings expanded their domains with relentless annual campaigns. These were absolute monarchs, who boasted of their conquests on their palace walls and lived in magnificent splendor, well aware of the value of conspicuous display (see chapter opener on page 218). When King Assurnasirpal completed his palace at Nimrud on the Tigris he threw a party for the 16,000 inhabitants of the city, 1,500 royal officials, "47,074 men and women from the length of my country," and 5,000 foreign envoys. The king fed this throng of more than 69,000 people for 10 days, during which time his guests ate 14,000 sheep and consumed more than 10,000 skins of wine.

The last of the great Assyrian kings was Assurbanipal, who died in approximately 630 B.C. Eventually, the Assyrian capital, **Nineveh,** fell to Persian and Babylonian warriors. For forty-three years, the mighty King Nebuchadnezzar of Babylon ruled over Mesopotamia and turned his capital into one of the showplaces of the ancient world. His double-walled city was adorned by huge mud-brick palaces with elaborate hanging gardens, a great processional way, and a huge ziggurat. It was to Babylon that a large contingent of Jews were taken as captives after Nebuchadnezzar's armies sacked Jerusalem. This event is immortalized in Psalm 137:1: "By the waters of Babylon we sat down and wept."

The Babylonian Empire did not long survive the death of Nebuchadnezzar in 556 B.C. The armies of Cyrus of Persia took Babylon in 539 B.C. The eastern Mediterranean world came under the sway of empires much larger than ever before. These were the centuries of classical Greece, when Rome began to emerge as a major power, when the basic foundations of Western civilization were laid. They came from a Mediterranean world that had been evolving economically, politically, and socially for thousands of years. What had begun as an adaptation to the realities of living in arid, but fertile flood plain environments had developed into a web of economic and political interdependency that was far larger than anything the world had seen before—the remote forerunner of the vast global economic system of today. As we shall see in Chapter 10, by the time the Roman Empire dominated the Mediterranean 2,000 years ago, new trade routes and markets as far east as India and China were linked to the western Asian world.

Summary

The Mesopotamian lowlands may have supported farmers before 6500 B.C., but their first traces appear in the 'Ubaid culture of the sixth millennium. They practiced small-scale irrigation and lived in groups of communities linked by trade networks. In time, some, like Eridu, became ceremonial centers and towns. A rapid evolution to urban life ensued— marked by fast population growth, the congregation of people in small cities, and the development of long-distance trade. This new urban society was organized in distinctive stratified social classes. Copper metallurgy developed at about the same time in the highlands and soon came into widespread use.

By 2900 B.C., Sumerian civilization was in full swing and was part of what we call a growing economic system, which linked kingdoms as far afield as the Iranian Plateau and the Indus in the east and the Mediterranean and the Nile Valley in the west. Mesopotamia never achieved political unification under the Sumerians. Rather, dozens of city-states vied for political and economic supremacy and competed with other societies in northern Mesopotamia and close to the Zagros Mountains. Sumerian civilization flourished until about 2000 B.C., when it was eclipsed by Akkadian and then Babylonian power.

To the north and west, the Minoans, and then the Mycenaeans, dominated the Aegean Sea and its lucrative wine and olive oil trade, while the Hittites rose to power in what is now Turkey. The centuries-old political order was disrupted by the Sea Peoples after 1200 B.C. In the late second millennium B.C., the city of Assur in the north nurtured the Assyrian Empire, which was extended by vigorous and despotic kings during the first half of the succeeding millennium. At one time, the Assyrian Empire stretched from the Mediterranean to the Persian Gulf. The Assyrian Empire fell in 612 B.C., and the power vacuum was filled by the Babylonians under the rule of Nebuchadnezzar. Babylon fell to Cyrus the Great of Persia in 539 B.C., and Mesopotamia became part of the Persian Empire.

10 Egypt and Africa

| 2.5 Million | 1.0 Million | 500,000 B.P. | 100,000 B.P. | 50,000 B.P. | 15,000 B.P. | A.D. 1 | A.D. 1950 |

PROLOGUE

"Nearly overcome, I . . . contrived to sit; but when my weight bore on the body of an Egyptian, it crushed it like a band-box. . . . I sank altogether among the broken mummies, with a crash of bones, rags, and wooden cases, which raised such a dust as kept me motionless for a quarter of an hour, waiting till it subsided again." Thus did the notorious Giovanni Belzoni, Italian circus performer turned tomb robber, explore ancient Egypt in 1817. Belzoni became a tomb robber by chance when a scheme to mechanize Egyptian agriculture collapsed. He contracted to move a large statue of the pharaoh Rameses II from Thebes to Alexandria. The tall Italian discovered he had a talent for bold discovery. In the course of three hectic years, he opened the great temple at Abu Simbel in Nubia, penetrated the inner chambers of the Pyramid of Kephren at Giza, and discovered the tomb of the pharaoh Seti I in the Valley of Kings. Belzoni and his ilk thought nothing of using gunpowder, even of going after rivals with a gun, for everyone was out for spectacular finds and all the loot they could gather. Eventually, he fled Egypt in danger of losing his life, exhibited his finds in London, then perished trying to find the source of the Niger River in West Africa.

Thanks to the adventures of Belzoni and his ilk, and magnificent discoveries like Tutankhamun's tomb, Ancient Egypt casts a magical spell over many people. All the ingredients of adventure and romance lie along the Nile: golden pharaohs' tombs, high pyramids, and spectacular temples. Of all ancient civilizations, Egypt is the best known, and perhaps the most misunderstood. Many people assume that Egyptian civilization developed and flourished in isolation in the Nile Valley, cut off from the rest of the ancient world. In fact, Egyptian civilization owed much to both Asia and tropical Africa and was a major political player in the eastern Mediterranean world of the second millennium B.C. This chapter describes the origins and development of this most remarkable of ancient civilizations and its relationships with the wider ancient world.

Predynastic Egypt: Ancient Monopoly (5000 to 3100 B.C.)

By 5000 B.C., a patchwork of simple village farming communities lay along both banks of the Nile River, from the delta of Lower Egypt to the First Cataract at Aswan and even further upstream. The river itself formed a natural highway between settlements near and far, the prevailing north winds allowing even sailing boats to stem the current. The villages soon became a patchwork of small kingdoms, each clustered under the rule of local leaders. Within two thousand years, these small polities had become a unified state, at the time the largest literate civilization in the world.

Most explanations for the origin of the state focus on population growth and competition for land and natural resources. In Egypt's case, state formation took place where population densities were still relatively low and there was plenty of vacant land, so neither of these factors played a significant role.

Egyptologist Barry Kemp believes that the village farmers of 4000 B.C. had strong ties to their ancestral lands, expressed in deeply symbolic terms. At first dozens of small communities, each with their own patchwork of farming land, competed and traded with their neighbors. Kemp likens the behavior and long-term effects to that in a game of Monopoly. In Monopoly, each player maximizes the opportunities thrown out by the dice. In Egypt, both individuals and entire villages took full advantage of favorable locations, of their access to desirable resources, like potting clay, and of chance breaks that came their way. At first the communities, like Monopoly players, were basically equal, but eventually some one, or some hamlet, gained an unforeseen advantage, perhaps from trading expertise, or by unusually high crop yields. Equilibrium gave way to a seemingly inevitable momentum, where some communities acquired more wealth, more power, than their neighbors— the prehistoric equivalent of building Monopoly hotels on Park Place. Inevitably victorious, they established a monopoly over local trade, food surpluses, and so on, which overrode any threat posed by other political or economic players.

In predynastic times, there were probably dozens of such "games" in progress. As time went on, the number of players grew fewer, but the stakes were higher as increasingly large chiefdoms vied for economic power and political dominance. Just like Monopoly, players changed over time, some acquiring great power, then losing it as charismatic individuals died or trading opportunities changed. Kemp points out that Egypt had more than enough fertile land and resources to enable such games to play out over many generations. Surplus resources like grain or toolmaking stone were the foundation of power. But he believes the Egyptians also had a genius for weaving a distinctive ideology that imbued leadership and authority with elaborate symbols and rituals. These ideologies became a powerful factor in promoting unification.

Archaeological excavations and surveys hint at a rapid, but complex consolidation of political power in fewer and fewer hands. By 3500 B.C., three predynastic kingdoms dominated the Nile: **Nagada, Nekhen,** and **This** near Abydos in Upper Egypt. These little-known kingdoms were the nucleus of a unified Egypt (Figure 10.1).[1]

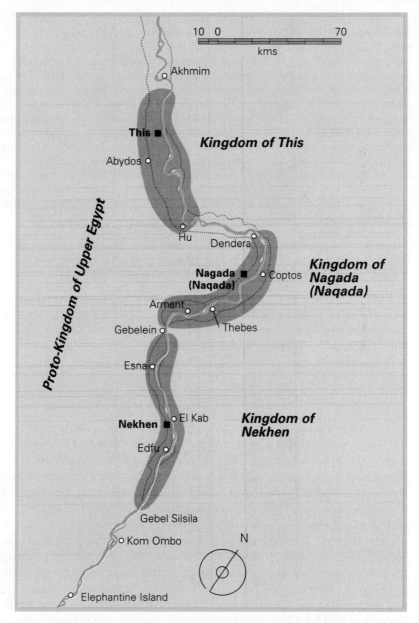

Figure 10.1 Map showing predynastic kingdoms in Upper Egypt in about 3300 B.C. This is a gross simplification of a complex, ever-changing political situation.

---

[1]Lower Egypt comprises the Nile Delta bordering the Mediterranean Sea and the valley to just upstream of the modern city of Cairo. Upper Egypt extends from there upstream to the First Cataract at Aswan. The ancient Egyptians themselves recognized this subdivision.

SCIENCE

Ancient Wine at Abydos

In 1988, German Egyptologist Günter Dreyer excavated the tomb of one of Egypt's first leaders at **Abydos** on the Middle Nile. Scorpion I lived in about 3150 B.C. His elaborate tomb contained four rooms stocked with at least 700 jars, which held a total of about 4,550 liters (1,200 gallons) of wine. Forty-seven of the jars contained wine pips, together with remains of sliced figs that were once suspended on strings in the wine, probably to sweeten it. The crusty residues adhering to the insides of the pots were analyzed with an infrared spectrometer and liquid chromatography, which revealed the remains of tartaric acids (found naturally in grapes), also of terebinth resin, which ancient vintners used to prevent wine from turning into vinegar. Neutron activation analysis of the jar clay yielded trace element clusters that were compared to a large database of samples from Egypt and the eastern Mediterranean. The database pointed to the southern hill country of Israel and Transjordan as the source of the vessels, an area where vine growing was well established in 3100 B.C. The wine probably traveled the Nile across an ancient trade route, "the Way of Horus," that linked southern Israel with Egypt via the Sinai Desert. By 3000 B.C., vine growing was well established in the Nile Delta in northern Egypt, the source of the pharaoh Tutankhamun's wines 1,500 years later.

New Kingdom tomb paintings show laborers picking bunches of grapes from laden vines supported with forked stick or on trellises. They empty heavy baskets into clay crushing vats. Teams of five or six men stomp the bunches by foot, hanging onto ropes to keep their balance. Tutankhamun enjoyed wines stored in short-handled red clay amphorae, mainly from vineyards in the western Delta far downstream. At least ten vintners produced the mainly dry wines enjoyed by the pharaoh. One Syrian wine maker named Khay made no less than six jars of fine wine for the king. A pharaoh enjoyed the pick of the vintages. At least 160 wine labels have come from the heretic king Akhenaten's palace at el-Amarna, some labeled "good," or "very good." Others, presumably inferior, were merely labeled "for merrymaking" or "for taxes."

Archaeology and myth combine for a hypothetical scenario for unification: By 3500 B.C., the kingdoms of Upper Egypt may have had direct contact with southern Arabia and Southwest Asia, bypassing Lower Egypt. Mesopotamian cylinder seals have come from Upper Egyptian sites, and gold was obtained from mines in the eastern desert. Conflict ensued, with the politically most-developed center, Nekhen, emerging victorious. The rulers of Nekhen, then This, finally embarked on a campaign of military conquest, which eventually engulfed all of Egypt between the Mediterranean and Aswan.

By 3100 B.C., a semblance of political unity joined Upper and Lower Egypt in the symbolic linking of the gods Horus and Seth depicted in later Egyptian art. As these events unfolded, a new state came into being, founded not only on physical, but on a symbolic geography, a harmony achieved by balanced opposites, of which Horus and Seth are but one manifestation. For thousands of years, the Egyptians were concerned with the potential of a world torn between potential chaos and order. They believed that disorder, disequilibrium, could be contained by the rule of kings and by the benign force of the power of the sun. Thus, the Egyptians' intellectual view of the universe coincided with the structure of political power. Unification was the culmination of local social and political developments that resulted from centuries of gradual change in economic and social life.

Predynastic villages were autonomous units, each with its local deities. During the fourth millennium B.C., the larger villages became the focal points of different territories, which in dynastic times became the nomes, or provinces, through which the pharaohs administered Egypt. The nomarchs (provincial leaders) were responsible for the gradual coalescence of Egypt into larger political and social units. Their deeds are recorded on ceremonial palettes that were used for moistening eye powder. Some of these palettes show alliances of local leaders dismantling conquered villages. Others commemorate the administrative skills of leaders who brought their villages through drought years by skillful management. The unification of Egypt was a gradual process of both voluntary and involuntary amalgamation. Voluntary unification resulted from common needs and economic advantage. Perhaps it was only in the final stages of unification that military force came into play to bring larger and larger political units under single rulers.

However the process of unification unfolded, there can be no question that unification was the pivotal, and fundamental concept upon which the institutions of ancient Egyptian civilization rested. Unification brought order from political chaos, serenity and rightness to a confused world. The king's task as shepherd of the people was to preserve *ma'at*, "rightness," derived in considerable part from unification, to maintain order in the face of a chaotic outside world.

The Egyptians themselves identified the first king as Narmer. (The universally used word *pharaoh*, from "great house": *par-aa*, came into use during the second millennium B.C.) In fact, a series of still-unknown rulers, Narmer among them, may have completed the process of unification. The famous Narmer palette (see Figure 10.2 on page 246) depicts the semblance of political unity achieved by this king and his successors, as a new state came into being, based on the symbolic balance of the forces of good and evil, unification and fragmentation. The Egyptians believed that only the rule of kings and the benign force of the sun could contain disorder. In reality, unification took several centuries to achieve through a process of deft political alliance and continual warfare.

Dynastic Egyptian Civilization (c. 3000 to 30 B.C.)

Egyptologists conventionally divide ancient Egyptian civilization into four broad periods: Archaic Egypt and the Old Kingdom, the Middle Kingdom, the New Kingdom, and the Late Period. The first three were separated by two intermediate periods that were interludes of political change and instability (see Table 10.1 on page 247).

Archaic Egypt and the "Great Culture" (3000 to 2575 B.C.)

The first ruler of a truly unified Egypt was King Horus Aha, who reigned in about 3100 B.C. The next four-and-a-half centuries were a long period of consolidation, the Archaic Period, when the pharaohs assumed the role of divine kings. They and their high officials invented Egypt's royal tradition, converting it into powerful architectural statements and artistic styles that endured for centuries. Just like Mesoamerican lords (Chapters 12 and 13), the pharaohs made a great play of their rare public appearances, developing spectacular settings for major ritual events and festivals. They also created a centralized bureaucracy that directed labor, administered food storage, and collected taxes. At the center of the state lay the concept of a great ruler on earth, who symbolized the triumph of order over chaos. In Egypt, the terms *father, king,* and *god* were metaphors for one another and for a form of political

Figure 10.2 The Narmer Palette, a slab carved on both sides with scenes commemorating King Narmer (Menes), whom legend credits with unifying Upper and Lower Egypt. He appears on the palette wearing the white and red crowns of these two regions, presiding over the conquest of the Delta. The central design of entwined beasts (right) symbolizes harmony, balancing images of conquest above and below.

power based on social inequality that was considered part of the natural order established by the gods at the creation.

The Archaic Period saw the birth of Egypt's "Great Culture," a distinctive ideology that systematized Egyptian civilization over wide areas at the expense of local religious cults. Such an ideology was essential in a society where only a minority could read and write. Scribes held enormous power in all early civilizations, and Egypt was no exception. "Be a scribe. . . . You will go forth in white clothes, honored, with courtiers saluting you," a young man is advised. Writing was power, the key to controlling the labor of thousands of people.

Old Kingdom (c. 2575 to 2134 B.C.)

The Old Kingdom saw society shaped in an image in which the well-being of the people depended on the ruler supported by their labors. The new image of kingship developed after the death in 2649 B.C. of the pharaoh Djoser, whose architect Imhotep built the first pyramid as a royal burial place—the celebrated Step Pyramid at **Saqqara.** The king was now absorbed into the mythic symbol of the sun. The sun god became a heavenly monarch, the pharaoh the deity's representative on earth. On his death, an Old Kingdom pharaoh "went to his double," joining the sun god in heaven. Thus it was that Djoser and his successors lavished enormous expenditure on their sepulchers—at first earthen mounds, then pyramids that became symbolic ladders to heaven, their sloping sides the rays of the sun widening after bursting through a gap in the clouds (see box on pages 248–249).

TABLE 10.1 Ancient Egyptian Civilization

Years B.C./B.P.	Period	Characteristics
30 B.C.	Roman occupation	Egypt an imperial province of Rome
332 to 30 B.C.	Ptolemaic period	The Ptolemies bring Greek influence to Egypt, beginning with conquest of Egypt by Alexander the Great in 332 B.C.
1070 to 332 B.C.	Late period	Gradual decline in pharaonic author-ity, culminating in Persian rule (525 to 404 and 343 to 332 B.C.)
1530 to 1070 B.C.	New Kingdom	Great imperial period of Egyptian history, with pharaohs buried in Valley of Kings; pharaohs include Rameses II, Seti I, and Tutankhamun, as well as Akhenaten, the heretic ruler
1640 to 1530 B.C.	Second intermediate period	Hyksos rulers in the delta
2134 to 2040 B.C.	Middle Kingdom	Thebes achieves prominence, also the priesthood of Amun
2040 to 1640 B.C.	First intermediate period	Political chaos and disunity
2575 to 2134 B.C.	Old Kingdom	Despotic pharaohs build the pyra-mids and favor conspicuous funerary monuments; institutions, economic strategies, and artistic traditions of ancient Egypt established
2920 to 2575 B.C.	Archaic period	Consolidation of state
3100 B.C.	Unification of Egypt under Narmer-Menes and Scorpion	

The court cemeteries and pyramid complexes of the Old Kingdom pharaohs extend over a 35-kilometer (22-mile) stretch of the western desert edge, most of them slightly north of Memphis.

The pharaohs lavished enormous resources on their pyramids, culminating in the reigns of Khufu and Khafre, who built the pyramid tombs of **Giza** (see Figure 1.2 on page 7). In about 2528 B.C., Khufu built the Great Pyramid of Giza, one of the spectacular wonders of ancient Africa and one of the Seven Wonders of the Ancient World. It covers 5.3 hectares (13.1 acres) and is 146 meters (481 feet) high. Well over 2 million limestone blocks, some weigh-ing 15 tons apiece, went into its construction. A long causeway linked each pyramid in the Giza complex to a royal mortuary temple. These were austere buildings that housed stat-ues of the king. The nearby sepulchers vested these temples with great authority, for they associated the ruler with what was, in effect, a powerful ancestor cult that linked them to their predecessors and to the gods (see Figure 10.4 on page 250).

SITE

The Step Pyramid at Saqqara, Egypt

Like other early Old Kingdom kings, Third Dynasty pharaoh Djoser (2668–2649 B.C.) grappled with internal political problems. He managed to extend his rule as far upstream as Aswan and laid great emphasis on his role as king and supreme territorial claimant, a role he celebrated within a large enclosure dominated by a unique structure: the Step Pyramid at Saqqara opposite the royal capital at **Memphis.**

Djoser's vizier Imhotep devised the architecture of the Step Pyramid (Figure 10.3). The great architect drew his inspiration from earlier royal tombs, rectangular structures like those at Abydos, which were eternal mansions for dead monarchs. Such tumuli (mounds) had associations with the primordial earthen mound that formed an integral part of the Egyptian legend of the creation. Imhotep erected a stepped pyramid instead of a mound as an area for the king's spirit. It rose in six diminishing steps to over 60 meters (372 feet) above the desert, the faces oriented to the cardinal points. Each step formed a bench or *mastaba,* resembling earlier royal tombs, here built into a stepped pyramid. The effect is like a giant double staircase rising toward heaven.

A thick stone wall with a palacelike façade over 1.6 kilometers (1 mile) in perimeter surrounded the entire mortuary complex, forming a huge courtyard, 108 by 187 meters (354 by 613 feet), with a main gateway at the southeastern corner. An entrance hall decorated with columns opened into a vestibule. The king's internal organs were buried in the so-called South Tomb facing the main pyramid on the south side of the enclosure. Thus, there were two sepulchers, for the Two Lands, Upper and Lower Egypt.

The substructure of the Step Pyramid is a honeycomb of shafts and tunnels, many dug by tomb robbers, others containing large numbers of often exquisite stone vases. Some of them bear the names of earlier kings, as if Djoser incorporated them into his pyramid as an act of piety to his predecessors. Only a mummified left foot remains of the king himself. Other members of the royal family were buried in some of the shafts and tunnels. As the pyramid grew, so these burial chambers were sealed off. Finally, the builders dug a new entrance for Djoser's burial chamber on the north side. They sealed it with a three-ton granite plug.

The Step Pyramid was an elaborate formal setting for the display of kingship—and of the ruler himself—either to his courtiers or the populace at large. The court before the pyramid was a setting for royal appearances, complete with ceremonial territorial markers, a throne platform, and a

---

We do not know why the pharaohs suddenly embarked on this orgy of pyramid construction, with all the accompanying demands that it made on the fledgling state. Their construction, like other major Egyptian public works, was a triumph of bureaucratic organization, of organizing and transporting food and building materials. Then officials marshaled skilled artisans and village laborers to quarry, dig, and drag stone into place, housing them nearby in a special pyramid town, where rations were prepared. What is staggering is the efficient management overview, achieved without computers, deploying and supporting thousands of villagers for short periods of time as they fulfilled their annual tax-by-labor obligations to the state.

Perhaps, as Kurt Mendelssohn has argued, the pyramids were built as a means of linking the people to their guardian, the king, and to the sun god, the source of human life and of bountiful harvests. The relationship between the king and his subjects was both reciprocal and spiritual. The pharaoh was a divine king, whose person was served by annual labor. In short, pyramid building created public works that helped define the

Figure 10.3 The Step Pyramid at Saqqara, Egypt.

token palace. On occasion, the pharaoh laid claim to his kingdom by striding around the limits of the court and its markers. The entire complex was an arena for the eternal pageantry of kingship on earth. The "appearance of the king" was an important occasion throughout Egyptian history.

authority of the ruler and make his subjects dependent upon him. Every flood season, when agriculture was at a standstill, the pharaohs organized thousands of peasants into construction teams, fed by a nearby pyramid workers' community. The permanent (year-round) labor force comprised relatively few people, mainly skilled artisans, the fruit of whose work was placed in position on the main structure once a year. As far as is known, the peasants worked off tax obligations. Their loyalty to the divine pharaoh provided the motivation for the work.

The construction of the pyramids helped institutionalize the state by trading redistributed food for labor. As construction proceeded from one generation to the next, the villagers became dependent on the central administration for food for three months a year, food obtained from surpluses contributed by the villages themselves in the form of taxation. After a while the pyramids fulfilled their purpose, and the state-directed labor forces could be diverted to other, less conspicuous state works. A new form of state organization had been created, one that both fostered and exploited the interdependence of Egyptian villages.

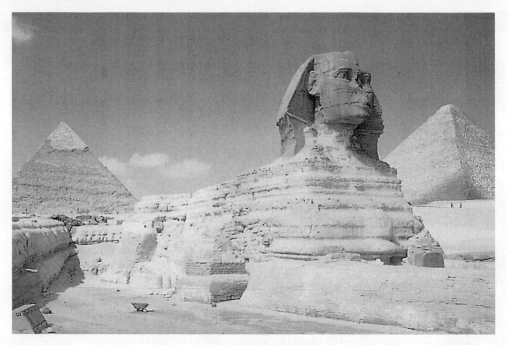

Figure 10.4 The Sphinx at Giza built by the Old Kingdom pharaoh Khafre in about 2500 B.C. Human-headed lions (sphinxes) were important symbols of royal power.

Old Kingdom Egypt was the first state of its size in history. The pharaohs ruled by their own word, following no written laws, unlike the legislators of Mesopotamian city-states. The pharaoh had power over the Nile flood, rainfall, and all people, including foreigners. He was a god, respected by all people as a tangible divinity whose being was the personification of *ma'at*, or "rightness." As previously mentioned, *ma'at* was far more than just rightness; it was a "right order" and stood for order and justice. *Ma'at* was pharaonic status and eternity itself—the very embodiment of the Egyptian state. As the embodiment of *ma'at*, the pharaoh pronounced the law, regulated by a massive background of precedent set by earlier pharaohs. A hereditary bureaucracy effectively ruled the kingdom, with rows of officials forming veritable dynasties. Their records tell us that much official energy was devoted to tax collection, harvest yields, and administration of irrigation.

Old Kingdom Egypt was a time of powerful, confident rulers, of a virile state governed by a privileged class of royal relatives and high officials. Their talents created a civilization that was for the benefit of a tiny minority. It was for this privileged elite, headed by a divine king, that Egyptian merchants traded for the famed cedars of Lebanon, mined turquoise and copper in Sinai, and sought ivory, semiprecious stones, and mercenaries for Egypt's armies from Nubia, present-day Sudan.

A prolonged drought cycle after 2180 B.C. undermined the Old Kingdom rulers' absolute powers. Three hundred years of repeated famines led to anarchy and a diminution of pharaonic authority (see Table 10.1 on page 247). Egypt splintered into competing provinces ruled by ambitious lords.

Middle Kingdom (2040 to 1640 B.C.)

In about 2134 B.C., the city of **Thebes** in Upper Egypt achieved supremacy and reunited Egypt under a series of energetic pharaohs. Middle Kingdom rulers were less despotic, more approachable, and less likely to see themselves as gods. They had learned lessons from the past and relied heavily on an efficient bureaucracy to stockpile food supplies and increase agricultural production (Figure 10.5). For over three centuries, Egypt enjoyed

(a)

(b)

Figure 10.5 Models of a boat and an estate granary belonging to a Middle Kingdom courtier named Meketre. **(a)** He rides in his boat sitting under a canopy. **(b)** On his estate, laborers fill bins with wheat as scribes in a neighboring office record the amounts being stored.

great prosperity and political stability under a series of able pharaohs. Their decisive leadership expanded overseas trade, while they secured Egypt's frontiers with vigorous military campaigns. The most able kings worked hard to create a highly centralized, controlled state both by able leadership and by bureaucratic supervision. At the same time, they strove to increase agricultural production as protection against drought by developing larger scale agriculture, especially on the shores of the fertile Fayum Depression west of the Nile.

Everything depended on charismatic leadership and a strong king. During the seventeenth century B.C., succession disputes engulfed the Theban court at a time when thousands of Asians were moving into the Delta region. Egypt soon fragmented into two kingdoms centered on Lower and Upper Egypt. Lower Egypt came under the control of Hyksos kings, nomadic rulers from Asia. This Second Intermediate Period was a turning point in Egyptian history, for the Hyksos brought new ideas to a civilization that was slowly stagnating in its isolated homeland. They introduced more sophisticated bronze technology, the horse-drawn chariot, and new weapons of war. All these innovations kept Egypt up to date and ensured that subsequent pharaohs would play a leading role in the wider eastern Mediterranean world.

New Kingdom (1530 to 1075 B.C.)

The New Kingdom began when a series of Theban rulers fought and finally conquered the Hyksos, thereby reunifying the kingdom (see box). An able pharaoh named Ahmose the Liberator turned Egypt into an efficiently run military state, tolerating no rivals and rewarding his soldiers with gifts of land, while retaining economic power and wealth in his own hands. Ahmose set the tone for the greatest era in Egyptian history. Now the king became a national hero, a military leader who sat on a throne midway between the Asiatic world in the north and the black Nubian kingdoms of the south (see page 257). He was an imperial ruler, a skilled general, the leader of a great power. As we saw in Chapter 9, Egypt now became a major player in the shifting sands of eastern Mediterranean politics, competing with the Hittites and Mitanni for control of lucrative trade routes and seaports. New Kingdom pharaohs financed their kingdom with Nubian gold, turning the lands beyond the First Cataract into a lucrative colony.

Thebes (known to the Egyptians as Waset) was now capital of Egypt, the "Estate of Amun," the sun god. The Temple of Amun at **Karnak,** built mostly between the sixteenth and fourteenth centuries B.C., was the heart of the sacred capital (see Figure 10.6 on page 254). Amun was the "king of the gods," a solar deity who conceived the pharaohs, then protected them in life and death. The "Estate of Amun" extended to the western bank of the Nile opposite Thebes, where the pharaohs erected an elaborate city of the dead. They themselves were buried in secret, rock-cut tombs in the arid Valley of Kings. Their sepulchers became models of the caverns of the underworld traversed by the night-sun.

The New Kingdom witnessed a brief period of religious unorthodoxy in 1353 B.C., when a heretic pharaoh, Akhenaten, turned away from Amun to a purer form of sun worship, based on the solar disk Aten. Akhenaten went so far as to found a new royal capital at **El-Amarna** downstream of Thebes, on land associated with no established deity. The capital was abandoned after his death, leaving a priceless archaeological legacy—a unique archive of New Kingdom society that archaeologists have excavated at intervals for over a century.

VOICES

The Warrior Ahmose, Son of Abana

The ancient Egyptians boasted loudly on their tomb walls, to the point that one does not know what to believe. Their stories of unrelenting success are much too good to be true, but, occasionally, we come across a truly remarkable individual. A doughty warrior named Ahmose, son of Abana, is a case in point. The old soldier must have been walking history. Ahmose was a soldier's son and followed in his footsteps, at first as a foot soldier, following the king as "he rode about on his chariot." His bravery was noted and "the gold of valor was given" to him. This was the beginning of an illustrious military career. Ahmose served five pharaohs, witnessed the expulsion of the Asian Hyksos kings from Egypt, was present at the ravaging of their capital Avaris in the Delta, at the siege of Sharuhen in Asia, and fought in several bloody Nubian campaigns. When the pharaoh Ahmose (no relative) laid siege to Avaris and fought three battles there, Ahmose (the soldier) noted: "took captive there one man and three women, total four heads, and His Majesty gave them to me for slaves." After bitter fighting and the complete destruction of Avaris, Ahmose's armies chased the Hyksos into Palestine and laid siege to the town of Sharuhen, their stronghold in southern Palestine.

Fresh from the slaughter at Sharuhen, the victorious Theban king turned his attention to Nubia, Ahmose, son of Abana, at his side. "Now when his majesty had slain the nomads of Asia, he sailed south . . . to destroy the Nubian Bowmen. His majesty made great slaughter among them, and I brought spoil from there: two living men and three hands. Then I was rewarded with gold once again, and two female slaves were given to me. His majesty journeyed north, his heart rejoicing in valor and victory. He had conquered southerners and northerners." Ahmose served in several later Nubian campaigns, ending up as a crew commander on a warship, promoted for his skill in organizing the towing of his ship through a turbulent cataract. "I brought a chariot, its horse, and him who was on it as a living captive. When they were presented to his majesty, I was rewarded with gold."

After Nubia, the battle-scarred veteran relaxed in honored retirement, lavished with honors and land. "The crew commander Ahmose, son of Abana, the justified. . . . I let you know what favors came to me. I have been rewarded with gold seven times in the sight of the whole land, with many male and female slaves as well. . . ."

I have always fantasized about sitting down for a long talk with Ahmose, son of Abana, in his old age. He died honored and respected, his deeds remembered on the walls of his sepulcher: "The name of the brave man is in that which he has done; it will not perish in the land forever" (quotes from Lichtheim, 1976, pp. 12–14).

In 1333 B.C., eight-year-old Tutankhamun succeeded to the throne. He presided over a troubled kingdom, so his advisers took the only course open to them. They restored the old spiritual order, reverting to the dynastic traditions of the early pharaohs. Tutankhamun himself ruled for a mere ten years, but achieved in death an immortality that transcends that of all other pharaohs, simply because Howard Carter and Lord Carnarvon found his intact tomb in the Valley of Kings (see Figure 10.7 on page 255).

The Rameside pharaohs of 1307 to 1196 B.C. labored hard to elevate Egypt to its former imperial glory. Rameses II (1290 to 1224 B.C.) campaigned far into Syria, financing his military campaigns and an orgy of temple building with Nubian gold (see chapter opener on page 240). He met his match at the Battle of Kadesh in Syria, where the Hittites fought his army to a standstill. From that moment on, Egypt lost political influence in southwestern Asia, and began a slow, at first barely perceptible, decline.

Figure 10.6 The Temple of the sun god Amun at Karnak.

Late Period (1070 to 30 B.C.)

With the death of Rameses III in 1070 B.C., Egypt entered a period of political weakness, during which local rulers exercised varying control over the Nile. The pharaohs were threatened by Nubian rulers from the south, who controlled Egypt for a time in the eighth century B.C. Assyrians, Persians, and Greeks all ruled over the Nile for varying periods of time until Rome incorporated the world's longest-lived civilization into its empire in 30 B.C. The Greeks brought much of Egyptian lore and learning into the mainstream of emerging Greek civilization, ensuring that ancient Egypt contributed to the roots of Western civilization.

Egypt and Afrocentrism

The ancient Greeks and Romans believed that Egypt was the fountain of all civilization. While archaeological discoveries have shown that urban civilization developed in both Egypt and Mesopotamia at the same time, most scholars believe that civilization developed in isolation along the Nile, in a fertile, if unpredictable, river valley that was a world unto its own.

Some African-American historians of the so-called Afrocentrism school disagree, for they believe that the institutions of Western civilization were born in tropical Africa and that ancient Egypt was a black African civilization. These arguments, which first surfaced in the 1950s, have reached a high level of sophistication in linguist Martin Bernal's celebrated "Black Athena" theory. Bernal presents archaeological, historical, and linguistic evidence to place ancient Egypt at the core of Western civilization. Egyptologists are almost

Figure 10.7 The antechamber of Tutankhamun's tomb, with his royal chariots in the foreground (left) and funerary beds to the right.

unanimous in demolishing his arguments on the grounds that they do not stand in the face of scientific data. For example, Afrocentrists claim that the ancient Egyptians were black-skinned tropical Africans. In fact, both tomb paintings and biological data point to a generally Mediterranean population, but one that became increasingly cosmopolitan in later centuries as Egypt enjoyed closer contacts with other lands, including tropical Africa. It is also worth mentioning that the ancient Egyptian social world thought of skin colors and races in distinctive ways quite different from our own—a point worth making about every human society.

Nubia: The Land of Kush (3000 to 633 B.C.)

If ancient Egypt was indeed a civilization unto itself, what connections did it enjoy with the people of the Nile Valley living south of the First Cataract at Aswan? The arid country that lay upstream was **Nubia,** the Land of **Kush,** famous to the ancient Egyptians for its gold, ivory, and slaves. Nubia straddled the Middle Nile, a narrow strip of fertile land that extended far upstream into modern-day Sudan as far as the borders of highland Ethiopia. The most fertile valley lands lie along the Dongola Reach between the Third and Fourth Cataracts. It was here that some of the earliest complex Nubian societies developed, among groups who had been herders and farmers since before 4000 B.C.

Old Kingdom pharaohs sent their armies to subdue Nubia and boasted of lucrative cattle raids. Egyptian prospectors journeyed far into the desert in search of fine rocks and semiprecious stones. The Middle Kingdom kings were more ambitious, for they discovered Nubian gold. In 1900 B.C. pharaoh Amenemhet fortified strategic reaches with ten strongholds, most of them at strategic points where trade routes intersected with the river. This trade lay in the hands of the Nubian chieftains of **Kerma** in the heart of the Dongola Reach, a small town with palaces and temples, fortified with elaborate defenses and four gates. Kerma's rulers enjoyed great wealth while alive and upon their death were buried under large burial mounds surrounded with as many as 400 sacrificial victims (Figure 10.8). All this wealth came from trade connections with people living in the desert and farther upstream, as well as with the Egyptians far downstream. But the New Kingdom pharaohs, who wanted this wealth for themselves, marched on Kush in 1500 B.C. and made it a colony. Nubia now changed from a country of village farmers and chiefdoms into something resembling a vast plantation state, worked for the benefit of absentee landlords to provide commodities of all types at the cheapest possible cost.

The economic and political shock waves that rolled over the eastern Mediterranean after 1200 B.C. not only overthrew the Hittites and weakened Egypt (see Chapter 9) but also

Figure 10.8 A royal tomb at Kerma—people rush to complete the mound as the burial takes place.

loosened the pharaohs' hold on Nubia. After four centuries of confusion, Nubian civilization achieved new heights. The rulers of the new Kush espoused ancient Egyptian religious beliefs and assumed the powers and ideology of the pharaohs. Their wealth came from the Egyptian export trade, from gold, ivory, and many other commodities.

Between 730 and 663 B.C. Nubian monarchs not only ruled over Kush, they presided over Egypt itself. King Piye marched north in 730, honored the sun god Amun at Thebes, then subdued rebellious rulers in the delta far downstream. Piye was content to rule Egypt from Kush, but his successors transferred their court to Thebes, as the servant became the master, the conquered the conquerors. The Nubian pharaohs did much to restore art and religion, but they were inexperienced in foreign affairs, which led to their downfall. In 663 B.C., King Assurbanipal of Assyria sacked Thebes and the ruler of the day fled to the safety of Kush. In 591, an Egyptian army marched upstream and "waded in Kushite blood." King Aspelta fled far upstream to Meroe, some 500 kilometers (300 miles) upstream, where Nubian monarchs ruled in peace for more than 800 years.

Meroe and Aksum

The move to **Meroe** came when the focus of Nubian trade was shifting away from the eastern Mediterranean to the Red Sea and Indian Ocean. This new commercial world linked the Red Sea, the Persian Gulf states, India, and ultimately Southeast Asia and China into a vast web.

The island of Socotra off northeast Africa and the mysterious Land of Punt on the coast of the southern Red Sea were spice-rich lands where Africans rubbed shoulders with Arabians, Indians with Egyptians. Well-traveled trade routes linked Red Sea coasts with the Nile and the eastern Mediterranean coastline, traversed by laden asses, and, increasingly, by camels, aptly named the "ship of the desert" by the Arabians who first domesticated them as early as 2500 B.C. By the third century B.C., camel breeders dominated the overland caravan trade and brought prosperity to Meroe.

Meroe (593 B.C. to A.D. 330)

Meroe lies on the east bank of the Nile, some 200 kilometers (124 miles) north of the modern city of Khartoum. Its rulers administered a string of villages and towns along the river from Lower Nubia to Sennar on the Blue Nile, controlling the gold, ivory, and slave trade with Egypt. The city also lay astride bustling caravan routes that linked the river with the Red Sea and extended far to the west, along the southern margins of the Sahara (see Figure 10.9 on page 258).

Some twenty-four kings and queens ruled over Meroe between 593 and 220 B.C. These black-skinned rulers were the descendants of the great pharaoh Piye and his successors. They preserved many of the conservative standards of ancient Egyptian civilization, while expressing distinctive African cultural traits. For centuries, they administered a complex, exploitative economic enterprise for their own benefit, controlling trade through a network of carefully policed trade routes and by force.

Ironworking was big business at Meroe, for iron ore was plentiful nearby. Huge slag heaps overlooked the temples and palaces of the city, accumulated over centuries of manufacture that began as early as the seventh century B.C. Iron-tipped tools and weapons gave Meroitic armies strategic advantages over their desert neighbors.

Figure 10.9 General view of Meroe, showing pyramids and iron slag heaps. Two thousand years ago Meroe lay amidst fertile grasslands; it is now desert, partly as a result of overgrazing and excessive tree cutting for charcoal burning by the city's inhabitants.

Meroe reached the height of its prosperity during the first century A.D., when it maintained regular trading contacts with the Roman Empire. A century later, the city was in decline, finally overthrown by the armies of King Ezana of the kingdom of Aksum in the nearby Ethiopian highlands between A.D. 325 and 350.

Aksum (A.D. 100 to 1000)

Aksum, which had prospered from the Red Sea trade, was an African kingdom, whose rulers adopted many ideas from south Arabia in the five centuries before Christ (Figure 10.10). Its highland homeland was a fertile, if unpredictable, environment where irrigated cereal crops, among them a native grass called teff, flourished, providing large food surpluses in good years. By the first century A.D., Aksum was a powerful kingdom, in regular contact with Rome, handling all manner of luxuries and commodities through its port at **Adulis** on the Red Sea. Adulis became so important that Aksum soon overshadowed Meroe, while the Nile trade declined.

The archaeology of Aksum is still little known, but we know that its rulers lived in imposing multi-story palaces and were buried under tall columns up to 33 meters (108 feet) high, carved to represent such buildings (see Figure 10.11 on page 260). At about the time he overthrew Meroe, King Ezana abandoned the religion of his forefathers and

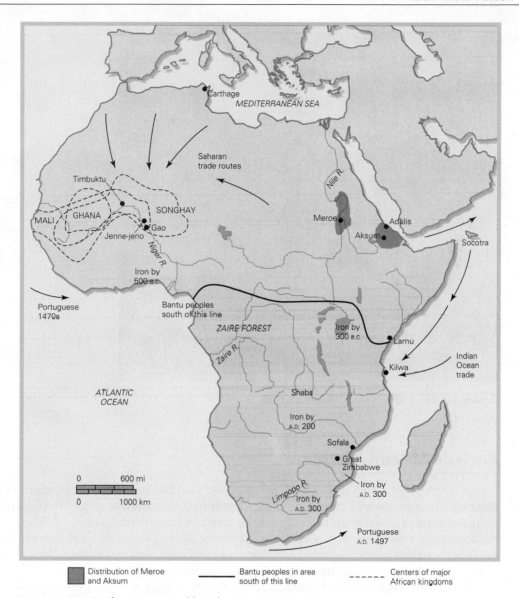

Figure 10.10 African states and kingdoms.

adopted Christianity, which had reached his domains through Aksum's widespread trading connections.

Christianity flourishes in Ethiopia to this day, but Aksum faltered as Islam acquired increasing influence over the Red Sea trade in the seventh century A.D. At the height of its powers, Aksum was a potent symbol of a new, much more international world, which sprang from the ruins of the Roman empire and linked Asia and Africa with lasting ties.

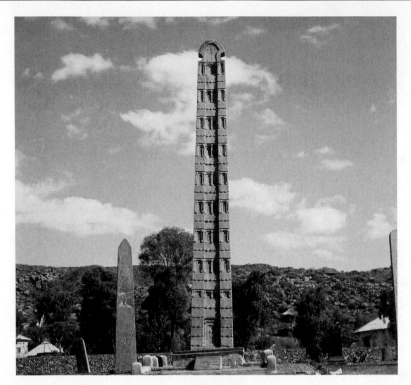

Figure 10.11 A royal stela at Aksum, Ethiopia.

Ancient African Kingdoms

The new trade networks of the Indian Ocean and Red Sea and the development of long-distance caravan routes across the Sahara Desert had an indelible effect on African history, linking tropical African kingdoms with a much larger foreign world. The cultural isolation of sub-Saharan Africa finally broke down during the early Christian era. The insatiable demands of its neighbors for copper, gold, ivory, and slaves brought Africans in touch with Mediterranean and Indian Ocean trading systems.

The camel revolutionized contacts across the desert. Camels are perfectly adapted to desert travel, so much so that North African merchants could organize regular caravans that crossed the Sahara from the Mediterranean to tropical West Africa. African gold and ivory eventually became important sources of medieval European wealth.

No one knows when mariners discovered the cycles of the Indian Ocean monsoon winds. The northeast monsoon brings sailors to Africa in winter. Then, in summer, the northwest monsoon returns them to their destination. These cycles are so regular that a sailing vessel can travel from India to Arabia or East Africa and back within twelve months. Egyptian and Greek navigators knew of the monsoon winds by A.D. 100, by which time the Indian Ocean was part of the vast trading networks that linked China with the Southeast Asian and Mediterranean worlds. There was an insatiable demand for African ivory, gold, silver, iron, and slaves in Arabia and India.

Arabian dhows, downwind sailing vessels, brought cargoes of Indian cotton, strings of cheap glass beads, Chinese porcelain, and other exotic goods to the East African coast. There they traded them for ivory and other raw materials brought to coastal ports and towns like Manda, Lamu, and **Kilwa.** From the coast, small parties of traders traveled far into the interior, along intervillage paths, developing trading contacts and relationships that were to endure for many centuries. By A.D. 300, villagers in the heart of Central Africa wore rare strings of Indian glass beads, more than 950 kilometers (600 miles) from the Indian Ocean.

The Spread of Iron (c. 500 B.C. to A.D. 250)

The Saharan trade brought iron and ironworking south of the desert for the first time, as early as the fifth century B.C. More a utilitarian than a decorative metal, and ideal for tropical forest clearance and agriculture, iron spread rapidly through sub-Saharan Africa as agricultural economies took hold for the first time. Farmers had settled in the great East African lakes region by the last few centuries B.C. and to the banks of the Zambezi and Limpopo Rivers in the early Christian era. The newcomers absorbed, eliminated, or pushed out the indigenous foragers. Today, forager populations survive only in areas that are too arid for farming, such as the Kalahari Desert in southern Africa.

The Kingdoms of Ghana, Mali, and Songhay (c. A.D. 800 to 1550)

Throughout the first millennium A.D., the Saharan gold trade continued to expand gradually, reflected by larger settlements south of the desert. Islamic conquerors took control of the Saharan trade at the end of the first millennium A.D., a development that brought literate and much-traveled Arab geographers to the lands south of the Sahara. There, the geographer al-Bakri described the Kingdom of Ghana as being so rich in gold that "it is said that the king owns a nugget as large as a big stone."

The Kingdom of **Ghana** straddled the northern borders of the gold-bearing river valleys of the upper Niger and Senegal. No one knows when it first came into being, but Arab writers described the kingdom in the eighth century A.D. The Ghanians prospered from the gold, ivory, and salt trade. They also exported kola nuts (used as a stimulant) and slaves. In return they, and their successors, received cloth, leather goods, glass beads, and weapons. The King of Ghana probably presided over a loosely knit alliance of minor chiefs and small towns and had little real power.

Ghana dissolved into its constituent chiefdoms during the eleventh century. Two centuries of incessant squabbling ensued, until the Kingdom of **Mali** came into being at the hands of an able ruler named Sundiata. Sundiata came to power in about 1230 and founded his new capital at Mali on the Niger River. A century later, Mali extended over much of sub-Saharan West Africa. The fame of the Mali kings spread all over the Islamic world (see Figure 10.12 on page 262). The city of Timbuktu on the fringes of the western Sahara became not only a famous caravan center but a celebrated place of Islamic scholarship. All this prosperity was based on the gold and ivory trade. Malian gold underpinned not only much of the Islamic world, but the treasuries of European kings, too. Before Columbus sailed to the New World, Mali and its lesser neighbors provided no less than two-thirds of Europe's gold.

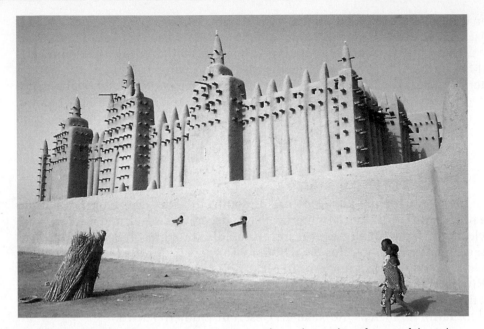

Figure 10.12 The Islamic mosque at Jenne, Mali, on the southern fringes of the Sahara Desert. Islam was a strong influence on West African kingdoms.

Mali's Islamic rulers governed with supreme powers granted by Allah and ruled their conquered provinces with carefully selected religious appointees, or even through clever slaves, chosen for their loyalty and political acumen. Islam provided a reservoir of thoroughly trained, literate administrators who believed that political stability resulted from efficient government and sound trading practices. So confident was the Malian king Mansa Musa that he left his kingdom and crossed the Sahara on a long pilgrimage to Mecca in 1324. He and his wealthy entourage spent so freely in Cairo that the price of gold was depressed for several years.

About a year later, Mansa Musa brought the great trading center at Gao on the Niger River under his control. The leaders of Gao resented Malian control and threw off its yoke in 1340, founding a rival kingdom, **Songhay.** The new state prospered as a series of able rulers expanded their domains. Most famous among them was Sonni Ali, who expanded Songhay's frontiers far into the Sahara and deep into Mali country between 1464 and 1494, monopolizing much of the gold and ivory trade at the same time.

Songhay was at the height of its powers when Columbus landed in the Bahamas. When Europe explored the Americas, its nations acquired new sources for precious metals that trebled the amount of gold and silver circulating in Europe in half a century. The annual output from America was ten times that of the rest of the world. The Saharan gold trade declined sharply. Cities like Gao and Timbuktu, as well as the Kingdom of Songhay, crumbled into relative obscurity. By 1550, Songhay had collapsed, and the center of political power moved south into the tropical forests and coastal regions that are now Ghana, Nigeria, and the Ivory Coast, where European ships traded for gold, ivory, and slaves.

Great Zimbabwe (A.D. 1100 to 1500)

The staple commodity of the Indian Ocean trade was elephant ivory. African ivory is softer and more easily carved than the brittle tusk of the Indian elephant. Tusks fed a flourishing market for Hindu bridal ornaments throughout India. This ancient commerce was well established by the late first millennium A.D., and it continued to prosper long after the discovery of the Americas. By A.D. 1100 a string of small Islamic towns flourished along the coast from Somalia in the north to Kilwa in southern Tanzania in the south. They formed a distinctive coastal civilization that was based entirely on the Indian Ocean trade. From places like the islands of Kilwa and Zanzibar, small caravans set off for the interior, carrying bundles of cotton, glass beads, and thousands of seashells from Indian Ocean beaches. These latter were prized as ornaments in the far interior. This trade was very one-sided in strict monetary terms, for the glass beads, cheap cloth, and other luxuries perceived as prestigious in the African interior were worth a fraction of the gold dust, copper ingots, ivory, and slaves that fueled the maritime trade of an entire ocean.

Much East African gold came from the highlands between the Zambezi and Limpopo Rivers in southern Africa. The coastal traders bartered with the **Karanga** peoples of the interior plateau, who were farmers and cattle herders organized into several powerful kingdoms headed by hereditary rulers. These chiefs acquired political power by controlling sources of copper, gold, and ivory and by redistributing imports from the coast to their subjects. Karanga chiefs were also important spiritual leaders, who acted as intermediaries between the people and their ancestral spirits.

One such chief built an imposing stone capital at **Great Zimbabwe** (see Figure 10.13 on page 264). His Great Enclosure with massive free-standing masonry walls lay in the shadow of a low hill at the head of a valley that brought moist winds and mist up from the distant Indian Ocean. It was here that the chief and his priests performed rainmaking ceremonies and interceded with the ancestors. Here, too, the chief traded with occasional parties of visiting coastal traders, probably men who were part Arabian, part African. There is no evidence that the Zimbabwe chiefs embraced Islam. Zimbabwe was the center of a truly indigenous African kingdom.

At least five stages of occupation have been recognized at Zimbabwe, the earliest dating to the fourth century A.D. The first settlement was a humble village, the four remaining occupations the work of Karanga peoples who built progressively more complicated stone enclosures and retaining walls. The heyday of Zimbabwe was between 1350 and 1450, just before Europeans arrived on the coast. The site was abandoned sometime after 1450, when the local grazing grass and farming land became depleted.

All these indigenous African kingdoms developed in response to economic and political opportunities from outside. But their political, social, and economic institutions were always adapted to local conditions and were logical developments of earlier farming cultures.

After the fifteenth century A.D., Africa was exploited not only for its raw materials, but for its slaves. The tentacles of the international slave trade touched not only African coasts, but reached into the deepest strongholds of the interior. It was not until the nineteenth century that Victorian explorers, in pursuit of elusive geographical prizes like the source of the Nile, revealed to a horrified world the full extent of the slave trade and its catastrophic effect on African society.

Figure 10.13 The walled enclosure at Great Zimbabwe.

Summary

Ancient Egyptian civilization arose out of complex processes of forced and voluntary integration along the Nile Valley. These processes were accelerated by increasing trade contacts with Southwest Asia, culminating in the emergence of the ancient Egyptian state somewhere around 3100 B.C. Egyptologists conventionally subdivide ancient Egyptian civilization into four main periods: the Archaic and Old Kingdom, the Middle Kingdom, the New Kingdom, and the Late Period, the first three of which were separated by brief intermediate periods of political chaos. The Old Kingdom was notable for its despotic pharaohs and its frenzy of pyramid construction, an activity that may be connected with pragmatic notions of fostering national unity. The Middle Kingdom saw a shift of political and religious power to Thebes and Upper Egypt. New Kingdom pharaohs made Egypt an imperial power with strong interests in Asia and Nubia. Ancient Egyptian civilization began to decline after 1000 B.C., and Egypt fell under Roman rule in 30 B.C.

Nubia, upstream of the First Cataract, was exploited by the Egyptians for centuries, but it came into its own as the pharaohs' power declined. Nubian kings from Kush actually ruled over Egypt in the eighth century B.C., but they were forced to retreat to Meroe, far upstream, two centuries later. Meroe became a center for the Red Sea and Indian Ocean trade, ruled by kings and queens who preserved Egyptian customs. It prospered until the fourth century A.D., when it was conquered and finally eclipsed by the kingdom of Aksum in the Ethiopian highlands.

The camel opened up the Sahara to regular gold and salt trade, thus fostering the development of powerful West African states such as Ghana, Mali, and Songhay. At the same time, the expanding Indian Ocean trade nurtured a network of trading towns on the East African coast. During the fourteenth and fifteenth centuries A.D., Great Zimbabwe in southern Africa controlled much of the gold and ivory trade in southeastern Africa.

11

South, Southeast, and East Asia

| 2.5 Million | 1.0 Million | 500,000 B.P. | 100,000 B.P. | 50,000 B.P. | 15,000 B.P. | A.D. 1 | A.D. 1950 |

PROLOGUE

In 1950, Sir Mortimer Wheeler, famed British excavator, assembled a team of young archaeologists, students, and local laborers to work on a confusion of mud bricks that projected out of a weathered citadel mound at Mohenjodaro on the banks of the Indus River, in Pakistan. The laborers removed meter after meter of sand, the few bricks grew into many, "until the stark walls of a huge platform began to emerge from the hillside. The aspect was of a fortress, towering grim and forbidding above the plain" (Wheeler, 1968, p. 317).

Wheeler puzzled over the mass of brickwork. He recorded a grid of narrow passages, signs of a timber superstructure, a carefully designed platform with an approach way. The enormous structure looked less and less like a fortress, but what was it? Suddenly a light went on in his brain. The narrow passages were ducts for air to dry the floor of the timber barn that once housed the city's grain, accessible only from the site, away from the teeming streets. The "fortress" was the municipal granary.

More recent excavations have thrown Wheeler's bold interpretation into doubt, but many details of the Harappan civilization of South Asia, one of the world's least known, came from his classic investigations of a half century ago. The world's earliest civilizations developed in the Nile Valley and western Asia. Within fifteen centuries, Egypt, the eastern Mediterranean, Mesopotamia, and the Iranian highlands were linked in a loosely structured and ever-changing economic system. States rose and fell, rulers achieved supreme power, only to see their domains collapse like a house of cards, armies battled over strategic ports and control of vital materials, but the web of interconnectedness adjusted and remained intact. Soon the tentacles of these economic contacts extended far to the east, into southern Asia and far beyond.

In Chapter 10, we saw how the emphasis of long-distance trade shifted southward into the Red Sea and Indian Ocean region after the decline of Ancient Egypt in about 1000 B.C. This chapter retraces chronological steps and describes how state-organized societies developed in South and Southeast Asia and China (Figure 11.1).

South Asia: The Harappan Civilization (c. 2700 to 1700 B.C.)

The Indus River, on the banks of which South Asian civilization began, rises in the snow-clad Himalayas of southern Tibet and descends 1600 kilometers (1,000 miles) through Kashmir before debouching onto the Pakistani plains. Here, as in Mesopotamia and the

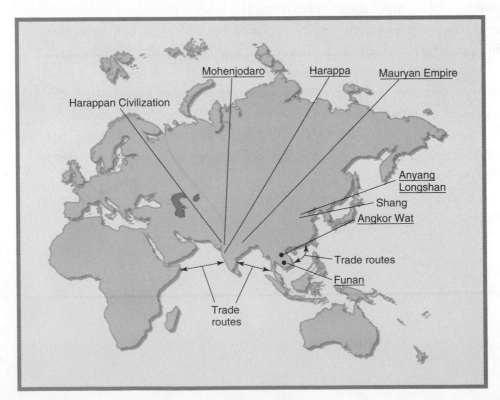

Figure 11.1 Map of Asian sites and societies in Chapter 11.

Nile valley, fertile flood plain soils played an important role in the development of state-organized society. Between June and September each year, the spring runoff from the distant mountains reaches the flat lands, inundating thousands of acres of good farming land and depositing rich flood-borne silts as a natural fertilizer, on soil soft enough to be cultivated without the aid of metal artifacts.

Hundreds of village settlements flourished across the Indus valley plains by 3000 B.C. Many of them were small fortified towns with carefully laid-out streets, built above the highest flood level but as close to the river as possible. The next 500 years saw irrigation canals and flood embankments transform the Indus valley environment into an artificial landscape. The obvious leaders for these new communities were the chieftains, traders, priests, and kin leaders, who acted as intermediaries between the people and their gods. Theirs was a philosophy that humans were part of an ordered cosmos that could be maintained by unremitting toil and a subordination of individual ambition to the common good. No one knows when this primordial philosophy developed, but it is probably as old as farming itself, always a risky undertaking in subtropical lands. By 2700 B.C., the most successful leaders of larger settlements presided over hierarchies of cities, towns, and villages.

The early stages of the **Harappan civilization** date to between 3200 and 2600 B.C. The people lived in small villages covering only a few acres, and there are no signs of social ranking. Their environment was like that of Mesopotamia: low-lying, hot, and with fertile soils but no metals. Thus, its inhabitants could not flourish in isolation. Long before the rise of Harappan civilization in the valley, the peoples of the lowlands interacted constantly with their neighbors to the north and west, especially in the highlands of southern Baluchistan in western Pakistan. Metals, semiprecious stones, and timber came from the highlands, where people depended for their subsistence on dry agriculture and sheep herding. Over the millennia, the relationship between lowlands and highlands was fostered not only by regular exchange of foods and other commodities but also by seasonal population movements that brought enormous herds of goats and sheep down from mountain summer pastures in Baluchistan to the lowlands during the harsh winters in the west. This symbiosis between Baluchistan and the Indus may have been a major catalyst in the rise of complex societies in both areas, a symbiosis that was vital not only in the Indus Valley but in distant Mesopotamia as well.

Early Harappan society was in sharp contrast to the complex, sometimes urban society that developed in the lowlands after about 2600 B.C. The transition from egalitarian to ranked society was an indigenous one, with a short period of explosive growth over a period of one or two centuries ending about 2500 B.C. This contrasts dramatically with the long period of increasing social, political, and economic complexity in Egypt and Mesopotamia.

Archaeologist Gregory Possehl believes that this growth may have coincided with a major shift in Sumerian trade patterns. After 2600 B.C., Mesopotamian city-states reorganized their trade in luxuries and raw materials and obtained many of their needs by sea from three foreign states—**Dilmun,** on the island of Bahrain in the Persian Gulf; **Magan,** a port farther east; and **Meluhha,** even farther away, where ivory, oils, furniture, gold, silver, and carnelian, among other commodities, were to be obtained. The Sumerians exchanged these goods for wool, cloth, leather, oil, cereals, and cedarwood. Possehl believes Meluhha to be the Indus Valley region. In about 2350 B.C., King Sargon of Agade in Mesopotamia boasted that ships from all these locations were moored at his city. There are even records of villages of Meluhhans near **Lagash** and elsewhere in Mesopotamia. This was a highly organized mercantile trade conducted by specialized merchants, a trade quite different from that of the exchange networks on the highlands far inland.

The sea trade increased the volume of Sumerian imports and exports dramatically. One shipment of 5,900 kilograms (13,000 pounds) of copper is recorded. The entire enterprise was very different from the basically noncommercial exchange systems of the Iranian Plateau. The trade was under Mesopotamian control, much of it conducted through Dilmun and, in Possehl's view, it had a major impact on the growth of Harappan civilization. Interestingly, its beginnings coincide with the growth of urban centers in both Mesopotamia and the Indus Valley. However, many scholars believe overseas trade was less important than sometimes claimed and that Harappan civilization was an entirely indigenous development.

Mature Harappan Civilization

Mature Harappan civilization developed and flourished over a vast area of just under 1.3 million square kilometers (0.5 million miles), a region considerably larger than modern Pakistan. The Indus and Saraswati Valleys were the cultural focus of the Harappan civilization, but they were only one part of a much larger, very varied civilization, whose influences and ties extended over the lowlands of Punjab and Sind, from the highlands of Baluchistan to the deserts of Rajastan, and from the Himalayan foothills to near Bombay. The age-old relationship between highland Baluchistan and the Indus plains placed the Harappans within a larger cultural system, as did their maritime links with the Persian Gulf.

Figure 11.2 The citadel at Mohenjodaro, with residential precincts in the foreground.

The Harappan civilization was different from that of the predominantly urban Sumerians in Mesopotamia, covering a core area of more than 777,000 square kilometers (3,000,000 square miles). Gregory Possehl makes an analogy with Egypt, where the Upper and Lower Nile were part of the same civilization, but there were always administrative, cultural, and social differences between the two regions. These were major regional subdivisions of the Harappan civilization, linked by common symbolism and religious beliefs, the foundations of a cultural tradition that endured, albeit in modified form, for many centuries. Like the Sumerians, the Harappans adopted the city as a means of organizing and controlling their civilization. We know of at least five major Harappan cities. The best known are **Harappa,** after which the civilization is named, and **Mohenjodaro.** Harappa and Mohenjodaro were built on artificial mounds above the floods at the cost of Herculean efforts. Mohenjodaro is by far the largest of the Harappan cities, six times the area of Harappa, and was rebuilt at least nine times, sometimes because of disastrous inundations (Figure 11.2). Widely accepted population estimates, based on densities of modern, somewhat similar settlements, place some 35,000 to 40,000 people at Mohenjodaro, 23,500 at Harappa.

The two cities are so similar that they might have been designed by the same architect. A high citadel lies at the west end of each city, dominating the streets below. Here lived the rulers, protected by great fortifications and flood works (Figure 11.3). Mohenjodaro's towering citadel rises 12 meters (40 feet) above the plain and is protected by massive flood embankments and a vast perimeter wall with towers. The public buildings on the summit include a pillared hall almost 27 meters (90 feet) square, perhaps the precinct where the rulers gave audience to petitioners and visiting officials. There are no spectacular temples or richly adorned shrines.

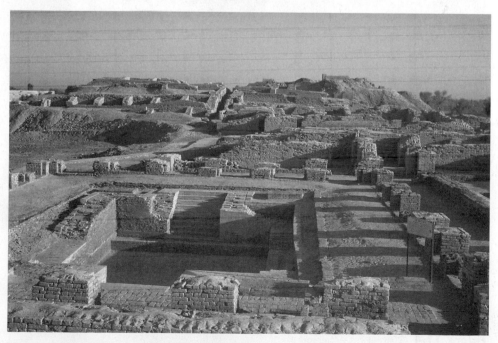

Figure 11.3 The great citadel at Harappa, Pakistan.

The rulers of each city looked down on a complex network of at least partially planned streets (Figure 11.4). The more spacious dwellings, perhaps those of the nobility and merchants, were laid out around a central courtyard where guests may have been received, where food was prepared, and where servants probably worked. Staircases and thick ground walls indicate that some houses had two or even three stories. There were also groups of single-rowed tenements or workshops at both Harappa and Mohenjodaro where the poorest people lived, many of them presumably laborers. Some areas of Harappa and Mohenjodaro served as bazaars, complete with shops.

We do not know the names of the rulers who controlled the major cities like Harappa and Mohenjodaro. The anonymity of the Harappan leaders extends even to their appearance (Figure 11.5). These were no bombastic rulers, boasting of their achievements on grandiose palace walls. Thus far, the evidence of archaeology reveals leadership by rulers, perhaps merchants, ritual specialists, or people who controlled key resources or large areas of land. They seem not to have led ostentatious lives; there was a complete lack of priestly pomp or lavish public display. There is nothing of the ardent militarism of the Assyrian kings or of the slavish glorification of the pharaohs.

One reason we know so little about Harappan leaders is that their script still has not been deciphered. Almost 400 different pictographic symbols have been identified from their seals. Linguists do not even agree on the language in the script, but they know it is a mixture of sounds and concepts, just like Egyptian hieroglyphs. Harappan seals depict gods, like a three-headed figure who sits in the yogic posture and wears a horned headdress. He

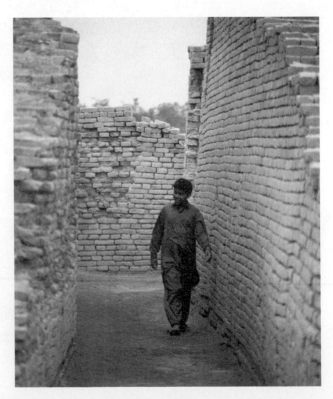

Figure 11.4 A street at Mohenjodaro, Pakistan.

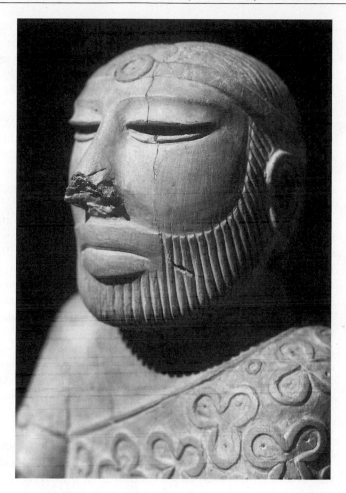

Figure 11.5 A bearded man from Mohenjodaro.

is surrounded by a tiger, elephant, rhinoceros, water buffalo, and deer. Some Harappan experts think the deity was a forerunner of the great god Shiva in his role of Lord of the Beasts. Many Harappan seals depict cattle, which may be symbols of Shiva, who was worshiped in several forms. To judge from later beliefs, he may have had a dual role, serving as a fertility god as well as a tamer or destroyer of wild beasts. In part he may symbolize the unpredictable dangers of flood and famine that could threaten a village or a city. If the evidence of figurines and seals is to be believed, the symbolism of early Indus religion bears remarkable similarities to that of modern Hinduism.

South Asia after the Harappans (1700 to 180 B.C.)

The Harappan civilization reached its peak in about 2000 B.C. Three centuries later, Harappa and Mohenjodaro were in decline and soon abandoned. Their populations dispersed into smaller settlements over an enormous area. The reasons for this change are still little understood, but may be due to a variety of factors, among them possibly flooding along the Indus, shifts in patterns of Mesopotamian trade, and changes in subsistence farming. One fundamental cause may have been major geological disturbances near the source of the all-important Saraswati River, which caused it to dry up and some tributaries to divert to new courses, thereby catastrophically disrupting farming life along its banks. Chronic deforestation and soil erosion may also have contributed to the demise of Indus cities.

Other changes followed soon afterward. By 1500 B.C., rice cultivation had taken hold in the Ganges Basin to the east, opening up a new environment for farming where conditions were unsuitable for wheat and barley cultivation. By 800 B.C., an indigenous iron technology was in full use throughout the subcontinent. Iron tools accelerated rice cultivation on the Ganges Plain. Two centuries later, sixteen major kingdoms were concentrated around urban centers in the Ganges Plain.

City life in the Ganges Valley marked the beginning of the classic period of South Asian civilization. The new cities became economic powerhouses and centers of great intellectual and religious ferment. Brahmanism was the dominant religion during the early first millennium, a form of Hinduism that placed great emphasis on ritual and sacrifice. But philosophers of the sixth century B.C., like Buddha and Makhali Gosala, challenged Brahmanism with revolutionary doctrines that militated against sacrifice. Buddhism, with its teachings of personal spiritual development, spread rapidly, becoming the dominant religion in the north within five centuries.

Meanwhile, outside powers eyed the fabled riches of the subcontinent. King Darius of Persia invaded the northwest in 516 B.C. and incorporated the Indus Valley into the Persian Empire. Two centuries later, Alexander the Great ventured to the Indus River and brought Greek culture to the area. The great ruler Chandragupta Maurya of Magadha benefitted from the power vacuum following Alexander the Great's conquests and carved out the **Mauryan Empire,** which extended from Nepal and the northwest deep into the Deccan (see Figure 11.1 on page 268). His grandson Asoka presided over the empire at its height between 269 and 232 B.C., seeking to unify its diverse people by a well-defined moral and ethical code based on Buddhist principles. As the Mauryan empire came to an end in 185 B.C., South Asia had become part of a vast trading network that linked the Mediterranean world to all parts of the Indian Ocean, and indirectly, to new sources of raw materials many sea miles to the east.

The Origins of Chinese Civilization (2600 to 1100 B.C.)

In Chapter 6, we described the origins of Chinese agriculture and the gradual elaboration of local society that resulted from cereal and rice cultivation. By 3000 B.C., China was a patchwork of kingdoms large and small, ruled by chieftains buried in considerable splendor. The origins of Chinese civilization in its traditional northern homeland are known only from legend. Such legends tell us that the celebrated ruler Huang Di founded civilization in the north in about 2698 B.C. This legendary warlord set the tone for centuries of the repressive, harsh government that was the hallmark of early Chinese civilization. About 2200 B.C., a Xia ruler named Yu the Great gained power through his military prowess and his knowledge of flood control, by which he could protect the valley people from catastrophic inundations. Like his successors, Yu appears to have used divination with the aid of ox shoulder blades as a way of making decisions (Figure 11.6).

Figure 11.6 Shang oracle bones, used for divination by early Chinese rulers. A heated point was applied to the ox shoulder blade, which cracked. The priest then "read" the cracks and recorded the findings.

What exactly do these legends mean? Who were the **Xia** and their successors, the **Shang?** In all probability they were dynasties of local rulers who achieved lasting prominence among their many neighbors after generations of bitter strife. Every chieftain lived in a walled town and enjoyed much the same level of material prosperity, but each ruler came from a different lineage and was related to his competitors by intricate and closely woven allegiances and kin ties. Each dynasty assumed political dominance in the north in turn, but for all these political changes, **Shang civilization** itself continued more or less untouched, a loosely unified confederacy of competing small kingdoms that quarreled and warred incessantly.

Royal Capitals

Shang settlements are stratified on top of less complex settlements at many places in northern China, and they represent a dramatic increase in the complexity of material culture and social organization. The same trends toward increasing complexity are thought to have occurred elsewhere in China at approximately the same time, for literate states may have emerged in the south and east as well. In form they probably resembled the Shang closely, but few details of the others are known. It seems likely that the Shang dynasty was dominant from approximately 1766 to 1122 B.C. but that other states continued to grow at the same time. The larger area of Chinese civilization ultimately extended from the north into the middle and lower courses of the Huang Ho and Yangtze rivers. In this account, we concentrate on northern Chinese civilization simply because more is known about the archaeology of the Shang than about any other early Chinese state.

Shang rulers lived in at least seven capitals, situated near the middle reaches of the Huang Ho River in the modern provinces of Henan, Shandong, and Anhui (see Figure 11.1 on page 268). The sites of all these towns are still uncertain, but in approximately 1557 B.C. the Shang kings moved their capital to a place named **Ao,** which archaeologists have found under the modern industrial city of Zhengzhou, some 150 kilometers (95 miles) south of **Anyang,** close to the Huang Ho River. The diggers have found traces of a vast precinct surrounded by an earthen wall more than 9.9 meters (33 feet) high, enclosing an area of 5 square kilometers (2 square miles). It would have taken 10,000 workers laboring 330 days a year for no fewer than 18 years to erect the fortifications alone. This walled compound housed the rulers, the temples, and the nobles. The residential quarters and craft workshops lay outside the Shang walls. These include two bronze factories, one of them covering nearly a hectare.

The capital moved to the Anyang area in approximately 1400 B.C., where it remained until the fall of the Shang more than 250 years later. This new royal domain was known as Yin and may have encompassed a network of compounds, palaces, villages, and cemeteries extending over an area some 310 square kilometers (120 square miles) on the northern bank of the Huang Ho River. The core of this "capital" was near the hamlet of **Xiao-tun,** 2.4 kilometers (1.5 miles) northwest of the modern city of Anyang. Years of excavations at Xiao-tun have revealed 53 rectangular foundations of stamped earth up to 36 meters (120 feet) long, 19.5 meters (65 feet) wide, and as much as 1.5 meters (5 feet) high, many of them associated with sacrificial burials of both animals and humans. One group of fifteen foundations on the north side of the excavated area supported timber houses with mud and stick walls, devoid of sacrificial victims. These are believed to be the royal residences that housed extended families of nobles living in large halls and smaller rooms closed off with doors.

Royal Burials

The Shang rulers at first buried their dead in a cemetery just over 1.6 kilometers (1 mile) northeast of Anyang. Eleven royal graves from this cemetery were excavated during the 1930s. They were furnished on a lavish scale and date to between 1500 and 1200 B.C. The best-known grave is in the shape of a crosslike pit approximately 9.9 meters (33 feet) deep with slightly sloping walls. Four ramps lead from the surface to each side of the pit. The coffin of the ruler, which was placed inside a wooden chamber erected in the burial pit, was accompanied by superb bronze vessels and shell, bone, and stone ornaments. One ceremonial halberd has an engraved jade blade set in a bronze shaft adorned with dragons and inlaid with malachite. Sacrificial victims and slaves accompanied the dead ruler, buried both in the chamber itself and on the approach ramps. Many were decapitated, so their bodies were found in one place and their heads in another.

The Shang kings surrounded their sepulchers with hundreds of lesser burials. No fewer than 1221 small graves have been dug up nearby, many of them burials of between 2 and 11 people in a single tomb. In 1976 archaeologists uncovered nearly 200 of these graves. Most of them contained decapitated, dismembered, or mutilated bodies. Some of the victims had been bound before death. These can only have been sacrificial offerings consecrated when the kings and their relatives died.

Bronzeworking

The Shang people are justly famous for their bronzework, best known to us from ceremonial artifacts found in royal tombs. The prestigious metal was not gold, which was in short supply, but bronze. Most Shang bronzeworks are food or drinking vessels, some are weapons, a few are musical instruments, and many are chariot and horse fittings. Bronzeworking was the guarded monopoly of the rulers, a complex art that the Chinese developed quite independently from the West before 2000 B.C. Their smiths produced some of the most sophisticated and elegant bronze objects ever crafted (Figure 11.7). Their elaborate display pieces were copies of clay prototypes carefully sculpted around a baked clay core and encased in a segmented mold. Once the clay version was completed, the baked outer mold was removed, the model broken away from the core, and the two parts reassembled to receive the molten bronze. This complex technique remained in use for at least five centuries.

Figure 11.7 Shang ceremonial bronzes.

Shang Warriors

Every early Chinese ruler stayed in power by virtue of a strong army. Shang society was organized on what might be called military lines, so that the royal standing army could be supplemented with thousands of conscripts on very short notice. The kings frequently were at war, protecting their frontiers, suppressing rebellious rivals, or raiding for sacrificial victims. In a sense, every early Chinese state was an armed garrison that could call on armies of more than 10,000 men. The secret was a sophisticated, permanent military establishment and a kin organization through which people were obligated to serve the king when called on. The same basic organization persisted long after the fall of the Shang dynasty in 1100 B.C.

Most surviving Shang weapons come from sacrificial chariot burials, such as the one excavated near Anyang in 1973. The archaeologists did not uncover the wooden chariot itself but a cast of the wooden parts preserved in the soil (Figure 11.8). They brushed away the surrounding soil with great care until they reached the hardened particles of fine sand that had replaced the wooden structure of the buried chariot. They were able to photograph not only the "ghost" of the chariot but also the skeletons of the two horses. The charioteer had been killed at the funeral and his body placed behind the vehicle. The charioteer rode on a

Figure 11.8 Chariot burial from the Shang royal cemetery near Anyang. The wooden parts of the chariot were excavated by following discolorations in the soil left by rotting wood.

wicker and leather car measuring between 0.9 and 1.2 meters (3 and 4 feet) across and borne on a stout axle and two spoked wheels with large hubs adorned with bronze caps. In all probability, the nail-free chariot was held together with sinew lashings, adorned with bronze and turquoise ornaments, and perhaps painted in bright colors.

The War Lords (1100 to 221 B.C.)

The Shang dynasty fell in about 1100 B.C. at the hands of the neighboring **Zhou**. The conquerors did not create a new civilization; rather, they took over the existing network of towns and officials and incorporated them into their own state organization, thus shifting the focus of political and economic power to the south and west, away from Anyang into the fertile Wei Valley near the modern city of Xi'an. By this time, the influence of what may loosely be called Shang civilization extended far beyond the north, into the rice-growing areas of the south and along the eastern coasts. The Zhou divided their domains into various almost independent provinces, which warred with one another for centuries. It was not until 221 B.C. that the great emperor Shihuangdi unified China into a single empire (Figure 11.9; see also chapter opener on page 266). His Han Dynasty successors traded with the Western world overland through the celebrated Great Silk Road across Central Asia, and also with newly powerful states in Southeast Asia.

Southeast Asian Civilization (A.D. 1 to 1500)

After 500 B.C. there are signs of major cultural and social change throughout Southeast Asia, which coincide with the introduction of iron technology between about 600 and 400 B.C. The new metallurgy was grafted onto existing bronze technology, but it is uncertain whether ironworking was introduced from India, where forging (smelting in a small furnace) was

Figure 11.9 A cart, its horses, and driver fabricated in cast-bronze with silver inlay, at one-third life size. From the precincts of the tomb of Emperor Shihuangdi, first emperor of China.

SITE

The Burial Mound of Emperor Shihuangdi, China

King Zheng, the "Tiger of Qin," was the First Sovereign Emperor (Shihuangdi) of China. He became ruler of Qin at the age of thirteen in 246 B.C., unifying China after a series of ruthless military campaigns in 221 B.C. Work may have begun on the emperor's tomb as early as 246 B.C., but it intensified with unification. The emperor considered himself unique, so his sepulcher was to be the largest ever built. Later court histories write of more than 700,000 conscripts, many of them convicts, who worked on the tomb, the capital, and the royal palace.

The great burial mound measures more than 335 meters (1,100 feet) on each side and rises 43 meters (140 feet) above the surrounding countryside, 40 kilometers (25 miles) east of Xianyang on the banks of the Wei River. Inside lies what is said to be a replica of the royal domains, with China's great rivers recreated in mercury flowing, by some mechanical device, into the ocean. The constellations of the heavens appear on the ceiling of the burial chamber, the earth's geography beneath. Scale models of palaces and pavilions contain the emperor's personal possessions, while models of courtiers attend him in death. Many concubines, who were also laborers on the tomb, were sacrificed and buried inside the tumulus. While Han Dynasty historians state that the mound was looted after the fall of the Qin line, Chinese archaeologists have detected unusually high concentrations of mercury in the soil chemistry of the mound and suspect Shihuangdi's grave goods may be intact. Chinese archaeologists decline to excavate the tomb, as they say they lack the resources and skills to dig it properly and conserve the contents. The mound once lay in the middle of a large funerary park surrounded by a 6.4-kilometer (4-mile) outer wall.

In the 1970s, Chinese archaeologists excavated a regiment of terracotta soldiers to the side of the funerary mound—armed cavalrymen, kneeling archers, and their officers, perhaps a ceremonial guard assigned to protect the eastern side of the tomb (see chapter opener on page 266). The molded figures were finished with individual hairstyles, mustaches, and other features and were fully armed. Other finds near the tumulus include two half-scale bronze chariots and their horses, as well as underground stables, some with mangers containing horses buried alive (see Figure 11.9 on page 279).

used, or from China, where sophisticated casting methods were commonplace, involving molten iron at very high temperatures. Larger communities developed, usually centers for craft production. The appearance of larger settlements may have coincided with both irrigation and the advent of plowing, which greatly magnified food production and produced much larger crop surpluses.

Toward the end of the first millennium B.C., some Southeast Asian societies had become highly ranked, centralized kingdoms, presided over by an aristocratic class to whom formal display, feasting, and ritual were of paramount importance. They ruled by virtue of their close relationships with their ancestors. The growing complexity of such societies came in part from the ability of their overlords to attract loyal followers and to organize people. In time, many such rulers aspired to even greater status, to presiding over far larger kingdoms carved out by force, charisma, or the creation of magnificent palaces and temples, which served as the focus for elaborate public ceremonials and prestigious displays.

These Southeast Asian kingdoms were in a constant state of political flux and without fixed boundaries. Alliances developed between neighboring rulers. Everything revolved around the principal overlord, whose ability to cement alliances and deal with potential enemies dictated his relationships with his rivals. Some experts use a Sanskrit word, *mandala*, an Indian political doctrine, to describe the relationships between these rulers, whose territories are thought of as circles. It is as if they were concertinas, which expanded and contracted as different kingdoms interacted with one another. Each society focused on its own center and on its own religious ruler and his retinue. The personal and spiritual qualities of each leader were important variables in a complex, ever-changing political equation.

Divine kingship revolutionized social and political organization in Southeast Asia. Kingdoms flourished in riverine and lowland areas, along the lower Mekong, and in the middle Mekong Valley, including the celebrated Tonle Sap plains, the homeland of Khmer-speaking peoples.

The Chinese called the lower Mekong region **Funan,** which meant "the port of a thousand rivers," but the term has little real historical meaning. According to Chinese records, the ports of the delta handled bronze, silver, gold, spices, and even horses brought by sea from Central Asia. Chinese accounts of Funan extol its rich trade. They tell of a drainage and transport system that rapidly transformed much of the delta from barren swamps into rich agricultural land. The development of these fields took the communal efforts of hundreds of people living off the fish that teemed in the bayous of the delta. Most Funanese lived in large lake cities fortified with great earthworks and moats swarming with crocodiles. Each major settlement was a port connected to the ocean and its neighbors by a canal network.

The coastal region prospered greatly from the third to the sixth centuries A.D., thanks to its long traditions of indigenous metallurgy and other crafts and trading expertise. But by the sixth century A.D., the center of economic and political gravity had shifted inland to the middle Mekong and the fertile Tonle Sap, an area the Chinese called Zhenla. Competing Zhenla rulers acquired sufficient food surpluses to embark on ambitious conquests and, eventually, to develop a new political concept of divine kingship that united their far-flung domains in a common purpose: the glorification of the god-king on earth. Devotion to the Hindu creator, Siva, became a mechanism that provided divine justification for kingship, as well as a focus for the loyalty and devotion of a ruler's retinue, who would endow temples in return for royal favors. Ambitious men would try and try again to raise themselves above others and their kingdoms to supreme rule. Throughout the centuries, these were never states in the Western sense of the word. Rather, the "concertina" effect of kingdom politics was constantly at work, with competing polities asserting independence at times, becoming tribute givers and vassals at others.

The Angkor State (A.D. 802 to 1430)

The overlords of the Tonle Sap all shared one ambition: to establish authority over as large an area as possible. The earlier kings were unable to hold the kingdom together until a dynamic Khmer monarch named Jayavarman II came to power in A.D. 802. He conquered his competitors and set up his new territories as tribute kingdoms, giving his loyal generals land grants.

Jayavarman II is said to have merged the cult of the ancestors with that of Siva in the form of a linga to consolidate his new kingdom. His subjects were taught to worship him as a god. All resources of an increasingly centralized government were devoted to the preservation of the cult of the god-king. Everyone, whether noble, high priest, or commoner, was

SITE

Angkor Wat, Cambodia

Four years after his succession in A.D. 1113, King Suryavarman II commenced building his masterpiece, an extraordinary shrine that is a spectacle of beauty, wonder, and magnificence, the largest religious building in the world. Angkor Wat (Figure 11.10) is 1,500 meters (5,000 feet) by 1,200 meters (4,000 feet) across. The central block measures 215 by 186 meters (717 by 620 feet) and rises more than 60 meters (200 feet) above the forest. It dwarfs even the largest Sumerian ziggurat and makes Mohenjodaro's citadel look like a village shrine.

Every detail of this extraordinary building reproduces part of the heavenly world in a terrestrial mode. The Khmer believed that the world consisted of a central continent known as Jambudvipa, with the cosmic mountain, Meru, rising from its center. The gods lived at the summit of Meru, represented at Angkor Wat by the highest tower. The remaining four towers depict Meru's lesser peaks; the enclosure wall depicts the mountain at the edge of the world, and the surrounding moat depicts the ocean beyond. Angkor Wat was the culminating attempt of the Khmer to reproduce a monument to the Hindu god Visnu, the preserver of the universe.

Angkor Wat's bas-reliefs show Suryavarman seated on a wooden throne wearing an elaborate crown and pectoral. He receives his high officials as they declare their loyalty. Next, the king progresses down a hillside on an elephant accompanied by the high priest and his generals. The court rides with him through a forest, with noble ladies in litters, everyone protected by heavily armed soldiers. Scattered throughout Angkor Wat are scenes of battles, and bas-reliefs of celestial maidens. Naked to the waist, slender and sensuous, the dancers wear skirts of rich fabric. Their flowered background, the subtle rhythm of their gestures, their jeweled necklaces and diadems bring to light the delights of paradise promised to the king after his death. Inscriptions also spell out the terrible punishments that awaited ill-doers.

Angkor Wat was constructed using a measurement of 0.435 meters (1.43 feet), a Khmer unit of measurement known as a *hat*. The length and breadth of the central structure of the temple corresponded to 365.37 *hat*, while the axial distances of the great causeway correspond with the four great eras of Hindu time. Someone standing in front of the western entrance on the spring equinox was able to see the sun rising directly over the central lotus tower. During his lifetime, Suryavarman

expected to subordinate his or her ambitions to the need to perpetuate the existence of the king on earth and his identity with the god in this life and the next. This remarkable leader reigned for forty-five years, the first of at least three dynasties of Khmer rulers, who often came to power after vicious fighting and presided over an ever-changing state that reached the height of its prosperity between A.D. 900 and 1200.

Previous monarchs had encouraged the worship of Siva in the form of the phallic image, but now Jayavarman II presented himself as the reincarnation of Siva on earth. He was the *varman*, the protector, and his priests were the instruments of practical political power. The high priests were invariably energetic, imposing nobles who presided over a highly disciplined hierarchy of religious functionaries. The ruler himself headed a bureaucracy of high status families, which included generals and administrators who settled land disputes. The bureaucracy supervised every aspect of Khmer life, from agriculture to warfare, tax collection, and the rituals of the state religion. As always with preindustrial civilizations, there was a close link between food surpluses and the control of the enormous labor forces needed to construct temples, reservoirs, and other public works.

Figure 11.10 Angkor Wat, Cambodia.

used Angkor Wat as the place where he, as a divine monarch, communicated with the gods. When he died, his remains were placed in the central tower, so that his soul entered his divine image and made contact with the royal ancestors. Here the immortal ruler became as one with Visnu, master of the universe.

The custom of building a new majestic and holy temple to house the royal linga of each king was the most important of all the religious rituals. As a result, many of the thirty monarchs who followed Jayavarman II left massive religious edifices to commemorate their reigns. These they built on artificial mounds in the center of their capitals, the hub of the Khmer universe, an area known today as Angkor. The Khmer's unique form of kingship produced, instead of an austere civilization like that of the Indus, a society that carried the cult of wealth, luxury, and divine monarchy to amazing lengths. This cult reached its apogee in the reign of Suryavarman II, who built the temple of **Angkor Wat** in the twelfth century (see box).

Angkor Wat taxed the resources of the kingdom severely at a time of increased strife with neighboring powers. In 1181, another ruler, Jayavarman VII, who was a Buddhist, started building a huge new capital at **Angkor Thom** nearby. A dark and forbidding 12.8-kilometer (8-mile) wall surrounds the capital. When visitors walked inside, they entered a symbolic Hindu world with the king's funerary temple at the center. The Grand Plaza of Angkor Thom was the scene of ceremonies and contests, of vast military reviews and massed bands.

It is said that a million people once lived in or near Angkor Thom. One temple dedicated to the king's father contained no fewer than 430 images, with more than 20,000 in gold, silver, bronze, and stone in the wider precincts. An inscription in the Ta Proehm temple nearby, dedicated to the king's mother in the image of the Buddha's mother, records that 306,372 people from 13,500 villages worked for the shrine, consuming 38,000 tons of rice a year. An inscription in the nearby temple of Ta Proehm inventories a staff of 18 senior priests, 2,740 minor functionaries, 615 female dancers, and a total of 66,625 "men and women who perform the service of the gods." All this royal construction was designed to make merit for the king and his followers. He also built fully staffed hospitals and pilgrims' shelters to gain further credit. The result of Jayavarman's building projects was a totally centripetal religious utopia in which every product, every person's labor, and every thought was directed to embellishing the hub of the universe and the kings who enjoyed it (Figure 11.11).

The impression of prosperity and stability was illusory in a society where the ruler's power depended on the granting of favors, on his successful patronizing of the major aristocratic families. The king mediated with the gods for rain, settled disputes, and used the rich resources of the land to redistribute wealth among his subjects. He sat at the center of the circle represented by the *mandala*, its boundaries defined only by the loyalties of the aristocrats who ruled the outlying provinces. A Khmer king's hold on the reins of power depended on the control of the center, the Angkor. Thus, when the central administration was weak, the kingdom tended to break up into regional units. In 1430–1431, Angkor was sacked by the Thai after a long siege and the great state finally dissolved.

Late in the thirteenth century, the strategic trade routes through the Malay Straits came under Islamic control in a new chapter of international trade. Melaka became an important port and stronghold on the northern shore of the straits. The rest of the kingdoms and ports

Figure 11.11 Ta Proehm in its current ruined state, where tree roots are uprooting the walls and exquisite sculptures.

of the islands soon adopted the new religion, which preached a message of religious egalitarianism in the face of centuries of Indian statecraft based on notions of divine kingship. Within three centuries, the rulers of inland Java had adopted Islam, perhaps to maintain control over their subjects, who were welcoming the new beliefs with open arms. Islam and trade went hand in hand in island Southeast Asia, until the arrival of Portuguese gun-bearing sailing ships at Melaka in 1519.

The Khmer state is a classic example of how a combination of cultural processes and able individuals can lead to the appearance of powerful, yet volatile states. Yet these same states face constantly the problem of controlling not only the center, but the periphery, especially in times of weak rule and menacing competition from outside.

Summary

State-organized societies on the Indian subcontinent developed from indigenous roots before 2700 B.C. The Harappan civilization of the lowland Indus Valley developed as the result of a major shift in Sumerian long-distance trade patterns and long-term interactions between the Harappan culture of the lowlands and the Baluchistan highlands. Harappan civilization flourished along the Indus for about a thousand years. It was an urban society with many smaller satellite settlements, carefully planned and ruled by priest-kings who controlled both religious and economic life. After 1700 B.C., the major cities went into decline, but Harappan society flourished in rural settings for a considerable time. The center of economic and political gravity moved eastward to the Ganges River valley, culminating in the Mauryan Empire of the first millennium B.C.

Early Chinese civilization emerged independently of state-organized societies in the West. The Shang civilization of the Huang Ho Valley is the best-known early Chinese state, flourishing from 1766 to 1122 B.C. It was probably the dominant state among several throughout northern China. Shang society was organized along class lines, with the rulers and nobles living in segregated precincts, whereas the mass of the people were scattered in townships and villages in the surrounding countryside. Shang civilization ended with the overthrow of the Shang Dynasty by Zhou rulers, who reigned over a wide area of northern China from 1122 to 221 B.C. China was unified under the emperor Shihuangdi in that year.

The process of forming Southeast Asian states began around the same time, but the first historical records of complex states date to the third century A.D. Many such states developed in and around the central Mekong Valley, and later the central Cambodian basin. There, after A.D. 802, flourished the flamboyant Khmer civilization, a society based on divine kingship and strong notions of conformity. After six centuries of spectacular development, the Khmer civilization came in contact with expanding Islamic trade networks and new religious doctrines, which caused its partial demise.

2.5 Million   1.0 Million   500,000 B.P.   100,000 B.P.   50,000 B.P.   15,000 B.P.   A.D. 1   A.D. 1950

PROLOGUE

By any standards, John Lloyd Stephens, New-York-lawyer-turned-traveler, was a remarkable man. In 1839, he and Scottish artist Frederick Catherwood journeyed deep into the Mesoamerican rain forest, following rumors of vanished civilizations and great ruins masked by primordial jungle. They came first to the tiny modern village of Copán, where "around them lay the dark outlines of ruins shrouded by the brooding forest. The only sound that disturbed the quiet of this buried city was the noise of monkeys moving around among the tops of the trees" (Stephens, 1841, p. 48). While Catherwood drew the intricate hieroglyphs he had found on the Maya stelae, Stephens tried to buy the ancient city of Copán for fifty dollars so that he could transport it block by block to New York. The deal fell through when he found he could not float the antiquities downstream. Stephens and Catherwood visited Palenque, Uxmal, Chichén Itzá, and other sites. They were the first to recognize the Maya as the builders of these great sites: "These cities . . . are not the works of people who have passed away . . . but of the same great race . . . which still clings around their ruins," Stephens wrote (1841, p. 222). All subsequent research into the Maya and into ancient Mesoamerican civilization has been based on his work.

Intricate calendars, great ceremonial centers and superb architecture, mysterious glyphs and spectacular shamanistic rituals—the colorful **Maya civilization** fascinates archaeologist and layperson alike. Exotic and, until recently, little understood, the Maya epitomize the ancient traditions of civilization in Central America. A search for its origins takes us back nearly four millennia to the village farming communities that flourished in Mesoamerica when Egyptian civilization was at its height and the Shang state dominated northern China. This chapter describes the origins and growth of Maya, and other, lowland civilizations in Central America. Chapter 13 surveys the peoples of the highlands, who interacted constantly with their lowland neighbors.

Beginnings: Preclassic Peoples in the Lowlands (2000 B.C. to A.D. 300)

Two great mountain chains form the backbones of highland Mesoamerica, running down the coastlines until they reach the east-west volcanic chain that forms the Mesa Central, the central plateau (Figure 12.1). The inland basin of the Valley of Mexico with its five lakes forms the heart of the plateau, for thousands of years the center of political and economic life in highland Mesoamerica. The highland regions of southern Mesoamerica are mountainous, with the highland plateau of Oaxaca offering some of the rare flat terrain in the region. Even further south, great mountain ranges enclose the highland plateau where modern Guatemala City lies. The peoples of the Basin of Mexico and the southern highlands enjoyed a cool climate with most rainfall falling between June and November, sufficient to allow a single crop a year. The more southerly plateaus were still fertile, but warmer.

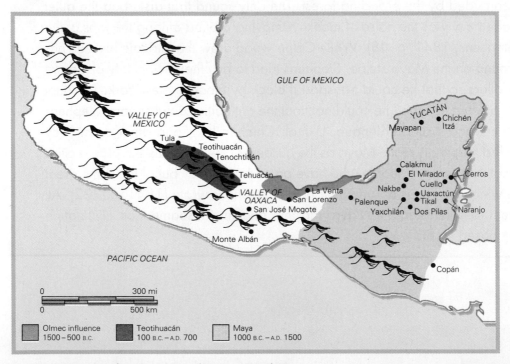

Figure 12.1 Map showing sites in Chapters 12 and 13.

To the north, the serried mountains of the highlands give way to the low-lying limestone peninsula of the Yucatán, the so-called Maya lowlands. Highland climatic conditions contrast dramatically with those in the lowlands, where conditions are hot and humid throughout the year. The southern two thirds of the Yucatán make up the Petén, hilly limestone formations covered with dense tropical forest intersected with lakes and swamps. The limestone plains of the northern Yucatán are much drier, with a drainage pattern based on underground water channels. The shores of the Gulf of Mexico are low-lying and hot: the low coastal plains of Veracruz and Tabasco, the Yucatán Peninsula, and the heavily forested coastal strip along the Gulf of Honduras.

By 2000 B.C., sedentary villages were common throughout Mesoamerica, dispersed in small communities across highly diverse agricultural environments in both lowlands and highlands. The very diversity of the Mesoamerican environment with its widely distributed food resources and raw materials made everyone dependent on their neighbors, on communities living in very different surroundings. From the earliest times, barter networks linked village to village, lowland groups to people living on the semi-arid highlands or in the Basin of Mexico. The same exchange networks also spread compelling ideologies, which were to form the symbolic foundation of ancient Mesoamerican civilization. Therein lies a crux of Mesoamerican civilization: the constant interactions and exchanges of both commodities and ideas between people living in dramatically contrasting environments, often within only a few hundred kilometers of one another.

The first signs of political and social complexity appear in many parts of highland and lowland Mesoamerica between about 2000 and 1000 B.C., during the so-called **Preclassic**, or **Formative**, era. In many regions, small, but often powerful, chiefdoms headed by a chief and a small nobility appeared. A similar pattern of greater social and political complexity appeared in Mesopotamia, Egypt, China, and other areas where early state-organized societies evolved. In Mesoamerica, as elsewhere, the new social complexity can be identified by differences in house designs, by the appearance of small shrines, and through prestigious trade goods such as fish spines and sea shells from the Gulf Coast used in bloodletting and other religious ceremonies. Here, as in other areas, control of trade in exotic, prestigious objects and knowledge of distant lands were vital to the ideology of chiefdoms. Such objects, and the ideology associated with them, symbolized and legitimized the authority of leaders to control both human and natural resources.

There was no one region where this emerging sociopolitical complexity occurred first. Rather, it was a development that took hold more or less simultaneously in many regions of Mesoamerica, not in isolation, but with each region interacting with others. The most famous of these early societies was the Olmec.

The Olmec (1500 to 500 B.C.)

The **Olmec** occupied a revered place in the legend and lore of later Mesoamerican civilizations. Maya priests recognized the great cultural legacy they owed to these little-known ancestral Mesoamericans. Earlier scholars thought in terms of a "mother civilization," of an Olmec state that was the ancestor of all later Mesoamerican civilizations. Today, we know that "Olmec" was a series of chiefdoms along the Gulf Coast of Veracruz and Tabasco, which may have exercised some influence over adjacent areas of Chiapas and central Mexico in early Preclassic times. Olmec society flourished during a period when art motifs, religious symbols, and ritual beliefs were shared between developing chiefdoms in many regions as a result of regular contacts between the leaders of widely separated communities and through day-to-day trade. Olmec art and artifacts have been found over an area twenty times that of the Gulf Coast heartland. Olmec-like artifacts have come from Cuello in the Maya lowlands, and with pre-Maya burials under the city of Copán (see pages 300–303). Archaeologist Arthur Demarest has called this phenomenon a "lattice of interaction," over many centuries that produced the complex and sophisticated traditions of Mesoamerican civilization that developed in later centuries.

Olmec peoples lived along the Mexican south Gulf Coast from about 1500 to 500 B.C. Their homeland is low-lying, tropical, and humid, with fertile soils. The swamps, lakes, and rivers are rich in fish, birds, and other animals, creatures that formed an important part of a new and remarkably sophisticated art style that was to leave a permanent imprint on Mesoamerican life. The origins of the Olmec are a complete mystery, but their culture undoubtedly has strong local roots.

Some of the earliest Olmec settlement comes from a platform at **San Lorenzo,** in the midst of frequently inundated woodland plains. The first village occupation shows few distinctive Olmec traits, but by 1250 B.C., the people of San Lorenzo were farming both dry gardens and fields located on river levees, which produced exceptional crop yields. Soon, San Lorenzo's leaders were erecting ridges and earthen mounds around their platform, on which they built pyramids and possibly ball courts. A century later, magnificent monumental carvings adorned San Lorenzo, apparently portraits of rulers that were often mutilated by the Olmec themselves, perhaps when they died (Figure 12.2). The people of San

Figure 12.2 Colossal Olmec head from San Lorenzo, with parrotlike glyph on the headdress.

Lorenzo traded obsidian and semiprecious stones with many parts of Mesoamerica until their center fell into decline after 900 B.C. and was superseded by La Venta, the most famous Olmec site, nearer the Gulf of Mexico.

Was Olmec society a large, homogeneous state or a series of smaller kingdoms linked together by king, religion, and trading connections? Current opinion favors the second alternative, where large kin groups originally owned village land. Over many generations, certain families probably acquired control of the most fertile lands, over prime fishing and waterfowl hunting preserves. They became the dominant elite in Olmec society. To give symbolic and ritual expression to their new-found power, the new elite built awe-inspiring artificial mountains and strategically placed open spaces, designed to give an impression of overwhelming power. It was here that the rulers performed carefully staged public rituals and displays designed to confirm supreme authority. Those who ruled over these settings adorned their precincts with colossal statues of themselves.

Nowhere are these buildings and sculptures more spectacular than at **La Venta,** built on a small island in the middle of a swamp. A rectangular earthen mound 120 meters long by 70 meters wide and 32 meters high (393 by 229 by 105 feet) dominates the island. Long, low mounds surround a rectangular plaza in front of the large mound, faced by walls and terraced mounds at the other end of the plaza. Vast monumental stone sculptures litter the site, including some Olmec heads bearing expressions of contempt and savagery (see Figure 12.2), perhaps portraits of actual rulers.

Thronelike blocks depict a seated figure, perhaps a ruler, emerging from a deep niche carved into stone (Figure 12.3). The sides bear stylized depictions of jaguars, perhaps symbolizing the mythic origins of the rulers among such animals. For about 400 years, La Venta people traded ceremonial jade and serpentine from as far away as Costa Rica, during a time

Figure 12.3 An Olmec altar at La Venta depicts a lord sitting below a schematic jaguar pelt. He emerges from a niche or cave holding a rope that binds prisoners carved on either side of the throne.

SITE

Maya Paintings at San Bartolo, Guatemala

William Saturno was thirsty and tired. He crawled into a shady looter's trench at San Bartolo, a small and remote Preclassic Maya center in Guatemala's Petén. The vandals had exposed part of a room covered by later construction. The one visible wall bore a colored mural, preserved because it was covered with mud and the room sealed off.

Careful recording uncovered nine mythological figures, the principal among them the bejeweled maize god, whose head replicates the foliation of the corn plant (Figure 12.4). His arms are outstretched as he turns his head and looks at the woman kneeling behind him, who also has her hands upraised. Another female figure with black hair seems to float above her. A kneeling man is in front of the Maize God, while other figures seem to form a procession. This narrative of the Maya Creation legend is the earliest known, although familiar from the mythological art of much later centuries. AMS radiocarbon dates for the paintings give readings between 400 and 200 B.C., making the San Bartolo paintings the earliest Maya wall art known. A line of ten hieroglyphs painted in black form part of the mural. So far, the experts have been unable to read them, even with their knowledge of later Maya writing, but at least one of the glyphs is thought to be a symbol of kingship.

San Bartolo is a Sistine Chapel of early Maya art, which extends back the origins of a civilization with an elaborate art tradition, writing, and religious beliefs. The distinctive cultural traditions of the Maya were developing rapidly as early as 400 B.C., much earlier than once believed.

when Olmec ideas of kingship and religious ideology spread far across the lowlands and highlands. Then, sometime around 400 B.C., La Venta was destroyed, its finest monuments intentionally defaced.

One of the most important institutions to come into being in Olmec society was kingship, known to us only from distinctive art styles centered on a mysterious half-jaguar, half-human figure. Olmec lords may have grafted the ancient ideology of the jaguar onto an emerging institution of kingship, where the ruler was a shaman-king, with awesome supernatural powers. The Olmec rain god may have been a half-human, half-animal figure with snarling jaguar teeth, but it was only one of many combinations of mythical beasts that came from the hallucinogenic mind as opposed to the forest itself. Olmec artists grafted eagles' feathers and claws onto serpents and other beasts to form mythical creatures, perhaps one of them the "Feathered Serpent," Quetzalcoatl, the most enduring of all Mesoamerican deities and central to highland civilization for many centuries.

By the time the classic Mesoamerican civilizations of highlands and lowlands arose, dynasties of lords had been ruling Mesoamerica along well-established lines for nearly 1,000 years.

The Origins of Maya Civilization (before 1000 B.C. to A.D. 300)

The roots of ancient Maya civilization lie in much earlier cultural traditions in the Mesoamerican lowlands. Boston University archaeologist Norman Hammond was able to trace the roots of Maya culture back to the second millennium B.C., at the Cuello site in northern Belize.

Figure 12.4 The Maize God appears in a Preclassic mural at San Bartolo, Guatemala.

Cuello is a small Maya ceremonial center, today comprising an acre-square, 3.6-meter (12-foot)-high platform with a low pyramid. Hammond excavated layer after layer of occupation, until he excavated a pole-framed, palm-thatched house set on a lime-plaster platform dating to about 1000 B.C. The Cuello people maintained the same basic plaza layout for many centuries, making it larger and larger until about 400 B.C. At this point, the villagers converted their ceremonial precinct with its wood and thatch temples into a large public arena. They filled the square with rubble to create a raised platform covering more than a hectare. Hammond unearthed the fragmentary skeletons of more than thirty sacrificial victims in the rubble, some with hacked-off skulls and limbs, others sitting in a circle around two young men. Six carved bone tubes buried with the victims bore the interlacing, woven mat motif symbolic of later Maya kingship. Such mats were royal thrones. The appearance of the motif here may document the appearance of a Maya elite by 400 B.C.

San Bartolo, Nakbé, and El Mirador (c. 1000 to 300 B.C.)

Preclassic life was much more complex than originally thought, witness a series of remarkable discoveries of important Maya centers dating to before the emergence of Classic Maya civilization about 2,000 years ago.

The **San Bartolo** site in Guatemala was occupied between 400 and 200 B.C., a little-known location marked by a small pyramid where wall paintings unexpectedly came to light on rooms inside it. Mayanists William Saturno and Boris Beltrán tunneled into the pyramid in 2005 and found a room richly decorated with polychrome murals (see box). Although epigraphers cannot yet read the hieroglyphs in the room, they are certainly evidence that Maya society was already literate 2,500 years ago, long before once believed.

Some Preclassic sites in Guatemala's Petén achieved considerable size and importance. **Nakbé** lies about 350 kilometers (215 miles) from Guatemala City, and 13.6 kilometers (8.5 miles) from the early Maya city at **El Mirador**, which covers 15.5 square kilometers (6 square miles). The two settlements were once linked by a causeway, but smaller Nakbé was occupied much earlier, by about 1000 B.C. Between 650 and 450 B.C., Nakbé's leaders built huge platforms over their earlier ceremonial structures, raising pyramids with blank facades atop them. The pyramids themselves were crowned with three small temples clustered at the top of a steep stairway bounded with panels and masks. Nakbé's temple facades reflect the emerging notion of *Ch'ul Ahau*, divine kingship, in Maya society. In lavish public ceremonies, important lords donned the masks of gods, symbolizing their role as living gods.

Nakbé reached the height of its powers around 300 B.C., but subsided into complete political and economic obscurity within a few generations, as its neighbor, El Mirador, rose to prominence.

Between 150 and 50 B.C., El Mirador grew to cover 15.5 square kilometers (6 square miles) of low, undulating terrain, part of which flooded during the wet season. El Mirador was a maze of pyramids and plazas, with more than 200 imposing structures including causeways, temples, and lords' dwellings. The city lies in a depressed zone, where water could be trapped for later use during the dry season. By this time, the Maya were also building large reservoirs for water storage. This careful management reflected a society that was well aware of the need to plan for drought years. The strategy seems to have worked, for Maya civilization developed rapidly into a complex mosaic of city-states.

Brigham Young University archaeologists have uncovered at least 200 buildings at El Mirador, including a great complex of pyramids, temples, and plazas. The Danta pyramid at the eastern end of the site rises from a natural hill more than 70 meters (210 feet) high. A

Figure 12.5 An artist's reconstruction of the Preclassic city of El Mirador, Guatemala.

little over 2 kilometers (1 mile) west rises the Tigre complex, a pyramid 55 meters (182 feet) high surrounded by a plaza and smaller buildings (Figure 12.5). El Mirador is yielding some of the earliest examples of Maya writing, inscribed on potsherds, and occasionally on stucco sculpture. A raised road connected El Mirador with another important Preclassic center, **Calakmul**, 38 kilometers (24 miles) to the northeast. This stupendous and still little-known city collapsed suddenly in the early Christian era. The dynamics of its collapse are little understood, but are mirrored at other Preclassic Maya communities where the institution of kingship rose and was then abandoned.

Kingship, Glyphs, and Political Cycles

Kingship was at the heart of lowland Maya civilization. Maya rulers linked their actions to those of the gods and ancestors, sometimes legitimizing their descent by claiming it reenacted mythical events. In a real sense, Maya history was linked to the present and to the Otherworld, and to the legendary Olmec of the remote past. Society was embedded in a matrix of sacred space and time.

Maya kingship unfolded within an intensely sacred setting, artificial landscapes where complex ceremonies took place throughout the year, and on longer cycles of time. Thus, the calendar was vital to Maya life, for the complex geography of sacred time was just as important as that of space for determining political strategies and social moves (Figure 12.6). At the heart of Maya life lay both the calendar and the elaborate hieroglyphic script used, among other things, to calculate the passage of time and regular religious observances.

Figure 12.6 The Maya calendar, showing the two interlocking cycles. The left wheel is the 260-day *tzolkin*, the sacred calendar with 13 numbers (inner wheel) and 20 day names (outer wheel). The right-hand wheel is the *haab*, the secular cycle, with 18 months of 20 days each.

Maya Script

The Maya inherited a long tradition of hieroglyphic writing from earlier times. Some Mesoamerican societies like the Olmec developed written scripts as early as 900 B.C., but we know little of them.

The decipherment of Maya script ranks among the greatest scientific achievements of the twentieth century. For generations, most Mayanists assumed that the intricate glyphs were used to record the calendar and that the ancient Maya lords were peaceful astronomer-priests. But in 1952, Russian epigrapher Yuri Knosorov demonstrated that Maya script was a phonetic and syllabic hieroglyphic script, just like Egyptian writing. Twenty years later, a group of scholars succeeded in assembling the dynastic histories of Maya lords at several important centers like **Palenque** and **Tikal**. More than twenty years of rapid-fire, intensive teamwork have since resulted in the decipherment of much Classic Maya script, although many difficulties await resolution.

Unlike Egyptian or Sumerian script, the Maya archive is limited in scope and confined to inscriptions on clay pots, monumental inscriptions on buildings and stelae, and only four codices (deer-skin documents) that survived the Spanish Conquest. These are public statements of royal accessions, triumphant military campaigns, and important ceremonies. They are the political propaganda of Maya lords, the "politically correct" literature of a nobility intent on justifying their deeds and their ancestry. Of the everyday literature of the Maya, we know nothing. But the surviving texts tell us Maya rulers were not peaceful astronomers, but bloodthirsty lords presiding over a patchwork of competing city-states. Decipherment has revealed Maya civilization as a constantly shifting quicksand of diplomatic marriages, political alliances, and brutal conquests. The account of Maya civilization that follows is based on both archaeology and deciphered glyphs.

Political Cycles

Archaeologist Joyce Marcus has observed a remarkable similarity in the ways in which Mesoamerican states rose, reached their peak, then collapsed. She notes a consistent scenario in both the lowlands and highlands, not only in Maya civilization, but with the great city of Teotihuacán and also Toltec and Aztec civilizations in the highlands (see Chapter 13).

This scenario unfolds as follows: First, a new city-state, say Maya Tikal or Teotihuacán, expands its territory through diplomacy, political marriages, and military conquest. The new state would reach its maximum territorial limits early in its history. Then, once some provinces reached a significant level of cultural complexity and development, they would break away from their nominal master and become an independent polity. Far from being weakened, the core state still prospered, investing its energy and resources in its own local area rather than in expansion. But sometimes the old provinces, now independent states, would ally themselves against their old overlord and conquer it, so the old state became a second center. This cycle of rise, expansion on the margins, fissioning, then decline at the expense of others repeated itself again and again, to the point that it can be considered a consistent pattern of Mesoamerican civilization. Marcus's scenario is well documented in Maya political history.

Classic Maya Civilization (A.D. 300 to 900)

Even as El Mirador collapsed, perhaps because its water supplies or trading connections faltered, two other centers, Tikal and **Uaxactún**, stepped into the resulting political and economic vacuum. The two centers were less than 20 kilometers (12 miles) apart, too close for bitter rivals to coexist. But their rivalry coincided with the blossoming of Classic Maya civilization.

The Classic Period of Maya civilization saw new adaptations to the challenging lowland environment. Many communities now lay at the summits of hillocks and ridges, so that the quarries at their base used to build pyramids, temples, and other structures became large reservoirs surrounded by artificial hills and plazas that were catchment pavements to funnel water into them. With brilliant ingenuity, the Maya architects built gravity canals that released water from the elevated central reservoir system into tanks and surrounding irrigation systems.

These elaborate water management systems developed over many centuries out of a need to store water in a land without seasonal river floods—or even major rivers—like those that watered the irrigation schemes of the Egyptians or Sumerians. The Maya developed what archaeologist Vernon Scarborough calls "microwatersheds" to make up for deficiencies in rainfall. But such systems have severe constraints. Inevitably, they can service only a limited area. Rainfall filled the reservoirs and tanks, but the rainfall fluctuated greatly from year to year, making the carefully controlled releases of floodwater typical of Mesopotamian irrigation impossible. Water management and irrigation in the lowlands required the right topography, highly flexible labor management, and a great deal of trial and error.

Over centuries, Maya agriculture slowly created a highly engineered infrastructure that became increasingly productive over time. Everything was slow and deliberate, set in a social and political context that accommodated the realities of a fragile tropical environment. The Maya were successful because they spent many centuries learning how to farm this environment. They worked successfully within environmental limitations they learned the hard way, kept their villages dispersed, and developed a level of interdependency that reflected the uneven distribution of soils and food resources across the landscape. As long as this system worked well, they were relatively immune to climatic stress. It was no coincidence that Maya civilization developed as a mosaic of much smaller city-states, each centered on microwatersheds, which gave it a flexibility and resilience to short-term climatic events that endured for many centuries.

As populations rose, especially on the outskirts of cities, the Maya expanded the scope of their agriculture. As early as the first century A.D., they began draining and canalizing swamps, turning hitherto unfarmable lands into grids of raised field systems elevated above low-lying, seasonally inundated land that bordered rivers. These plots resembled the well-known swamp gardens used by the Aztecs of highland Mexico centuries later to feed their great capital, Tenochtitlán. As populations climbed even further, the Maya began terracing steep hillsides to trap silt that cascaded downslope during heavy rainstorms.

By A.D. 800, immediately before the collapse, perhaps 8 to 10 million Maya lived in the lowlands, a staggeringly high density for a tropical environment with low natural carrying capacity.

The Rise of Tikal and Uaxactún

Tikal had expanded greatly during the first century B.C. as large public buildings rose on the foundations of earlier, more humble structures. Clearly, the intent was to rival, and outdo, El Mirador's splendor. During this century an elite emerged at Tikal, people represented by the burial of a noblewoman under a shrine and tomb paintings of richly decorated nobles. Uaxactún just to the north underwent a similar transition during the same century. Here, Preclassic temples bear stucco masks and facades that depict the Maya world and the king who built the structures. The two centers were political and economic equals during this century (Figure 12.7).

Tikal's inscriptions are the chronicle of a remarkable dynasty that ruled one of the four Maya capitals from the Early Classic period until the ninth century A.D. The earliest recorded monarch is Yax Ch'aktel Xok ("First Scaffold Shark"), who is thought to have reigned around A.D. 200, although the city had a long, and much earlier history. During his reign, strong influences from Teotihuacán on the highlands appear, shown by pottery styles and green obsidian from the city's closely controlled sources. This strong influence on political, military, and religious affairs at Tikal continued until A.D. 550.

Yax Ch'aktel Xok was not the earliest king, but was the one who served as founding ancestor for the great royal clan of Tikal that ruled in coming centuries. Tikal's hieroglyphic texts identify thirty-one rulers (eighteen known by name) after the founder, the earliest dating to A.D. 292, the last known one to A.D. 869, making for 577 years of recorded history. Uaxactún also fostered a powerful royal dynasty, whose monuments, like those of the Tikal kings, soon depicted rulers with sacrificial victims cowering at their feet, noble victims taken in hand-to-hand combat for later sacrifice in public rituals. These portraits signal a crucial development in Maya history: the increasing role of warfare and campaigns of deliberate conquest.

Figure 12.7 The central area of Tikal.

Between A.D. 320 and 378, Great Jaguar Paw, the ninth successor of Yax-Moch-Xoc, sat on the throne of Tikal, at a time when rivalries with nearby Uaxactún came to a head. He died in 378, at a moment when a warrior named Fire-Born arrived, a warrior from the "west," perhaps the city of Teotihuacán on the highlands (see Chapter 13). The connection between Great Jaguar Paw's death and Fire-Born's arrival is unclear, but it was the former who defeated the armies of Uaxactún on January 16, A.D. 378. His army ignored long-established rules of combat and sacked Uaxactún, setting up Fire-Born as the founder of a new dynasty. Tikal's military expansion took place with assistance from Teotihuacán during a period of regular trading contacts between the great highland city and many Maya centers, marked by many finds of the distinctive green obsidian mined by the great city. The same contacts may have brought new philosophies of war and conquest and the rituals associated with them. These rituals were to become part of the Mesoamerican religious tradition for many centuries.

Tikal's royal dynasty prospered in the coming centuries. It eventually headed a multi-center polity, extending its influence by conquest and long-distance trade and by judicious political marriages that gave neighboring rulers maternal kin ties to the center. At the height of its powers, Tikal's territory may have supported an estimated population of as many as 300,000 people, the city and its immediate hinterland 62,000; these are perhaps high estimates, however.

In about A.D. 557, Tikal went into decline after its defeat by the lord of a new rising state, Caracol, then prospered anew during the Late Classic period.

Caracol and Calakmul

Caracol lies in south-central Belize, 70 kilometers (43 miles) southeast of Tikal, controlled important crystalline rock supplies, and was an important rival. Its imposing ceremonial core covered at least 2.25 square kilometers (0.9 square mile) during the seventh century, when between 30,000 and 50,000 people lived there, and as many as 100,000 lived in the surrounding countryside. Caracol commenced hostilities against Tikal in A.D. 557, soon after Tikal had captured and executed a prominent lord. The Caracol ruler Lord Water defeated Tikal, apparently capturing the city's then-ruler, Double Bird. Tikal now became a tribute dependency of Caracol, which grew in size and prestige as its vassal declined. Lord Water's successors dominated Tikal for at least 150 years and embarked on ambitious conquests against neighboring Calakmul and Naranjo. But eventually Caracol paid the price for its military adventures, only to rise again during the Late Classic period.

The ever-shifting diplomatic and military landscape in the lowlands involved dozens of city-states and cities, large and small, whose relationships with the major centers and lesser kingdoms are a tangle of claims, counterclaims, and archaeological data. In addition to Caracol, both Tikal and Calakmul, also in the southern lowlands, were rival regional capitals during the Early Classic. At its height, Calakmul had a ceremonial precinct covering about 2 square kilometers (0.7 square mile) and a surrounding residential area over 20 square kilometers (7.7 square miles) in extent. More than 50,000 people lived in the urban core of a great city and important rival of Tikal between at least A.D. 514 and 814. Like Tikal, Calakmul sat astride an important overland trade route. The rivalry between the two cities may have been both a power play and a struggle for dominance of long-distance exchange. There may have been family ties between the two cities. The rivalry was intense, culminating in warfare and constant shifts in allegiance between Tikal, Calakmul, and Caracol.

Tikal had few allies in its immediate vicinity, but maintained friendlier relations with two more distant city-states—Palenque and Copán.

Palenque and Copán

The city of Palenque, another Maya capital, but in the western lowlands, is remarkable not only for its fine buildings but also for its rulers' obsession with their ancestry. Two Palenque rulers, Pacal the Great ("Shield") and his oldest son, Chan-Bahlum ("Snake-Jaguar"), who ruled in the seventh century A.D., stand out for their vision and wisdom. Palenque's dynastic history began on March 11, A.D. 431, when Bahlum-Ku'k ("Jaguar-Quetzal") became ruler, and lasted until sometime after A.D. 799.

Toward the end of his long reign, which lasted sixty-seven years, Pacal built the Temple of the Inscriptions, a masterpiece of Maya architecture under which his tomb lies (Figure 12.8). His sarcophagus lid bears his royal genealogy. Palenque dominated the southwestern lowlands between A.D. 603 and 702.

Copán in Honduras is adorned with pyramids and plazas covering 12 hectares (30 acres), rising from the vast open spaces of the Great and Middle Plazas to an elaborate complex of raised enclosed courtyards, pyramids, and temples known to archaeologists as the

Figure 12.8 The tomb at Palenque of the Maya ruler Pacal, who died in A.D. 683. The lid of his tomb commemorates his genealogy.

Acropolis (Figure 12.9). Here successive rulers built their architectural statements atop those of their predecessors in an archaeological jigsaw puzzle of the first magnitude.

The earliest inscription at the site dates to December 11, A.D. 435, and was the work of ruler Yax-Ku'k-Mo' ("Blue Quetzal Macaw"), although there may have been earlier rulers. For four centuries, Blue Quetzal Macaw's successors formed a powerful dynasty at Copán and became a major force in the Maya world. At one point, Copán ruled over neighboring **Quirigua**. More than 10,000 people lived in the surrounding valley. On May 3, 738, the subordinate ruler of Quirigua turned on his master and captured and sacrificed him, but Copán seems to have maintained a measure of independence and survived. In 749, a new ruler, Smoke Shell, ascended to the throne of the once-great city. He embarked on an ambitious campaign of rehabilitation, even marrying a princess from distant Palenque. He also embarked on a building frenzy that culminated in the Temple of the Hieroglyphic Stairway, built in 755. Smoke Shell's son from his Palenque marriage, Yax-Pac ("First Dawn") ruled during troubled times, with internal factionalism on the rise. By this time, the city was top-heavy with privilege-hungry nobles and rife with political intrigue. Collapse was imminent.

Today's Maya archaeologist works closely with epigraphers, using carefully deciphered glyphs and inscriptions to reconstruct complex architectural events, as well as the ritual or political motives behind them. Archaeologists William and Barbara Fash combined both lines of evidence to reconstruct Smoke Shell's Hieroglyphic Stairway at Copán, erected by the ruler on one of the city's most sacred precincts. In the 1930s, archaeologists of the Carnegie Institution restored much of the ruined stairway, replacing the glyph blocks in approximate order. They were unable to read the inscriptions, which made the task difficult.

Figure 12.9 Artist Tatiana Proskouriakoff's reconstruction of Copán.

In 1986, a team of archaeologists and epigraphers headed by the Fashes set out to restore and conserve the building, while establishing the true meaning of the stairway. Using meticulous excavation, the archaeologists recovered thousands of tenoned mosaic fragments, which were drawn and photographed, then pieced together in a precise reconstruction of the building. They recovered a powerful political statement (Figure 12.10).

More than 2,200 glyphs ascend the sides of the stairway and provide an elegant statement of the Maya kings' supernatural path. William Fash believes the building was an attempt by Smoke Shell to relegitimize the conquered dynasty of earlier times. Portraits on the stairs depict Copán's lords as warriors carrying shields, with inscriptions recounting their deeds. A figure, perhaps Smoke Shell himself, stands where an altar forms the base of the stairway, in the form of an inverted head of the rain god Tlaloc. Tlaloc seems to be belching forth the inscriptions, his lower jaw forming the top of the stairs. Inside his head lay an offering of decorated flints in the form of portraits and artifacts perhaps used by Smoke Shell himself in the sacrificial and bloodletting ceremonies that dedicated the stairway. Unfortunately, the stairway was shoddily, and hastily, built. It soon collapsed, at a time when Copán was rapidly losing its political authority (Figure 12.11).

The diplomatic and military landscape was constantly changing as alliances were formed and just as rapidly collapsed again. During the very Late Classic era, after A.D. 771, a new political pattern emerged, indicative of changed conditions and stressful times. Carved inscriptions began to appear in the houses of local nobles at Copán and other sites, as if the rulers were now granting the privilege of using inscriptions to important individuals, perhaps as a way of gaining their continued support in times of trouble. This proliferation of inscriptions in the southern lowlands and elsewhere may also reflect minor nobles' taking

Figure 12.10 Tatiana Proskouriakoff's rendering of the Hieroglyphic Stairway at Copán.

Figure 12.11 Artist's reconstruction of a ball game at Copán.

advantage of confused times and a disintegrating political authority to claim their own brief independence. The confusion accelerated. By A.D. 800, Maya populations were declining sharply, and both monument carving and major construction soon came to an end.

The central institution of Maya civilization was kingship, for it was the concept that unified society as a whole. Maya kings lived and carried out their deeds in the context of a history they recorded in building projects at Copán, Palenque, Tikal, and elsewhere. Maya elites lived out their lives in the context of the kings who ruled them, and in turn, thousands of commoners lived their lives with respect to the nobility. We are only beginning to understand the tapestry of their history.

The Classic Maya Collapse

Maya civilization reached its peak after A.D. 600. Then, at the end of the eighth century, the great ceremonial centers of the Petén and the southern lowlands were abandoned, the long court calendar was discontinued, and the structure of religious life and the state decayed. Within a century, huge sections of the southern lowlands were abandoned, never to be reoccupied. At Tikal, perhaps the greatest Maya center, the elite vanished and the population declined to a third of its earlier level. The nonelite survivors clustered in the remains of great masonry structures and tried to retain a semblance of their earlier life. Within a century, even they were gone. All this is not to say that Maya civilization vanished completely, for new centers may have emerged in neighboring areas, taking in some of the displaced population. Maya civilization continued to flourish in the northern Yucatán.

SITE
A Tragedy at Cerén, San Salvador

We would know little of the lives of commoners but for an ancient natural disaster. One August evening in the sixth century A.D., a sudden rumble shook the quiet Maya village at **Cerén** in El Salvador. An underground fissure less than a mile away erupted without warning. A fast-moving cloud of ash darkened the twilight sky. The villagers fled for their lives, leaving everything behind. Minutes later, their houses lay under a thick layer of volcanic debris. Fifteen hundred years later, archaeologist Payson Sheets used subsurface radar to locate several buried houses deep under the ash. He then excavated the dwellings. Plotting every artifact, even individual wall fragments, seeds, and pieces of thatch, he discovered households where the people fled cascading ash at the end of their evening meal.

One household lived in a complex of four buildings: a kitchen, a workshop, a storehouse, and a residence, where the residents socialized, ate, and slept. The residence had a front porch open on three sides. The main room covered 4 square meters (43 square feet), with storage pots against the back wall. One pot contained a spindle whorl for making cotton thread. A large adobe bench on the east side of the room served as a sleeping place. During the day, people rolled up their mats and stored them among the rafters. Even the sharp-edged obsidian knife blades, stored high in the roof for safety, still lay among the thatch. A walkway linked the dwelling to a nearby storehouse, passing by a food-grinding area where a metate (grinding stone) still stood on forked sticks about 50 centimeters (20 inches) above the ground. The household owned a well-tended garden along the side of the storehouse, with carefully spaced rows of three species of medicinal herbs standing about a meter (3 feet) apart, each plant standing in a small mound of soil. Just to the south, an ash-covered field contained ridges of young maize plants about 20 to 40 centimeters (8 to 15 inches) high, typical corn growth for August in this environment. Some of the maize plants were doubled over, the ears still attached to the stalk, a "storage" technique still used in parts of Central America today.

Everyone studying this ninth-century collapse agrees that a multiplicity of factors—some ecological, some political and social—led to catastrophe in the southern lowlands. The theories of the 1970s argued that the collapse of Teotihuacán gave the Maya a chance to enlarge their managerial functions in Mesoamerican trade. According to these theories, the elite became increasingly involved in warfare and competition between regions. The Late Classic era saw a frenzy of public building and increased pressure on the people, the source of both food and labor for prestige projects. Agricultural productivity fell, disease may have reached epidemic proportions, and population densities plummeted, so that recovery was impossible. There is some evidence of disease, stature decline, and malnutrition, but the evidence is incomplete.

More recently, endemic warfare has been invoked as a powerful factor in the collapse. At **Dos Pilas** in northern Guatemala, 105 kilometers (65 miles) from Tikal, and founded by a renegade noble from Tikal in A.D. 645, Arthur Demarest uncovered evidence of civil war and prolonged conflict. Dos Pilas's later rulers embarked on campaigns of expansion, which had enlarged their territory to more than 3,884 square kilometers (1,500 square miles) by the mid-eighth century. Dos Pilas now controlled major jade and obsidian routes. Its lords lavished wealth on ornate palaces and a pyramid topped by three temples. Demarest and Juan Antonio Valdés dug deep under a small temple behind a stela that commemorated "Ruler 2," who reigned between A.D. 698 and 726, and uncovered the ruler's burial chamber. He wore a shell mosaic headdress adorned with monster faces, a heavy jade necklace, and jade bracelets. Hieroglyphs associated with the grave tell of the lord's carefully contrived diplomatic marriages with neighbors and of his delicate political marriages and his military campaigns.

Dos Pilas flourished until A.D. 761. By then, its rulers had overextended themselves, despite frantic efforts to maintain their domains. In that year, nearby **Tamrindo** attacked its former sovereign and killed "Ruler 4," despite desperate resistance by the Dos Pilas inhabitants. The invaders tore down the royal palace and robbed temple facades to build rough defensive walls with wooden palisades to surround the central precinct. Here, the people clustered in a small village of crude huts while the nobles fled and built a new center at **Aguateca.** The new center lay atop a steep cliff above a deep chasm, protected on three sides by natural features, as well as by massive defense walls. The Aguatecans held out for another half century, despite repeated attacks. In the early ninth century A.D., Demarest believes, intensive warfare drove these survivors of Dos Pilas into fortified towns and villages, where they erected defensive walls even around large tracts of agricultural land. Local conditions may have become so insecure that farmers were limited to defended acreage, so that crop yields may have been affected dramatically. In a last desperate stand, the remaining Aguatecans dug three moats, one 140.2 meters (460 feet) long, across a peninsula in Lake Petexbatun, creating an island fortress. The bedrock from the canals became defensive walls and a walled wharf for a canoe landing. The outpost did not last long, for the inhabitants abandoned it in the 800s.

The various collapse theories have been subjected to exhaustive analysis by researches that involve both simulation studies and examinations of trading patterns and demographic and ecological stresses that could have affected population densities. Patrick Culbert has examined population densities and the potential for agricultural production in the southern lowlands. He has shown that population densities rose to as many as 200 persons per square kilometer (518 per square mile) during the Late Classic period over an area so large that it was impossible for people to adapt to bad times by moving to new land or emigrating. He believes that the magnitude of the population loss during the two centuries after A.D. 800 was such that social malfunction alone cannot account for it. Failure of the agricultural base must have been an important component in the collapse equation at the local level.

Maya agriculture became increasingly intense as populations rose, and both terrace and raised-field systems covered large areas in many parts of the lowlands. At some of the larger sites like Tikal, the people may have been transporting great quantities of foodstuffs from distances of between 50 and 100 kilometers (31 and 62 miles) away. In the short term, the intensification strategies worked, but they carried the seeds of collapse. The risks of climatic change, plant disease, erosion, and long-term declines in soil fertility are always present in such enterprises. To continue functioning efficiently, the newly intensified systems would have had to have been managed constantly. Just the repair of field systems after floods and rains would have required watchful effort on a large scale. There are no signs that the Maya made any social changes that enabled them to achieve such a level of management, especially when so many people were engaged in public construction projects and apparently in military activity (perhaps the Maya were under pressure from the north).

Culbert believes that long-term environmental degradation was an important element in the scenario, where short-term gains in productivity were followed by catastrophic declines. For example, as populations rose, fallow cycles may have been shortened, so that there was increased competition between crop plants and weeds; this is a problem that can be solved only by constant weeding, a very labor-intensive activity. Shortened fallow cycles also lead to lower levels of plant nutrients and declining crop yields, and we do not know whether the Maya tried to counteract these trends by systematic mulching or by planting soil-restoring crops. The problem of erosion may have been even more acute. There are signs that the people lost much soil to runoff in the lowlands, for they did not build the terraces needed in time to retain the soil. Some of this erosion may have resulted from extensive deforestation.

Newly collected paleoclimatic data from cores bored into lowland lake deposits and from a deep sea core in the Carioco Basin off Venezuela provide a potential "smoking gun" for the collapse. They show that three major droughts spread over the Yucatán during the 2,500-year period of Maya civilization. The first was from 475 to 250 B.C., when Maya civilization was still forming. Another lasted from 125 B.C. to A.D. 210, coinciding with the heyday of El Mirador, the greatest of the early Maya cities. The abandonment of El Mirador in about A.D. 150 may have resulted, at least in part, from the continuing drought. The most severe drought of all, from A.D. 750 to 1025, coincided with the great Maya collapse of the southern lowlands. Carioco's core is so fine-grained that it chronicles four major droughts *within* this last period of much drier conditions, spaced at about forty-five-year intervals. This may account for the gradual nature of the collapse, which toppled city after city in the central and southern lowlands. The northern Yucatán fared better, because collapsed sink holes provided access to deep groundwater.

If one sets the history of Maya civilization against this background of recurring drought, there are some remarkable coincidences. The first of the three dry cycles occurred while Maya agriculture was still providing sufficient flexibility to accommodate drier years. The second cycle descended on the Maya just as the first efflorescence of cities and civilization appeared in the lowlands. Cities like El Mirador were situated in low-lying areas, where water could be trapped and stored. At first, the system worked, but soon the city grew too large, the vulnerability threshold was crossed, El Mirador's lords lost their spiritual credibility in the face of environmental disaster, and the people dispersed—there was still enough space for them to do so.

When the drought ended, growth resumed, and Maya civilization entered an astounding trajectory of rapid expansion. By the time the greatest drought of all settled over the lowlands, essentially all the arable land was under cultivation, and Maya agriculture was very close to the critical threshold where even a slight drop in agricultural productivity would mean serious trouble. For nearly three centuries, intense drought lowered the water table, produced inadequate rains, and ravaged an agricultural economy that already had trouble satisfying the accelerating demands of the nobility.

A fundamental cause of the Maya collapse, then, was at least four major droughts that brought hunger and catastrophic social change. In city after city, the great lords were powerless to bring rain; perhaps unrest erupted. Archaeology shows us that these cities' populations either perished or dispersed into small hamlets. Having overreached themselves, the unfortunate Maya saw their civilization come down around their ears.

Surveys of Copán and its hinterland have shown how dramatic the settlement shifts were (see box).

Ecological factors lay at the center of the collapse. The expanding Maya population was dependent on an agricultural system that made no allowance for long-term problems. Eventually, the system could produce no further riches, could not expand, and could only decline—with catastrophic results. But it would be a mistake to think of the Maya "collapse"

SCIENCE

Studying the Maya Collapse at Copán, Honduras

How and why did Copán collapse? Archaeologists David Webster and William Sanders and many colleagues working on a long-term investigation of the city decided to investigate the collapse by studying changing settlement patterns and shifting population densities around the abandoned city. They developed a large-scale settlement survey modeled after the famous Basin of Mexico survey of some years earlier to examine more than 135 square kilometers (52 square miles) around the urban core. Using aerial photographs and systematic field surveys, the research team recorded more than 1,425 archaeological sites containing more than 4,500 structures. Team members mapped and surface-collected each location. Two hundred fifty-two sites were test-pitted to obtain artifact and dating samples so they could be placed within the general chronological framework for the valley.

As the data flowed into the laboratory, the researchers developed a classification of site types using size and other criteria, classifying them in a hierarchy from simple to complex as a way of developing a portrait of shifting landscape use over many centuries. At the same time, they obtained 2,300 dates, using volcanic glass fragments that could be dated using the obsidian hydration method. The survey yielded a bird's-eye view of dramatic population changes as human settlement expanded and contracted over the valley landscape.

The earlier sites found in the survey documented rapid population growth, especially in the city itself and nearby. There was only a small, scattered rural population. Between 700 and 850, the Copán valley reached its greatest sociopolitical complexity, with a rapid population increase to between 20,000 and 25,000 people. These figures, calculated from site size, suggest the local population was doubling every 80 to 100 years, with about 80 percent of the people living within the urban core and immediate periphery. Rural settlement expanded outward along the valley floor, but was still relatively scattered. Now people were farming foothill areas, as the population density of the urban core reached over 8,000 people per square kilometer (0.3 square mile), with the periphery housing about 500 people per square kilometer (0.3 square mile). Some 82 percent of the population lived in relatively humble dwellings, an indication of the pyramidlike nature of Copán society.

After A.D. 850, the survey showed dramatic shifts. The urban core and periphery zones lost about half their population, while the rural population increased by almost 20 percent. Small regional settlements replaced the scattered villages of earlier times, a response to cumulative deforestation, overexploitation of even marginal agricultural land, and uncontrolled soil erosion near the capital. By 1150, the Copán Valley population had fallen to between 2,000 and 5,000 people.

The Copán research does not explain why the city collapsed, but it chronicles the dramatic impact of rapidly growing populations on ecologically fragile landscapes. The evidence hints that environmental degradation was a major factor in the Maya collapse. Maya writings tell us that Maya lords considered themselves the intermediaries between the living and supernatural worlds. However, when the inexorable forces of environmental decline took hold, their authority evaporated and a centuries-old spiritual relationship between farmers and an elaborate cosmic world vanished into near-oblivion.

as a universal phenomenon. Rather, the collapse in the ninth century was a marked episode in a long series of periodic flowerings and collapses characteristic of Maya civilization—indeed, of Mesoamerican civilization generally.

Postclassic Maya Civilization (A.D. 900 to 1517)

Despite the collapse in the southern lowlands, Maya religious and social orders still endured in the more open country of the northern Yucatán. Just as Tikal and other famous cities collapsed, northern centers like **Chichén Itzá** in the northeast came into prominence during the Postclassic period. Chichén Itzá itself has never been fully mapped, so its area and exact population remain a mystery. The city's central core is well known, its central plaza dominated by the Castillo, the Temple of Kukulcán (Quetzalcoatl), a square, stepped pyramid about 23 meters (75 feet) tall, crowned with a temple, with stairways on all four sides (Figure 12.12). The Temple of the Warriors lies west of the Castillo, an inner temple with sculpted pillars masked by a later, more elaborate structure. The mosaics, carved facades, and sculpted serpents and warriors on the later temple show Toltec influence from the highlands. During its heyday, this great city maintained contacts with the Maya of the Gulf Coast lowlands, and through them with the Valley of Oaxaca and the highlands.

Postclassic Maya civilization was marked by as much volatility as that of earlier years. Political infighting and ecological problems may have been part of the cause. As Chichén Itzá collapsed in the thirteenth century, the city of **Mayapan** moved into the economic and political vacuum and dominated the northern Maya world. Mayapan lies in the center of the northern Yucatán, a densely populated, walled city with about 12,000 inhabitants, built near a series of natural wells. It was a trading center, dependent on an expanding waterborne trade in bulk goods like cacao, salt, and obsidian. Her confederacy fell apart in the mid-fifteenth century. Three quarters of a century later, in 1519, Spaniard Hernan Cortés

Figure 12.12 Tatiana Prouskouriakoff's sketch of Chichén Itzá at its height, looking south from the Sacred Cenote.

and his conquistadors landed on the Gulf lowlands, to change the face of Mesoamerica forever. His objective was not the lowland Maya but the gold-rich kingdom of the Mexica, or Azteca, in the distant highlands, described in Chapter 13.

Summary

The Preclassic period of Mesoamerican prehistory lasted from approximately 2000 B.C. to A.D. 250, a period of major cultural change in both lowlands and highlands. Sedentary villages traded with each other in raw materials and exotic objects. These exchange networks became increasingly complex and eventually came under the monopolistic control of larger villages. Increasing social complexity went hand in hand with the appearance of the first public buildings and the evidence of social stratification. These developments are well chronicled in the Olmec culture of the lowlands, which flourished from approximately 1500 to 500 B.C. Olmec art styles and religious beliefs were among those that spread widely over lowlands and highlands during the late Preclassic period.

Religious ideologies, ritual organization, and extensive trading networks were key factors in the development of Maya society in the lowlands after 1000 B.C. Classic Maya civilization flourished from A.D. 250 to 900 and consisted of an ever-changing patchwork of competing states. Maya glyphs show that Maya civilization was far from uniform. Religious beliefs rather than political or economic interests unified Maya society. Until about A.D. 600, the largest states were in northeast Petén, with a multicenter polity headed by the "Sky" rulers of Tikal. Maya civilization reached its height in the southern lowlands after the seventh century, collapsing suddenly in the Yucatán after A.D. 900. The reasons for the collapse are still uncertain, but environmental degradation, pressure on the labor force, and food shortages were doubtless among them. After the collapse, the focus of Maya civilization moved into the northern Yucatán, where Maya civilization flourished at Chichén Itzá and other centers right up to the Spanish conquest of the sixteenth century. Many Maya communities still flourish in the lowlands today.

Highland
Mesoamerica

PROLOGUE

"*And when we saw all those cities and villages* built in the water, and other great towns on dry land, and that straight and level causeway leading to Mexico, we were astounded. These great towns and pyramids and buildings rising from the water, all made of stone, seemed like an enchanted vision. . . . Indeed some of our soldiers asked whether it was not all a dream. . . ." Spanish conquistador Bernal Diaz was one of the 600 soldiers and adventurers who accompanied Hernan Cortés on his hazardous march from the Gulf Coast to the heart of the Aztec empire. He was an impressionable youth when he gazed out over the Valley of Mexico in 1519 and saw the Aztec capital, Tenochtitlán, stretched out before him. Half a century later he wrote: "I stood looking at it, and thought that no land like it would ever be discovered in the whole world, because at that time Peru was neither known nor thought of." Then he added: "All that I then saw has been destroyed." Cortés reduced Tenochtitlán to rubble in a brutal siege in 1521, founding Mexico City on its ruins. Aztec civilization collapsed. Thousands of Indians perished from smallpox and other exotic diseases introduced by the conquistadors. But Diaz knew he had witnessed a unique moment in history, a sight of a well-ordered preindustrial city at the height of its powers. His memories of his first sighting of the Aztec capital were as fresh in his seventies as they were when he glimpsed the Valley of Mexico for the first time (Cohen, 1963, pp. 214–215).

The roots of Aztec civilization went back at least 1,500 years, and sprang from both indigenous and lowland roots. Throughout the long history of Mesoamerican civilization, lowlands and highlands were linked inextricably to one another. This chapter describes the highland Mesoamerican civilizations, which culminated in the complex, rapidly changing world of the Aztecs, disrupted catastrophically by the Spanish conquest of A.D. 1519 (see Figure 12.1 on page 288).

The Rise of Highland Civilization: The Valley of Oaxaca (2000 to 500 B.C.)

Many of the foundations of highland Mesoamerican civilization were laid in two areas: the Valley of Oaxaca and the Valley of Mexico.

The warm, semiarid Valley of Oaxaca is the homeland of the modern-day Zapotec people. By 2000 B.C., maize and bean agriculture supported dozens of small villages and hamlets of 50 to 75 people. In time, some of these settlements grew to considerable size, with as many as 500 inhabitants, some of them nonfarming artisans and priests. The earliest farming villages lie on the valley floors, where water supplies were more plentiful. As local population densities rose, the Oaxacans expanded onto slopes and into more arid lands. Eventually, argues Kent Flannery, the economic power generated by these rising farming populations gave highland areas like this an edge over their neighbors.

The evolution of larger settlements in Oaxaca and elsewhere was closely connected with the development of long-distance trade. Simple barter networks of earlier times evolved into sophisticated regional trading organizations in which Oaxacan and other village leaders controlled monopolies over sources of obsidian and its distribution. Soon magnetite mirrors (important in Olmec ritual), tropical feathers, and ceramics were traded widely between highlands and lowlands. The influence of the lowlands was felt most strongly in Oaxaca, where Olmec pottery and other ritual objects appear between 1150 and 650 B.C. Many of them bear the distinctive human-jaguar motif of the lowlands, which had an important place in Olmec ideology (see Chapter 12).

In 1300 B.C., the largest settlement in the Valley of Oaxaca was **San José Mogote,** which lay at the junction of three side valleys, a village of thatched houses with about 150 inhabitants, sharing one lime-plastered public building. During the next century, San José Mogote grew rapidly into a community of 400 to 600 people living in rectangular houses with clay floors, plastered and white-washed walls, and thatched roofs over an area of about 20 hectares (50 acres). Public buildings then appeared in larger Oaxacan settlements, built on adobe and earth platforms. Fragments of conch shell trumpets and turtle shell drums come from these structures. Clay figurines of masked, costumed dancers lie in San José Mogote's ceremonial buildings (Figure 13.1). There are marine fish spines, too, almost certainly used in personal bloodletting ceremonies performed before the gods. By 400 B.C., there were at least seven small chiefdoms in the Valley of Oaxaca.

The basic Mesoamerican pattern of civilization came into being over more than 1,000 years in the highlands. In the Valley of Mexico, in Oaxaca, and elsewhere, a larger center was ruled by an elite and served by a rural population living in lesser villages scattered throughout the surrounding countryside. By 50 B.C., at least some of the centers, like Monte Albán in the Valley of Oaxaca, achieved considerable size and complexity. The new highland elites presided over hierarchies of priests and officials and had the ability to command the labor of hundreds, if not thousands, of farmers to build and maintain temples, pyramids, and

Figure 13.1 Four masked and costumed dancers from San José Mogote, Valley of Oaxaca, placed deliberately to make a scene, early evidence of ceremonial activity in the community.

palaces. They controlled large food surpluses, which supported a growing population of nonfarmers, merchants, and artisans. Their political power rested on their ability to coerce others, on well-established notions of social inequality, and, above all, on a complex, and often publicly reenacted, social contract between rulers and their subjects. The people saw their leaders as intermediaries between the living and the ancestors, between their plane of existence and the spiritual world. An elaborate calendar and, soon, writing, regulated every aspect of ceremonial and daily life, and helped generations of rulers presiding over many kingdoms to legitimize their dynastic origins and their relationship to the gods. Highland civilization, with its carefully regulated agriculture, marketplaces, and lucrative trade monopolies, was to flourish for 2,000 years.

Monte Albán (500 B.C. to A.D. 750)

Two major city-states dominated the Mesoamerican highlands in the early first millennium A.D., at the time when classic Maya civilization flourished in the lowlands: Monte Albán in the Valley of Oaxaca, and Teotihuacán in the Valley of Mexico.

Monte Albán was founded in about 900 B.C. on a hill overlooking three arms of the Valley of Oaxaca 400 meters (1,300 feet) below (see Figure 13.2 on page 314). The new settlement grew rapidly, soon boasting of more than 5,000 inhabitants. The chosen hill commands a spectacular view and a unique setting, but it did not make economic sense as a site for a

Figure 13.2 Monte Albán, Valley of Oaxaca.

major ceremonial center, lying as it does far from fertile agricultural lands in the valley below. Perhaps nearby San José Mogote's leaders simply chose an imposing site overlooking their domains as a symbol of their power and political domination. In any event, Monte Albán soon assumed great importance, becoming a major state by 150 B.C. Between 200 and 350 B.C., more than 16,000 people lived in the city, the population rising to a peak of 30,000 during the Late Classic period, between A.D. 500 to 700. Here, again, the Marcus model of rapid expansion, then growth in the center before decline (see Chapter 12) may hold true.

Between 300 and 100 B.C., Zapotec rulers laid out the Main Plaza atop the artificially flattened hilltop. Monte Albán became an elaborate complex of palaces, temples, and plazas, some of which served as ritual settings, others as markets. The city straddled three hills, with at least fifteen residential subdivisions, each with their own plazas. Most inhabitants lived in small houses erected on stone-faced terraces built against the steep terrain. Years of archaeological excavation and survey have mapped more than 2,000 houses and an enormous ceremonial precinct centered around the paved Main Plaza. This ritual ward evolved over more than 1,000 years of continuous rebuilding and modification, which had the effect of progressively isolating the plaza and those who lived around it from the rest of the city. The Late Classic plaza of A.D. 500 to 720 was 300 meters long and 150 meters wide (975 by 480 feet), bounded on its north and south sides by 12-meter (37-foot)-high platform mounds with staircases leading to buildings atop them (Figure 13.2). The rulers and their families lived in a complex of buildings on the north platform, which also served as the formal settings for meetings with high officials, and with emissaries from other states such as Teotihuacán.

Monte Albán reached the height of its power after 200 B.C., when it rivaled another expanding state, Teotihuacán to the north. The two great cities coexisted peacefully and traded with one another for centuries. Parts of Monte Albán were still occupied until the Spanish conquest.

Valley of Mexico: Teotihuacán (200 B.C. to A.D. 750)

As early as 600 B.C., a series of chiefdoms ruled over the Valley of Mexico. Five centuries later, two of them, Cuicuilco in the west and Teotihuacán to the east, were vying for leadership of the Valley. At that moment, nature intervened with a major volcanic eruption that buried and destroyed Cuicuilco completely, leaving Teotihuacán the master of the Valley of Mexico and adjacent parts of the central highlands.

Teotihuacán grew rapidly during the ensuing centuries as thousands of people moved from outlying communities into the metropolis. Whether they moved voluntarily or as a result of conquest and compulsory resettlement is unknown. At least 80,000 people lived in the city by A.D. 100. Like Monte Albán, Teotihuacán may have grown from constant military conquest, in another example of the Marcus model of initial rapid expansion. Between A.D. 200 and 750, Teotihuacán's population grew to more than 150,000 people, making it similar in size to all but the very largest cities of contemporary western Asia and China.

Archaeologist René Millon's map of the city reveals an enormous community that grew over many generations according to a long-term master plan. Over more than eight centuries, the Teotihuacanos built 600 pyramids, 500 workshop areas, a great marketplace, 2,000 apartment complexes, and precinct plazas, all laid out on a grid plan anchored by the 5-kilometer (3-mile)-long Street of the Dead, which bisects the city on a north-south axis, oriented exactly 15.5 degrees east of north, an orientation established by astronomical observation (Figure 13.3).

The Teotihuacán map suggests that the city was grouped into wards based on both kin ties and commercial considerations. Most people lived in standardized, walled residential compounds up to 60 meters (200 feet) on each side, connected by narrow alleyways and

Figure 13.3 Teotihuacán, showing the Pyramid of the Sun (back left) and the Avenue of the Dead, with the Pyramid of the Moon in the foreground.

compounds (see box). Some of these barrios (neighborhoods) were home to craftspeople like obsidian workers or potters. There were also military quarters. Foreigners from the Valley of Oaxaca, also lowland Veracruz, lived in their own neighborhoods. More important priests and artisans lived in dwellings built around small courtyards. Prominent nobles occupied elaborate palaces with central, sunken courts.

At the very core of Teotihuacán's being was the Sacred Cave under the 64-meter (210-foot)-high Pyramid of the Sun, an entryway to the Underworld. The cave was the focus of the powerful creation myth perpetuated by the city's leaders. A sight line from the mouth of the cavern to the western horizon may have associated such astronomical phenomena as the setting sun to specific dates in the local calendar. Teotihuacán's first, and very able, leaders used this cave and the creation myth associated with it as the catalyst for putting their city on the political and religious map. They laid out their entire city as a symbolic landscape commemorating the creation and their principal gods. Their architects laid out the Avenue of the Dead perpendicular to the Sacred Cave and built a small pyramid dedicated to what scholars call "the Great Goddess," associated with the Sun, on the site of the present Pyramid of the Moon, framing it with a sacred mountain on the horizon. They then constructed a Pyramid of the Sun on the site of the Sacred Cave, dedicated to the Great Goddess and to a deity of fire, rain, and wind.

The broad avenue extends southward for 3.2 kilometers (2 miles), where it intersects an east-west avenue, thereby dividing the city into four quadrants. The huge, square enclosure known as the Ciudadela, with sides over 400 meters (1,300 feet), long lies at the intersection. Here lies the Temple of Quetzalcoatl, the Feathered Serpent, a six-level pyramid adorned with tiers of inset rectangular panels placed over a sloping wall (Figure 13.4). The architects took Teotihuacán's centuries-old symbolism of the Sacred Cave as a passageway and

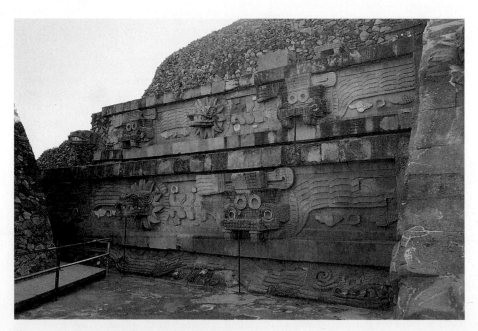

Figure 13.4 Temple of Quetzalcoatl, Teotihuacán.

SITE

Life in Teotihuacán's Barrios

Teeming neighborhoods of single-story, flat-roofed, rectangular apartment compounds complete with courtyards and passageways lay beyond Teotihuacán's ceremonial precincts. Narrow alleyways and streets about 3.6 meters (12 feet) wide separated each compound from its neighbors. Each housed between 20 and 100 people, perhaps members of the same kin group. Judging from artifact patternings, some sheltered skilled artisans, families of obsidian and shell ornament makers, weavers, and potters.

What was life like inside Teotihuacán's anonymous apartment compounds (*barrios*)? Mexican archaeologist Linda Manzanilla has investigated one such complex close to the northwest edge of Teotihuacán, searching for traces of different activities within the complex. The stucco floors in the apartments and courtyards had been swept clean, so Manzanilla and her colleagues used chemical analyses of the floor deposits to search for human activities. She developed a mosaic of different chemical readings, such as high phosphate readings where garbage had rotted, and dense concentrations of carbonate from lime (used in the preparation of both tortillas and stucco) that indicated cooking or building activity. Manzanilla's chemical plans of the compound are accurate enough to pinpoint the locations of cooking fires and eating places where the inhabitants consumed such animals as deer, rabbits, and turkeys. She was able to identify three nuclear families of about thirty people who lived in three separate apartments within this community inside a much larger community. Each apartment had specific areas for sleeping, eating, religious activities, and funeral rites.

Teotihuacán's barrios have revealed intense interactions between people who knew one another well and between these tight-knit communities and the wider universe of the city itself. Walking along one of the cleared streets, you can imagine passing down the same defile 1,500 years earlier, each side bounded by a bare, stuccoed compound wall. Occasionally, a door opens onto the street, offering a view of a shady courtyard, of pots and textiles drying in the sun. The street would have been a cacophony of smells and sounds—wood smoke, dogs barking, the monotonous scratch of maize grinders, the soft voices of women weaving, the passing scent of incense.

Teotihuacán was a vast urban community made up of hundreds of smaller communities, with a market that sold commodities and exotic luxuries from all over the Mesoamerican highlands and lowlands. The Teotihuacános valued their foreign trade so highly that they allowed foreigners to settle among them in special barrios occupied over many centuries. Immigrants from the Veracruz region of the lowlands lived in a neighborhood on the city's eastern side, identified from the remains of distinctive circular adobe houses with thatched roofs identical to those of the inhabitants' Gulf Coast homeland (see Figure 1.10 on page 25). These people, easily identified by their orange-, brown-, and cream-painted pots, probably traded in exotic tropical luxuries such as brightly colored bird feathers. Another neighborhood on the western side housed Zapotec traders from the Valley of Oaxaca, 400 kilometers (250 miles) south of Teotihuacán. Potsherds from their segregated compounds allow us to identify their presence in the crowded city.

built it into the Temple of the Feathered Serpent. The facade is thought to depict the moment of creation, when opposed serpents, one representing lush greenness and peace, the other desert, fire, and war, cavort in the primordial ocean, painted blue in the background. The Temple of Quetzalcoatl was built to the accompaniment of at least 200 human sacrifices, young warriors with their hands tied behind their backs sacrificed in groups of 18 individuals, the number of 20-day months in the year.

A powerful cult of sacred war and human sacrifice, sometimes called "Star Wars" by modern scholars, became associated with the Feathered Serpent, the Storm God, and the cyclical movements of the planet Venus. The beliefs associated with this "Star Wars" cult spread widely in Mesoamerica and had a profound effect on Maya civilization (see Chapter 12). The Ciudadela lay at the very center of Teotihuacán, at the crossroads of the city, and the symbolic center of the cosmos, the axis around which the universe revolved.

Teotihuacán was a unique city, covering at least 21 square kilometers (8 square miles), and it was a major place of pilgrimage, a sacred city of the greatest symbolic importance. Its prosperity came from trade, especially in the green obsidian found nearby, which Teotihuacán's merchants exchanged for all manner of tropical products, including bird feathers, shells, and fish spines from the lowlands. Food supplies came from the intensive cultivation of valley soils, and from acres of swamp gardens built up in the shallow waters of the nearby lakes. This was a brightly colored city, a landscape painted in every hue, the houses adorned with polished whitewash, which still sticks to wall fragments. But above all, the great city spoke a powerful symbolic language, which comes down to us in architecture, art, and ceramics. Its leaders perpetuated an origin myth that had their great city as the place where the cosmos and the present cycle of time began. Every ritual within Teotihuacán's precincts fostered the belief that its people were honored and responsible for maintaining the cosmos. A cult of war and sacrifice governed by an eight-year cycle ensured the well-being of the cosmos, the city, and its inhabitants. Teotihuacán's armies were formidable in battle, their victories the source of the prisoners sacrificed to the gods.

To be a Teotihuacano was to be honored, for one dwelt at the very center of the world. But this honor carried important obligations to the city, the lords, and the gods. Every citizen served the state, through artisanship, through laboring on public works, and by serving in Teotihuacán's armies. These obligations were fulfilled through the ties of kinship that underlay every household, every apartment compound, every royal palace, linking everyone in the great city in the common enterprise of maintaining the cosmos. On occasion, the government attempted planned resettlement of city dwellers on adjacent, underutilized lands, where agricultural production could be maximized, especially on irrigable lands near the lakes. But most people still lived in the city, the heart of a large, loosely knit state about the size of the island of Sicily in the Mediterranean, some 26,000 square kilometers (10,000 square miles).

Teotihuacán's rulers controlled the destinies of about half a million people, but its main impact on lowland and highland Mesoamerica was economic, ideological, and cultural rather than political. Its power came from conquest and trade, and, above all, from a carefully nurtured ideology that made the great city the place of creation, the very cradle of civilization. So successful was this religious propaganda that a ruined Teotihuacán was still deeply revered by the Aztecs and other highland peoples at the time of the Spanish conquest seven centuries later.

After about A.D. 650, Teotihuacán's ideology became increasingly militaristic, at a time when the state may have become more oppressive. The city's enormous population combined with uneven exploitation of the Valley of Mexico's resources may have created serious economic problems that threatened to undermine the state. The end, when it came, was cataclysmic. The Ciudadela was attacked in about A.D. 750, its temples and palaces burned and razed. The destruction was part of a systematic desanctification of Teotihuacán both politically and ritually, to prevent new rulers from rising from the ashes. No one knows who the agents of total destruction were, but Teotihuacán and its state vanished from history, only to be remembered in legend as the place where the Toltec and Aztec world of later times began.

The Toltecs (A.D. 650 to 1200)

Teotihuacán had acted as a magnet to the rural populations of the highlands for many centuries. When the great city collapsed, her inhabitants moved outward as other central Mexican cities expanded into the political vacuum left by her conquerors. Political authority passed rapidly from one growing city to the next. Eventually, one group achieved a semblance of dominance: the Toltecs.

Early Toltec history is confusing at best, but, like other highland peoples, they were composed of various tribal groups, among them the Nahua-speaking Tolteca-Chichimeca, apparently semicivilized people from the fringes of Mesoamerica. (Nahuatl was the common language of the Aztec empire at the Spanish Conquest.) A ruler named Topiltzin Quetzalcoatl, born in the year A.D. 935 or 947, moved the Toltec capital to Tollan, "the Place of Reeds" (the archaeologists' **Tula**), in its heyday a city of some 30,000 to 60,000 people, far smaller than Teotihuacán. Here bitter strife broke out between the followers of the peace-loving Topiltzin Quetzalcoatl and those of his warlike rival Tezcatlipoca, "Smoking Mirror," god of warriors and of life itself. The Tezcatlipoca faction prevailed by trickery and humiliation. Topiltzin and his followers fled Tula and eventually arrived on the shores of the Gulf of Mexico. There, according to one account, the ruler set himself on fire decked out in his ceremonial regalia. As his ashes rose to heaven, he turned into the Morning Star. The Spanish conquistadors learned another version of the legend in which Topiltzin Quetzalcoatl fashioned a raft of serpents and sailed over the eastern horizon, vowing to return in the year 1 Reed, of which you will read more (on page 327).

In the years following Topiltzin Quetzalcoatl's departure, the Toltec state reached its greatest extent, controlling much of central Mexico from coast to coast. By A.D. 900, Tula was a prosperous town of artisans that soon grew into a city of as many as 40,000 people covering 16 square kilometers (5.4 square miles). By A.D. 1000, the Toltec lords had laid out their capital on a grid pattern with a wide central plaza and ceremonial center bordered by imposing pyramids and at least two ball courts. Four colossal warriors carrying spearthrowers and incense bags supported the roof of a temple atop a pyramid (see Figure 13.5 on page 320). A grim "Serpent Wall," 40 meters (131 feet) long, runs along the north side of the pyramid, bearing friezes of serpents consuming skeletal humans. Everything points to a now militaristic society, obsessed with human sacrifice.

Tula's temples, pyramids, and ball courts were torn to the ground in about 1200, when the Toltec empire fell apart.

Aztec Civilization (A.D. 1200 to 1521)

During the next century, a political vacuum existed in the Valley of Mexico, where a series of moderate-sized city-states prospered and competed. Into this settled and competitive world stepped a small and obscure group, the Azteca, or Mexica. Within a mere two centuries, these insignificant players on the highland stage presided over the mightiest pre-Columbian empire in the Americas.

The Aztecs' history, as they told it, reads like a rags-to-riches novel. They claimed they came from Aztlan, an island on a lake west or northwest of Mexico, migrating into the Valley under the guidance of their tribal god Huitzilopochtli, "Hummingbird on the Left," who was soon reborn as the Sun God himself. This was the official version perpetuated by official Aztec historians and recorded by the Spaniards. Such migration legends

Figure 13.5 Colossal warriors atop Pyramid B at Tula, the Toltec capital.

were common in ancient Mesoamerica and should not be taken at face value. The Aztecs had certainly settled in the Valley by the thirteenth century, but they were unwelcome arrivals in the densely settled valley. Eventually they settled on some swampy islands in the marshes of the largest lake in the Valley, where they founded twin capitals, Tenochtitlán and Tlatelolco, sometime after 1325. Fierce and ruthless warriors, the Aztecs became mercenaries for the lord Tezozomoc of the expanding Tepanec kingdom in 1367. The Aztecs shared in the spoils of his expanding domains, soon adopting the institutions and empire-building strategies of their employer.

After Tezozomoc's death in 1426, an Aztec ruler named Itzcoatl and his exceptionally able adviser Tlacaelel attacked the Tepanecs and crushed them in one of the great battles of Aztec history. The Aztecs became the masters of the Valley of Mexico and set out to rewrite society and history itself. The great Tlacaelel ordered all the historical codices of the Aztecs' rivals to be burnt, creating a mythic, visionary history of the Mexica in their place. The Aztecs were now the chosen of the Sun God Huitzilopochtli, the true heirs of the ancient Toltecs, great warriors destined to take prisoners in battle to nourish the sun in its daily journey across the heavens. A series of brilliant and ruthless leaders embarked on aggressive campaigns of conquest, destined to fulfill Aztec destiny. The greatest Aztec ruler was Ahuitzotl (1486–1502), the sixth *tlatoani,* or "speaker." His armies marched far beyond the Valley, to the borders of Guatemala. Just like Teotihuacán and Tikal, the initial conquests rapidly delineated the broad outlines of their domains.

The Aztec empire covered both highlands and lowlands and affected the lives of over 5 million people. Brilliant strategist and able administrator, Ahuitzotl was a single-minded militarist, who believed fervently in his divine mission to nourish the Sun God. Twenty thousand prisoners are said to have perished in 1487 when he inaugurated a rebuilt Great Temple of Huitzilopochtli and the Rain God Tlaloc in the central precincts of Tenochtitlán.

Tenochtitlán

In its late-fourteenth-century heyday, **Tenochtitlán** was a sophisticated and cosmopolitan city with a social, political, and economic organization flexible enough to integrate large numbers of outsiders—merchants, pilgrims, and foreigners—as well as thousands of laborers into its already large permanent population. The Aztec capital reflected a society that depended on military strength and on its ability to organize large numbers of people to achieve its end. Thousands of hectacres of carefully planned swamp gardens (*chinampas*) that intersected with canals provided food for the large urban population.

The city originally consisted of two autonomous communities, Tenochtitlán and Tlatelolco, each with their own ceremonial precincts. By 1519, Tenochtitlán was the center of religious and secular power, while the main market was at Tlatelolco. The capital was divided into four quarters, which intersected at the foot of the stairway up the Great Temple of Huitzilopochtli and Tlaloc within the central walled plaza. The rectangular plaza was about 457 meters (500 yards) square, large enough to accommodate nearly 10,000 people during major public ceremonies (Figure 13.6).

Thanks to excavations by Eduardo Matos Moctezuma, we know that the Great Temple stood on the north side of the plaza, a stepped pyramid with two stairways and two shrines, dedicated to Huitzilopochtli and Tlaloc respectively (see box on page 322). Huitzilopochtli's red chapel lay to the right, Tlaloc's blue shrine to the left. Moctezuma unearthed no less than six earlier phases of the temple, the second dating to about 1390 and

Figure 13.6 Artist's reconstruction of the central precincts of Tenochtitlán, the Aztec capital. The great temple of Huitzilopochtli is at the left.

SITE

The Aztec Templo Major at Tenochtitlán

The focal point of Aztec religious life was the Great Temple of the gods Huitzilopochtli and Tlaloc in the heart of Tenochtitlán. Until quite recently our knowledge of this hub of the Aztec universe came largely from documentary sources. The Spaniards demolished the final temple at the conquest and built Mexico City's cathedral on much the same site. In 1978 electricity workers digging a pit came across a gigantic oval stone, over 3.2 meters (10 feet 7 inches) in diameter, not far from the cathedral. Reliefs carved on the stone depicted the dismembered body of the goddess Coyolxauhqui who, according to myth, had been killed by her brother, Huitzilopochtli. Five years of excavations on the site led by archaeologist Matos Moctezuma and his colleagues unearthed the remains of the Great Temple (Templo Major). Little survived of the final building razed by the Spanish, but beneath it lay no less than six earlier phases of the temple, the second dating to about A.D. 1390, virtually complete.

The original temple structure had been a small and crude construction, later enclosed within successively larger shells, new pyramids each with their own shrines, sculpture, offerings, and other artifacts. In all, about 6,000 objects were excavated from 86 separate offering caches—some of them objects of Aztec manufacture, but the great majority clearly tribute or spoils of war from different parts of the empire buried here as a sacred expression of Aztec power and might. They included magnificent artifacts of obsidian, jade, and terra-cotta—and even ancient stone masks from Teotihuacán. Perhaps the Aztecs were themselves amateur archaeologists, who dug up the masks at this ruined city.

The Great Temple depicted the Aztec vision of the cosmos. The platform that supported the whole structure of the temple corresponded to the terrestrial level of existence. The four tapering tiers of the pyramid itself rose to the summit and represented the celestial levels. At the summit was the supreme level, with the two shrines to the two supreme gods, Huitzilopochtli and Tlaloc. The Underworld lay beneath the platform. Most of the offerings come from below it. These offerings include a very large number associated with Tlaloc—not just depictions of him, but extraordinary quantities of fish and marine animal bones appropriate for this god of water and rain.

According to the Aztecs, the earth lay in the center of the universe, encircled by a ring of water. Above lay the heavens with the gods and beneath lay the Underworld. The terrestrial level of existence had a central point, located at the Great Temple, from which radiated the four directions of the Aztec world. The Great Temple was the symbolic pivotal point, the place where a vertical channel led both to the heavens and to the Underworld. The symbolism went even further, for Tenochtitlán itself lay in the midst of a lake. Indeed it was sometimes called Cemanahuac, "Place in a Circle of Water," thought of as a turquoise ring. Such, also, was Aztlan, the mythical Aztec island homeland to the northwest, surrounded by water. Thus, Tenochtitlán was the symbolic center of the universe and the place where the supreme ruler interceded with the gods.

virtually complete. Moctezuma points out that the great pyramid depicts the four celestial levels of the Aztec cosmos, the original ground surface being the earthly plane of existence. It was from this point that the four cardinal directions of the Aztec world radiated, each associated with colors, different personifications of gods and goddesses. From here a vertical channel led to the heavens above and the Underworld below.

Tenochtitlán was the symbolic center of the universe, a city set in a circle of water, Aztlan itself, the mythic island surrounded by water. The greatest festivals of the Aztec world unfolded at the great pyramid, ceremonies marked by rows of brightly dressed prisoners climbing the steep stairway to their death. The victim was stretched out over the sacrificial stone. In seconds, a priest with an obsidian knife broke open his chest and ripped out his still-beating heart, dashing it against the sacrificial stone. The corpse rolled down the steep pyramid into the hands of butchers at the foot, who dismembered the body and set the skull on the great skull rack nearby (Figure 13.7). Despite a reputation for cannibalism, most experts believe the Mexica consumed only small amounts on ritual occasions, perhaps as acts of spiritual renewal.

The World of the Fifth Sun

The Aztecs were militaristic, but every deed, every moment of living, was filled with symbolic meaning and governed by ritual (see box on page 324). They inherited the cyclical view of time, established by the movements of the heavenly bodies, which had lain at the core of Mesoamerican civilization for millennia. Their 365-day secular calendar measured the passing of seasons and market days. A ritual calendar on a 260-day cycle consisted of 20 "weeks" of 13 days each. Each week, each day, had a patron deity, all of them with specific good and evil qualities. Once every 52 years, the two calendars coincided, a moment at which time was thought to expire until rekindled by the priests lighting a sacred fire in a sacrificial victim's chest. Then a new cycle began amidst general rejoicing.

Figure 13.7 Aztec human sacrifice. A victim's heart is torn out at the Temple of Huitzilopochtli.

VOICES

Aztec Thoughts on Human Existence

For all their well-ordered lives, Aztec wise men puzzled over the meaning of life and probed into the nature of reality and the verities of life. They wondered if life was all a dream:

> "Do we speak the truth here, Giver of Life?
> We merely dream, we are only wakened from dreams.
> All is like a dream. . . .
> No one speaks here of truth. . . ." (Leon-Portilla, 1963, p. 220)

These same philosophers had more practical missions, too, to "place a mirror before the people, that they might become wise and prudent: to endow with wisdom the countenances of others." Their task was to give people born faceless a purpose and an identity. So they sought a meaning for human existence. Was there a truth to human life? Were humans real beings or just transitory illusions?

The wise men taught that one's self attempted to fill its own emptiness by searching for wisdom and art, for its own image, the "face and heart," the Aztec image of the individual. So deeply traditional was this notion that the Aztec teacher was called "teacher of peoples' faces."

Beyond attempting to influence their pupils' wills, Aztec wise men taught self-discipline through strict education. They well knew the dilemma confronting a people who have a measure of personal freedom while at the same time facing a world controlled by the Creator. "We are but toys to him; He laughs at us," speculated one sage. Humans existed to serve the gods. Existence on earth was but transitory. With death, one entered the world of the beyond, the region of the dead. Here, those favored by Tlaloc, the god of rain, went to an earthly paradise called Tlalocan, where "never is there a lack of green corn, squash, sprigs of amaranth . . . and flowers." (Anderson and Dibble, 1963 (6): p. 122).

Most people lived well-regulated, humdrum lives, for which they were well prepared by the wise men:

> "Our forefathers, the old men, the old women . . . went saying that on earth we travel, we live along a mountain peak. Over here there is an abyss, over there is an abyss. Wherever thou art to deviate, wherever thou art to go astray, there wilt thou fall, there wilt thou plunge into the deep. Continue with caution on earth, for thou hast heard that moderation is necessary." (Anderson and Dibble, 1963 (6), pp. 121–126.)

Aztec creation legends spoke of four suns preceding their own world, that of the Fifth Sun. A cataclysmic flood destroyed the world of the Fourth Sun. Primordial waters covered the earth. The gods gathered at the sacred city, Teotihuacán, where they took counsel. Two gods were chosen to represent the Sun and Moon. They did penance for four days, then immolated themselves in a great fire in the presence of the other gods. They emerged as the Sun and Moon, blown on their cyclical courses by the wind god Ehecatl. Thus was born the world of the Fifth Sun, but a world doomed to inevitable, cyclical extinction. A strong sense of fatalism underlay Aztec existence, but they believed they could ensure the continuity of life by nourishing the sun with the magic elixir of human hearts. This was the reason why human sacrifice was so prevalent in Mesoamerican society, as a means of returning food and energy from living people to the earth, the sky, and the waters. Feeding the sun was warriors' business, for they were the chosen people of the sun, destined to conquer, or to suffer the "Flowery Death" (death on the sacrificial stone) when captured in battle. From birth, in formal orations, in schools, through art, architecture, poetry, even in dress codes, the Aztecs were told theirs was a divine quest—to carve out an empire in the name of Huitzilopochtli.

The Aztec State

The Aztec empire was a mosaic of ever-changing alliances, cemented together by an elaborate tribute-gathering machine, and controlled by a tiny group of rulers, the lord of Tenochtitlán being principal among them. Everything was run for the benefit of a growing elite, who maintained their power by ruthless and efficient taxation campaigns, political marriages, and the constant threat of military force. Tribute was assessed on conquered cities and taken in many forms, as raw materials like gold dust, metal artifacts, or tropical bird feathers for ceremonial mantles and headdresses (Figure 13.8). Fine ornaments, even capes, were assessed from communities specializing in such products. Twenty-six cities did

Figure 13.8 Aztec tribute. An inventory, preserved in the *Codex Mendoza*, an account of Aztec society compiled after the Spanish Conquest for the Viceroy of New Spain, lists, among other items from the province of Tochtepec: "1,600 rich mantles, 800 striped red, white, and green mantles, 400 warrior's tunics and shorts. . . ." The tribute included colored bird feathers, cacao, and tree gum.

nothing but provide firewood for one royal palace alone. Expert smiths made musical instruments like bells, and alloyed copper to bring out shimmering gold and silver hues. Both color and sound were central parts of Mesoamerican ideology, commemorating the sun and moon, the sounds of rain, thunder, and rattlesnakes, helping bring symbolic order to the world. Both settlement data and other archaeological data suggest that the Aztec empire was less centralized, as both a society and an economy, than its great predecessor, Teotihuacán. To what extent it originated through decision making at the top, as opposed to market dynamics such as supply and demand, is still unknown.

Under the highly visible and much touted imperial veneer lay a complex foundation of small kingdoms, towns, and villages, all integrated into local economies. Many of them existed before the Aztec state, or even earlier; civilizations came into being and continued after the Spanish Conquest. At the same time, the economic and political patterns of the empire were highly variable, both regionally and socially, in everything from land tenure to craft specialization, patterns of urbanization to merchants and markets. This intricate social mosaic, only now being revealed by a new generation of archaeological research, lay behind a facade of seeming political and economic uniformity and centralization.

Tribute and trade went together, for the Aztec empire depended heavily on professional merchants, *pochteca.* The Aztec merchants formed a closely knit class of their own, serving as the eyes and ears of the state, and sometimes achieving great wealth. Tenochtitlán's great market at Tlatelolco was the hub of the Aztec world, attended, so the Spanish chroniclers record, by at least 20,000 people a day, and 50,000 on market days. There were gold and silver merchants, dealers in slaves and tropical feathers, sellers of capes and chocolate, every kind of merchandise imaginable. Specially appointed officials supervised the market to ensure that fair practices prevailed.

The state itself was run for the benefit of the rulers and the nobility, a privileged class who controlled land and had the right to make use of communal labor. Through birthright, tribute levies, and appointed positions, nobles controlled nearly every strategic resource in the empire and the trade routes that handled them. An elaborate dress code covered everything from ornaments to cape and sandal styles, regulations designed to restrict the size of the nobility. The tribute and labor of tens of thousands of commoners supported the state. The humble commoners with their coarse capes and work-worn hands supplied a small number of people with an endless supply of food, firewood, water, fine clothing, and a host of luxury goods that came from all over the lowlands and highlands. Only slaves and prisoners were lower in the social hierarchy.

Every Aztec was a member of a **calpulli**, or "big house," a kin-based group of families that claimed descent through the male line from a common ancestor. The four quarters of Tenochtitlán were organized into neighborhoods based on such groups. The *calpulli* served as the intermediary between the individual commoner and the state, paying taxes in labor and tribute, and allocating people to carry out public works. Most important, the *calpulli* held land communally and allocated it to its members. An elected leader maintained special maps showing how the land was being used and dealt with government tribute collectors. The *calpulli* provided a measure of security to every member of society, while providing an efficient device for the state to govern a teeming and diverse urban and rural population and to organize large numbers of people for armies or work projects at short notice. None of the Aztecs' social and political institutions was new, for they inherited them from the Toltecs and the rulers of Teotihuacán, even if, in the Aztec case, they worked within a more flexible and diverse milieu.

The Spanish Conquest (A.D. 1517 to 1521)

The Aztec empire was at its height when the aggressive and militaristic ruler Ahuitzotl died in 1501. The following year, Moctezuma Xocoyotzin ("the Younger") was elected to the throne, a complex man, said to be a good soldier, but given to introspection. When reports reached Tenochtitlán in 1517 of mountains moving on the Gulf of Mexico, of white-bearded visitors from over the eastern horizon to the Maya of the distant Yucatán, Moctezuma became obsessed with ancient Toltec legends, with the departure of Topiltzin Quetzalcoatl, who had sailed over the eastern horizon vowing to return in the year 1 Reed. By grotesque historical coincidence, Hernan Cortés landed in Vera Cruz in the year 1519, 1 Reed, convincing Moctezuma that Topiltzin Quetzalcoatl had returned to claim his kingdom.

The story of the Spanish conquest that followed unfolds like a Greek tragedy. The conquest pitted an isolated, battle-hardened expeditionary force of about 600 men against a brave, driven people who were convinced, like their illustrious predecessors, that every act of war was imbued with deep symbolism. The Aztecs had long used war to feed the relentless appetite of the gods and to keep a loose patchwork of vassal states in order. With a skilled enemy exploiting their uneasy allies, they found themselves on their own. All they could do was to defend themselves desperately against a puzzling foe quite unlike any adversary they had encountered. This small and determined band of gold-hungry adventurers was accustomed to long and arduous military campaigns, and it was inevitable that they would prevail.

Ten years passed before the whole of Mexico (New Spain) was under secure Spanish control. Tens of thousands of people died in bloody encounters, hundreds of thousands more from exotic diseases like influenza and smallpox introduced by the newcomers. Instead of the divine benevolence of Quetzalcoatl, the conquerors brought suffering, death, exotic diseases, and slavery. More than 3,000 years of Mesoamerican civilization passed rapidly into centuries of historical obscurity.

Summary

Highland Mesoamerican civilization stemmed from both indigenous and lowland roots. Olmec influence was strong, but small kingdoms developed in the Valley of Oaxaca by at least 1000 B.C. These coalesced into the Monte Albán state, which reached its heyday during the first millennium A.D. and coexisted with Teotihuacán on the edge of the Basin of Mexico.

Teotihuacán was the dominant political and economic force on the highlands and in the Basin of Mexico for the first seven centuries of the first millennium A.D. Its rulers traded constantly with the Maya, and its militaristic philosophies and religious beliefs permeated much of Mesoamerica. The great city with its huge pyramids and sacred precincts was an intensely sacred place, credited with being the birthplace of Aztec civilization.

The Toltec civilization, also based on the Valley of Mexico, filled the political vacuum left by the collapse of Teotihuacán, but fell apart in A.D. 1200. By the fourteenth century, the Aztecs, who originated to the northwest of the Basin, were becoming the dominant force in the highlands. Over the next two centuries, their rulers created a vast tribute-paying empire, which extended into the lowlands and as far south as Guatemala. Aztec civilization depended on militaristic doctrines and human sacrifice to further the ambitious goals of the sun god Huitzilopochtli. The empire was already showing signs of strain when Hernan Cortés and 600 conquistadors entered the Aztec capital, Tenochtitlán, in 1519. Two years later, the city was in ruins after a bitter siege. Aztec civilization collapsed abruptly in the face of superior military technology helped by rebellious vassals who rose against their hated masters.

Andean Civilizations

2.5 Million   1.0 Million   500,000 B.P.   100,000 B.P.   50,000 B.P.   15,000 B.P.   A.D. 1   A.D. 1950

PROLOGUE

The year was 1911. American explorer Hiram Bingham was high in the Andes, struggling along precipitous, densely forested paths, slipping ankle-deep in mud at every corner. Bingham was searching for Vilcabamba, the last refuge of the Inca ruler Manca Inca when he fled from the Spaniards in 1537. With a local farmer as a guide, he and his men climbed in places on all fours, high above the tumbling Urubamba River. Suddenly, he emerged into the open, high atop a mountain ridge. He wandered through "a maze of beautiful granite houses . . . covered with trees and moss and the growth of centuries." He wandered for hours among "walls of white granite . . . carefully cut and exquisitely fitted together." Stone terraces climbed like giant staircases up the hillside. A twisting path led to ruined houses built with fine Inca stonework. A granite stairway led Bingham to a plaza with two temples, one containing a large altar stone. "The sight held me spellbound," declared Bingham. On this mountain ridge, the Incas had built Machu Picchu, a settlement in such a remote, inaccessible setting that Bingham claimed it was the "lost city of the Incas" (see Figure 14.14 on page 350). For three years, Bingham worked at Machu Picchu, clearing, excavating, and mapping houses and temples.

Machu Picchu is one of the most spectacular archaeological sites in the world, but was never a lost city, for the local farmers were well aware of its existence. Bingham himself believed he had found Vilcabamba, but in 1964 explorer Gene Savoy identified the remote Inca settlement of Espiritu Pampa in the forested Pamaconas Valley as the last Inca capital (Bingham, 1964, p. 212).

In its late-fifteenth-century heyday, the vast Inca empire, known as **Tawantinsuyu** ("The Land of the Four Quarters"), extended from high-altitude mountain valleys in the **Andes** through dry highland plains to foothills to tropical rain forests and to coastal deserts, some of the driest landscape on earth (Figure 14.1).

Over many centuries, two "poles" of **Andean** civilization developed, the one along the north coast of what is now Peru, the other in the south-central Andes. Only the Inca succeeded in joining the two into one vast empire. The northern pole was centered on the bleak and effectively rainless Peruvian desert plain, which extends south nearly 550 kilometers (350 miles) along the coast as far as Collasuyu, reaching a width of up to 100 kilometers (62 miles) in the area of the Lambayeque River. Some forty rivers and streams fueled by mountain runoff flow across the plain, but they can be used for irrigation only in areas where the surrounding desert is low enough.

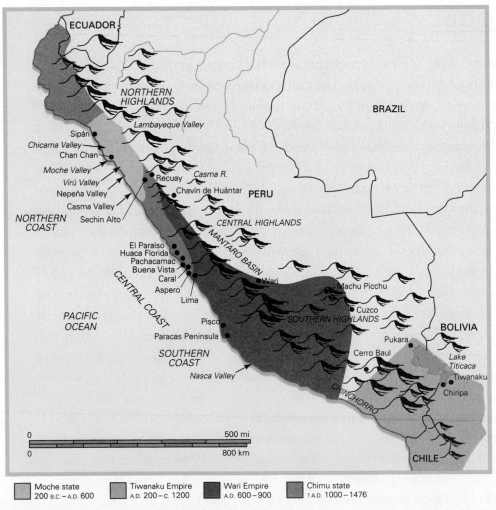

Figure 14.1 Map showing archaeological sites in Chapter 14.

The southern pole embraced the high plains of the Lake Titicaca Basin, highland Bolivia, and parts of Argentina and northern Chile in the south-central Andes. Much of this region was too dry and cold to sustain dense human populations. The northern end of the Lake Titicaca Basin was somewhat warmer and better watered, making both alpaca and llama herding and potato and quinoa agriculture possible.

Andean civilization pursued many different evolutionary pathways, which came together in a remarkable mosaic of states and empires, in large part as a result of widely held spiritual beliefs and by constant interchange between the coast and the highlands and between neighboring valleys and large population centers. Tawantinsuyu itself was a unique political synthesis sewn together by the Inca lords of the Andes in the centuries just before European contact. It was the culmination of many centuries of increasing social complexity throughout the Andean area.

This chapter describes the development of Andean civilization, which culminated in the Inca empire.

The Maritime Foundations of Andean Civilization

The rugged central Andean mountains are second only to the Himalayas in height, but only 10 percent of their rainfall descends the Pacific watershed. The foothill slopes and plains at the western foot of the mountains are mantled by one of the world's driest deserts, which extends virtually from the equator to 30 degrees south, much of it along the Peruvian coast. At the opposite extreme, the richest fishery in the Americas hugs the Pacific shore, yielding millions of small schooling fish such as anchovies. These easily netted shoals support millions of people today, and they supported dense prehistoric populations. In contrast, the cultivation of this dry landscape requires controlling the runoff from the Andes with large irrigation systems that use long canals built by the coordinated labors of hundreds of people. Only 10 percent of this desert can be farmed, so its inhabitants rely heavily on the bounty of the Pacific, including the enormous shoals of easily netted anchovies. Surprisingly, perhaps, this apparently inhospitable desert was a major center of complex early states, which traded with neighbors in the highlands and built large ceremonial centers.

In the 1970s, archaeologist Michael Moseley proposed what he called the "maritime foundations of Andean civilization" hypothesis. He argued that the unique maritime resources of the Pacific coast provided sufficient calories to support rapidly growing, sedentary populations, which clustered in large communities. In addition, the same food source produced sufficient surplus to free up time and people to erect large public monuments and temples, work organized by the leaders of newly complex coastal societies. This scenario runs contrary to conventional archaeological thinking, which regards agriculture as the economic basis for state-organized societies. In the Andes, argued Moseley, it was fishing. For thousands of years, coastal populations rose, and their rise preadapted them to later circumstances, under which they would adopt large-scale irrigation and maize agriculture.

Several critiques of the maritime foundations hypothesis have appeared, all of them based on the assumption that large coastal settlements could not have been supported by maritime resources alone. Most of these critiques have tended to ignore the potential of anchovies. Overall, the maritime foundations hypothesis has stood the test of time well, provided it is seen as a component in a much broader evolutionary process, which also took place inland, in the highlands, and in areas where the width of the coastal shelf precluded extensive anchovy fishing.

Richard Burger argues that changing dietary patterns in the highlands, where agriculture became increasingly important, would have created a demand among farmers for lowland products—salt, fish, and seaweed. Seaweed is rich in marine iodine and could have been an important medicine in the highlands, used to combat endemic goiter and other conditions. By the same token, carbohydrate foods like white potatoes that could not be grown on the coast have been found in sites in the Pacific lowlands. Thus, the formation of states in both lowlands and highlands may have been fostered by continuous interchange between coast and interior.

Michael Moseley believes that the reliance on maritime resources led to a preadaptation in the form of large, densely concentrated populations, whose leaders were able to organize the labor forces needed not only for building large ceremonial centers but also for transforming river valleys with sizable irrigation schemes. Under this scenario, irrigation farming was in the hands of a well-defined group of authority figures, who took advantage of existing simple technology and local populations to create new economies. This transformation, based as it was on trade, maize agriculture, and a maritime diet, acted as a "kick" for radical changes in Andean society. But the transformation was based on ancient fishing traditions, which can be documented thousands of years earlier at early coastal villages.

Coastal Foundations (2600 to 900 B.C.)

Agriculture remained a secondary activity until comparatively recently in the lowlands. Despite this, sedentary villages of several hundred people flourished along the north coast between 2500 and 1800 B.C. This Initial Period of Andean civilization was a critical millennium, for new concerns both with the cosmos and with religion permeated the Andes. The new beliefs manifested themselves in a wave of monumental construction in both lowlands and highlands, notably of U-shaped ceremonial structures.

We do not know when the first more-complex societies developed along the coast, but it was before 3000 B.C. **Aspero**, a settlement covering at least 15 hectares (37 acres) flourished at the mouth of the Supe River by 3055 B.C. By 2600 B.C., a large kingdom was ruled by a center named **Caral** in the hot Supe Valley about 193 kilometer (120 miles) north of modern-day Lima. There were as many as seventeen centers in the Supe region, supported by cultivating guavas, beans, peppers, and fruit grown with skilled irrigation agriculture. The farmers also grew cotton, but not maize and potatoes, the two later staples of Andean life. The kingdom may have prospered by growing and trading cotton for net manufacture. Much of its subsistence came from anchovies, which occur in desiccated human feces from the site.

Caral is dominated by six large stone platforms with structures atop them built of quarried stone and filled in with cobbles from the nearby river. The largest is 152 by 137 meter (500 by 450 feet) and 18 meter (60 feet) high (Figure 14.2). A small elite governed this important kingdom, but we still know almost nothing about them, or about the ways in which they commanded the loyalty of the hundreds, if not thousands, of people who built their imposing centers. Caral was abandoned for unknown reasons between 2000 and 1500 B.C., just as other kingdoms came into prominence along the coast to the north. **Buena Vista,** by the Chillon River near Lima, has yielded a stepped pyramid temple with distinctive sculpture dating to 2200 B.C. The shrine is aligned with the sun and constellations on the equinox and at the summer and winter solstices, used by the Andeans to schedule their agricultural activities.

El Paraíso, built close to the mouth of the Chillón River near Lima in about 1800 B.C., is the oldest of these U-shaped ceremonial complexes and the closest one to the Pacific (Figure 14.3). This vast site consists of at least six huge square buildings constructed of roughly shaped stone blocks cemented with unfired clay. The people painted the polished clay-faced outer walls in brilliant hues. Each complex consisted of a square building surrounded by

Figure 14.2 A terraced Caral pyramid.

Figure 14.3 El Paraíso.

tiers of platforms reached by stone and clay staircases. The largest is more than 250 meters (830 feet) long and 50 meters (166 feet) wide, standing more than 10 meters (30 feet) above the plain. The rooms apparently were covered with matting roofs supported by willow posts. Perhaps as many as 100,000 tons of rock excavated from the nearby hills were needed to build the El Paraíso buildings. There are few signs of occupation around them, though, as if they were shrines and public precincts rather than residential quarters. The two largest mounds of collapsed masonry lie parallel to one another, defining a vast, elongated patio covering more than 2.5 hectares (6 acres).

What is most surprising is that people from dozens of scattered villages erected these huge structures. For reasons not yet understood, they united in a building project that channeled most of their surplus energies into a vast monumental center, a place where few people lived but where everyone apparently congregated for major public ceremonies.

El Paraíso's U-shaped layout coincides with the florescence of similarly shaped ceremonial centers in the interior, at a time when coastal people began to consume much larger amounts of root crops, to make pottery, and to shift their settlements inland to river valleys. Some scholars believe that this move coincided with the introduction of large-scale canal irrigation. Perhaps the spread of U-shaped ceremonial centers reflects a radical restructuring of society that accompanied major economic change.

What does this mean in ritual terms? In many parts of the Americas the ritual manipulation of smoke and water served as a way of bridging stratified layers of air, earth, and bodies of water in the cosmos. The early ceremonial centers of the coast and highlands may reflect an ancient tradition of using these substances to maintain communication with the cosmos.

The Early Horizon and Chavín de Huántar (900 to 200 B.C.)

In 1943, archaeologist Julio Tello identified a distinctive art style in stone, ceramics, and precious metals over a wide area of highland Peru, a style he named Chavín after a famous prehistoric ceremonial center at Chavín de Huántar in central Peru. Tello's research led to a long-held belief among Peruvianists that the widespread Chavín art style was a "mother culture" for all later Andean civilizations, somewhat equivalent to the Olmec phenomenon in Mesoamerican prehistory. This became a distinctive "Early Horizon" in Peruvian prehistory, dating to about 900 B.C., when there was a great expansion of indigenous religious belief by conquest, trade, and colonization when civilization began.

Chavín de Huántar is testimony to an elaborate, well-developed iconography. The site had a long history, beginning in at least 1500 B.C. From small beginnings as a shrine, the builders expanded the site. The temple area is terraced with an impressive truncated pyramid on the uppermost level (Figure 14.4a). The 10-meter (32-foot)-high pyramid appears solid but is in fact hollow, a honeycomb of stone passages and rooms. The galleries are ventilated by special rectangular tubes. The temple housed a remarkable carving of a jaguarlike human with hair in the form of serpents, the famous "Lanzón," which may have served as an axis joining the heavens, the earth, and the Underworld (Figure 14.4b). The deity seems to be acting as an arbiter of balance and order. The entire center was a place of mediation with the heavens and the Underworld. Chavín's priests and religious functionaries served as intermediaries between the living and the supernatural. In this shamanlike role, they transformed themselves into supernatural jaguars and crested eagles.

Huachecsa

Subterranean gallery—
location of the Lanzón

New temple

Old temple

U-shaped plaza and
sunken circular
courtyard

Mosna

Black-and-white
portal and stairs

U-shaped plaza with
sunken rectangular
courtyard

(a)

(b)

Figure 14.4 Chavín de Huántar. **(a)** Plan of the ceremonial center with major architectural features. **(b)** The "Lanzón" god carved on a pillar set in the midst of the temple interior.

Chavín art reflects these transformations. Jaguar motifs predominate; humans, gods, and animals have jaguarlike fangs or limbs; snakes flow from the bodies of many figures. The art is both grotesque and slightly sinister. Many figures were carved in stone, others in clay or bone, their nostrils dripping with mucus from ingesting hallucinogenic substances. The principal god may have been a nature deity, associated with thunder and other powerful meteorological phenomena of the nearby high mountains.

Conceivably, theorizes Richard Burger, Chavín de Huántar was a four-stage artificial mountain, where rituals surrounded the circulation of water. Under these beliefs, the earth floated on a vast ocean. From there, water circulated through mountains to the Milky Way in the heavens, where it became rain to water human fields before flowing back into the ocean. Peruvian archaeologist Luis Lumbreras has replicated the deep roaring sound of water flowing through the elaborate stonelined tunnels and canals of the great shrine. He believes that the roar of the water would have echoed through the temple during the rainy season, a symbolic link between the rain-giving mountains, the temple, and the layers of the cosmos. With its tangled animal and human motifs, Chavín art has all the flamboyance and exotic touches of the tropical forest. The animals depicted—cayman, jaguar, and snake—are all forest animals. The art may have originated in the tropical forests to the east of the Andes, but the Early Horizon Chavín temple has a U shape with a sunken central plaza, an architectural design documented centuries earlier at other coastal and highland sites.

Chavín represents a coalescence of traits and ideas from both the coast and the forest that formed a flamboyant cultural manifestation over a local area of the highlands. The Early Horizon may have been a long period of cultural change and political adjustment.

The Initial Period

The Initial Period saw the development of distinctive coastal and highland societies at either end of the Andean world, on the North Coast and on the shores of Lake Titicaca far to the south.

The Coast (after 1800 B.C.)

After 1800 B.C., a set of interacting kingdoms developed in the Moche, Casma, Chillón, and other river valleys where irrigation agriculture flourished. Centuries before, communication networks had arisen that linked not only neighboring coastal river valleys but lowlands and highlands as well. These trade routes, which straddled all manner of environmental zones, helped spread technology, ideology, pottery making, and architectural styles over large areas, giving a superficial sense of unity that was reflected in the widespread use of common art motifs.

By this time, people had moved from the coast inland. The subsistence base changed from fishing to large-scale irrigation agriculture. Even the first farmers probably made some limited use of canals to water their riverside gardens. However, the new works were on a far larger scale, spurred by the availability of an army of workers fed by abundant Pacific fish; by the presence of gentle, cultivable slopes inland; and by the expertise of the local people in farming cotton, gourds, and many lesser crops such as squashes and beans.

At first, each family may have worked together to irrigate its own sloping gardens, but gradually each community grew so much that essential irrigation works could be handled only by cooperative effort. Organized irrigation perhaps began as many minor cooperative works between individual families and neighboring villages. These simple projects eventually evolved over many centuries into elaborate public works that embraced entire inland valleys, controlled by a corporate authority that held a monopoly over both the water and the land it irrigated.

Lake Titicaca Basin: Chiripa and Pukara (1000 B.C. to A.D. 100)

As Chavín de Huántar rose to prominence in the northern highlands, a separate Early Horizon tradition of complex society developed around Lake Titicaca far to the south. The plains landscape of the basin was gradually transformed by ever more intensive agriculture and herding.

At **Chiripa** on the southern shore of the lake, farming and herding were integrated into much earlier hunter-gatherer traditions. Chiripa itself remained a small village until about 1000 B.C., when a platform mound was built in the community, then modified many times over the centuries. Eventually, carved stone plaques set into the walls depicted serpents, animals, and humans, the earliest appearance of a stone-carving tradition that persisted along the shores of the lake for many centuries. Sixteen rectangular buildings surrounded the court. Many features of the Chiripa shrine, especially the stepped doorways, sunken courts, and niche-like windows, are ancestral to the later Tiwanaku architectural tradition, which used the same devices for its ceremonial architecture. The religious beliefs associated with this architecture have been grouped under the Yaya-Mama religious tradition, which flourished for many centuries.

Another major center flourished at **Pukara,** 75 kilometers (47 miles) northwest of Lake Titicaca, with a large residential area and an imposing ceremonial complex on a stone-faced terrace, complete with rectangular sunken court and one-room structures on three sides. Judging from the distribution of Pukara pottery styles, the kingdom's power was confined to the northern Titicaca Basin, but ceramics and other artifacts from as far afield as the north coast reflect widespread trade connections. Tiwanaku, then a smaller center than in later centuries, presided over the southern shores of the lake between 400 B.C. and A.D. 100. There is no evidence that Pukara incorporated its southern neighbor.

From the Initial Period onward, the Andean region witnessed an extraordinary array of state-organized societies that displayed a remarkable diversity of culture, art, organization, and religious belief. At the same time, there were broad similarities in cosmology and culture that distinguish these societies from states elsewhere in the prehistoric world.

The Moche State (200 B.C. to A.D. 700)

By 200 B.C., the Moche state had begun in northern coastal Peru, flourishing for 800 years. Its origins lay in the Chicama and Moche valleys, with great ceremonial centers and huge irrigation works.

The spectacular discovery of undisturbed Moche tombs near the village of Sipán about 680 kilometers (420 miles) northwest of Lima has revolutionized our knowledge of Moche's elite. Peruvian archaeologist Walter Alva has excavated three unlooted royal burials. The sepulchers contained plank coffins holding the extended skeletons of men wearing gold nose and ear ornaments, gold and turquoise bead bracelets, and copper sandals. A ceremonial rattle, crescent-shaped knives, scepters, spears, and exotic seashells surrounded each body (see box on pages 338–339).

SITE

The Lords of Sipán, Peru

The discovery of the undisturbed Moche burials at **Sipán**, on Peru's northern coast, ranks as one of the greatest archaeological discoveries of all time. Peruvian archaeologist Walter Alva spent months painstakingly excavating the royal tombs, using conservation laboratories in Peru and Europe. The result is a triumph of scientific archaeology.

Figure 14.5 A mannequin wearing a Lord of Sipán's regalia.

Tomb I held the body of a warrior-priest in his late 30s or early 40s (Figure 14.5). The mourners had built a brick burial chamber deep in the pyramid (Figure 14.6), building the sepulcher like a room with solid mud-brick benches along the sides and at the head end. They set hundreds of clay pots in small niches in the benches. Priests dressed the dead lord in his full regalia, including a golden mask, and wrapped his corpse and regalia in textile shrouds. Then they placed him in a plank coffin and set it in the center of the burial chamber, the lid secured with copper straps. They laid out more ceramics, mainly fine spouted bottles, at the foot and head of the coffin. Next, someone sacrificed two llamas and placed them on either side of the foot of the coffin. At some point, the priests also sat the body of a nine- or ten-year-old child in poor health at the head of the warrior-priest.

Five cane coffins were then lowered into the grave, each containing the body of an adult. The two male dead, perhaps bodyguards or members of the lord's entourage, were each laid on top of one of the llamas. One was a strongly built male, over thirty-five years old, adorned with copper ornaments and laid out with a war club. The other bore a beaded pectoral and was between thirty-five and forty-five years old. Two of the three women's coffins lay at the head of the royal casket; in the third, at the foot of the coffin, the woman had been turned on her side. Interestingly, the women's disarticulated and jumbled bones suggest they were not sacrificial victims, for they had died long before the lord, and were partly decomposed at the time of their burial. Perhaps they had been wives, concubines, or servants. Once the coffins had been positioned, a low beam roof was set in place, too low for someone to stand inside the chamber. Then the tomb was covered, a footless male victim being laid out in the fill. Finally, a seated body with crossed legs watched over the burial chamber from a small niche in the south wall, about 1 meter (3 feet) above the roof.

Figure 14.6 Artist's reconstruction of Tomb I at Sipán, showing the lord in his regalia set in his coffin, also male and female attendants.

Comparing the objects found in the tomb with people depicted in Moche art, Christopher Donnan has identified the man as a warrior-priest. Such individuals are depicted on Moche pots presiding over sacrifices of prisoners of war (Figure 14.7). Apparently, Moche warriors went to war specifically to take captives. They would strip the captives of their armor and weapons, then lead them in front of the Warrior-Priest. Then the prisoner's throat was cut and the Warrior-Priest and others drank the blood of the slain victim while the corpse was dismembered. On pot after pot, the Warrior-Priest wears a crescent-shaped headdress atop a conical helmet, exactly the regalia found in the Sipán tombs. Such men were a priesthood of nobles living in different parts of the kingdom, who enacted the Sacrifice Ceremony at prescribed times.

Moche society consisted of farmers and fisherfolk as well as skilled artisans and priests, who are depicted on pots with felinelike fangs set in their mouths and wearing puma-skin headdresses. A few expert craft potters created superb modeled vessels with striking portraits of arrogant, handsome men who can only have been the leaders of Moche society (Figure 14.8). The potters modeled warriors, too, complete with shields and war clubs, well-padded helmets, and colorful cotton uniforms. Moche burials show that some members of society were much richer than others, lying in graves filled with as many as fifty vessels or with weapons or staffs of rank.

We do not know exactly how Moche society was organized, but we can assume that the ruler wielded authority over a hierarchical state of warriors, priest-doctors, artisans, and the mass of the agricultural population. For instance, there was at least one Moche-style settlement in each subject valley.

By this time the coastal people were expert metalworkers. They had discovered the properties of gold ore and extracted it by panning in stream beds rather than by mining. Soon they had developed ways of hammering it into fine sheets and had learned how to emboss it to make raised designs (see Figure 14.9 on page 342). They also had worked out the technique of annealing, making it possible to soften the metal and then hammer it into more elaborate forms, and they joined sheets with fine solder. The smiths used gold as a setting for turquoise and shell ornaments, crafted crowns, circlets, necklaces, pins, and tweezers.

Figure 14.7 A Moche lord presides over a parade of prisoners who are being sacrificed. A frieze from a painted pot "unrolled" photographically.

Figure 14.8 A Moche portrait head.

The Moche was a multivalley state that may have consisted of a series of satellite centers that ruled over individual valleys but owed allegiance to the great centers of the Moche Valley. At one time the Moche Valley presided over the coast as far south as the Nepeña Valley. Where possible, the Moche extended their ambitious irrigation systems to link several neighboring river valleys and then constructed lesser copies of their capital as a basis for secure administration of their new domains.

Like all Andean coastal societies, the Moche lived at the mercy of droughts and El Niños. Michael Moseley believes that a series of natural disasters struck Moche domains in the late sixth century. The first may have been a major drought cycle between A.D. 564 and 594, identified from the growth rings deep in mountain glaciers between Cuzco and Lake Titicaca. Crop yields in some valleys may have fallen as much as 20 percent. Sometime between 650 and 700, a great earthquake struck the Andes, choking rivers with debris from landslides. Within a half century Moche civilization collapsed.

The Middle Horizon: Tiwanaku and Wari (A.D. 600 to 1000)

The Middle Horizon flourished between A.D. 600 and 1000 in the southern highlands. This period saw the beginnings of monumental building at a highland site—Tiwanaku—that would influence much of the Peruvian world.

Figure 14.9 A Moche pendant from Huaca de la Luna.

Tiwanaku

Between A.D. 600 and 1000, the wealthiest highland districts lay at the southern end of the central Andes, in the high flat country surrounding Lake Titicaca. This was fine llama country. The local people maintained enormous herds of these beasts of burden and were also expert irrigation farmers. The altiplano supported the densest population in the highlands, and almost inevitably, the Titicaca region became an economic and demographic pole to the prosperous northern coast.

By A.D. 450 **Tiwanaku,** on the eastern side of the lake, was becoming a major population center as well as an economic and religious focus for the region. The arid lands on which the site lies were irrigated and supported a population of perhaps 20,000 around the monumental structures near the center of the site. By A.D. 600 Tiwanaku was acquiring much of its prosperity from trade around the lake's southern shores. Copper working probably developed independently of the well-established copper technology on the northern coast.

Tiwanaku was not only an economic force; it was a religious one as well. The great enclosure of Kalasasaya is dominated by a large earth platform faced with stones. Nearby, a rectangular enclosure is bounded with a row of upright stones, and there is a doorway carved with an anthropomorphic god, believed to be the staff god, sometimes called Viracocha (Figure 14.10).

The striking Tiwanaku art style is related to earlier iconography found at Pukara. So powerful was the iconography and, presumably, the political and economic forces behind Tiwanaku that there was a serious political vacuum in the south after A.D. 1200, when Tiwanaku inexplicably collapsed into obscurity.

Wari

Wari in the Ayacucho Valley is a highland urban and ceremonial center that stands on a hill. It is associated with huge stone walls and many dwellings that cover several square miles. The Wari art styles show also some Pukara influence, especially in anthropomorphic, feline, eagle, and serpent beings depicted on ceramic vessels. Like their southern neighbors, the Wari people seem to have revered a Viracocha-like being. By A.D. 800, their domains extended from Moche country in the Lambayeque Valley on the northern coast to south of Nasca territory, down the Moquequa Valley of the south-central Andes and into the highlands south of Cuzco. They were expert traders, who probably expanded their domain through conquest, commercial enterprise, and perhaps religious conversion. Storehouses and roads probably were maintained by the state. As with the Inca of later centuries, the state controlled food supplies and labor.

Figure 14.10 The Gateway of the Sun at Tiwanaku, Bolivia. The central figure is known as the Gateway God. Note its jaguar mouth and serpent-ray headdress. The running figures flanking the god are often called messengers.

Wari itself was abandoned in the ninth century A.D., but its art styles persisted on the coast for at least two more centuries. Both Wari and Tiwanaku were a turning point in Peruvian prehistory, a stage when small regional states became integrated into much larger political units. There was constant and often intensive interaction between two poles of Andean civilization in the highlands and lowlands, each with quite different food resources and products. This interaction, long a feature of Andean life, was to intensify in the centuries that lay ahead.

The Late Intermediate Period: Sicán and Chimu (A.D. 700 to 1460)

The highland states traded regularly with several emerging polities on the coast, each of them founded on extensive irrigation systems. The decline of Moche in the Lambayeque Valley had left somewhat of a vacuum, filled by the **Sicán** culture after A.D. 700. Sicán reached its peak between 900 and 1100, centered on the Lambayeque Valley and remarkable for its magnificent gold work. Elite burials from its capital rival those from Sipán. Between 1050 and 1100, an El Niño caused widespread flooding and disruption. In 1375, an expanding Chimu state overthrew Sicán and absorbed its domains into a new empire.

The Moche Valley had long been densely cultivated, but the **Chimu** people now embarked on much more ambitious irrigation schemes; they built large storage reservoirs and terraced hundreds of miles of hillside to control the flow of water down steep slopes. So effective were these irrigation techniques that the Chimu controlled more than twelve river valleys with at least 50,600 hectares (125,000 acres) of cultivable land, all of it farmed with hoes or digging sticks.

The focus of the Chimu state was **Chan Chan,** a huge complex of walled compounds lying near the Pacific at the mouth of the Moche Valley. Chan Chan covers nearly 10.3 square kilometers (4 square miles), the central part consisting of nine large enclosures laid out in a sort of broken rectangle. Each enclosure probably functioned as the palace for the current ruler of Chan Chan, who probably built himself a new headquarters near those of his predecessors (Figure 14.11). The adobe walls of these compounds once stood as high as 10 meters (33 feet) and covered areas as large as 200 by 600 meters (670 by 2,000 feet). The walls were not constructed to defend the rulers but to provide privacy and some shelter from the ocean winds. Each enclosure had its own water supply, a burial platform, and lavishly decorated residential rooms roofed with cane frames covered with earth and grass. The same enclosure that served as a palace during life became the ruler's burial place in death. The common people lived in tracts of small adobe and reed-mat houses on the western side of the city. Similar dwellings can be seen on the coast to this day.

Oral traditions tell us that the Chimu rulers practiced the institution of split inheritance, whereby each ruler inherited no material possessions to finance his reign. Split inheritance was to play a major role in Inca civilization (both described in the next section). Chimu rulers had access to and control of a huge labor pool. They employed laborers to expand and maintain irrigation works, and they served as military levies to acquire new lands and expand the tax base.

Rulers soon learned the value of officially maintained roadways that enabled them to move their armies from one place to the next rapidly. They constructed roads that connected each valley in their domain with the capital. These were the roads that carried gold ornaments and fine hammered vessels to Chan Chan and textiles and fine, black-painted

Figure 14.11 Chan Chan, the Chimu capital, showing a royal compound.

vessels throughout the empire. All revenues and tribute passed along the official road-ways, as did newly conquered peoples being resettled in some area far from their original homeland. This draconian resettlement tactic was so successful that the Inca adopted it. The ruler then would install his own appointee in the new lands, in a compound palace that was a smaller version of Chan Chan itself.

The Chimu state **(Chimor)** extended far south, at least to Casma and perhaps reaching to the vicinity of modern Lima, but the main focus of civilization lay on the northern Peruvian littoral, where the soils were fertile and large-scale irrigation was a practical reality.

For all its wide-ranging military activities and material wealth, Chimor was vulnerable to attack from outside. The massive irrigation works of the northern river valleys were easily disrupted by an aggressive conqueror, for no leader, however powerful, could hope to fortify the entire frontier of the empire. The Chimu were vulnerable to prolonged drought, too, for the storage capacity of their great irrigation works was sufficient to carry them over only one or two lean seasons. Perhaps, too, the irrigated desert soils became too saline for agriculture, so that crop yields fell drastically when population densities were rising sharply. Since the Chimu depended on a highly specialized agricultural system, once that system was disrupted—whether by natural or artificial causes—military conquest and control of the irrigation network were easy, especially for aggressive and skillful conquerors such as the Inca, who conquered the Chimu in the 1460s.

The Late Horizon: The Inca State (A.D. 1476 to 1534)

The Late Horizon of Peruvian archaeology was also the shortest, dating from A.D. 1476 to 1534, embracing the heyday of the Inca Empire. The Inca were born into an intensely competitive world, their homeland lying to the northwest of the Titicaca basin in the area around Cuzco. They were a small-scale farming society living in small villages, organized in kin groups known as **ayllu,** groups claiming a common ancestry and also owning land in common.

The later Inca rulers clothed their origins in a glorious panoply of heroic deeds. It is likely, however, that the Inca were a fractious, constantly quarreling petty chiefdom. The chronicles of early conquest reflect the constant bickering of village headmen, and the earliest Inca rulers were probably petty war leaders (*sinchi*), elected officials whose success was measured by their victories and booty. To stay in office, they had to be politically and militarily adept so that they could both defeat and appease their many potential rivals. The official Inca histories speak of at least eight Inca rulers between 1200 and 1438, but these genealogies are hardly reliable.

During the fourteenth century, the Inca flourished in this competitive atmosphere because their leaders were expert politicians as well as warriors. A leader named Viracocha Inca rose to power at the beginning of the fifteenth century. Unlike his raiding predecessors, however, he turned to permanent conquest and soon presided over a small kingdom centered in **Cuzco**. Viracocha Inca became the living god, the first in a series of constant religious changes that kept the new kingdom under tight control.

Around 1438, a brilliant warrior named Cusi Inca Yupanqui was crowned *Inca* (the term *Inca* can refer to both the ruler and the people) after a memorable victory over the neighboring Chanca tribe. He immediately took the name Pachakuti ("He Who Remakes the World") and set about transforming the Inca state. In particular, he and his henchmen developed a form of royal ancestor cult. This in itself was not especially significant since Pachakuti simply reworked an age-old Andean tradition, but the law of split inheritance that went along with it had a lasting and profound significance. A dead ruler was mummified. His palace, servants, and possessions were still considered his property and were maintained by all his male descendants except his successor, normally one of his sons. The deceased was not considered dead, however. His mummy attended great ceremonies and would even visit the houses of the living (Figure 14.12).

Figure 14.12 Inca ancestor worship. A drawing by seventeenth-century native Andean chronicler Felipe Guaman Poma de Ayala.

Those entrusted to look after the king ate and talked with him, just as if he were still alive. This element of continuity made the royal mummies some of the holiest artifacts in the empire. Dead rulers were visible links with the gods, the very embodiment of the Inca state and of the fertility of nature.

Meanwhile, the ascending ruler was rich in prestige but poor in possessions. The new king had to acquire wealth so he could both live in royal splendor and provide for his mummy in the future—and the only wealth in the highland kingdom was taxable labor. Therefore, every adult in Inca country had to render a certain amount of labor to the state each year after providing for the basic subsistence needs of his own *ayllu*. This *mit'a* system repaired bridges and roads, cultivated state-owned lands, manned the armies, and carried out public works. It was a reciprocal system. The state, or those benefiting from the work, had to feed and entertain those doing it. Since the Inca rulers needed land to provide food for those who worked for them and the earlier kings owned most of the land near Cuzco, the only way a new ruler could obtain his own royal estates was by expansion into new territory. The conquest had to be permanent, the conquered territory had to be controlled and taxed, and the ruler's subjects had to be convinced of the value of a policy of long-term conquest.

A complicated set of benefits, economic incentives, rewards, and justifications fueled and nourished the Inca conquests. Inca rulers turned into brilliant propagandists, reminding everyone that they were gods and that the welfare of all depended on the prosperity of all rulers, past and present, and on constant military conquest. There were initial economic advantages, too, in the form of better protection against famine. Also, the rulers were careful to reward prowess in battle. Nobles were promoted to new posts and awarded insignia that brought their lifestyle ever closer to that of the king, and a brave warrior could even become a member of the secondary nobility.

The Incas' successful ideology provided them with a crucial advantage over their neighbors. Within a decade of Pachakuti's accession they were masters of the southern highlands. Their army had become an invincible juggernaut. In less than a century the tiny kingdom taken over by Pachakuti had become a vast empire. Topa Inca (1471–1493) extended the Inca Empire into Ecuador, northern Argentina, parts of Bolivia, and Chile. Another king, Wayna Capac, ruled for thirty-two years after Topa Inca and pushed the empire deeper into Ecuador.

Tawantinsuyu, the empire, was divided into four large provinces known as *suyu* ("quarters"), each subdivided into smaller provinces, some of them coinciding with older, conquered kingdoms. Inca nobles held all the really important government posts. The Inca rulers realized, however, that the essence of efficient government in such varied topography was efficient communications, so the road builders commandeered a vast network of age-old highways from the states they conquered. They linked them in a coordinated system with regular rest houses so that they could move armies, trade goods, and send messengers from one end of the kingdom to the other in short order.

The Inca passion for organization impinged on everyone's life. Their society was organized into twelve age divisions for the purposes of census and tax assessment, divisions based on both physical changes like puberty and major social events like marriage. The most important stage was adulthood, which lasted as long as one could do a day's work. Census and other data of the empire were recorded not on tablets but on knotted strings. These *quipu* were a complex and sophisticated record-keeping system that seems to have been so efficient that it more than made up for the lack of writing. They also were a powerful instrument for codifying laws and providing data for the state's inspectors, who regularly visited each household to check that everyone was engaged in productive work and living in sanitary conditions.

SITE

Cuzco, the Inca Capital

At the heart of Tawantinsuyu lay Cuzco, the home of the sun god Inti, its patron. The royal families lived in the capital itself, they and their dependents numbering perhaps 40,000 people. A further 200,000 or so lived within 50 kilometers (30 miles), many of them artisans, minor officials, or engineers. The highest nobles had fine estates close to the city, the navel of the universe that was Tawantinsuyu.

In the days of Pachacuti, a brilliant architect named Huallpa Rimachi Inca laid plans for a massive fortress to be built against a hill named Sacsahuaman, which means "Speckled Hawk." The great rocky headland and its fort dominate Cuzco, looking eastward toward the rising sun. Sacsahuaman is bathed in sunlight long before the rest of the city, so it was a logical place for the House of the Sun, Intihuasi. Intihuasi was the *pukara,* or place of refuge, for Cuzco. A close relative of the ruler commanded the fortress, a position of great trust, for he was responsible for the royal treasury and a vast array of weaponry stored in an armory close to the soldiers' barracks. The great walls that brood over Cuzco today are but a shadow of the original edifice, which was wrecked by the Spaniards soon after the Conquest (Figure 14.13).

The Inca called the city Topa Cuzco, "royal Cuzco." Their capital lay along the spine of a narrow ridge between two deep gullies, in a landscape shaped like a triangle facing to the southeast. The great compounds of the living ruler and his deceased predecessors lay within this triangle. Each compound was a world unto its own, close to its neighbors yet separate, an invitation to the ardent factionalism that marked the Inca court.

The central plaza of Cuzco was called Huacaypata, today the Plaza de Armas. The Inca plaza was about 120 meters on its long axis along the river and 91 meters across (400 by 300 feet). The Sapi River defined the southern side, paved over with stone slabs to join Huacaypata with Cusipata, a square on the other bank. Huacaypata was where the four main roads of the empire met, defining the four quarters of Tawantinsuyu and merging them into the heart of the empire. Imposing buildings and royal palaces surrounded the plaza. Pachacuti's palace stood on the west side. The Yuchahuasi, the House of Learning, the school for young nobles and scribes, adjoined the palace. The entire area was an architectural commemoration of Inca rulers and their deeds.

The Inca royal palaces were much enlarged and elaborated versions of rural farm enclosures. The entrance led to a courtyard where a regiment of guards was stationed. Soldiers in ceremonial uniform bearing war clubs protected the entry to the palace proper. The guard room led to an antechamber where high officials awaited their audiences in the nearby audience room. Here the Sapa Inca sat on the stool of state to receive ambassadors and delegations. The storage area and treasury lay in the heart of the palace, where they were most protected. A "House of Spoils" contained trophies from the ruler's victories and sometimes the dried and stuffed bodies of conquered enemy leaders. The harem quarter was the most sequestered of all, where the royal women lived in adjoining, cell-like rooms, close to lush gardens hidden from the outside world. The royal living quarters were close by, where the Inca was looked after by carefully selected young women. During the Inca's life, the palace was a labyrinth of important happenings, ceremonies, and intrigue.

At the time of the Spanish conquest, the Inca controlled the lives of as many as 6 million people, most of them living in small villages dispersed around larger centers. Inca political and religious power was based on major ritual locations like Cuzco in the Andes, where the ceremonial precincts were built of carefully fitted stone blocks (Figure 14.13). The Inca ruler held court in Cuzco, surrounded by plotting factions and ever-changing political tides. One villain was the very institution of split inheritance that fueled Inca military

Figure 14.13 An entrance to the Sacsahuaman fortress near Cuzco. Inca architecture was based on closely fitted stone blocks. They were moved by human hands since Andean llamas could only carry loads of about 45 kilograms (100 pounds).

When the ruler died, the palace continued to function as if nothing had happened, except that no one debated policy there.

The Coriancha was the largest palace of all, the place where the gods resided, each with their own thatched house and patio. At least 4,000 people were attached to the divine households, some 200 to 300 of them the virgin women who served as Inti's wives. They prepared his food and fermented maize beer, wove his clothes, and drummed for him at major festivals. The manaconas also symbolically satisfied Inti's sexual desires as his consorts. The walls of the Coriancha were built on precipitous terraces in the oldest part of the city. The tapered wall with its beautifully fitted blocks give a powerful illusion of height and strength, still towering 3 meters (10 feet) above the highest level of the temple platform inside. The temple itself was clad with gold sheet and housed the golden image of the sun, with a garden of golden plants before the room where the symbol lay.

Cuzco was also a vast storehouse filled with the incredible wealth of the empire. The storehouses of Cuzco held gigantic stocks of raw materials and finished goods that poured into the capital from all corners of Tawantinsuyu, stocks of cloaks, wool, weapons, metals, and food supplies neatly arranged in hundreds of stores.

conquest. Every ruler faced increasingly complex governance problems as a result. The need for more and more conquests caused great military, economic, and administrative stress. The logistics of long-distance military campaigns were horrendous, and the soldiers had to be fed from state-owned land, not royal estates. Moreover, although their tactics were well adapted to open country, where their armies were invincible, the rulers eventually had to start fighting in forest country, where they fared badly.

Meanwhile the empire had grown so large that communication became an increasingly lengthier process, compounded by the great diversity of people living within Inca domains (Figure 14.14). Under its glittering facade, Tawantinsuyu was becoming a rotten apple. In the end, the Inca Empire was overthrown not by Peruvians but by a tiny band of foreigners with firearms who could exploit the inherent vulnerability of such a hierarchical, conforming society.

The Spanish Conquest (A.D. 1532 to 1534)

This vulnerability came home to roost in 1532, when a small party of rapacious Spanish conquistadors landed in northern Peru. When Francisco Pizarro arrived, the Inca state was in some political chaos, its people already decimated by smallpox and other diseases introduced by the first conquistadors. Inca Wayna Capac had died in an epidemic in 1525. The empire was plunged into a civil war between his son Huascar and another son, Atahuallpa, half brother to Huascar. Atahuallpa eventually prevailed, but as he moved south from Ecuador to consolidate his territory, he learned that Pizarro had landed in Peru.

The Spaniards had vowed to make Peru part of Spain and were bent on plunder and conquest. Pizarro arrived in the guise of a diplomat, captured Atahuallpa by treachery, ransomed him for a huge quantity of gold, and then brutally murdered him. A year later the Spaniards overthrew the Inca capital with a tiny army. Despite pockets of resistance, the world's last preindustrial state collapsed.

Figure 14.14 Machu Picchu high in the Andes, once thought to have been the last city of the Incas. In fact it was occupied much earlier.

Summary

The earliest complex societies of coastal Peru may have developed as a result of the intensive exploitation of maritime resources, especially small fish easily netted from canoes. In time, abundant food surpluses, growing population densities, and larger settlements preadapted coastal people to intensive irrigation agriculture. These societies were organized in increasingly complex ways. During the Initial Period, large monumental structures appeared, many of them U-shaped, just before and during the transition toward greater dependence on maize agriculture. This was also a period of continuous interaction and extensive trade between the coast and the highlands.

The culmination of this trend is seen in various local traditions, among them the famous Chavín style. Chavín de Huántar, once thought to have been the source of Peruvian civilization, is now known to be a late manifestation of cultural trends that began as early as 2000 B.C. After the Early Horizon ended in about 200 B.C., a series of coastal kingdoms developed until about A.D. 700, the political and economic influence of which spread beyond their immediate valley homelands. These states included Moche, remarkable for its fine pottery styles and expert alloy and gold metallurgy, which flourished in the period between 200 B.C. and A.D. 700.

About A.D. 1375, Chimu, with its great capital at Chan Chan on the northern coast, dominated a wide area of the lowlands. Its compounds reflect a stratified state with many expert craftspeople and a complex material culture. During the Late Horizon of Peruvian prehistory (1400 to 1534), there was unification of the highlands and the lowlands under the Inca Empire, which may have emerged as early as 1200 and lasted until the Spanish Conquest in 1532–1534. The Inca rulers were masters of bureaucracy and military organization and governed a highly structured state—one, however, that was so weakened by civil war and disease that it fell easily to the conquistador Francisco Pizarro and his small army of adventurers.

Epilogue

Our journey through the long millennia of prehistory ends on the very threshold of modern times. It ends with the so-called Age of Discovery that saw European explorers sailing ever further from their homelands in search of gold and spices, to serve God, or simply out of compelling curiosity.

Western Europe was born 3,000 years ago. For thousands of years it had been a geographical outpost of Asia, on the fringes of civilizations and empires based in the Near East and Mediterranean lands. Twenty-five centuries ago, Europe became a western peninsula with a consciousness and identity all its own. Born of Greek civilization, this consciousness matured still further in much later European victories against Huns, Turks, and Moors. It was a Christian enclave, driven by doctrines that encouraged a deep sense that the individual was as important as the state. A growing sense of individualism and adventure bred an intense curiosity about the outside world. What peoples lived south of the endless sands of the Sahara Desert? Were there distant lands beyond the boundless horizons of the western ocean?

During the 1420s and 1430s, Henry the Navigator, Prince of Portugal, organized annual voyages of exploration southward from Europe, deep into tropical latitudes. His captains coasted down the west coast of Africa and rounded the great western bulge in 1433. Then, in 1488, Bartolemeu Dias rounded the southern tip of Africa. He came in contact with the **Khoe Khoe,** simple cattle herders who appeared to wander aimlessly with their herds. The Khoe Khoe made a profound impression on the Western mind, for they appeared more primitive in their customs than any other people on earth. For centuries, the Khoe Khoe were thought of as half-apes, half-humans, lower on the Great Chain of Being than other human beings. They vanished a mere seventy years after European settlement at the Cape of Good Hope in 1652, their herding adaptation destroyed by encroaching white farmers.

Dias was followed in 1497 by Vasco da Gama, who sailed up the east African coast to what is now Kenya, then followed the trade winds to India. Thus, Europeans found an alternative route to the rich gold and spice markets of South and Southeast Asia. They sailed along ancient seaborne routes that linked Africa, with its seemingly inexhaustible exports of gold, ivory, and slaves, with markets that had an insatiable demand for such commodities. In the centuries that followed, Africa was exploited for human and material wealth, not only by European nations but by Islam. The burgeoning international slave trade decimated African populations far from the continent's familiar coastlines. European explorers did not penetrate the far interior until the nineteenth century, by which time Africa was already part of a vast and complex world economic system.

As Dias and da Gama explored African shores, so did Christopher Columbus sail west to the "Indies" in 1492. He thought he was at the threshold of Asia. In fact, he revealed a

New World teeming with new species of animals and plants and a great diversity of American Indian societies. As we have seen, the great civilizations of Mexico and Peru collapsed rapidly in the face of the conquistadors, while epidemics of smallpox and other exotic diseases decimated Native American populations within a few generations of the first European visitors wherever they appeared.

With the rounding of the Cape of Good Hope and the discovery of the Americas, the final chapter of human prehistory began, a complex and long-drawn-out clash between increasingly elaborate Western civilization and a myriad of non-Western societies in all parts of the world. The basic scenario was relived again and again. A small party of European explorers would arrive, as did Captain James Cook in Tahiti and New Zealand, or French voyager Marion du Fresne in Tasmania, Australia. Usually the first encounter was a fleeting kaleidoscope of curiosity, sometimes horrified fascination, and often romantic excitement. Sometimes spears were thrown and muskets fired. At others there was friendly trading of furs for cheap glass beads and other trinkets. Almost invariably, however, there was total incomprehension on both sides.

Sometimes the people thought that their strange visitors were gods, as did Moctezuma with Hernan Cortés at the gates of Tenochtitlán. An elderly **Maori** chief in New Zealand told a nineteenth-century official that the priests had told him the whites were spirits with eyes in the backs of their heads, an apparent reference to Cook's oarsmen facing the stern in their boats. All too soon, and wherever they appeared, the strangers proved not to be gods, but to be only too human—aggressive, warlike, and acquisitive.

At first the contacts were brief ones. But soon Europeans came in larger numbers to trade for furs, to refit their ships, or to search for gold. Then the missionaries arrived, seeking to convert the heathen and to save their souls. Australia became a dumping ground for convicts, many of whom escaped and brutalized Australian Aboriginal groups. In many places a flood of colonists followed the first visitors. They were often impoverished, land-hungry farmers from Europe who sought a better life in the fertile soils of the African interior, British Columbia, New Zealand, or Tasmania.

These were permanent residents, people with iron tools and firearms in search of new homes and lush acreage. They competed with the indigenous populations for prime land, elbowing them aside, sometimes hunting them down, or often acquiring large farms through shady land sales or illegal treaties. Almost inevitably, the indigenous population lost their land, territory that had often been vested in the same kin groups for centuries, if not millennia. They had few options open to them, except to retreat onto remote, marginal lands where they preserved a shadow of their former culture and lifeway, if they were able to survive at all. The only alternative was to assimilate themselves into the newcomers' society, where they almost always lived on the margins, often employed as agricultural laborers or domestic servants.

The spread of Western civilization around the world accelerated dramatically after the Industrial Revolution of the late eighteenth century. This revolution was another catalyst in human history, which created industrial societies driven not by human hands but by fossil fuels. It fostered insatiable demands for raw materials of all kinds, gave birth to the steamship and the railroad, and led to large-scale human migrations from Europe to America, and from Asia to all parts of the Pacific and North America on an unprecedented scale. The mass population movements of recent times have had catastrophic effects on non-Western societies large and small.

Today, there are no parts of the world where traditional lifeways survive untouched by modern civilization. There are a handful of groups deep in the Amazon Basin and in highland New Guinea who have still not come into sustained contact with industrialized civilization. These are endangered societies, as rain forests are felled and landscapes modified beyond recognition by the insatiable maw of industrial civilization. To all intents and purposes, however, the ancient world, which began over 2.5 million years ago in Africa, has vanished into near-oblivion except insofar as we know it from modern scientific research.

Glossary of Technical Terms

Accelerator Mass Spectrometry (AMS) Radiocarbon Dating A radiocarbon dating method that uses a mass spectrometer, which is more accurate than conventional radiocarbon dating.

Adaptive radiation The proliferation of variants following the appearance of an evolutionary innovation, which typically occurs with the establishment of a new clade, a group of species that contains the common ancestor and all its descendants.

Agricultural Revolution A term coined by V. Gordon Childe to refer to the beginnings of food production, caused by drought and close associations between animals, humans, and plants.

Andes (Andean) Term used by archaeologists to refer to those areas of Peru and adjacent countries where state-organized societies developed.

Anthropoid The taxonomic suborder of apes, humans, and monkeys.

Arboreal Tree-living.

Archaeological culture The material remains of a human culture preserved at a specific space and time at several archaeological sites.

Archaeology The study of the human past using the surviving material remains of human behavior.

Artifact A humanly manufactured or modified object.

Atlatl Throwing stick used by early North American hunters, a spear-thrower.

Ayllu Andean kin group claiming descent from a common ancestor.

Band Egalitarian associations of families knit together by close social ties.

Bipedal Walking upright on two feet.

Blade core technology A stone tool technology involving the use of preshaped cores and long, parallel-sided blades produced with the aid of a punch. Characteristic of many Upper Paleolithic peoples.

Burin A chisel-like stone tool made on a blade used for grooving stone, antler, bone, and wood, also for making rock engravings.

Calpulli An Aztec kin grouping used to organize rural and urban populations.

Chiefdom Societies headed by leaders with exceptional entrepreneurial, political, or ritual powers, which are still kin-based.

Civilization See State-organized society.

Cladistics An analytical system for reconstructing evolutionary relationships that emphasizes diversity over homogeneity.

Clan A group of people from many lineages who live in one place and have a common line of descent from a kin grouping.

Cognitive archaeology The "archaeology of mind," using archaeological methods to study human motives, ideologies, and intangibles.

Composite tool An artifact made up of more than one component, such as a stone spear point and its shaft.

Context In archaeology, the exact location of a site, artifact, or other archaeological find in time and space.

Cultural ecology The study of the ways in which human societies adapt to, and transform, their environments.

355

Cultural process The ways in which human cultures change over time.

Cultural system The adaptive mechanism, made up of many parts, that humans use to adapt to their physical and social environment.

Culture as adaptation See Cultural ecology.

Culture history Descriptions of human cultures derived from archaeological evidence.

Culture The primary nonbiological means by which humans adapt to their natural environment.

Cuneiform From the Greek word *cuneus*, "wedge." Mesopotamian script made by stamping clay tablets with a wedge-shaped stylus. Long used as an international diplomatic script in the ancient eastern Mediterranean world.

Dendrochronology Tree-ring dating.

Diffusion The spread of ideas over short or long distances.

Ethnoarchaeology The study of living societies to aid in the interpretation of ancient ones.

Ethnographic analogy Comparison of artifacts and other culture traits from living societies with those of ancient ones.

Ethnographic present A term used to describe prehistoric societies at their moment of contact with Europeans. It is not based on reality, because no culture was ever static, and a momentary portrait of a culture is misleading.

Fertile Crescent The crescent of territory from the Nile Valley through the Iranian highlands to Mesopotamia, where agriculture and civilization first began.

Flotation A method of recovering plant remains by passing them through screens and water.

Fluting A term used to describe the vertical thinning flake removed from the base of Paleo-Indian projectile points in North America with a punch. The thinned base made it easier to mount the point on the shaft.

Food production Agriculture and animal domestication.

Groove-and-splinter technique Longitudinal grooving of antler and bone to produce long, parallel-sided grooves for making spear points, harpoons, and other artifacts. Used by Upper Paleolithic and Mesolithic peoples.

Ground stone Artifacts manufactured by pecking the surface and edges with a stone, then grinding them smooth, to form sharp working edges. A technique used for axes and adzes employed for felling trees and woodworking.

History The study of the past using written records.

Holocene From the Greek word for "recent." Refers to the millennia since the end of the Pleistocene (Ice Age) about 10,000 B.C.

Hominoid A primate superfamily that includes apes and Hominins.

Hominin/Hominidae Primates of the family Hominidae, which includes modern humans, earlier human subspecies, and their direct ancestors.

Inevitable variation Cumulative culture change due to minor differences in learned behavior over time.

Invention New ideas that originate in a human culture by accident or design.

Kiva Sacred ceremonial room built by prehistoric peoples in the American Southwest.

Knuckle walking Specialized way of getting around on four limbs, which uses the backs of the hands for supporting body weight.

Loess Fine, glacial wind-blown sand distributed over vast areas of Central Europe and the Eurasian steppe during Ice Age glaciations, especially during the late Ice Age.

Mandala A Hindu conception of the state used in Southeast Asian archaeology.

Matuyama/Brunhes A moment of reversal of the earth's magnetic field, c. 730,000 years ago.

Megalith From the Greek for "large stone." A term applied to stone-built graves widespread during early farming times in western Europe, generally in the fifth millennium B.C.

Mesoamerica   A term used by archaeologists to refer to those parts of Central America where state-organized societies arose.

Microlith   From two Greek words for "small stone." Diminutive stone artifacts manufactured on tiny blades and used as barbs and points for spears and later arrows. Characteristic of the late Ice Age and early Holocene societies.

Migration   The movement of people from one area to another.

Mitochondrial DNA   DNA that is inherited through the female line, which is of great value in establishing ancient evolutionary relationships.

Monophyletic   In evolution, a phylum whose members are all descended from a single ancestor.

Multilinear cultural evolution   Cultural evolution along many diverse tracks.

Neolithic Revolution   See Agricultural Revolution.

Obsidian   Volcanic glass.

Phytoliths   Minute particles of silica from plant cells produced throughout the life of a plant and used to identify species in archaeological sites.

Pleistocene   The last geological epoch, sometimes called the Ice Age or Quaternary.

Pongidae   The family of non-human primates closest to human.

Post-processual archaeology   Approaches to the past that examine ideology, motives, and nonenvironmental aspects of culture change.

Potassium-argon dating   A radiometric dating method that dates geological strata and early archaeological sites from volcanic rocks. Used to date prehistory from the earliest times up to about 100,000 years ago.

Prehistory   Human history before the advent of written records.

Preindustrial civilization   See State-organized societies. Also, a civilization organized without the use of fossil fuels.

Prestate societies   Small-scale societies based on the community, band, or village.

Primordium   The very beginning. The starting point of creation myths.

Prosimian   The taxonomic suborder that includes lemurs, tarsiers, and other so-called pre-monkeys.

Quaternary   See Pleistocene.

Rachis   A hinge that joins a seed to a plant.

Radiocarbon dating   An absolute dating method based on measuring the decay rate of the carbon isotope carbon-14 to stable nitrogen. The resulting dates are calibrated with tree-ring, ice core, and tropical core chronologies to convert radiocarbon ages into dates in calendar years.

Settlement pattern   The distribution of human settlement on the landscape and within archaeological communities.

Shaman or spirit medium   The word comes from the Siberian Tungus word *saman*, meaning "priest."

Sinodonty   A distinctive cluster of tooth features associated with Siberian and Native American populations.

Spear-thrower   A hooked and sometimes weighted stick or equivalent device used for hurling spears.

State-organized society   A large-scale society with strongly centralized government and marked social stratification. Synonymous with preindustrial civilizations.

Sundadont   Teeth characteristics shared by ancient Eurasian and European populations.

Tribe   Clusters of bands linked by formal kin groups.

Urban Revolution   V. Gordon Childe's concept of an Urban Revolution was based on the assumption that metallurgy, specialists, and food surpluses caused a revolution in human life and urban civilization.

World prehistory   The study of human prehistory, from human origins to the advent of literate civilization, from a global perspective.

Glossary of Archaeological Sites and Cultural Terms

This glossary covers major cultural terms and archaeological sites. It does not include names of leaders and other individuals.

Abri Pataud, France   A rock shelter used by Upper Paleolithic foragers in southwestern France during the late Ice Age. Famous for its evidence of reindeer hunting.

Abu Hureyra, Syria   A village site by the Euphrates River occupied first by foraging groups before 10,500 B.C., then by very early farmers. Famous for its excellent botanical evidence for agricultural origins.

Abydos, Egypt   Burial place of Egypt's earliest pharaohs, considered a sacred entry to the underworld.

Acheulian stone technology   A technology based on hand axes, cleavers, and flake artifacts that flourished in Africa, Europe, southwestern Asia, and parts of Southeast Asia between about 1.8 million and 200,000 years ago. Named after the town of St. Acheul in northern France.

Adena culture   A culture dating between 500 B.C. and A.D. 400, centered on the Ohio valley and famous for its elaborate earthworks.

Adulis, Ethiopia   A Red Sea port associated with the Aksum civilization.

Aguateca, Guatemala   Late Classic Maya settlement of the ninth century A.D.

'Ain Ghazal, Syria   Early farming village of the eighth millennium B.C.

Aksum, Ethiopia   Ethiopian highland civilization of the first millennium A.D. that traded with the Mediterranean and Indian Ocean worlds.

Ali Kosh, Iran   A farming settlement on the Khuzistan Plains occupied between 9000 and 6000 B.C.

Allia Bay, Kenya   Early hominin site by Lake Turkana, which yielded *Australopithecus anamensis* about 4 million years ago.

Altamira, Spain   Magdalenian painted cave dating to about 15,000 years ago. Famous for its polychrome bison paintings.

Ambrona, Spain   An Acheulian butchery site dating to between 200,000 and 400,000 years ago.

Ancestral Pueblo (Anasazi)   Major Southwestern cultural tradition centered on the Four Corners region, which reached its greatest efflorescence after A.D. 1100.

Angkor Thom and Angkor Wat, Cambodia   Royal capitals and shrines built by the Khmer rulers of Cambodia between A.D. 1000 and 1200.

Anyang, China   Central core region of Shang civilization of northern China between 1400 and 1122 B.C.

Ao, China   Shang civilization capital in northern China occupied in about 1560 B.C.

Aramis, Ethiopia   Site on the Awash River where *Ardipithecus ramidus* was discovered and dated to 4.5 million years.

Archaic   Generalized label given to later forager cultures in the Americas, highly diverse and often sophisticated cultures dating from 6000 B.C. into recent times. In Egypt, refers to the first few centuries of dynastic Egyptian civilization.

Aspero, Peru   A large settlement with platform mounds dating to c. 3055 B.C. at the mouth of the Supe River.

Assur, Iraq Assyrian capital on the Tigris River, which was powerful after 900 B.C.

Atapuerca, Spain Cave system that has yielded fossils of 300,000-year-old humans, probable ancestors of the Neanderthals.

Avebury, England A large circular earthwork with stone circles that was the focus of a Stone Age landscape, reaching its final form in about 2500 B.C.

Babylon, Iraq Major early city-state, and later capital of the Babylonian empire under King Nebuchadnezzar in the sixth century B.C.

Bandkeramik complex A cultural label describing the first farmers of central and northwestern Europe of about 6000 B.C. Distinguished on the basis of line-decorated pottery.

Benin, Nigeria A West African forest kingdom with a capital of the same name, which flourished before the fourteenth century A.D. until recent times.

Boghazkoy, Turkey Capital of the Hittite empire, second millennium B.C.

Boxgrove, England Hunting site in southern England used by *Homo erectus* some 500,000 years ago.

Broken Hill See Kabwe.

Buena Vista, Peru An important religious center in the Chillon Valley near Lima, with distinctive astronomical alignments, dating to c. 2200 B.C.

Cahokia, Illinois Major ceremonial center of the Mississippian culture built after A.D. 900.

Calakmul, Guatemala Major Maya political and religious center from Preclassic times to A.D. 800.

Caracol, Belize An important Maya center in the seventh century A.D. A rival of Calakmul and a major center of stone trade.

Caral, Peru An early coastal ceremonial center on the Peruvian coast, built c. 2600 B.C. and abandoned between 2000 and 1500 B.C.

Çatalhöyük, Turkey Early farming town that prospered on the obsidian trade between 6000 and 5000 B.C.

Çayönü Tepesi, Turkey Early farming settlement with ritual buildings and evidence of an ancestor cult, c. 8600 to 7000 B.C.

Cerén, San Salvador A small Maya village destroyed by a volcanic eruption in the sixth century A.D., the ash preserving many details of domestic life.

Chaco Canyon, New Mexico See Chaco phenomenon.

Chaco phenomenon Generic name given to the Ancestral Pueblo sites and associated phenomena of Chaco Canyon, New Mexico, in the eleventh and twelfth centuries A.D.

Chan Chan, Peru Capital of the Chimu civilization, after A.D. 1000.

Chauvet See Grotte de Chauvet.

Chavín de Huántar, Peru Ceremonial center in Peru's Andes foothills dating to between 900 and 200 B.C. Source of much Andean art and ideology.

Chichén Itzá, Mexico Postclassic Maya center in the northern Yucatan, especially in the thirteenth century A.D.

Chilca, Peru A semipermanent foraging settlement on the Peruvian Coast dating to after 4000 B.C.

Chimor, Peru The domains of the Chimu civilization.

Chimu civilization Lowland civilization in Peru's Lambayeque valley, which flourished between c. A.D. 1000 and 1476.

Chiripa, Peru A ceremonial center near Lake Titicaca founded in 1000 B.C.

Cliff Palace, Mesa Verde, Colorado Major Ancestral Pueblo site, which reached its greatest extent after A.D. 1200.

Clovis tradition Widespread Paleo-Indian tradition associated with very early settlement throughout North America. Dates to the eleventh millennium B.C.

Copán, Honduras Major Maya center during the mid-first millennium A.D.

Coxcatlán Cave, Mexico A rock shelter in the Tehuacán Valley that yielded desiccated maize cobs dating to about 2000 B.C.

Cro-Magnon, France   A rock shelter near Les Eyzies in southwestern France where the first late Ice Age people were found in 1868. The Upper Paleolithic people of western and central Europe are often called Cro-Magnons.

Cuello, Belize   An early Maya settlement and ceremonial center, occupied as early as 1500 B.C., which contains shrines dating to the early second millennium B.C.

Cuzco, Peru   Capital of the Inca empire in highland Peru.

Dilmun, Bahrain   Important transshipment port between Mesopotamia and the Indus valley in the Persian Gulf as early as 2500 B.C.

Diuktai Cave, Siberia   The best-known site for a widespread, very late Ice Age culture in northeastern Siberia, which may have been the ancestor of some early Native American groups. Dates to as early as 18,000 years ago.

Dmanisi, Georgia   A site dating to c. 1.7 million years ago, which has yielded crania of *Homo erectus*, the earliest known in Europe and Eurasia.

Dos Pilas, Guatemala   Important Classic Maya center after A.D. 600.

East Turkana, Kenya   Location where fossil hominins and their sites date to c. 2.5 million to 1.6 million years ago.

El Mirador, Guatemala   Preclassic Maya center dating to between 250 and 50 B.C.

El Paraíso, Peru   Ceremonial center in Peru's Chillón Valley dating to c. 1800 B.C.

El-Amarna (or Akhetaten), Egypt   Capital of the New Kingdom pharaoh Akhenaten, occupied for only about twelve years, c. 1340 B.C.

Erech, Iraq   Early Sumerian city-state of about 2800 B.C.

Eridu, Iraq   One of the world's earliest cities, famous for its shrine, c. 4000 B.C. and later.

Fort Rock Cave, Oregon   A site with possible evidence of human occupation in North America as early as 12,000 B.C.

Funan, Cambodia   Prosperous city-state region in Southeast Asia between the third and sixth centuries A.D.

Ganj Dareh, Iran   A seasonal foraging camp of 10,500 B.C. in the Zagros Mountains.

Ghana, Kingdom of   West African state on the southern fringes of the Sahara Desert, which controlled much of the West African gold trade as early as the eighth century A.D.

Giza, Egypt   Major pyramid site of Old Kingdom Egypt dating to c. 2600 B.C.

Göbekli Tepe, Turkey   Shrine site dating to c. 9500 B.C., boasting of semisubterranean structures and carved monoliths.

Great Zimbabwe, Zimbabwe   Major religious and trading center and Karanga chiefdom between about A.D. 100 and 1500.

Grotte de Chauvet, France   Painted late Ice Age cave with remarkable depictions of lions, rhinoceroses, and other animals, dating to as early as 31,000 B.C.

Guilá Naquitz, Mexico   A cave occupied by a small band of foragers between 8750 and 6670 B.C. Important for the study of early bean and squash cultivation.

Hadar, Ethiopia   Location where many specimens of *Australopithecus afarensis* have been found, dating to about 3 million years ago.

Harappa, Pakistan   Major city of the Harappan civilization, c. 2500 B.C.

Harappan civilization   Indigenous Indian civilization of the Indus valley of what is now Pakistan, c. 2700 to 1700 B.C.

Hatti, Turkey   Hittite kingdom centered on Anatolia in the second millennium B.C.

Herto, Ethiopia   Location where three anatomically modern skulls dating to 160,000 years ago were found, northeast of Addis Ababa.

Hidden Mammoth site, Alaska   A hunting camp in central Alaska dating to about 9700 B.C.

Hittites   See Hatti.

Hohokam, Arizona   A widespread desert farming culture centered on southern Arizona, which flourished from about 300 B.C. to A.D. 1500.

Hopewell tradition A religious and burial cult centered on Illinois and the eastern United States, which flourished from 200 B.C. to A.D. 400.

Huon Peninsula, New Guinea Site where 40,000-year-old ground stone axes offer early evidence of human settlement on the island.

Jarmo, Iraq Early farming village in the Zagros Mountains occupied before 5000 B.C.

Jericho, Jordan Biblical city and famous archaeological site with evidence of an early fortified town of the eighth millennium B.C. and of farming settlements as early as 7800 B.C.

Kabwe (Broken Hill), Zambia Site in Central Africa where a robust form of early *Homo sapiens* was discovered. Exact age unknown.

Kalambo Falls, Zambia Lake bed site where Acheulian occupation levels over 200,000 years old were found.

Kanapoi, Kenya See Allia Bay.

Kanesh, Turkey Hittite settlement founded in the seventeenth century B.C., famous in later centuries for its Assyrian trading quarter.

Karanga Generic name given to the Shona-speaking peoples of Zimbabwe.

Karnak, Egypt Temple of the sun god, Amun, New Kingdom, Egypt. After 1500 B.C.

Kerma, Sudan Nubian kingdom of the third millennium B.C.

Khoe Khoe Pastoral cattle herders of the southernmost tip of Africa, encountered by Portuguese explorers in the fifteenth century A.D.

Kilwa, Tanzania East African coastal trading port, which was a major transshipment point for African gold and ivory after A.D. 1200.

Kish, Iraq Early Sumerian city-state of about 2800 B.C. and later.

Knossos, Crete The Palace of Minos at Knossos was a major center of Minoan civilization. The site was occupied from before 2000 B.C. to about A.D. 1400.

Koobi Fora, Kenya Location of some of the earliest traces of stone manufacture in the world, some 2.5 million years ago.

Koster, Illinois A stratified site in the Illinois River valley of the North American Midwest inhabited from about 7500 B.C. to A.D. 1200 by foragers, then maize farmers.

Koto Toro, Chad *Australopithecus afarensis* site south of the central Sahara dating to about 3 to 3.5 million years ago.

Kush An African state in the Sudan, which flourished along the Nile River after 900 B.C. (See Nubia.)

Laetoli, Tanzania Site where hominin footprints were preserved in hardened volcanic ash 3.6 million years ago.

La Ferrassie, France A rock shelter near Les Eyzies in southwestern France, where evidence of Neanderthal burials was found.

Lagash, Iraq Major Sumerian city-state of the third millennium B.C.

La Madeleine, France See Magdalenian culture.

Langebaan Lagoon, South Africa Site where 117,000-year-old footprints of an anatomically modern human are preserved in a fossilized sand dune.

Lapita culture A cultural tradition in the southwestern Pacific, responsible for colonizing much of the offshore Pacific after 2000 B.C.

Lascaux, France Major site of Magdalenian cave painting in southwestern France dating to about 15,000 years ago.

La Venta, Mexico Olmec ceremonial center dating to after 900 B.C.

Le Tuc d'Audoubert, France A Magdalenian ceremonial site famous for its clay bison figures.

Liang Bua Cave, Flores A cave site occupied by *Homo floresiensis,* a diminutive human, c. 13,000 to 13,000 years ago.

Machu Picchu, Peru Inca settlement high in the Andes occupied during and after the Spanish conquest.

Magan, Persian Gulf Transshipment port between Mesopotamia and the Indus Valley.

Magdalenian culture Late Ice Age culture with sophisticated technology and art tradition found in southwestern France, parts of central Europe, and northern Spain. Flourished between 15,000 and 12,000 years ago. Named after the La Madeleine rock shelter, Les Eyzies, Dordogne.

Mali, Kingdom of West African state that succeeded Ghana in about A.D. 1200 and became internationally famous for its gold during the next century.

Maori people New Zealand's indigenous inhabitants, with ancestry in Polynesia dating back to at least A.D. 1000.

Mauryan Empire, India Early Indian empire centered on the Ganges River during the mid-first millennium B.C.

Maya civilization Major lowland Mesoamerican civilization from before 1000 B.C. until the fifteenth century A.D., with the Classic period ending in about A.D. 900.

Mayapan, Mexico Postclassic Maya center ruled by the Cocom family after the 13th century A.D.

Meadowcroft Rock Shelter, Pennsylvania A long-occupied rock shelter, with possible evidence of human occupation as early as 12,000 B.C.

Meer, Belgium A Stone Age camp of 6000 B.C., used by stoneworkers.

Meluhha Important Persian Gulf transshipment port for the Indus civilization. Location unknown.

Memphis, Egypt Capital of Ancient Egypt.

Merimda Beni Salama, Egypt A farming settlement in the Egyptian delta dating to about 4500 B.C.

Meroe, Sudan Royal capital of the kingdom of that name on the Nile River from about 500 B.C. to A.D. 400. A major trading center.

Mesa Verde, Colorado A series of canyons in Colorado famous for their multiroom Ancestral Pueblo pueblos of the thirteenth and fourteenth centuries A.D.

Mesa, Alaska A forager camp site in the Brooks Range of northern Alaska, occupied in about 9700 B.C.

Mezhirich, Ukraine Late Ice Age forager camp with elaborate mammoth bone houses on the Ukraine's Dnieper River, dating to about 17,000 years ago.

Minoan civilization Bronze Age kingdom centered on Crete, which reached its height between 1900 and 1400 B.C.

Mississippian tradition A maize and bean farming culture in the midwestern and southeastern United States dating from A.D. 900 to 1500, remarkable for its large ceremonial centers, elaborate religious beliefs, and powerful chiefdoms.

Mitanni, Syria Bronze Age state of the second millennium B.C., east of the Euphrates River. Contemporary with the Hittites.

Moche civilization Coastal Peruvian civilization centered on the Chicama and Moche valleys, dating from 200 B.C. to A.D. 600.

Mogollon Southwestern cultural tradition of about 300 B.C. to about A.D. 1100. A highland farming culture without major population centers.

Mohenjodaro, Pakistan Major city of the Harappan civilization. See Harappan civilization.

Monte Albán, Mexico Major city and state in the Valley of Oaxaca during the first millennium A.D.

Monte Verde, Chile A streamside forager site in northern Chile dating to about 10,000 B.C.

Mound City, Ohio A Hopewell mound complex covering 13 acres (5.26 hectares) in the Ohio River valley.

Moundville, Alabama Major Mississippian town and ceremonial center after A.D. 900.

Mousterian technology Stone tool technology associated with Neanderthal peoples of Europe, Eurasia, and the Near East after about 100,000 years ago. Based on carefully prepared disk cores. Named after the French village of Le Moustier.

Mycenae, Greece Citadel of Mycenaean kings, c. 1500 B.C.

Mycenaean civilization Bronze Age civilization on mainland Greece, which reached its height between 1500 and 1200 B.C.

Nagada, Egypt Predynastic Egyptian kingdom in Upper Egypt dating to the fourth millennium B.C.

Nakbé, Guatemala Early Maya ceremonial center of 600 to 400 B.C., occupied as early as 1000 B.C.

Nekhen, Egypt Ancient Egyptian town, center of an important Predynastic kingdom.

Nevali Çori, Turkey Settlement and cult center dating to c. 9600 B.C.

Nineveh, Iraq Capital of Assyrian Empire under King Assurbanipal, c. 630 B.C.

Nubia "The Land of Kush," which lay upstream of Ancient Egypt in the present-day Sudan.

Oldowan The earliest known human stone tool technology, based on simple flakes and choppers, which appeared about 2.5 million years ago and remained in use for nearly a million years. Named after Olduvai Gorge.

Olduvai Gorge, Tanzania A site where stratified early hominin archaeological sites are associated with long-dried-up Lower and Middle Pleistocene lakes dated to between 1.75 million and 100,000 years ago.

Olmec Lowland Mesoamerican art style and series of cultures, which formed one of the foundations of later civilizations in the region, c. 1500 to 500 B.C.

Palenque, Guatemala Maya city and ceremonial center ruled by the Shield Dynasty for many centuries, and powerful in the seventh century A.D.

Paleo-Indian Generalized label given to the earliest forager cultures in North America. Approximate time span from before 12,000 to 6000 B.C.

Paloma, Peru A large foraging settlement with limited agriculture on the Peruvian Coast, dating to after 4000 B.C.

Panalauca Cave, Peru A site that has yielded evidence of early quinoa cultivation and llama herding, dating to about 2500 B.C.

Phoenicians Expert traders who controlled much Mediterranean trade after 500 B.C. Founders of the city of Carthage in North Africa, they became hated rivals of Rome.

Preclassic The early stages of Maya civilization, c. 1500 B.C. to A.D. 250. Sometimes called the Formative Era.

Pueblo Bonito, New Mexico A major Ancestral Pueblo "great house" in Chaco Canyon, occupied in the twelfth century A.D.

Pukara, Peru Center of a small kingdom in the north Lake Titicaca Basin in the early first millennium A.D.

Pylos, Greece Mycenaean palace famous for its archives of clay tablets, dating to c. 1500 B.C.

Quirigua, Honduras Maya city subordinate to Copán, which conquered its neighbor in A.D. 738.

Sahul Australia, New Guinea, and area surrounding the continental shelf during the late Ice Age.

San Andrés, Mexico Site of early maize cultivation, c. 5100 B.C.

San Bartolo, Guatemala A Preclassic Maya center with murals depicting the Maya creation legend, c. 400 to 200 B.C.

San José Mogote, Mexico Important Valley of Oaxaca farming village of the second millennium B.C.

San Lorenzo, Mexico Major Olmec center dating to c. 1250 B.C.

San Marcos Cave, Mexico Important Tehuacán Valley site for the early history of maize.

Santorini, Greece Island some 113 kilometers (70 miles) north of Crete, site of a violent eruption in the fifteenth century B.C. (The date is disputed and could be a century and a half earlier.)

Saqqara, Egypt Ceremonial complex on the west bank of the Nile in Lower Egypt, where many Old Kingdom pharaohs were buried. Site of the Step Pyramid of Djoser, c. 2600 B.C. Also a center of the important Apis bull cult, which flourished during the Late Period.

Schoningen, Germany Stone Age archaeological site, about 400,000 years old, which yielded the earliest known wooden spears.

Sea Peoples Traders and pirates, who dominated much of the eastern Mediterranean for 300 years after 1200 B.C.

Shang civilization Early civilization centered on the Huang Ho River of northern China, dating to c. 1766 to 1122 B.C.

Sicán, Peru Coastal Andean culture c. A.D. 700 to 1375.

Sipán, Peru Major ceremonial center of the Moche people, celebrated for its spectacular royal burials and dating to about A.D. 400.

Snaketown, Arizona Major Hohokam settlement near the Gila River; an important ceremonial center.

Songhay, Kingdom of West African state, which succeeded Mali after A.D. 1450 and collapsed after 1500, partly because of the new supplies of gold that reached Europe from the Americas.

Southern Cult A term given to a series of artistic motifs and associated religious beliefs of the Mississippian culture found over a wide area of the Midwest and southeastern United States.

Stonehenge, England A stone circle complex dating to the Neolithic and Bronze Age, which flourished as early as 2950 B.C. and reached its apogee in about 1600 B.C.

Sunda Continental shelf of Southeast Asia during the late Ice Age.

Swanscombe, England A Thames valley site that yielded Acheulan hand axes and a skull of an archaic hominin, c. 230,000 years old.

Taima Taima, Venezuela A site with possible evidence of early human occupation in the 12,000 B.C. range.

Tamrindo, Guatemala Maya center, which attacked nearby Dos Pilas, c. A.D. 760.

Tawantinsuyu Inca name for their empire, "The Land of the Four Quarters."

Tehuacán Valley, Mexico A dry valley in Mexico where some of the earliest evidence of maize cultivation has been discovered.

Tenochtitlán, Mexico Capital of the Aztec civilization from about A.D. 1325 to 1521, estimated to have had a maximum population of about 250,000 people.

Teotihuacán, Mexico Major city in the Valley of Mexico that flourished from about 200 B.C. to A.D. 750.

Thebes, Egypt Capital of Middle and New Kingdom Egypt after 1520 B.C. and a major center of the worship of the sun god Amun, known to the Egyptians as Waset.

This, Egypt Predynastic Egyptian kingdom in Upper Egypt in the fourth millennium B.C.

Tikal, Guatemala Classic Maya city, which reached the height of its power in A.D. 200 to 600.

Tiwanaku, Bolivia Highland Andean state near Lake Titicaca, which traded with a wide region, dating to between A.D. 200 and 1000.

Toro-Menalla, Chad Site of fossil-bearing beds that yielded the cranium of *Sahelanthropus tchadensis*, said to be 6 to 7 million years old.

Torralba, Spain See Ambrona.

Trinil, Java, Indonesia Gravel deposits up to 1.8 million years old, which have yielded the fossil remains of *Homo erectus*.

Trois Frères, France Magdalenian painted cave, famous for its sorcerer figures.

Tula, Mexico Capital center of the Toltec civilization, c. A.D. 900 to 1160.

Uaxactún, Guatemala Classic Maya city in the Mesoamerican lowlands defeated by its neighbor Tikal in A.D. 378.

'Ubaid culture Early farming culture of about 5000 B.C. in southern Iraq.

Ugarit, Syria Major port and commercial kingdom in the northern Levant during the Bronze Age, c. 1200 B.C. and later.

Uluburun, Turkey Bronze Age shipwreck site off southern Turkey, dating to the fourteenth century B.C.

Ur (Ur-of-the-Chaldees), Iraq Biblical Calah, Ur was a major city of the Sumerian civilization in the third millennium B.C.

Uruk, Iraq The world's first city, flourishing from 4500 B.C. for more than 2,000 years.

Valsequillo, Mexico A site where mastodon bones and artifacts date to about 12,000 B.C.

Verkhene-Trotiskaya, Siberia The earliest known Diuktai site in Siberia, dating to about 18,000 years ago.

Wallacea Sulawesi and Timor, Southeast Asia, during the late Ice Age.

Wangdong, China See Xianrendong.

Wari, Peru Major highland Andean kingdom centered on an urban and ceremonial center of that name, c. 800 A.D.

Willandra Lakes, Australia Shell middens and camp sites dating from 37,000 to about 26,000 years ago.

Xia Early dynasty of northern Chinese rulers dating to before 1700 B.C., known from both archaeological evidence and legend.

Xianrendong, China An early site used for rice-farming, c. 9220 and 7550 B.C. The exact date of the earliest rice cultivation is unknown.

Xiao-tun, China Capital of Shang civilization, 1400 to 1122 B.C., located in the Anyang region of northern China.

Yangshao, China A widespread farming culture in the Huang Ho River Valley of northern China after 5000 B.C.

Zhou An important Chinese dynasty that ruled over much of northern China after 1122 B.C.

Zhoukoudian, China Cave site famous for its *Homo erectus* fossils dating to as early as 600,000 years ago.

Zimbabwe See Great Zimbabwe.

The literature of world prehistory is enormous and scattered in dozens of languages. The references that follow provide a way of exploring in more detail the topics covered in this book. I tend to emphasize general works, all of which contain comprehensive bibliographies that summarize the specialist literature. For more detailed information, please consult one of the major summaries listed here or ask a specialist. The emphasis here is on English-language sources, simply because most readers are English-speaking. For all the furor over the World Wide Web, the printed page continues to be the primary source of information on world prehistory. However, you can sometimes glean valuable information by searching for Web domains of individual sites where research is ongoing.

Two major college textbooks offer more comprehensive summaries of world prehistory. My *People of the Earth,* 12th ed. (Upper Saddle River, N.J.: Prentice Hall, 2006) is a much-expanded version of this book. T. Douglas Price and Gary Feinman, *Images of the Past,* 4th ed. (New York: McGraw Hill, 2004) is a world prehistory based on site case studies. Chris Scarre, ed. *The Human Past* (London: Thames and Hudson, 2005) is a comprehensive, multi-authored account of prehistory for the more advanced reader. The best atlas of archaeology for the general reader is Chris Scarre, ed. *Past Worlds: The Times Atlas of Archaeology* (London: Times Books, 1988). The same author's *Timelines* (London: Dorling Kindersley, 1993) is a magnificently illustrated chronological guide to human history from the earliest times to A.D. 1500. Brian Fagan, ed. *The Oxford Companion to Archaeology* (New York: Oxford University Press, 1996) is a reference book that tells you everything you ever wanted to know about archaeology—and more. Paul Bahn, *The Penguin Archaeology Guide* (London: Penguin Books, 2000) is an excellent dictionary, especially strong on individual sites. Brian Fagan, ed. *Eyewitness to Discovery* (New York: Oxford University Press, 1997) is an anthology of firsthand accounts of archaeological discoveries. Tim Murray, ed. *The Great Archaeologists,* 2 vols. (Santa Barbara, CA: ABC-CLIO, 1999) provides excellent biographies of major figures in the field.

Dozens of local, national, and international journals cover the subject matter of this book, most of them aimed at specialists. Among those carrying popular articles are *National Geographic, Natural History, Smithsonian,* and *Scientific American. Archaeology* is a popular journal aimed at the enthusiast and professional archaeologist alike. *Antiquity, The Journal of World Prehistory,* and *World Archaeology* carry articles of wide interest to serious archaeologists and informed laypeople. American archaeologists rely heavily on *American Antiquity* and *American Anthropologist.* Old World archaeologists often publish in the *Proceedings of the Prehistoric Society,* while the latest hominin discoveries often appear in *Nature* or *Science. The Journal of Field Archaeology* is of high technical value and often contains definitive field reports. *Current Anthropology* often carries valuable survey articles on major topics.

Chapter-by-Chapter Literature

Chapter 1: Introducing World Prehistory

The history of archaeology is widely accessible through the National Geographic Society's *The Adventure of Archaeology* (Washington, D.C.: National Geographic Society, 1985), also through Paul Bahn, ed. *The Cambridge Illustrated History of Archaeology* (Cambridge, England: Cambridge University Press, 1996). A short college text: Brian Fagan, *A Brief History of Archaeology* (Upper Saddle River, NJ: Prentice Hall, 2005). For American archaeology, see Gordon Willey and Jeremy Sabloff's, *A History of American Archaeology*, 2nd ed. (New York: W. H. Freeman, 1994). Popular books on science and archaeology include: Brian Fagan, *Time Detectives* (New York: Simon & Schuster, 1995) and the National Geographic Society's *Into the Unknown* (Washington, D.C.: National Geographic Society, 1997). Archaeological theory enjoys an enormous literature. Bruce Trigger's *History of Archaeological Interpretation*, 2nd ed. (Cambridge, England: Cambridge University Press, 2006) is definitive. Lewis Binford's *In Pursuit of the Past*, rev. ed. (Berkeley: University of California Press, 2001) and David Meltzer, Don Fowler, and Jeremy Sabloff, eds. *American Archaeology Past and Future* (Washington, D.C.: Smithsonian Institution Press, 1986) are useful assessments.

Method and theory in archaeology are well covered in a series of widely available college textbooks. These include the companion volume to this work, my *Archaeology: A Brief Introduction*, 9th ed. (Upper Saddle River, NJ: Prentice Hall, 2006) and a more comprehensive treatment: *In the Beginning*, 11th ed. (Upper Saddle River, NJ: Prentice Hall, 2005). Robert Sharer and Wendy Ashmore, *Archaeology: Discovering the Past*, 4th ed. (New York: McGraw Hill, 1999) is another useful book. Paul Bahn and Colin Renfrew, *Archaeology*, 4th ed. (New York: Thames and Hudson, 2004), is a magisterial handbook of archaeological method and theory that is an essential reference book for any serious student of the past. Ian Hodder, *The Archaeological Process* (Oxford, England: Blackwell, 1999) offers a thoughtful assessment of archaeology. Robert Layton, ed. *Who Needs the Past?*, 2nd ed. (London: Routledge, 1994) contains essays on the relationship between indigenous people's values and archaeology.

Finally, the following is a major source book that is essential for all serious students of world prehistory. It comprises a series of essays on the current state of different aspects of the subject: Gary M. Feinman and T. Douglas Price, eds. *Archaeology at the Millennium: A Sourcebook* (New York: Plenum/Kluwer, 2000).

Chapter 2: Human Origins

The literature is enormous and sometimes polemical. Roger Lewin's *Bones of Contention* (New York: Simon & Schuster, 1987) offers an excellent historical survey for the lay reader. The same author's *Principles of Human Evolution*, 4th ed. (Oxford, England: Blackwell, 1998) gives an excellent summary of what we know about human evolution. Donald Johanson and Maitland Edey's *Lucy: The Beginnings of Humankind* (New York: Simon & Schuster, 1981) is a popular account of the Hadar finds. Donald Johanson, Lenora Johanson, and Blake Edgar's *Ancestors: In Search of Human Origins* (New York: Villard Books, 1994) covers the main developments of human evolution in a book written to accompany a television series entitled *Ancestors*. Richard Klein with Blake Edgar, *The Dawn of Human Culture* (New

York: John Wiley, 2002) picks up the story from there. Ian Tattersall, *The Fossil Trail: How We Know What We Think We Know about Human Evolution* (New York: Oxford University Press, 1996) is a closely argued account of human origins for a general audience. At a more technical level, Robert Foley's *Humans Before Humanity* (Oxford, England: Blackwell, 1995) discusses the ecological background to human origins. Steven Mithen's *Prehistory of the Mind* (London: Thames and Hudson, 1997) is a brilliant essay on the evolution of human intelligence for a general audience. Kathy Schick and Nicholas Toth's "Palaeoanthropology at the Millennium," in Gary M. Feinman and T. Douglas Price, eds. *Archaeology at the Millennium: A Sourcebook* (New York: Plenum/Kluwer, 2000), pp. 39–108, is a useful synthesis of research into the archaeological record of early prehistory with an excellent bibliography. Richard Klein's *The Human Career,* 2nd ed. (Chicago: University of Chicago Press, 1999) is an advanced textbook. For scavenging research, see Robert Blumenschine and John Cavallo's "Scavenging and Human Evolution," *Scientific American* 257 (10) (1992): 90–96.

Chapter 3: African Exodus

There are few general summaries of the long millennia covered by this chapter. Richard Klein with Blake Edgar, *The Dawn of Human Culture* (New York: John Wiley, 2002) provides an authoritative summary. See also the relevant portions of Steven Mithen's *The Prehistory of the Mind,* already cited, also Philip Lieberman's, *Uniquely Human: The Evolution of Speech, Thought, and Selfless Behavior* (Cambridge, MA: Harvard University Press, 1991). Clive Gamble's *The Palaeolithic Societies of Europe* (Cambridge, England: Cambridge University Press, 2000) is an excellent overall summary of developments in Chapters 3 and 4. More specialist contributions include J. Desmond Clark and Jack Harris's "Fire and Its Roles in Early Hominid Lifeways," in *African Archaeological Review* 3 (1985): 3–28. Robert Foley's "Hominid Species and Stone-Tool Assemblages: How Are They Related?" in *Antiquity* 61 (1987): 380–392 is a provocative essay on the relationship between stone tools and biological evolution. For bamboo and archaic humans, see Geoffrey Pope's "Bamboo and Human Evolution," *Natural History* 10 (89) (1989): 49–56. A popular account of modern human origins is Christopher Stringer and Robin McKie's *African Exodus: The Origins of Modern Humanity* (New York: Henry Holt, 1997). Chris Stringer and Paul Mellars, eds. *The Human Revolution,* 2 vols. (Edinburgh: Edinburgh University Press, 1989, 1990) provides specialist essays on the controversies surrounding the subject, including an important article by Gunter Braüer on archaic *Homo sapiens* in Africa. See also M. H. Nitecki and V. Nitecki, eds. *Origins of Anatomically Modern Humans* (New York: Plenum Press, 1994). Anthony Marks's "The Middle to Upper Palaeolithic Transition in the Levant," in *Advances in World Archaeology* 2 (1983): 51–98, covers the technological changeover associated with modern humans. Chris Stringer and Clive Gamble's *The Search for the Neanderthals* (London: Thames and Hudson, 1993) and Erik Trinkaus and Pat Shipman's *The Neanderthals: Changing the Image of Mankind* (New York: Alfred Knopf, 1992) are excellent popular accounts of these archaic humans.

Chapter 4: Diaspora

Brian Fagan, *The Journey from Eden* (New York: Thames and Hudson, 1990) carries a somewhat outdated summary of the material in this chapter, which can be amplified from numerous references of both a general and more specialist nature. Australia and New

Guinea are well summarized by Derek Mulvaney and John Kamminga, *Prehistory of Australia* (Washington, D.C.: Smithsonian Institution Press, 1999). Early discoveries are discussed by Jim Allen in "When Did Humans First Colonize Australia?" *Search* 20 (5) (1989): 149–154. See also David Frankel, *Remains to Be Seen: Archaeological Insights into Australian Prehistory* (Melbourne: Longman Cheshire). The Cro-Magnons have been described by many popular authors. Randall White, *Dark Caves and Bright Visions* (New York: American Museum of Natural History, 1986) is a useful summary, especially when amplified by Paul Bahn and Jean Vertut, *Images of the Ice Age* (New York: Viking, 1988), which is an invaluable analysis of Stone Age art. Clive Gamble, *Timewalkers: The Prehistory of Global Colonization* (Stroud, Glos: Alan Sutton, 1994) offers a broad and provocative view of the topics in this chapter. Jean Clottes, *Chauvet Cave: The Art of Earliest Times*, trans. Paul Bahn (Salt Lake City: University of Utah Press, 2003) is a brilliant description of this important cave. Olga Soffer, *The Upper Palaeolithic of the Central Russian Plains* (New York: Academic Press, 1985) describes Mezhirich in detail. For Eurasia generally, see John Hoffecker, *Desolate Landscapes* (New Brunswick, NJ: Rutgers University Press, 2001). For the controversies surrounding the first settlement of the Americas and the Clovis people, see Brian Fagan, *The Great Journey* (Gainesville: University of Florida Press, 2004). Tom Dillehay, *The Settlement of the Americas* (New York: Basic Books, 2000) is an important survey. See also James Adovasio with Jake Page, *The First Americans* (New York: Random House, 2002).

Chapter 5: The Origins of Food Production

For forager archaeology and the issue of social complexity among them, see R. L. Bettinger, "Archaeological Approaches to Hunter-Gatherers," *Annual Review of Archaeology* 16 (1987): 121–142. *A Pleistocene Revolution,* edited by Paul Martin and Richard Klein (Tucson: University of Arizona Press, 1984), summarizes evidence for extinction of big game in many parts of the world. Douglas Price and James Brown edited *Complexity among Prehistoric Hunter-Gatherers* (Orlando, FL: Academic Press, 1985), which contains valuable essays on the issue of social complexity. Douglas Price's "The Mesolithic of Western Europe," in the *Journal of World Prehistory* 1 (3) (1987): 225–305, describes complex hunter-gatherers in Europe, while Stuart Struever and Felicia Holton's *Koster: Americans in Search of Their Past* (New York: Anchor Books, 1979) is a popular account of that famous site. Further descriptions of Archaic cultures in North America, and of the Chumash Indians of California, can be found in my *Ancient North America,* 4th ed. (New York: Thames and Hudson, 2005). Also see Stuart Fidel, *Prehistory of the Americas,* 2nd ed. (Cambridge: Cambridge University Press, 1992).

The classic theories surrounding the origins of agriculture are gathered in Stuart Struever's anthology *Prehistoric Agriculture* (Garden City, NY: Natural History Press, 1971). Bruce D. Smith's *The Emergence of Agriculture* (New York: W. H. Freeman, 1999) summarizes what we know of early agriculture and animal domestication throughout the world, as well as the remarkable results being obtained from AMS radiocarbon dating of grain. Graeme Barker, *The Agricultural Revolution in Prehistory* (Oxford: Oxford University Press, 2006) is an authoritative, global synthesis with excellent theoretical insights. Kent Flannery's *Guilá Naquitz* (Orlando, FL: Academic Press, 1986) is an exemplary monograph, which is essential reading, if for nothing else, for its hypothetical dialogues, which contain a multitude of wisdoms about archaeology and archaeologists.

Chapter 6: The Earliest Farmers

Andrew Moore's *Village on the Euphrates* (New York: Oxford University Press, 2000) describes the Abu Hureyra excavations and is the finest and most comprehensive monograph on an ancient farming settlement ever written. Ian Hodder, *The Leopard's Tale* (London and New York: Thames and Hudson, 2006) is a fascinating analysis of the beliefs behind the early farming settlement at Çatalhöyük, Turkey. For Europe, see I. J. Thorpe, *The Origins of Agriculture in Europe* (London: Routledge, 1996) and Barry Cunliffe, ed. *The Oxford Illustrated Prehistory of Europe* (Oxford: Oxford University Press, 1996). Early farming in Asia: Li Liu, *The Chinese Neolithic* (Cambridge: Cambridge University Press, 2004). Charles Higham's *The Archaeology of Mainland Southeast Asia* (Cambridge, England: Cambridge University Press, 1989) is comprehensive and authoritative, while his article coauthored with Tracey L. D. Lu, "The Origins and Dispersal of Rice Cultivation," *Antiquity* 72 (1998): 867–877, is a good source for early rice agriculture. The Americas: See Bruce Smith, *The Emergence of Agriculture,* already cited. For everything you want to know (and perhaps don't want to know) about maize, turn to John Staller, Robert Tykot, and Bruce Benz, eds. *Histories of Maize* (New York: Academic Press/Elvesier, 2006). See also S. H. Wills, *Early Prehistoric Agriculture in the Southwest* (Santa Fe, NM: School of American Research Press, 1989), which covers the introduction of maize in that region.

Chapter 7: Chiefs and Chiefdoms

For Pacific voyaging, the interested reader can do no better than to start with Geoffrey Irwin's *The Prehistoric Exploration and Colonization of the Pacific* (Cambridge, England: Cambridge University Press, 1992). This remarkable study is based not only on archaeology and computer simulations, but on the author's own voyages. Patrick Kirch, *On the Road of the Winds: An Archaeological History of the Pacific Islands Before European Contact* (Berkeley: University of California Press, 2002) summarizes the first colonization of the Pacific Islands. Kirch's *The Evolution of the Polynesian Chiefdoms* (New York: Cambridge University Press, 1989) describes complex societies in the Pacific. New Zealand archaeology: See Janet Davidson, *The Prehistory of New Zealand* (Auckland: Longman Paul, 1984). Southwestern archaeology is well analyzed by Linda Cordell, *The Prehistory of the Southwest,* 2nd ed. (Orlando, FL: Academic Press, 1999). For the Eastern Woodlands, see George R. Milner, *The Moundbuilders* (London: Thames and Hudson, 2004), also the same author's *The Cahokia Chiefdom* (Washington, D.C.: Smithsonian Institution Press, 1998). Cahokia and the Mississippian tradition receive thorough examination in Timothy R. Pauketat and Thomas E. Emerson, eds. *Cahokia: Domination and Ideology in the Mississippian World* (Lincoln: University of Nebraska Press, 1997). Also see Judith Bense, *Archaeology of the Southeastern United States* (San Diego: Academic Press, 1994). Lastly, Susan Keech McIntosh, ed. *Beyond Chiefdoms: Pathways to Complexity in Africa* (New York: Cambridge University Press, 1999) contains a collection of essays that are essential to anyone interested in the archaeology of chiefdoms.

Chapter 8: State-Organized Societies

The literature is enormous. Charles Redman, in *The Rise of Civilization: From Early Farmers to Urban Society in the Ancient Near East* (San Francisco: W. H. Freeman, 1978), critiques theories up to the late 1970s. Christopher Scarre and Brian Fagan's *Ancient Civilizations,* 3rd ed. (Upper Saddle River, NJ: Prentice Hall, 2008) summarizes the world's early civilizations for beginning readers. See also Kent Flannery's "The Cultural Evolution of Civilizations," in the *Annual Review of Ecology and Systematics* (1972): 399–426, which is good on ecological and systems approaches. Elizabeth Brumfiel's "Aztec State Making: Ecology, Structure, and the Origin of the State," *American Anthropologist* 85 (2) (1983): 261–284 discusses social approaches. Two definitive works: Bruce Trigger, *Understanding Early Civilizations: A Comparative Study* (Cambridge: Cambridge University Press, 2003) and Norman Yoffee, *Myths of the Archaic State: Evolution of the Earliest Cities, States, and Civilizations* (Cambridge: Cambridge University Press, 2005). Writing: Andrew Robinson's *The Story of Writing* (London: Thames and Hudson, 1995) is a lavishly illustrated essay for beginners.

Chapter 9: Mesopotamia and the Eastern Mediterranean World

Two books summarize the Sumerians admirably. Samuel Kramer's *The Sumerians* (Chicago: University of Chicago Press, 1963) is a well-deserved popular classic. Harriett Crawford's *Sumer and the Sumerians,* 2nd ed. (Cambridge, England: Cambridge University Press, 2004) is an up-to-date synthesis. Nicholas Postgate's *Early Mesopotamia: Economy and Society at the Dawn of History* (London: Kegan Paul, 1992) is also definitive. See also Seton Lloyd's *The Archaeology of Mesopotamia,* 2nd ed. (London: Thames and Hudson, 1983) and Hans J. Nissen's *The Early History of the Ancient Near East,* 9000 to 2000 B.C. (Chicago: University of Chicago Press, 1990). Susan Pollock, *Ancient Mesopotamia* (Cambridge, England: Cambridge University Press, 1999) focuses on origins. The Hittites: See J. G. MacQueen, *The Hittites,* 3rd ed. (New York: Thames and Hudson, 1996) and Trevor Bryce, *The Kingdom of the Hittites* (Oxford: Oxford University Press, 1998). For later events, see Manuel Robbins, *Collapse of the Bronze Age: The Story of Greece, Troy, Israel, Egypt, and the Peoples of the Sea* (New York: Author's Choice Press, 2001) and Robert Drew, *The End of the Bronze Age* (Princeton: Princeton University Press, 1995). The Assyrians are described in Nicholas Postgate's *The First Empires* (Oxford: Phaidon, 1977). The Minoans and Mycenaeans: See Oliver Dickinson, *The Aegean Bronze Age* (Cambridge, England: Cambridge University Press, 1994); J. Lesley Fitton, *Minoans (Peoples of the Past)* (London: British Museum Press, 2002); and Robert Castleden, *Mycenaeans: Life in Bronze Age Greece* (London: Other, 2005).

Chapter 10: Egypt and Africa

The ancient Egyptians have attracted an enormous literature. Three volumes provide a good general summary. Cyril Aldred's *The Egyptians,* 3rd ed. (New York: Thames and Hudson, 1998) is a concise account, while Barry Kemp's *Ancient Egypt: The Anatomy of a Civilization,* 2nd ed. (London: Routledge, 2006) is destined to become a classic. For the latest discoveries, see Vivian Davies and Rene Freedman, *Egypt* (London: British Museum Press, 1998). Nicholas Reeves's *The Complete Tutankhamun* (New York: Thames and Hudson, 1990) is a magnificent tour of the golden pharaoh's sepulcher. Nubia is little known to anyone but specialists, but the following are useful starting points: William Adams's *Nubia: Corridor to Africa* (London: Alan Lane, 1977) is a comprehensive, if outdated, monograph that is still useful. David O'Connor's *Ancient Nubia: Egypt's Rival in Africa* (Philadelphia: University of Pennsylvania Museum, 1993) offers an update. Meroe and Kush: Derek Aelsby, *The Kingdom of Kush: The Napatan and Meroitic Empires.* (London: Marcus Weiner, 1999. Aksum: David Phillipson, *Ancient Ethiopia: Aksum, Its Antecedents and Successors*

(London: British Museum Press, 1998). Graham Connah's *African Civilizations,* 2nd ed. (Cambridge, England: Cambridge University Press, 2001) is a superb account of early African kingdoms, including Nubia, Meroe, and Aksum. Nehemiah Levetzion's *Ancient Ghana and Mali* (London: Methuen, 1971) and Peter Garlake's *Great Zimbabwe* (New York: Thames and Hudson, 1973) provide beginning summaries.

Chapter 11: South, Southeast, and East Asia

Mortimer Wheeler's *The Indus Civilization,* 2nd ed. (Cambridge, England: Cambridge University Press, 1962) is still a major, if outdated, source on the Harappan Civilization. Gregory Possehl's *Indus Age: The Beginnings* (Philadelphia: University of Pennsylvania Press, 1999) is the first volume in what will be a definitive account of the Harappans. The same author's *Harappan Civilization: A Recent Perspective* (New Delhi, India: Oxford and IBH Publishing, 1993) also provides updates, as does Jean R. McIntosh, *A Peaceful Realm* (Boulder, CO: Westview Press, 2002). Raymond Allchin's *The Archaeology of Historic South Asia* (Cambridge, England: Cambridge University Press, 1995) covers the Mauryan and later societies. Chinese prehistory is well summarized by Sarah Allen, ed. *The Formation of Chinese Civilization: An Archaeological Perspective* (New Haven, CT: Yale University Press, 2005). K-C Chang's *Shang Civilization* (New Haven, CT: Yale University Press, 1980) is still authoritative. See also Li Liu, *State Formation in Early China* (London: Duckworth, 2003). Gina Barnes's *China, Korea, and Japan* (London: Thames and Hudson, 1993) is a general summary in English. For Southeast Asia generally, see Charles Higham, *Early Cultures of Mainland Southeast Asia* (London and New York: Thames and Hudson, 2002); also see the same author and Rachanie Thosarat's *Prehistoric Thailand* (Bangkok: River Books, 1998), which describes recent excavations. Charles Higham, *The Civilization of Angkor* (Berkeley: University of California Press, 2000) is an excellent summary of this important site.

Chapters 12 and 13: Mesoamerican Civilizations

The definitive summary is Susan Toby Evans, *Ancient Mexico and Central America* (London and New York: Thames and Hudson, 2004). Kent Flannery's edited *The Early Mesoamerican Village* (New York: Academic Press, 1976) contains a rich foundation of wisdom about archaeology generally, as well as valuable information on early complexity in the Valley of Oaxaca. For the Olmec, see Richard Diehl, *The Olmecs: America's First Civilization* (London and New York: Thames and Hudson, 2004). Joyce Marcus and Kent Flannery's *The Zapotec Civilization* (London: Thames and Hudson, 1996) is a richly illustrated account of Monte Albán and the origins of civilization in the Valley of Oaxaca. Teotihuacán is well described in René Millon, R. B. Drewitt, and George Cowgill's *Urbanization at Teotihuacán* (Austin: University of Texas Press, 1974), and by Esther Pasztory, *Teotihuacán: An Experiment in Living* (Norman: University of Oklahoma Press, 1997). William Saunders, Jeffrey Parsons, and Robert Santley's *The Basin of Mexico* (New York: Academic Press, 1979) describes the comprehensive archaeological surveys carried out in this highland region.

The Maya literature is rich and often contradictory. Michael Coe's *The Maya,* 7th ed. (New York: Thames and Hudson, 2005) is the most widely read summary. See also Arthur Demarest, *Ancient Maya: The Rise and Fall of a Rainforest Civilization* (Cambridge: Cambridge University Press, 2005). Linda Schele and David Freidel's *A Forest of Kings* (New York: Morrow, 1990) is a popular synthesis of Maya history based on both archaeology and glyphs, which is seminal, if controversial in places. Their *Maya Cosmos* (New York: Morrow, 1993) discusses Maya astronomy and world views. Jeremy A. Sabloff's *The Cities of Ancient Mexico* (New York: Thames and Hudson, 1989) provides a guide to major Mesoamerican sites. David Webster, *The Fall of the Ancient Maya* (London and New York: Thames and Hudson, 2002) is an excellent up-to-date account of the collapse. For climate change and Maya agriculture, see Vernon L. Scarborough, "Resilience, Resource Use, and Socioeconomic Organization: A Mesoamerican Pathway," in Garth Bawdon and Richard Martin Reycraft, eds. *Environmental Disaster and the Archaeology of Human Response* (Albuquerque: Maxwell Museum of Anthropology, 2000), pp. 195–212. For a summary of lake and deep-sea core research, see Gerald Haug and others, "Climate and the Collapse of Maya Civilization," *Science* 299 (2003): 1731–1735.

The Toltecs are summarized by Richard Diehl in *Tula, the Toltec Capital of Ancient Mexico* (New York: Thames and Hudson, 1983). The Aztecs: Geoffrey W. Conrad and Arthur A. Demarest, *Religion and Empire* (Cambridge, England: Cambridge University Press, 1984). Their civilization is described in Michael Smith, *The Aztecs (The Peoples of America)*, 2nd ed. (Oxford England: Blackwell, 2002). Inga Clendinnon's *Aztecs: An Interpretation* (Cambridge, England: Cambridge University Press, 1991) is a valuable analysis of Aztec history, which is especially good on sources. For the Spanish Conquest, see Charles Dibble and Arthur Anderson's *The Florentine Codex* (Salt Lake City: University of Utah Press, 12 vols., 1950–1975).

Chapter 14: Andean Civilizations

Michael Moseley's *The Incas and Their Ancestors*, 2nd ed. (New York: Thames and Hudson, 2000) is an excellent summary of Andean archaeology for the general reader. Jonathan Haas, S. Pozorski, and T. Pozorski, eds. *The Origins and Development of the Andean State* (Cambridge: Cambridge University Press, 1987) is a somewhat technical edited volume. *Early Ceremonial Architecture in the Andes*, edited by Christopher Donnan (Washington, D.C.: Dumbarton Oaks, 1985), brings together articles on early architecture on the coast and in the highlands. Richard Burger's *The Prehistoric Occupation of Chavín de Huántar* (Berkeley: University of California Publications in Anthropology, 1984) describes excavations at this most important of sites. Lawrence Sullivan's monumental excursion into traditional Latin American religions, *Icanchu's Drum* (New York: Macmillan, 1988), is essential for any student of Andean archaeology. The Moche are well described by Christopher Donnan and Donna McClelland in *The Burial Theme in Moche Iconography* (Washington, D.C.: Dumbarton Oaks, 1987). Christopher Donnan and Walter Alva's *Royal Tombs of Sipán* (Los Angeles: Fowler Museum of Cultural History, UCLA, 1994) is the definitive account of one of the most spectacular archaeological finds of the twentieth century. For Tiwanaku, see Alan Kolata, *Tiwanaku* (Oxford, England: Blackwell, 1993). See also the same author's "The Agricultural Foundations of the Tiwanaku State," *American Antiquity* 51 (4) (1986): 748–762. For information on Huari, see William Isbell, and Katharina Schreiber, "Was Huari a State?" *American Antiquity* 43 (1978): 372–389. Chimu: See Michael Moseley and C. Kent Day, eds. *Chan Chan: Andean Desert City* (Albuquerque: University of New Mexico Press, 1982).

The best starting point for the Inca civilization is Conrad and Demarest's *Religion and Empire*, already cited. Terence D'Altroy, *The Incas (The Peoples of America)* (Oxford, England: Blackwell, 2002) is a useful summary. John Rowe's *Inca Culture at the Time of the Spanish*

Conquest (Washington, D.C.: Smithsonian Institution Handbook of South American Indians, vol. 2, 1946) is still a thorough account. John Hemming's *The Conquest of the Incas* (Baltimore: Pelican Books, 1983) describes Pizarro's ravages.

Epilogue

Three books cover the closing centuries of prehistory from different perspectives. John Bodley's *Victims of Progress*, 4th ed. (New York: McGraw Hill, 1998) is a widely consulted college textbook on culture change and modernization. My *Clash of Cultures*, 2nd ed. (Walnut Creek, CA: Alta Mira Press, 1997) describes contact between Westerners and a series of non-Western societies for a general audience. Eric Wolf's *Europe and the People Without History* (Berkeley and Los Angeles: University of California Press, 1984) is the authoritative account, with a strong anthropological bias.

References in the Text

Anderson, A. O., and Charles Dibble, trans. 1963. *A General History of the Things of New Spain.* Vol. 7. Salt Lake City: University of Utah Press.

Bingham, Hiram. 1964. *Lost City of the Incas.* New York: Athenaeum.

Chauvet, Jean-Marie, Eliette Brunel Deschamps, and Christian Hillaire. 1996. *Dawn of Art: The Chauvet Cave.* New York, Harry Abrams.

Cohen, J. M. Trans. 1963. *The Conquest of New Spain.* Baltimore: Pelican Books.

Cushing, Frank. 1979. *Zuni.* Lincoln: University of Nebraska Press.

Fagan, Brian M. 1979. *Return to Babylon.* Boston: Little Brown.

Foley, Robert. 1995. *Humans Before Humanity.* Oxford: Blackwell.

Kürten, Bjorn. 1986. *How to Deep-Freeze a Mammoth.* New York: Columbia University Press.

Kramer, Samuel. 1963. *The Sumerians.* Chicago: University of Chicago Press.

Kramer, Samuel. 1981. *History Begins at Sumer.* Philadelphia: University of Pennsylvania Press.

Leakey, Mary D., and Jack Harris. 1990. *Laetoli: A Pliocene Site in Northern Tanzania.* Oxford: Oxford University Press.

Leon-Portilla, Miguel. 1963. *Aztec Thought and Culture: A Study of the Ancient Nahuatl Mind.* Jack Emory Davis, trans. Norman, OK: University of Oklahoma Press.

Lichtheim, Miriam. 1976. *Ancient Egyptian Literature: A Book of Readings. Vol. 2: The New Kingdom.* Berkeley: University of California Press.

Mithen, Steven. 1996. *Prehistory of the Mind.* London: Thames and Hudson.

Schele, Linda, and David Freidel. 1990. *A Forest of Kings.* New York: William Morrow.

Stephens, John Lloyd. 1941. *Incidents of Travel in Chiapas and Yucatan.* New York: Harpers.

Sullivan, Lawrence. 1988. *Icanchu's Drum.* New York: Free Press.

Tedlock, Dennis, trans. 1985. *Popol Vuh.* New York: Doubleday.

Wheeler, Sir Mortimer. 1968. *The Indus Civilization.* Rev. ed. Cambridge: Cambridge University Press.

Photo Credits

Museum, London; page 157 (a) and (b): Deutsches Archaeologisches Institut–Orientabteilung, © Courtesy Dr. Klaus Schmidt; page 158: Michael Holford/ Michael Holford Photographs; page 165: Robert Harding World Imagery; page 169: © Robert S. Peabody Museum of Archaeology, Phyllips Academy, Andover, Massachusetts, All Rights Reserved; page 170: John W. Rick.

Chapter Seven: page 172: Archaeological Museum, Photograph from the Arthur Sackler Gallery, Washington, D.C., and reproduced with the permission of the Jordan Department of Antiquities; page 177: The Granger Collection; page 178: Courtesy of the Library of Congress; page 179: Courtesy of the Library of Congress; page 181: Arizona State Museum, University of Arizona, Helga Teiwes, Photographer; page 184: David Muench/Corbis/ Bettmann; page 185: Muench Photography, Inc.; page 186: © George H. H. Huey/Corbis, All Rights Reserved; page 189: Werner Forman/Art Resource, NY; page 190: Van Bucher/Photo Researchers, Inc.; page 191: © Richard Schlecht/National Geographic Image Collection; page 193: Gordan Gahan/ National Geographic Image Collection; page 194: Courtesy National Museum of the American Indian, Smithsonian Institution, Heye Foundation, Neg. #15/0853, Photo by David Heald.

Chapter Eight: page 198: AP Wide World Photos; page 207: Courtesy Department of Library Services, American Museum of Natural History; page 211: Peter Menzel/Stock Boston; page 213: Art Resource/The British Museum Great Court Ltd, Copyright The British Museum; page 215: Kenneth Garrett/NGS Image Collection.

Chapter Nine: page 218: Art Resource/The British Museum Great Court Ltd, Copyright The British Museum; page 225: Art Resource/The British Museum Great Court Ltd, Copyright The British Museum; page 228: Richard Ashworth/ Robert Harding World Imagery; page 229: Art Resource/The British Museum Great Court Ltd, © Copyright The British Museum; page 231: Borromeo/Art Resource, NY; page 233: Institute of Nautical Archaeology/D. Frey; page 234: Hirmer Fotoarchiv, Munich, Germany; page 235:

Hirmer Fotoarchiv, Munich, Germany; page 236: Ira Block/Getty Images Inc.—Image Bank; page 237: Nimatallah/Art Resource, NY.

Chapter Ten: page 240: O. Louis Mazzatenta/ National Geographic Image Collection; page 246 (left): Pharaonic, 1st dynasty, c. 3100–2890 B.C., Nekhen (Hierakonlolis), Greywacke, H = 63, W = 42 cms., The Egyptian Museum, Cairo, Copyright Werner Forman/Art Resource, NY; page 246 (right): Egyptian Museum, Cairo, Egypt, Copyright Erich Lessing/Art Resource, NY; page 249: Robert Harding World Imagery; page 250: John Ross/ Robert Harding World Imagery; page 251 (a): The Metropolitan Museum of Art, Museum Excavations, 1919–1920, Rogers Fund and Edward S. Harkness Gift, 1920 (20.3.5); page 251 (b): The Metropolitan Museum of Art, Museum Excavations, 1919–1920, Rogers Fund and Edward S. Harkness Gift, 1920 (20.3.11); page 254: Hirmer Fotoarchiv, Munich, Germany; page 255: Art Resource/Photography by Egyptian Expedition, The Metropolitan Museum of Art; page 258: Peter Shinnie; page 260: Copyright Werner Forman/ Art Resource, NY; page 262: Angel Martinez Bermejo/Corbis/Sygma; page 264: Robert Holmes/ Corbis/Bettmann.

Chapter Eleven: page 266: Corbis/Bettmann, © Asian Art & Archaeology, Inc./Corbis; page 270: Paul Almasy/Corbis/Bettmann; page 271: Paulo Koch/Photo Researchers, Inc.; page 272: © J. M. Kenoyer, Courtesy Dept. of Archaeology and Museum, Govt. of Pakistan; page 273: Robert Harding/Robert Harding World Imagery; page 275: Peabody Museum, Harvard University; page 277: Shang bronzes, Courtesy of the Freer Gallery of Art, Smithsonian Institution, Washington, D.C. (F1923.1, F1959.15); page 278: National Archives and Records Administration; page 279: An Ceren/ Sovfoto/Eastfoto; page 283: Tim Hall/Getty Images, Inc.—Photodisc; page 284: Brian M. Fagan.

Chapter Twelve: page 286: Barbara & Justin Kerr Studio, K1184 © Justin Kerr; page 290: Lee Boltin Picture Library; page 291: Robert & Linda Mitchell Photography; page 293: Kenneth Garrett/National Geographic Image Collection; page 294: National Geographic Image Collection; page 298: Robert

Index

Page numbers followed by *f* indicate figures. Page numbers followed by *t* indicate tables. Page numbers followed by *n* indicate notes.